A substance-free framework for phonology

Edinburgh Studies in Theoretical Linguistics

Series Editors: Nikolas Gisborne, University of Edinburgh and Andrew Hippisley, University of Kentucky

Books in the series address the core sub-disciplines of linguistics – phonology, morphology, syntax, semantics and pragmatics – and their interfaces, with a particular focus on novel data from various sources and their challenges to linguistic theorising.

Series Editors
Nikolas Gisborne is Professor of Linguistics at the University of Edinburgh.

Andrew Hippisley is Professor of Linguistics and Linguistics Programme Director at the University of Kentucky.

Editorial Board
Umberto Ansaldo, University of Hong Kong
Balthasar Bickel, Universität Zürich
Olivier Bonami, Université Paris Diderot
Heinz Giegerich, University of Edinburgh
Jen Hay, University of Canterbury
Stefan Müller, Humboldt-Universität zu Berlin
Mitsuhiko Ota, University of Edinburgh
Robert Truswell, University of Edinburgh
David Willis, University of Cambridge
Alan Yu, University of Chicago

Titles available in the series:
1 *Lexical Structures: Compounding and the Modules of Grammar*
   Heinz J. Giegerich

2 *A Substance-free Framework for Phonology: An Analysis of the Breton Dialect of Bothoa*
   Pavel Iosad

Visit the Edinburgh Studies in Theoretical Linguistics website at www.euppublishing.com/series/esitl

A substance-free framework for phonology
An analysis of the Breton dialect of Bothoa

Pavel Iosad

Edinburgh University Press is one of the leading university presses in the UK. We publish academic books and journals in our selected subject areas across the humanities and social sciences, combining cutting-edge scholarship with high editorial and production values to produce academic works of lasting importance. For more information visit our website: edinburghuniversitypress.com

© Pavel Iosad, 2017

Edinburgh University Press Ltd
The Tun – Holyrood Road, 12(2f) Jackson's Entry, Edinburgh EH8 8PJ

Typeset in Sabon by
Servis Filmsetting Ltd, Stockport, Cheshire

A CIP record for this book is available from the British Library

ISBN 978 1 4744 0737 3 (hardback)
ISBN 978 1 4744 0738 0 (webready PDF)
ISBN 978 1 4744 0739 7 (epub)

The right of Pavel Iosad to be identified as the author of this work has been asserted in accordance with the Copyright, Designs and Patents Act 1988, and the Copyright and Related Rights Regulations 2003 (SI No. 2498).

Contents

Acknowledgements		x
Chapter 1 Introduction		1
Chapter 2 Conceptual foundations of substance-free phonology		5
2.1	The modular enterprise	5
	2.1.1 Domain-specificity	6
	2.1.2 Encapsulation and inaccessibility	8
2.2	No phonetics in (modular) phonology: the autonomy of phonological representations	8
	2.2.1 Cross-linguistic phonetic variation	9
	2.2.2 Phonological and phonetic arguments for representations	10
	2.2.3 Emergent features and the nature of the evidence	12
	2.2.4 The role of contrast	14
	2.2.5 Markedness	15
	2.2.6 Rule scattering	16
	2.2.7 Crazy rules	16
	2.2.8 Sign languages	17
	2.2.9 Conclusion on autonomy	17
2.3	The status of the interfaces	18
	2.3.1 Two approaches to the interface	18
	2.3.2 Domain-specificity and external interfaces	19
	2.3.3 Interfacing as interpretation	21
	2.3.3.1 Incomplete neutralisation	22
	2.3.3.2 Near-mergers and listener-agnostic phonological patterns	24
	2.3.3.3 Phone subsetting	26
	2.3.4 The interface and sound change	26
	2.3.5 Conclusion on interfaces	26
2.4	Substance-free phonology and overgeneralisation	27
	2.4.1 Crazy patterns	27
	2.4.2 Frequency of occurrence	28

2.5	The status of Universal Grammar in phonological theory		30
2.6	Summary and outlook		31

Chapter 3 Representational assumptions — 36
- 3.1 The Parallel Structures Model — 36
- 3.2 Tier organisation — 37
  - 3.2.1 Tier structure in the PSM — 37
  - 3.2.2 Feature typing — 38
  - 3.2.3 Locality — 39
- 3.3 Featural structure — 39
  - 3.3.1 Feature geometry and the contrastive hierarchy — 40
  - 3.3.2 Bare nodes as contrastive non-specification — 40
  - 3.3.3 Empty segments and hierarchy subversion — 42
  - 3.3.4 Further consequences of gradualness — 44

Chapter 4 Computational assumptions — 45
- 4.1 The power of computation — 45
- 4.2 Towards a substance-free computation — 46
  - 4.2.1 No fixed rankings — 46
  - 4.2.2 The importance of constraint schemata — 47
  - 4.2.3 Non-exhaustive markedness — 48
  - 4.2.4 Complex structure faithfulness — 50
  - 4.2.5 The augmentation constraint schema — 52
  - 4.2.6 The role of MaxLink and DepLink — 54
- 4.3 Stratal aspects of the computation — 56
  - 4.3.1 Tri-stratal organisation — 57
  - 4.3.2 The stem-level syndrome — 58
  - 4.3.3 Stratal aspects of Richness of the Base — 58

Chapter 5 Complexity and markedness in substance-free phonology — 61
- 5.1 Structural markedness: a review — 61
- 5.2 Markedness and contrast — 62
- 5.3 Geometry and markedness — 64
- 5.4 Partial markedness orders and augmentation — 65

Chapter 6 The Breton language — 67
- 6.1 Dialectal divisions — 67
- 6.2 The dialects and the written language — 68
- 6.3 Sources — 69
  - 6.3.1 General descriptions — 69
  - 6.3.2 Sources: dialect descriptions — 70
  - 6.3.3 Theoretical studies — 71
- 6.4 The dialect of Bothoa — 72

Chapter 7	Segments and representations		74
7.1	Vowel inventory		74
	7.1.1 Oral monophthongs		74
		7.1.1.1 Mid vowels	74
		7.1.1.2 The schwa	76
	7.1.2 Nasal vowels		78
	7.1.3 Diphthongs		78
7.2	Consonants		79
	7.2.1 Laryngeal contrasts		79
	7.2.2 Velar palatalisation		81
	7.2.3 Coronal palatalisation and overlap		82
	7.2.4 The 'glottal' fricative		83
	7.2.5 Voiceless sonorants		85
7.3	Sandhi		85
	7.3.1 Lack of release		85
	7.3.2 Laryngeal phenomena		87
7.4	Featural representations		89
	7.4.1 Laryngeal contrast		90
	7.4.2 Manner contrasts		90
	7.4.3 Nasal vowels		93
Chapter 8	Suprasegmental phonology		95
8.1	Stress		95
	8.1.1 Types of stress		96
	8.1.2 Stress placement		97
	8.1.3 Morphological factors in stress placement		99
	8.1.4 Multiple stressed elements		100
8.2	Foot structure		102
	8.2.1 The generalisations		102
	8.2.2 Stress on dominant elements		103
	8.2.3 Stress with no dominant elements		103
	8.2.4 Doubly stressed words		104
	8.2.5 Stratal aspects of Bothoa Breton stress		105
	8.2.6 Edgemost degenerate feet: lapses and segmental structure		107
8.3	Syllabic structure and phonotactics		108
	8.3.1 Syllable size restrictions		108
		8.3.1.1 Data	108
		8.3.1.2 Analysis	111
	8.3.2 The trough pattern		113
	8.3.3 Consonant sequences		115
	8.3.4 The distribution of vowel length		115
	8.3.5 Extrametricality and (sub)minimality		120

viii   Contents

Chapter 9 The phonology of vowels   124
9.1   Stress-related alternations   124
       9.1.1   Data   125
       9.1.2   Analysis   127
9.2   Vowel raising   129
9.3   Diphthongs   130
9.4   Morphologically conditioned alternations   130
9.5   Summary: vowels   131

Chapter 10 The phonology of consonants: palatalisation and
            gliding   132
10.1   Palatalisation   132
       10.1.1 Velar palatalisation   132
               10.1.1.1 Data   133
               10.1.1.2 An aside: the evidence from article
                         allomorphy   135
               10.1.1.3 Analysis   136
       10.1.2 Coronal palatalisation   138
               10.1.2.1 Data   138
               10.1.2.2 Analysis   141
10.2   Gliding   146
       10.2.1 The back rounded vowel   146
       10.2.2 The front unrounded vowel   146
               10.2.2.1 The stem level: gliding   147
               10.2.2.2 The word level   150
               10.2.2.3 Later levels   152
       10.2.3 The front rounded vowel   154
10.3   Discussion: the case for cyclicity   157
       10.3.1 Parallel approaches with Free Base Priority   157
       10.3.2 Optimal Paradigms   159

Chapter 11 Laryngeal phonology   163
11.1   Final laryngeal neutralisation   163
       11.1.1 The ternary contrast on the surface   164
       11.1.2 Geometric analysis   165
       11.1.3 OT analysis   167
               11.1.3.1 Final neutralisation   168
               11.1.3.2 Onset enhancement   169
11.2   Provection   171
       11.2.1 Morphologically restricted provection   171
               11.2.1.1 Adjectives   172
               11.2.1.2 Verbs   174
               11.2.1.3 Autosegmental analysis   175
               11.2.1.4 OT analysis   176

	11.2.2	Phonological provection	177
		11.2.2.1 Data	178
		11.2.2.2 Analysis: laryngeal similation	179
		11.2.2.3 Boundary effects in provection	182
		11.2.2.4 OT analysis	185
11.3	Initial consonant mutations		189
	11.3.1	Spirantisation	189
		11.3.1.1 Analysis	190
		11.3.1.2 Full spirantisation	191
	11.3.2	Provection	193
		11.3.2.1 Analysis: stops	193
		11.3.2.2 The status of voiceless sonorants	196
		11.3.2.3 Sonorant provection: analysis	196
		11.3.2.4 The status of [hr]	197
	11.3.3	Lenition	198
		11.3.3.1 Data	198
		11.3.3.2 Analysis	200
		11.3.3.3 The 'failure of lenition'	203
		11.3.3.4 OT analysis	206
		11.3.3.5 Lexical insertion and the stratal affiliation of lenition	207
	11.3.4	Lenition-and-provection	208
11.4	Ternary contrasts and markedness relations in Bothoa Breton laryngeal phonology		208
	11.4.1	Surface ternarity in Breton	210
		11.4.1.1 Further evidence for ternarity	211
		11.4.1.2 Surface underspecification and (lack of) contrast	216
	11.4.2	The evidence against underspecification in binary contrasts	219
		11.4.2.1 Laryngeal realism and essentialism	220
		11.4.2.2 Variability in laryngeal contrast realisation	221
		11.4.2.3 A substance-free interpretation	222
11.5	Markedness relationships in Breton		225
	11.5.1	Ternary contrast with binary features: Krämer (2000)	225
		11.5.1.1 The analysis	225
		11.5.1.2 Empirical issues	226
	11.5.2	Ternary contrast with privative features: Hall (2009)	229
	11.5.3	Laryngeal markedness in Breton	230

Chapter 12	Conclusion	234
References		239
Index		271

Acknowledgements

This book is substantially based on my University of Tromsø PhD thesis *Representation and computation in substance-free phonology: A case study in Celtic*. I am grateful to my supervisor, Bruce Morén-Duolljá, for his patient and insightful direction of the work that led to the thesis, and to everyone at the Centre for Advanced Study in Theoretical Linguistics and elsewhere at the University of Tromsø for providing the best possible environment for doctoral study. Particular thanks are due to Patrik Bye, Martin Krämer, Curt Rice, and Marit Westergaard, who played key roles in getting the project to completion at various stages. Thanks also to my external examiners, Keren Rice and S. J. Hannahs, for their valuable input.

The book version builds in important respects on feedback I have received on the thesis and on related work. I am grateful to Ricardo Bermúdez-Otero, Daniel Currie Hall, Steve Hewitt, Bill Idsardi, Yuni Kim, Máire Ní Chiosáin, Jim Scobbie, Patrycja Strycharczuk, and Marc van Oostendorp for valuable discussions.

I am very grateful to my erstwhile colleagues at the University of Ulster – Raffi Folli, Alison Henry, Catrin Rhys, and Christina Sevdali – for all their friendship and help during my time in Northern Ireland.

I am also grateful to all my colleagues at the University of Edinburgh for their help and support in too many ways to name. This book has particularly benefited from discussions with (in alphabetical order) Josef Fruehwald, Heinz Giegerich, Patrick Honeybone, Bob Ladd, Warren Maguire, Ben Molineaux, and Michael Ramsammy. Nik Gisborne has been extremely supportive of the book project (and not only the book project) throughout. Richard Strachan and Laura Williamson at Edinburgh University Press have been extremely helpful throughout the production process. I would also like to thank Jean Le Dû for his permission to use the recordings collected for the *Nouvel atlas linguistique de la Basse-Bretagne* to produce Figure 7.1.

Finally, my deepest thanks to Irina, Dina, and Úna for all their unstinting love and support over the past few years.

1

Introduction

As the title indicates, this book has two principal aims. As is hopefully appropriate for a series called *Edinburgh Studies in Theoretical Linguistics*, it aims to present a coherent, relatively compact account of a particular theoretical approach to phonology – what I call the substance-free framework. A theoretical approach, however, is worthless unless can be applied to produce new insights into specific phonological data. To this end, I offer a fairly detailed account of the phonological system of a variety of Breton. This language is currently not only very fragile in a sociolinguistic perspective but also underdescribed, at least in the sense that available descriptions are frequently not informed by newer theoretical developments. This description thus serves both as a testing ground for the theoretical approach and as a way of introducing a range of new data into relevant theoretical debates.

The substance-free approach, presented in detail in the following four chapters of the book, seeks to address a growing concern regarding the scope and place of phonological knowledge in the overall architecture of the language faculty. On the one hand, we have witnessed an increased appreciation of the gradient and variable nature of much of the data that have traditionally been interpreted as reflecting categorical symbolic operations, coupled with an increased interest in accounting for variation within the speech of individuals and across entire communities. These developments have led to increased scrutiny of the foundations of formal phonology, including fundamental concepts such as 'category', 'contrast', and 'computation'. On the other hand, within formal phonology itself there appears to be a perception that the momentum behind theoretical innovation has stalled somewhat following the burst of activity in the late 1990s and early 2000s following the introduction of Optimality Theory (OT) to the scene.[1] While significant amounts of work continue to be done both in OT (and cognate theories such as Harmonic Serialism and MaxEnt grammar modelling) and in other formal frameworks, such as Rule-Based Phonology or Government Phonology, it does not always seek to address major architectural questions or indeed to defend the necessity of formal, symbolic phonology in the face of the very real empirical challenges that it faces.

It is the ambition of this book to contribute to these debates. Here, I seek first and foremost to propose a viable theory of what the proper purview of the phonological computation should be. To this end, I emphasise architectural *modularity* and the *autonomy* of the phonological component. The substance-free framework as envisaged here seeks to restrict the flow of information between phonology and other cognitive components involved in linguistic behaviour. In common with other 'substance-free' approaches to phonology, notably those offered by Hale and Reiss (2008) and Samuels (2011), this inevitably leads to a 'leaner' system that does not aim to account for many phenomena that phonologists have historically been happy to see falling within the scope of phonological grammar. The approach offered here shares the concerns of Hale and Reiss, and Samuels regarding the explanatory value of 'functional' factors as drivers of phonological *processes*. However, my primary focus in this book is *representational*: unlike both Hale and Reiss, and Samuels (but like authors such as Morén 2006; Blaho 2008; Odden 2010, 2013; Youssef 2013), I reject the dominant view in mainstream generative phonology whereby the properties of phonological objects such as segments are trivially connected with their physical realisations (see also Dresher 2009; Scheer 2014). Instead, I advocate a system where the relationship between phonological representations and phonetic substance is also an extraphonological, learned mapping.

Despite the emphasis on representations, I recognise that a full theory of the phonological component also requires an explicit theory of computation: without a demonstration that a given representational hypothesis can be reconciled with an adequate computational account of relevant phonological phenomena, the representational proposal is at best incomplete. Thus, the possibility of a computational analysis serves as an empirical 'sanity check' for hypotheses regarding phonological representations. In addition, conceptually, adopting a modular representational system is only part of the job of establishing a modular phonological architecture: if proposed representations cannot be used to account for the data without violations of modularity in the computational system, then the entire project fails.

To provide such an explicit computational account, it is imperative that we determine the proper scope of phonology. One of the tenets of the substance-free approach is that many phenomena that are possible to express in transcription are in fact not products of symbolic operations effected by the phonological module. Throughout this book, I will offer assessments of whether a particular phenomenon falls within the purview of the phonological grammar. This is a necessary component of the methodological groundwork within the substance-free approach.

Another important aspect of an explicit computational account is the choice of a computational framework. In this book, I use a stratal version of Optimality Theory. It is not my purpose here to argue specifically for OT over other phonological models (although I do argue that a stratal version of OT is superior to fully parallel ones). There are two reasons for this. First, the representational proposals are hopefully robust enough to stand on their own, and they could probably be incorporated into a different computational framework (such as Rule-Based Phonology) without significant changes. Second, a fair comparison between OT and other phonological theories also requires comparability in representational assumptions. It is no doubt true that OT has been faced with very real challenges on empirical grounds (see in particular Vaux 2008); however, it appears that they are often concerned with the inability of OT to accommodate a straightforward translation of a particular analysis, and could perhaps be resolved if closer attention were paid to representational assumptions.[2] I will therefore proceed with OT, fully aware of the dangers of embracing a framework that is nothing if not controversial.

Finally, this book offers a wide-ranging account of several aspects of the phonology of a single language. This genre, while widespread in earlier generative phonological literature, seems to have rather fallen into abeyance with the advent of OT. This is perhaps understandable given OT's excellent tools for cross-linguistic comparison, but represents, I believe, an important gap in the scholarship.[3] In particular, the consideration of a wide range of phenomena in a single language is a very important check on the adequacy of any OT account of an isolated phenomenon, since the rankings must all be consistent with each other. Hence, the analysis of Breton is important not just for the sake of informing future work on that language but also for making sure that the book's theoretical contribution holds water.

The overall organisation of the book reflects its dual nature. In the four following chapters, I lay out the general motivations for the approach and some representational and computational specifics. In Chapter 2, I discuss the conceptual motivation for adopting a substance-free approach to phonology, with an emphasis on modularity. I describe the place of phonology in the overall architecture, and the nature of its interface with physical realisation ('phonetics'), and address some common objections to the substance-free approach. Chapter 3 presents the core of the representational system used here, which is a version of Morén's (2003, 2006) Parallel Structures Model of feature geometry. In Chapter 4, I go on to discuss some ways in which the OT computational system is used here to provide a better fit with the representational model, and in Chapter 5 I argue that the model's representational and computational properties conspire to provide a contentful, non-trivial view of the vexed question of 'markedness'.

The subsequent chapters focus on the Breton data. After a brief overview of the language and existing literature in Chapter 6, I describe its consonantal and vocalic inventories in Chapter 7, with a focus on discovering those aspects of the system that must be accounted for phonologically. Chapter 8 provides an analysis of the language's suprasegmental phonology, focusing on phonotactics and foot structure. Chapter 9 describes phonological phenomena involving vowels, while Chapter 10 concentrates on the phonology of glides and palatalisation in Bothoa Breton (with some excursions into other varieties). In that chapter I argue that a stratal OT approach is particularly well suited to the data. Finally, Chapter 11 considers laryngeal phonology by offering the argument that Breton provides strong evidence for the complete arbitrariness of the connection between phonological behaviour and phonetic realisation.

Notes

1. This perception seems to be shared widely enough for a well-attended debate to have been organised in conjunction with the 23rd Manchester Phonology Meeting in May 2015, entitled *W(h)ither OT?*
2. For more discussion of this point, see Iosad (forthcoming a).
3. By this I do not mean, of course, to neglect those examples of the whole-language approach that do exist; see, for instance, Picanço (2005) or Jaker (2011).

2

Conceptual foundations of substance-free phonology

In this chapter I discuss the basic assumptions underlying the framework presented in this book and give a brief overview of the modular approach to grammar that provides the conceptual motivation for the theory.

2.1 The modular enterprise

At the heart of the substance-free approach is the thesis that phonology is an autonomous *module*; that it exists as a component of grammar and possesses domain-specific representational and computation systems that are, in principle, independent of the representational and computational systems operating in morphosyntax or phonetics. Arguably, in this view phonology must be substance-free almost by definition: in the classic modular approach (Fodor 1983), modules are defined by characteristics such as *information encapsulation* and *domain specificity*. If phonology is a module, then the alphabet of phonological symbols and the types of operations available for these symbols *must* be independent of considerations that properly belong to other domains, despite the fact that such considerations are often relevant to the shape of phonological systems.

The substance-free approach takes autonomy and modularity seriously, resting on the assumption that the phonological grammar operates independently of external factors, similarly to recent work by authors such as Reiss (2007); Scheer (2010); Bermúdez-Otero (2012). Specifically, phonology is defined as a module that effects *categorical computation* over proprietary phonological symbols. The focus in this book is on segmental phonology, so the majority of such symbols encountered here are phonological features.

With respect to the identification of features, I follow the main tenet of the Contrastivist Hypothesis as expressed in structuralist phonology (e.g. Trubetzkoy 1939; Martinet 1955; Hjelmslev 1975) and recently revived in the 'Toronto school' of contrastive specification (e.g. Dresher et al. 1994; Dresher 2003, 2009; Hall 2007; Mackenzie 2013). I operate with the assumption that the set of features available to a language's phonological grammar is coextensive with the set of features used to make distinctions among segments found in lexical (underlying) representations for that language's morphemes. In this formulation, the Contrastivist Hypothesis is arguably the default assumption for a minimalist conception of phonology: if a feature is necessary to express lexical contrast, its existence is justified 'outside' the phonological grammar, and therefore appealing to it in our analysis of phonological patterns does not require special pleading.

Before we discuss the issue of contrast in more depth, it might be worth our time setting the approach more firmly in the landscape of modular theories of cognition. Fodor (1983) proposes the following set of characteristics of modules of the human mind:

- domain-specificity
- mandatory operation
- limited central accessibility
- fast processing
- informational encapsulation
- 'shallow' outputs
- fixed neural architecture
- characteristic and specific breakdown patterns
- characteristic ontogenetic pace and sequencing.

For various reasons, I will not have much to say here about mandatory operation, fast processing, neural architecture, breakdown patterns, or ontogenetic aspects of phonology. Other properties do deserve some comment.

2.1.1 *Domain-specificity*

The modular property of most relevance to the present work is domain-specificity. Its importance chimes in well with the suggestion by Coltheart (1999) that it is in fact the defining property of a modular system.

A module shows domain-specificity if there is a requirement that the computation it performs be concerned with objects that are not encountered in other modules – in our case, phonological features and sub- and suprasegmental organising nodes. If phonology is to be modular, we immediately disqualify some approaches current in the literature, especially in the OT framework. A domain-specific phonology cannot operate on non-phonological objects, such as formant values (e.g. Flemming 2002) or morphological indices (e.g. Pater 2000, 2009) – although it can operate on phonological objects that are the result of interface translation.

If phonology has no access to phonetic information such as the acoustic properties or gestural interpretation of phonological representations, there is no requirement for features to be defined in phonetic terms.

Phonetic definitions help explain the cross-linguistically frequent near-isomorphism between the features emerging from phonological analysis ('natural classes') and certain phonetic properties, but logically there is no need to include phonetic grounding as a constraint on possible phonological grammars. It can, of course, be stipulated that a feature like [+high] corresponds to a high concentration of energy in the region of about 200–400 Hz, or to a high position of the tongue body. By now, however, it is well known that many well-established phonological features elude such straightforward definitions, especially if they are to be made universally applicable.

A similar point is made at length by Ladd (2014: ch. 2), who also argues for the even stronger proposition that universal phonetic categories do not exist, and therefore neither does a universal mapping between phonology and phonetics. He suggests that the confusion between phonological and phonetic phenomena can be rectified by abandoning the 'systematic phonetic' level that serves *simultaneously* as the output of phonological computation ('surface representation') and a bona fide phonetic representation. Ladd's ultimate conclusion in favour of a distinction between a symbolic, abstract representation (approximately 'phonology') and a continuous signal describable in quantitative terms (approximately 'phonetics') is consonant with the main thrust of substance-free phonology as conceived here.

Insufficient domain-specificity is also at the heart of Foley's (1977) attack on early generative phonology as 'transformational phonetics'. Foley views the entanglement between the analysis of alternations and the description of how distinctive units are realised phonetically as a category mistake. Instead, for him phonology operates on units defined in entirely non-phonetic terms, using a scale of 'strength'. These units are converted to more familiar phonetic entities at a later, non-phonological stage. Although one need not agree with the proposal to put the concept of 'strength' at the centre of phonology, the main insight is sound: if phonology is a module, it must have a proprietary alphabet of symbols to compute.

A similar concern underlies the approach to phonological architecture offered by Reiss (2007); Hale et al. (2007); Hale and Reiss (2008). They argue that any description of the phonological component should include a description of the phonological alphabet, which they suggest to be sensitive to the presence of certain perceptible cues (such as formant values or transitions, periodicity, durational properties, etc.) but insensitive to others (for instance, the use of real-world objects such as bananas). Although these authors' ultimate conclusions are often very different from those reached here, I share their conviction that a phonological analysis must include a description of a universe of discourse which is specific to phonology.

To conclude, a modular approach must recognise the following null hypothesis: phonological symbols are defined without reference to phonetics, morphology, and other grammatical domains. A similar consideration applies with respect to the computation, as I discuss in the next section.

2.1.2 Encapsulation and inaccessibility

The properties of encapsulation and inaccessibility refer to the flow of information between modules. *Encapsulated* systems cannot access information stored in other modules: they can only refer to information contained in the input, and to module-internal information. Thus, a phonological module encapsulated with respect to, say, syntax, should not be able to access syntax-internal facts about linguistic objects. Similarly, phonology-internal information is not necessarily accessible to other modules, as evidenced by the frequently cited principle of 'phonology-free syntax'.

It must be noted that encapsulation is not necessarily absolute, in that a module can be encapsulated with respect to some modules but not to others (cf. Prinz 2006). For instance, it is reasonably clear that speech perception is encapsulated with respect to, say, conscious beliefs (i.e. it is not possible to consciously perceive a [t] as a [w]). On the other hand, speech perception can be influenced by input from modules other than hearing, as in the case of sign languages or of the McGurk effect, although this could simply be a sign that the perception mechanism is multimodal in nature and not restricted to the aural mode of transmission (Robbins 2010).

Thus, a modular phonology should operate without reference to information available in other modules. A modular view of phonology is incompatible with approaches that seek the *proximate* causes of phonological behaviour in extraphonological domains, such as ease of perception: for instance, it should not be possible to say that 'non-peripheral vowels tend to be disallowed in unstressed positions [a statement about a phonological phenomenon] because they are more difficult to perceive than peripheral vowels [a statement about the perceptual system]'. It is, of course, highly plausible that such factors play a role in synchronic systems by shaping them over time: they can be ultimate causes – but not proximate ones.

2.2 No phonetics in (modular) phonology: the autonomy of phonological representations

The most important theoretical foundation of the present framework is the *autonomy of phonology*. In the modular approach, phonology must possess a proprietary alphabet and a proprietary computation, which are *in principle* independent of considerations related to substance. There are two aspects of the substance-free principle.

At the bare conceptual level, the autonomy of representation means that the phonological alphabet is entirely abstract and defined without any reference whatsoever to phonetics. The physical realisation of phonological units is not the concern of the *phonological grammar* as such – although a theory of this realisation is a necessary complement to the theory of grammar. The job of phonology is to match input strings provided by the lexicon to output strings which can be interpreted by the interface (in production mode) and perform the opposite operation in perception mode (Keating 1988a; Morén 2007). There is no logical requirement for the metalanguage of these strings to make any reference to non-phonological entities, and in fact, given the constitutive role of domain-specificity, we do not expect any such reference. Some authors (e.g. Burton-Roberts 2000) have pointed out that phonology appears to deal with substance, and flagged this as a contradiction: if it is part of specifically linguistic competence, it *should* be substance-free. For this reason, Burton-Roberts (2000) argues for the exclusion of phonology from the 'core' linguistic component. Here, I agree with the latter but not the former premise: phonology is linguistic, but it does not deal with substance.

In a modular architecture of grammar, it is incumbent on the proponent of a phonetically oriented approach to representations to show that phonology operates on symbols defined in phonetic terms. Traditionally (i.e. since at least Jakobson et al. 1951), the argument made to this effect is essentially typological (inductive) rather than principled (deductive). This argument, however, is weaker than it appears.

2.2.1 Cross-linguistic phonetic variation

The broad diversity in the phonetic realisation of what appear to be 'the same' phonological representations (which, in practice, means that the two segments are transcribed using the same IPA symbol) is by now an established fact (Ladefoged 1984; Ladd 2014). The variation ranges from '[r]', which covers an extreme diversity of sounds (Sebregts 2014), to cases like the degree of variation permitted in the realisation of [i] in languages with small vowel inventories: from relatively large as predicted by dispersion theorists (e.g. Liljencrants and Lindblom 1972; Flemming 2002) to quite small, as found in Amis by Maddieson and Wright (1995).

This sort of variation is plausibly *not* a purely mechanic matter outside cognitive control: it should be reflected in our model of the human capacity for language. However, whether these facts should be *phonological* is another question altogether. A common assumption is that phonology includes all non-trivial (non-mechanical) aspects of human behaviour in the domain of speech sounds (e.g. Hammarberg 1976; Pierrehumbert et al. 2000; Pierrehumbert 2002). However, I suggest that defining phonology (or indeed any component of the human linguistic capacity) in terms of the *behaviour* it is 'responsible' for is a category mistake within the generative enterprise. Phonology is computation over phonological symbols; whether other components of grammar also happen to produce cognitively controlled phenomena that look similar to phonological ones is not necessarily a concern *in* the phonology. Hale et al. (2007) and Hale and Reiss (2008) express a similar insight by introducing a distinction between 'variation' (cross-linguistic differences expressed in terms of phonological symbols) and 'microvariation' (differences introduced 'either by the transduction process, individual physical properties, or external physical events', Hale et al. 2007: 650).

Of course, introducing a language-specific phonetic realisation component (or 'interface') also means increasing the number of 'moving parts' in a complete theory of sound-related behaviour. On the other hand, it also allows establishing a firmer division of labour between the various components: phonology, phonetic implementation, and what has been termed the 'usage component' in the literature; I treat this issue in more detail later in the chapter. In the meantime, I will explore the consequences of the modular approach for identifying evidence for and against phonological features.

2.2.2 *Phonological and phonetic arguments for representations*

Starting at least from the acoustic feature theory of Jakobson et al. (1951) and the 'universal phonetics' of Chomsky and Halle (1967), phonological computation was assumed to produce as its ultimate output representations of physical events. A frequent corollary is that the mapping from phonology to physical events is simple and universal (cf. the 'transduction' of Hale et al. 2007; Hale and Reiss 2008). Very roughly, there are three broad approaches in this tradition:

- The SPE tradition, building on the set of features proposed by Chomsky and Halle (1967), or conceived as an alternative to that particular formalism without significant differences in terms of modular organisation. Here, we can include both SPE-style attribute-value matrices and autosegmental and geometrical approaches (e.g. Sagey 1986; McCarthy 1988; Clements and Hume 1995; Halle 1995).
- The 'realist' tradition, which strives to bring the output of phonology as close to physical events as possible, often without particular regard

to issues such as lexical contrast and morphophonological alternations that have traditionally been at the centre of theoretical attention. Examples include Articulatory Phonology (e.g. Browman and Goldstein 1990; Silverman 2003) and many declarative approaches (e.g. Scobbie et al. 1996; Scobbie 1997; Coleman 1998; Lodge 2009), as well as recent approaches based on rich-memory models (e.g. Pierrehumbert 2001, 2002; Scobbie 2007).

- The element-based tradition (e.g. Anderson and Ewen 1987). Especially in the relatively recent guise of Element Theory (Harris 1994; Harris and Lindsey 1995; Backley 2011), this framework emphasises that phonological elements are in principle abstract but also have direct acoustic (or rather perceptual) correlates, making it relatively easy to recover element-based phonological representations from the phonetics.

Relatively few phonologists pay more than lip service to the abstract, non-substance-bound nature of phonological features. Structuralist phonology recognised, following Saussure, that the prime factor defining phonological representation was not phonetic, since representations were based on contrast (Trubetzkoy 1939; Hjelmslev 1943, 1975; see also the overview by Dresher 2009). Most work in the generative tradition, however, has not embraced truly abstract representation, with a few exceptions such as Foley (1977), discussed above, and the recent growth of various 'substance-free' approaches (Hale and Reiss 2000a, 2008; Morén 2006, 2007; Hale et al. 2007; Blaho 2008; Youssef 2010; Odden 2010, 2013; Samuels 2011).

In addition, although Element Theory was described as substance-bound above, much work in that tradition gives more weight to phonological patterning rather than phonetic realisation; for recent examples of sophisticated representational argumentation on the basis of (morpho)phonological alternations, see Gussmann (2007); Cyran (2010). Even the textbook treatment by Backley (2011), which largely relies on the perceptual approach to elements, contains numerous ambiguous passages such as the following: 'Adding |ʔ| makes no difference to the phonetic shape of laterals [...] It does make a difference phonologically, however, as it links *l* to the class of stops' (2011: 182).

The ambivalent behaviour of laterals in terms of (phonological) continuancy is well known (Mielke 2005); the point of the example is that Element Theory, despite the insistence of some of its adherents on the recoverability of phonological representation from phonetics, arguably cannot avoid what is essentially substance-free argumentation. This indicates that phonetic evidence might not (always) be sufficient to determine the phonological representation in each particular case.

2.2.3 Emergent features and the nature of the evidence

If a fully phonetically based representational system is not viable, we ought to examine the possibility that phonological argumentation alone might suffice to establish the nature of phonological representations. Under such a regime, phonological representations – including phonological features – must be *emergent*, in the sense that they do not exist a priori and must be extracted from the data.

There are two main objections to this idea. The first has to do with learning: having a hard-wired universal set of features can make phonological acquisition easier. However, numerous studies have shown that categories can be formed without reference to a priori features, on the basis of iterated learning procedures (e.g. Boersma 1998; de Boer 2000, 2001; Boersma et al. 2003; Escudero and Boersma 2003; Oudeyer 2005; Boersma and Hamann 2008; Zuidema and de Boer 2009; see also Kirby et al. 2014 for a more general overview).

A second argument is typological: certain contrasts seem to recur cross-linguistically, which is not surprising if the set of possible distinctions as expressed by a fixed feature set is (relatively) small. Conversely, some contrasts are unattested, and presumed impossible for a principled reason, namely that the fixed feature set cannot express the relevant contrast.[1] Emergent feature theory, on the other hand, predicts the existence of segment classes that share some phonological properties but do not necessarily cohere phonetically.

This is usually treated as an undesirable prediction, but Mielke (2007) argues it is in fact correct (see also Mielke et al. 2010). By examining what he calls 'phonologically active classes' – sets of segments that participate in alternations as targets or triggers – he is able to quantify how well the predictions of various feature theories correspond with typological reality. Even the best-performing systems cover only up to 75 per cent of the attested phonological classes: the rest fall within the category of 'unnatural' classes (see also Mielke 2013).

Mielke (2007) identifies several types of uncharacterisable segment sets:

- 'Crazy' classes, e.g. Evenki /v s g/ as the targets of nasal assimilation. If real, these are important evidence for emergent features: as Mielke (2007: §6.1) discusses, innate feature theory puts a strict limit on how arbitrary a phonological class can be, thus predicting the non-existence of some of these 'crazy' classes.
- Phonetically natural classes that happen to be impossible to capture due to the specifics of individual feature theories. These clearly cannot be used as an argument against innate and/or phonetically defined features, but only as an argument against these feature theories.

- 'Generalisation in two directions', or 'L-shaped' classes. Diachronically, these involve a phonologically active class extending to comprise two subclasses similar to the 'core' class in some dimension, without necessarily being similar to each other.

Mielke's results are highly suggestive. However, to be fully convincing, they must be supplemented by closer analysis of individual languages, with particular attention to the computational processes in each individual language. Hall (2010) provides several examples of how Mielke's unnatural classes may dissolve under such closer scrutiny.

The lack of attention to whole-language analysis also undermines the criteria for class status used by Mielke. For instance, one of the examples of an 'L-shaped' class is the set of Navajo segments that are labialised before [o]: [t k k' x ɣ], i.e. all voiceless stops irrespective of place (generalisation of [voiceless stop]) and dorsals irrespective of manner (generalisation of [dorsal]).[2] Crucially, the pattern cannot be described by a simple conjunction of features without covering other segments: the Navajo class clearly has to allow both coronals (e.g. [t]) and voiceless fricatives (e.g. [x]), but voiceless coronal fricatives [s ɬ] are excluded.

Mielke excludes the segments [kʷ xʷ ɣʷ] from the class, yet it is not obvious that they do not undergo vacuous labialisation. Identifying whether a segment 'participates' in an alternation without considering the analysis in detail is difficult. Computationally, a segment whose representation changes is clearly part of the class defined by the change, even if it is phonetically vacuous. It is not entirely obvious how such cases could be identified using Mielke's comparative method.

Second, as Mielke concedes, L-shaped classes can be account for in (some versions of) Optimality Theory (Flemming 2005), since it allows multiple constraints to block the appearance of certain segments or the application of certain processes: in this case, constraints against the labialisation of coronal fricatives could be created by constraint conjunction.[3] Similarly, 'class subtraction' (i.e. a situation when only a non-characterisable subset of a predicted featural class is phonologically active, but adding some other featural class to this subset results in a characterisable class) is trivial to achieve in OT via constraints against the co-occurrence of relevant features.

Mielke's (2007: 166) answer to these concerns is essentially typological: 'If factorial typology is taken seriously, then classes which are defined with fewer interacting constraints are expected to be more common, and this in turn depends on the feature set which is used to formulate the constraints'. He suggests that this prediction is not borne out by his data, casting doubt on the adequacy of the OT approach. However, the prediction holds only if the distribution of attested surface grammars is influenced only by the *set* of constraints. This implies that the probability of different *rankings* is approximately equal; below, I will argue that this is untenable.

These objections are not meant to invalidate Mielke's arguments against innate, substance-based features. As Mielke recognises, the 'phonologically active classes' gleaned from a list of alternations are important as *a* source of evidence for the nature of phonological computation, but they are not *the* evidence. In any approach with emergent features, the evidence should come from a detailed consideration of the pattern, including an explicit statement of the division of labour, an explicit set of features used in the individual language, and a detailed analysis of the phonological evidence. Only such analysis can show whether a given 'phonological class' is defined by a certain feature or whether it is an epiphenomenon of the interaction of several patterns (Hall 2010).

In this book I argue that a framework with language-specific, emergent, substance-free features is superior to one with innate, substance-bound features, on the grounds of empirical adequacy: the former, but not the latter, predicts the existence of 'crazy' phonologically classes. However, conclusive evidence for 'crazy classes' cannot come from a broad analysis of trends in featural inventories – it requires detailed consideration of specific languages, and this book provides just such a study.

2.2.4 *The role of contrast*

The constitutive role of contrast in phonological specification has been recognised in structuralist approaches (Trubetzkoy 1939; Martinet 1955; Jakobson and Halle 1956; Hjelmslev 1943, 1975). Thus, for Trubetzkoy (1939), phonemes are defined by their distinctive function; yet 'distinctive function can [...] only be ascribed to a sound property inasmuch as it is opposed to another sound property'.[4] Most importantly for structuralists, phonological representation was *language-specific* almost by definition, since the phonological content of any element could only be established on the basis of its relationship to other members of the same system, and not to a priori, potentially universal considerations. Somewhat similar motivations underlie various theories of underspecification (Steriade 1987, 1995; Archangeli 1988), especially Modified Contrastive Specification (Dresher et al. 1994; Dresher 2003, 2009; Hall 2007), where the primary function of phonological features is to implement contrast in the lexicon. A strong form of the Contrastivist Hypothesis is formulated by Hall (2007: 20): 'The phonological component of a language L operates only on those features which are necessary to distinguish the phonemes of L from one another.'

As discussed in more detail in Chapter 5, this book attempts to reconcile the Contrastivist Hypothesis with the generative notion of significant computational freedom. The motivation behind strong contrastivist approaches is essentially parsimony: entities whose existence cannot be independently demonstrated should be avoided. Lexical contrast provides irrefutable evidence of the phonological significance of a feature; thus, it can be argued that contrastivism is a good null hypothesis. The question of whether phonological grammar can add material that is *not* necessary for lexical contrast is empirical.

2.2.5 Markedness

Ever since Trubetzkoy (1939) it has been recognised that the relationships between phonological elements may be asymmetrical: some phonemes can be distinguished from others by the presence of elements. Starting out as a purely formal notion defined by the presence of the 'mark' (*Merkmal*), markedness quickly accrued many additional connotations as a property used to describe various aspects of human language competence (for recent overviews, see Haspelmath 2006; Rice 2007; Hume 2011).

I discuss the relevant notions of markedness in more detail in Chapter 5. The importance of markedness for the autonomy of phonology lies in the question of whether markedness-related phonological behaviour is directly tied to phonetic substance. Positive answers to this question in formal phonology have tended to dedicate a special markedness 'submodule' that ensures that certain phonological elements behave in a particular way, as in Chomsky and Halle (1967: ch. 9) or Calabrese (2005), and in work on underspecification theory with redundancy rules (e.g. Archangeli and Pulleyblank 1994). De Lacy (2002, 2004, 2006) makes a more nuanced distinction, ascribing markedness-related behaviour to structural factors (his *xo* Theory of features) but including the close relationship to substance as an additional postulate of the theory. Given that such markedness statements have tended to allow functional and/or diachronic explanations, it has also been proposed that they merely recapitulate these explanations and are thus unnecessary, or that markedness is in some sense emergent from such factors and thus not very interesting for phonological theory (cf. Blevins 2004, 2006).

However, markedness-related behaviour of what appear to be 'identical' sounds can be both language-specific and not necessarily functionally driven. The first line of attack is particularly prominent in work by Keren Rice (1992, 1994, 1996, 2003, 2007, 2011), who shows that standard markedness diagnostics may designate most types of segments as 'marked' or 'unmarked' with no apparent functional motivation. The mapping between markedness classes and substance is driven by phonology-internal (i.e. functionally arbitrary) considerations, which is exactly what we expect under an approach with autonomous phonology. A second approach, exemplified, for instance, by Hume (2004), derives markedness-related behaviour from frequency. Whether or not that is true, it still implies this behaviour is *learned*, and thus potentially not universal but language-specific.

2.2.6 Rule scattering

The autonomy of phonology is also demonstrated by the possibility of making a distinction between categorical (and potentially phonological) and continuous (potentially non-phonological) versions of similar processes. A distinction between superficially similar processes has been repeatedly demonstrated in domains such as vowel harmony vs vowel-to-vowel coarticulation (e.g. Przezdziecki 2005), vowel reduction (Barnes 2006; Kingston 2007), consonant palatalisation (Zsiga 1995, 2000), and tone spreading vs peak delay (Myers 2000).

An important special case of this situation is found when *the same language* possesses both versions of some sound pattern, dubbed 'rule scattering' by Bermúdez-Otero (2015).[5] Examples include vowel reduction in Russian (Barnes 2007; Iosad 2012a), palatalisation in English (Zsiga 1995) and in Bothoa Breton (section 7.2.3), English [l]-darkening (Turton 2014), and gemination in Hungarian (Pycha 2009, 2010). The existence of rule scattering is an important argument for a phonology that is separate from the phonetics, establishing that the two can coexist but produce different outcomes.

2.2.7 Crazy rules

A frequent argument for the autonomy of phonology is the existence of 'crazy rules' (Bach and Harms 1972) – phonological patterns that have no obvious synchronic rationale but represent the accrual of successive historical changes. Anderson (1981) makes this argument in the context of the naturalness controversy, arguing that an abstract phonological computation is necessary to represent the knowledge of the relevant facts.

This argument has come under fire from functionalist approaches. One prominent example is Evolutionary Phonology (Blevins 2004, 2006), which all but does away with synchronic abstract computation by declaring it a mere duplicate of the historical explanation: if a historical account of some sound pattern is available, no explanatory synchronic devices are necessary. However, this view presupposes there are no abstract biases in speakers' knowledge of language, in effect meaning that they can learn any pattern from the ambient data, as long as it has been produced by a certain sequence of changes; factors ensuring the non-attestation of certain patterns are purely functional.

The position that humans can learn basically anything using domain-general mechanisms as long as there is sufficient ambient data is also buttressed by the burgeoning study of statistical learning. However, as emphasised by authors such as Yang (2002, 2004), statistical learning still relies on a well-defined problem domain: as Yang (2004: 452) puts it, 'Although infants seem to keep track of statistical information, any conclusion drawn from such findings must presuppose that children know *what kind* of statistical information to keep track of.'[6]

Functionally unmotivated sound patterns ('crazy rules') require a mechanism of learning and representation that is distinct from the functional biases active in acquisition, production, and perception. That mechanism can be either domain-general (e.g. general learning capabilities) or domain-specific (an autonomous phonology). The question of whether domain-general mechanisms are sufficient to achieve the requisite knowledge is an empirical one, of course; the present book attempts to provide a set of hypotheses consonant with the autonomous-phonology view.

2.2.8 Sign languages

Further evidence for the autonomy of phonological representations comes from languages that do not use the aural modality (first and foremost sign languages). As discussed by van der Hulst (1993) and Morén (2003), if the phonologies of spoken and sign languages share the same computational module (call it 'Universal Grammar', UG) (Sandler 1993), then the mapping between phonological representations and phonetic realisations provided by UG cannot be modality-bound (and thus cannot be the 'universal phonetics' of Chomsky and Halle 1967). It follows that the mapping between phonology and phonetics is, in principle, language-specific and must be learned, buttressing the emergent-feature hypothesis.

2.2.9 Conclusion on autonomy

In this section I have summarised some arguments for phonological representations that are both distinct in kind from a phonetic representation and not trivially recoverable from the signal. The two major points are the autonomy of phonological representation from phonetic reality and the existence of phonology-specific representational and computational principles.

The first point has major consequences for phonological analysis. If phonological representation cannot be easily recovered, any analysis must first make explicit the procedure used for the discovery of these representations. In this book I defend a minimalist approach that rejects a relatively strong conception of Universal Grammar with a narrowly defined set of representational primitives, and subscribe to an emergentist approach where phonological representations are learned on the basis of ambient data.

The second point is that the functioning of phonology cannot entirely be derived from domain-general or functionally driven mechanisms. Most of the evidence given so far has concentrated on the existence of phonological categories. A significant amount of work exists that recognises the existence of categories alongside more finely grained 'gradient' phenomena (see Pierrehumbert et al. 2000; Pierrehumbert 2006), although sometimes it is argued that categorical behaviour can emerge from bottom-up interactions (e.g. Wedel 2007). The working assumption here is that the potential of categorical phonology has been far from exhausted, and that an explicit theory of how phonological categories may interact once they are in place still remains desirable (see also Cohn 2006, 2010, 2011). Only offering such a theory may put us in a position to explicitly compare the formalist, modular approach with frameworks seeking a non-modular integration between different types of the knowledge of sound patterns.

2.3 The status of the interfaces

If we accept a modular view of the language faculty, we are faced with a dilemma regarding the type of interaction between modules. Barring a complete disavowal of the modular perspective, there are two possible positions, which I shall call the 'poor' versus the 'rich' interface model.

2.3.1 Two approaches to the interface

The 'poor' interface model is more akin to Fodor's (1983) original conception, where the translation between the symbolic alphabets specific to each module is undertaken by the simple and deterministic mechanism of *transduction* (e.g. Pylyshyn 1984). In phonological scholarship, this position has been taken most explicitly by Hale et al. (2007), Reiss (2007) and Hale and Reiss (2008): 'these two transducers [perception → phonology and phonology → articulation] are innate and invariant – they are identical in all humans (barring some specific neurological impairment) and do not change over time or experience (i.e., they do not "learn")' (Hale et al. 2007: 647).

In this approach, the roots of which go back to at least Jakobson et al. (1951) and Chomsky and Halle (1967), the mapping between phonological units such as features and articulatory and/or perceptual entities is relatively simple and highly consistent cross-linguistically, although Hale et al. (2007) do have a place for language-specific mechanisms in the mapping from signal to phonology. This approach does not exclude a substance-free view of phonological computation, in that computation may still proceed without reference to extraphonological considerations (Hale and Reiss 2000a, 2000b, 2008; Hale et al. 2007; Reiss 2003, 2007;

Samuels 2011), but it does significantly reduce the amount of crosslinguistic variation in sound patterns due to factors other than phonology, by drastically simplifying the interface.

A contrasting view, expressed perhaps most prominently by Jackendoff (1987, 1992, 1997, 2000, 2002),[7] sees both 'modules' and 'interfaces' as essentially similar entities. There is no significant difference in complexity: both perform some kind of computation. Jackendoff (2002) calls the different types 'integrative' and 'interface' modules: the difference is that the former have objects of identical types as inputs and outputs, while the latter translate between different types of objects. In phonological terms, this means that the interface between phonetics and phonology differs from both 'phonetics' and 'phonology' in that it takes as its input phonological representations – perhaps 'phones' as envisaged by Ladd (2014) – and produces phonetic entities, for instance gestural scores à la Browman and Goldstein (1990), Silverman (1997) and Hale and Reiss (2008) (in production mode), or vice versa, taking some perceptual representation and translating it into a surface-phonological representation (in perception mode).[8] In other respects, it behaves like any other module in the grammar. In particular, it is not necessarily innate, but may be learned, so that there is no expectation of universality. In other words, under the 'rich' interface approach it is only to be expected that 'similar' phonological representations should demonstrate some language-specific variation in their phonetic realisation.

In this book, I subscribe to a version of the rich interface model. I assume that the translation between phonological and non-phonological representations is not trivial and, in particular, that it is not crosslinguistically consistent. It still remains a module, with the implications that modularity has for encapsulation. Specifically, the phonetics–phonology interface has no access to information that is not somehow accessible via the output of the phonological module, such as underlying forms of morphemes, contrasts obscured in the course of phonological computation, and the morphological affiliation of phonological objects.[9]

2.3.2 Domain-specificity and external interfaces

Under domain-specificity, each module only manipulates symbols of a certain type, and cannot access symbols belonging to other domains. It is important because an integrative module is essentially defined by the type of elements it can 'see'. Simplifying somewhat, we could say that the definition of phonology is 'the module that takes strings of phonological objects (such as features and suprasegmental structure, which should then be defined independently) and outputs strings of phonological objects'.

This feed-forward model has been claimed to be problematic in view of various interactions between phonology and other modules. Some examples include category-specific effects, the effects of lexical frequency, various 'cophonology' effects (e.g. the special behaviour of borrowings), and the influence of social information.

Many of these remain controversial. For instance, Bermúdez-Otero (2012) offers an extended discussion of morphology–phonology interactions within a strictly modular framework, while MacKenzie (2013), MacKenzie and Tamminga (2013), and Tamminga et al. (2016) demonstrate that the interaction between phonology and the 'usage component' sensitive to social information may be serial rather than parallel. Resolving these issues fully is far beyond the scope here. However, one aspect of the Jackendovian parallel architecture that is worth mentioning here is the status of the lexicon in the model. For Jackendoff (2002), the lexicon is not a module within the feed-forward pipeline, but rather a 'mediator' between other modules: lexical activation links the activation of different phonological, syntactic, and semantic representations, which are themselves confined to their respective modules. Under this view, modularity does not necessarily preclude at least the interface modules from being more weakly encapsulated with respect to non-grammatical knowledge, such as knowledge of social networks.

It is also possible that what is influenced by social information is not necessarily phonological computation, but rather the mechanism that effects the mapping from the phonetics to the lexical representation. Lexical recognition is known to be sensitive to various types of non-phonological knowledge. In our terms, the relevant mechanism is the phonology–phonetics interface, which takes whatever representations the phonetic module operates with and matches them with a phonological string, with input – via short- and long-term memory – from other components involved in lexical recognition. This allows for both bottom-up mechanisms (e.g. the matching of phonetic substance to plausibly related phonological representations) and top-down pressures, such as those related to lexical frequency and extralinguistic (e.g. encyclopaedic or social) knowledge. It is reasonable that such mechanisms, which implicate overall knowledge of the lexicon (e.g. frequency, neighbourhood density) in the interface mappings, enable the existence of less than straightforward interactions between the integrative modules. However, they require *no* reference to social factors or lexical knowledge *in the phonological computation*. In other words, extralinguistic knowledge may affect the *input* to phonology, but it is not necessarily true that it intrudes on the phonological operations as such.

Once again, a grand theory of extralinguistic knowledge in formal phonology is far beyond the scope of this book. Such a theory is necessary if modular assumptions are to be upheld. However, it appears that a theory providing for *both* extralinguistic influence of phonological patterns *and* the existence of an encapsulated phonological module is not impossible. This tallies well with approaches such as that of Cohn (2006, 2011), who suggests that phenomena such as frequency or prototype effects in perception are powerful, but perhaps not powerful enough to explain the categoricity found in sound patterns cross-linguistically.

A categorical computation may exist, 'emerging' perhaps in some sense from the ambient data, but still possessing a proprietary universe of discourse and its own rules rather than forming one end of a continuum of phenomena with no difference in kind between smaller-scale gradient effects and larger-scale categorical behaviour. This argument will arise repeatedly in the course of this book (cf. also Barnes 2006; Moreton 2006; Bermúdez-Otero 2007a; Becker et al. 2011 for related discussion).

2.3.3 *Interfacing as interpretation*

If interfaces are as complex as integrative modules, we need a restrictive theory of how much an interface can do. Information *can* be lost or introduced by the computation in integrative modules: for instance, in most models morpheme boundaries are not part of the phonological output, while metrical structure is mostly introduced by the computation. It is not unthinkable that interface modules could then significantly reduce the informational content compared with their input. However, such an approach essentially obliterates the difference between the integrative phonological module and the interface, allowing for equally powerful transformations in both. As a restrictive working hypothesis, I suggest the following principle:

(1) **The Interface Interpretation Principle:** An interface module cannot obligatorily collapse contrasts present in its input.

In phonology–phonetics interactions, the Interface Interpretation Principle (IIP) entails that all contrasts present in the surface phonological representation must be available to the phonetics, at least in principle. Specifically, it forbids effecting absolute neutralisation of phonological contrasts in the interface, ruling out a large class of potential approaches to issues such as absolute neutralisation and certain types of opacity.

If neutralisation by the interface were permitted, many classic cases of absolute neutralisation and opacity could be resolved without recourse to a multi-level phonological computation (a major objective of phonological study in the recent past), just by using the feed-forward modular architecture. To take a couple of familiar examples, one could assume that *surface-phonological* representations in Hungarian contain the [–low +back –round] vowels [ɯ(ː)] and [ɤ(ː)], with the [ɯ]~[i] and [ɤ]~[e] contrasts collapsed at the interface. Similarly, a conceivable analysis of the opaque interaction between PRICE raising and flapping in North American English would postulate surface-phonological representations such as [ɹəɪtɚ] for *writer* and [ɹaɪdɚ] for *rider*, with the stop contrast neutralised to [ɾ] at the interface and the raising transparently triggered *in the phonology*. The principle in (1) prohibits such analyses, since they allow the interface to effect *obligatory* neutralisation of contrasts present in the output of the phonology.[10]

However, I do not propose that categories that are distinct in the phonology will always be mapped to the phonetics in a way that makes them clearly distinct: quite to the contrary, the phonetics–phonology interface does allow for situations where tokens belonging to distinct categories are realised with a very high degree of overlap between the permitted ranges of realisation of the two categories. There are at least three types of such non-bijective relationships between phonological symbols and areas of the phonetic space: incomplete neutralisation, listener-agnostic patterns, and phone subsetting.

2.3.3.1 Incomplete neutralisation

Incomplete neutralisation arises when several categories are distinct in the phonological output but are realised in extremely similar ways on the surface. Thus, it has been argued that 'final devoicing' in many languages, normally treated as the neutralisation of the laryngeal contrast (Trubetzkoy 1939), actually preserves the distinction, since it is recoverable by speakers, in Catalan (Dinnsen and Charles-Luce 1984; Charles-Luce and Dinnsen 1987), Polish (Slowiaczek and Dinnsen 1985; Slowiaczek and Szymanska 1989), Russian (Dmitrieva et al. 2010), Dutch (Ernestus and Baayen 2007), German (Port and O'Dell 1985), and Friulian (Baroni and Vanelli 2000). Similarly, North American English flapping has been argued to involve incomplete neutralisation, since the laryngeal feature specification of the coronal stop is recoverable from the length of the preceding vowel (and other cues normally associated with laryngeal contrast), and presumably from vowel quality in dialects with 'Canadian' Raising (Fisher and Hirsch 1976; Fox and Terbeek 1977; Zue and Laferriere 1979; Braver 2011).

Incomplete neutralisation has been cited in support of particular approaches to phonological representation (e.g. van Oostendorp 2008), but also of a complete rejection of formal phonology (Port and Leary 2005). On the other hand, some cases of incomplete neutralisation have been criticised as unduly influenced by laboratory conditions, orthography, and similar confounding factors (Fourakis and Iverson 1984; Manaster Ramer 1996; Warner et al. 2004), and van Rooy et al. (2003) show that complete neutralisation of the laryngeal contrast in word-final position in Afrikaans is progressively more likely as the experimental conditions approach naturalistic settings.[11] (However, as Jansen 2004 points out, not all of the experiments reported in the literature are open to such criticisms.)

The modular framework advocated here can accommodate both complete and incomplete neutralisation, if the interface between phonetics and phonology is learned and language-specific. Incomplete neutralisation arises when the range of variation allowed in the realisation of a phonological category becomes so large as to overlap the range of realisations permitted for a different phonological category. In other words, the existence of ambiguous tokens does not preclude the existence of distinct categories, but does require an explicit statement of the range of variation permitted by the interface in a particular language in a particular context. A similar approach is envisaged by Scobbie (1995), who says:

> The English words *sip* and *zip* contrast, so surface structure *must* provide feature bundles, say /s/ and /z/, to differentiate them. The /z/ in *buzz* is usually partially devoiced, being prepausal. General (but not necessarily universal) phonetic interpretation rules account for this, so we do not need a feature bundle [...] for 'partly devoiced /z/'. (Scobbie 1995: 305)

This approach can be very naturally paired with the 'window' model of (co)articulation proposed by Keating (1988b, 1990a). She suggests that the phonetics–phonology interface assigns to each phonological feature specification a range of values along certain dimensions – a window – into which the relevant phonetic tokens must fall. Formulated in these terms, the Interface Interpretation Principle requires that distinct phonological categories cannot be assigned identical windows in the implementation – although it says nothing about the windows overlapping. Prototypical cases of incomplete neutralisation are those where most realisations of one of the categories tend to fall into an area where its window overlaps with the window for the other category, at least along one of the relevant parameters: thus, in a language where devoicing is not yet part of the phonology, we can expect the word-final voiced obstruents to be realised without voicing *most of the time* (with the process still potentially under cognitive control, e.g. in response to social factors), but still retain the possibility of having a voiced realisation. Crucially, such a language should not allow the converse pattern: phonological voiceless obstruents cannot be realised with voicing,[12] just as in Scobbie's *buzz* example a partially devoiced [z] is allowed in *buzz* but generally not in *bus*.

This approach allows for several patterns of neutralisation, which are given below using final devoicing as an example. Here, as elsewhere in this book, I use the notation $[\![x]\!]$ to refer to the phonetic implementation of the phonological expression x, itself written as $[x]$ when the output of the phonology is at stake and as $/x/$ when the form is not a surface representation:[13]

- No neutralisation either in the phonology or the phonetics: /t ~ d/ → [t ~ d] → ⟦t ~ d⟧. Attested widely, e.g. in English.
- Neutralisation in the phonology: /t ~ d/ → [t] → ⟦t⟧. Traditionally assumed as the widespread case of neutralisation, e.g. in German or Russian.
- Near-neutralisation in the interface: /t ~ d/ → [t ~ d] → ⟦t ~ t/ḑ(/d)⟧. This is 'incomplete neutralisation', characterised by overlap between the realisations of the two phonological categories. Preferences within both categories can be driven by controlled and uncontrolled factors, for instance speech rate, aerodynamic considerations, social pressures, and so on.

The mappings predicted to be impossible are /t ~ d/ → [t ~ d] → ⟦t⟧, where the contrast is collapsed by the interface, and /t ~ d/ → [t ~ d] → ⟦t/t̞/ḑ/d⟧, where all possible realisations are ambiguous with respect to their phonological interpretation. The IIP entails that if *all* tokens are phonetically ambiguous – they can equally well correspond to any of the underlying phonological categories – then the output of the phonology must also have neutralised the underlying contrast.

From the perspective of a substance-free theory, the most important corollary of this approach is that apparent neutralisation can have a number of sources: either phonological neutralisation or partial neutralisation by the interface. Determining the type of neutralisation that a given language exhibits requires either empirical study, with careful disentangling of the various phonological, phonetic, and sociolinguistic factors, or evidence from the phonological behaviour of the relevant elements that would show that they are distinct in the phonology. Ideally, of course, the two types of evidence should converge. In Chapter 11, I argue that Breton shows just such a case of convergence, with both phonetic and phonological evidence of incomplete neutralisation in the output of the phonology.

To conclude, a model of the phonology–phonetics interface organised along the lines sketched here is able to deal with incomplete neutralisation and also implies a meaningful restriction on the architecture of phonological patterns: contrasts present in the output of phonology cannot be obligatorily neutralised by the interface.

2.3.3.2 Near-mergers and listener-agnostic phonological patterns

One type of pattern where the interface seems to collapse phonological distinctions is the case of the so-called near-mergers. In a near-merger situation, speakers claim to be unaware of a difference in the realisation of two distinct categories, but still produce a consistent contrast, which can also be identified in perception experiments (see, for instance, Gordon 2002; Maguire et al. 2013). In this case, the interface neutralisation only seems to affect perception, and perhaps incompletely at that: although hearers are not conscious of a difference, they may be able to attend to it in commutation tasks, and clearly do not implement a merger in production.

Near-mergers afford a glimpse into the nature of overlapping windows. As demonstrated especially by Milroy and Harris (1980), near-mergers often involve a significant overlap in possible realisations, i.e. a large number of genuinely ambiguous tokens.[14] As suggested by Milroy and Harris (1980), it is this large set of ambiguous realisations that leads the speakers to claim the lack of contrast; nevertheless, the range of realisation is not *identical*, meaning that the interface fails to fully neutralise the phonological contrast found on the surface.

The crucial point is, again, that near-mergers still presuppose a clear separation between the cognitive representation in terms of lexically contrastive units (i.e. phonology) and the phonetic implementation of these representations. The fact that some contrasts may appear to be neutralised due to factors such as social pressures does not invalidate the existence of the distinction: the interface always provides at least the *potential* for expressing these contrasts phonetically. Research has shown that such suboptimal contrasts can develop either towards a full merger (which obliterates the contrast at the level of phonology, and eventually of the lexicon) or to a situation where the realisations of the phonological categories drift apart, leading to an apparent 'merger reversal'. The crucial factor here is the preservation of the contrast *in the phonology*, despite the phonetic realisations making it difficult.[15]

A similar argument for the independence of phonological representation and the properties of its phonetic realisation can be made on the basis of phonological patterns that persist despite leaving no audible trace. An example is phrase-initial geminate obstruents in Thurgovian German. As described by Kraehenmann (2001, 2003), this language has no laryngeal contrast, but clearly contrasts long and short ('geminate' and 'singleton') consonants. This contrast is extremely difficult to maintain in non-postvocalic contexts. It is thus not surprising that it should be neutralised, for instance, adjacent to another consonant (Kraehenmann 2003). In word-initial position, geminates and singletons clearly contrast following a vowel in a phrasal context, but at the acoustic level there is no way of distinguishing the two classes in absolute phrase-initial position (Kraehenmann 2003). Nevertheless, as Kraehenmann and Lahiri (2008) demonstrate, Thurgovian German speakers do make a durational distinction phrase-initially, even though it is vacuous acoustically.

This case shows that speakers do not just pick up generalisations from acoustic data, since there is no possibility for them to learn from the acoustics that there are two classes for phrase-initial stops: rather, they must make an abstract generalisation, tying the two classes of stops in phrase-medial position to the two phrase-initial classes of stops. Phonological representation cannot be simply identified with the phonetic form, but rather requires abstraction.

2.3.3.3 Phone subsetting

A final case of overlapping windows is found when the range of realisations permitted for one category is a complete subset of the range allowed for a different category. For instance, Flemming and Johnson (2007) show that the '[ɨ]' in *roses* occupies a subset of the space allotted to the '[ə]' of *Rosa's* in American English. Following Ladd (2011), this fact can be interpreted in terms of two separate phonological categories (Ladd calls them 'phonemes') mapping to two separate regions of the phonetic space. The Interface Interpretation Principle allows this, because there is no *obligatory* neutralisation: *roses* can be homophonous with *Rosa's*, but does not have to be.

2.3.4 *The interface and sound change*

The autonomy of the interface vis-à-vis surface phonological representation can also be observed in the existence of gradual, regular ('Neogrammarian') sound change (Labov 1994, 2010; Labov et al. 2013; Fruehwald 2013). In changes such as vowel shifts, individuals differ in the phonetic implementation of what are essentially the same phonological categories. Fruehwald (2016) provides a particularly instructive example in his analysis of the raising of the PRICE vowel in Philadelphia English. Fruehwald shows that the change proceeds gradually over time, without categorical variation between the original and the raised allophone. This suggests that there exists a language-specific mechanism that maps the PRICE phonological category to phonetic realisation, and that speakers in different generations show subtle differences in the operation of this mechanism. Further, Fruehwald (2016) argues that at essentially all stages of the change the raised versions of PRICE represent the phonological category of a 'clipped' vowel, separate from the one to which the non-raised tokens belong, and it is the realisation of that category that undergoes change over time. This is a very clear example of cross-linguistic, language-specific variation in the phonetics–phonology interface.

2.3.5 *Conclusion on interfaces*

In this section I have argued that the phonetics–phonology interface is best viewed not as a transducer effecting a highly deterministic mapping between phonological and phonetic representation, but rather as something akin to a module translating phonological representations into phonetic ones (and vice versa). Such a view of the interface is necessary to uphold the autonomy of phonological representation and computation, since a transducer along the lines of Hale et al. (2007) and Hale and Reiss (2008) cannot account for the range of variation found in the realisation of phonological phenomena.

This view of the interface makes some types of interaction between the components of grammar (such as morphologically conditioned phonetics) an architectural impossibility. I have suggested that a limiting condition on the operation of the phonetics–phonology interface is the impossibility of obligatory neutralisation of phonological contrasts, or of obligatory introduction of contrasts not present in the phonology. As we shall see throughout this book, these conditions are a useful heuristic for distinguishing phonological patterns from interface mappings.

2.4 Substance-free phonology and overgeneralisation

An important argument against substance-free phonology is that it overgenerates, i.e. that the set of grammars deemed possible within this framework is substantially larger than the set of grammars that are attested. I deal with two possible versions of this argument: the existence of crazy patterns and the failure to make quantitative predictions about frequency.

2.4.1 Crazy patterns

With an essentially arbitrary mapping between phonetics and phonology and no built-in grounding conditions, substance-free phonology appears open to the criticism of being unable to distinguish between attested, or at least attestable, languages and languages that are allowed by the theory but are not attested, and perhaps felt highly unlikely to be attested ('pathological predictions'). However, as others have pointed out (Blaho 2008; Hale and Reiss 2008; Samuels 2011), this argument is valid only if the distribution of attested grammars is determined only by the mechanics of the formal grammar. Clearly, however, other factors have an influence on both the set of attested patterns and on their distribution.

First, the set of attested languages is strongly influenced by externalities such as the exigencies of population movements, language extinction, the availability of fieldworkers in a certain time and place, and so on; many gaps in the record created in this way are obviously accidental (although it is worth pointing out that these gaps might seep into phonologists' intuitions of what '(im)possible' and '(im)plausible' patterns look like). It is also worth noting that a body of research has argued that small speaker communities tend to preserve typologically unusual structures, including those which functionally based frameworks would treat as dispreferred, much better than large communities (Nettle 1999a, 1999b; Wohlgemuth

2010; Trudgill 2011).[16] Given the high rate of extinction of languages with small community size, both in the very recent past and, presumably, in connection with events such as the rapid expansion of agriculture, it is likely that 'unusual' patterns were disproportionately represented among these accidental gaps unattested in research in theoretical linguistics. This warrants caution in the deployment of the non-attestation argument. Several cautionary tales are provided by the history of metrical typology, where ternary rhythm (C. Rice 1992), initial extrametricality (Buckley 1992), and quantity-insensitive iambs (Altshuler 2009) have all at some point been assumed not to exist.

Trends in diachronic development are another widely recognised filter. If phonological change is not random but driven in part by functional and formal biases in production, perception, and acquisition, it is only to be expected that some types of sound change should be much more frequent than others, and thus that grammars favoured by these biases will be over-represented cross-linguistically. As emphasised, among others, by Blevins (2004), the synchronic grammar does not need to encode these preferences. On the other hand, the same mechanism of diachronic change can produce 'unintuitive' or functionally unmotivated patterns (see also Anderson 1981; Mielke 2007; Yu 2007).

Finally, as Reiss (2007) argues, some patterns are predicted to be possible under a certain permutation of representational and/or computational prerequisites but unlearnable under other, independent, assumptions. One such factor is the acquisition system, which might lead the learner to interpret the data produced by the 'implausible' grammar in terms of a different grammar. If such a theory of learning is available, it is not necessary to exclude these computable but unlearnable languages via some grammatical device. For concrete implementation of similar ideas, see Alderete (2008) and, with less bias towards OT, Heinz (2009).

2.4.2 *Frequency of occurrence*

The relatively low importance accorded to non-attestation in a substance-free framework brings into even sharper relief the necessity of distinguishing between accidental non-attestation of phenomena that the theory should allow for and principled non-attestation of patterns that cannot be generated by the grammar. On the other hand, there are no commitments from the grammar to model the frequency of the occurrence of some pattern either within a language (synchronic variation) or cross-linguistically.

In much of the OT literature, treating unattested patterns as accidental gaps is undesirable, since the ultimate aim is to achieve the tightest possible fit between the set of attested phenomena and the set of mappings allowed by the grammar. Thus, a grammar allowing some unattested pattern is considered inferior to a grammar that excludes that pattern via harmonic bounding.

Factorial typology has also been used to model not just the set of attested languages but also their expected frequency: if multiple rankings can lead to a single input–output mapping, then, *ceteris paribus*, it is expected that grammars favoured by more rankings should be more frequent cross-linguistically, providing an additional restriction on choosing the 'correct grammar'. Similar thinking underlies some attempts to derive quantitative aspects of within-speaker variation from the workings of the OT grammar (Coetzee and Pater 2011).

Both of these arguments, if valid, undermine the substance-free framework, since it is unable to make the necessary sort of specific, quantitative predictions. However, both arguments rely on the assumption that the distribution of constraint rankings is random, which is necessary for arguments of the following form: 'If grammar G were the correct grammar, we would expect there to exist a language L exhibiting undesirable property P; such languages are unattested, therefore G is not to be preferred if alternatives excluding P are available.' This argument suffers not just from assuming impossibility based on lack of attestation, but also from treating all conceivable rankings as having approximately equal probabilities: otherwise, it is not at all clear why we 'should expect' L to exist.

Since language is learned from ambient data, we expect the distribution of attested grammars to be skewed towards rankings that are similar to those attested in synchronic systems at any given time. This distribution, in turn, is far from random. It is thus not at all obvious when we should 'expect' a pattern to be attested: it may be accidentally unattested due to language extinction, or for lack of a description, or it may only arise as the result of a chain of highly unlikely diachronic changes, etc. None of these cases requires building an explanation for the lack of the pattern into the formal grammar.

In fact, the question of whether accounting for the cross-linguistic *frequency* of patterns is a primary aim of the theory of grammar is an open one. Arguably, this frequency is not an aspect of the human knowledge of language, but instead a function of a variety of factors, including diachronic changes and biases active in language use and acquisition. The theoretical linguist's primary object of study is not behaviour, although it is used as a window on knowledge of language. Typological frequency is not part of that knowledge, and may lie outwith the remit of grammar (for more discussion on this point, see Newmeyer 2005; Harris 2008, 2010). Thus, possibly, the fact that substance-free phonology does worse than orthodox approaches at accounting for the precise quantitative characteristics of cross-linguistic variation may not be quite as problematic.

2.5 The status of Universal Grammar in phonological theory

The rejection of straightforwardly typological approaches argued for above does not make substance-free phonology unfalsifiable; instead, it represents a different approach to what the remit of Universal Grammar should be. Substance-free phonology does predict that certain types of phonological patterns (input–output mappings effected by the phonological module) should be impossible. However, extracting the right generalisations is not straightforward. Whatever universals exist in phonology, they are, in Hyman's (2008) terms, analytic rather than absolute. Since the sources of variation in sound patterns are numerous in almost any theoretical approach (except the most expansionist ones), 'It is misguided to attribute every accidentally true statement about human language to U[niversal] G[rammar]' (Odden 1988: 461).

Any pronouncements on whether a theory of the phonological component should allow a particular pattern require a precise statement of the pattern in representational and computational terms, with an explicit discussion of the division of labour between phonological grammar and other participating mechanisms.[17]

For example, a substance-free phonological theory has nothing to say about the behaviour of specific, concrete features: it is not possible to formulate universal, hard-wired asymmetries such as those between 'place' and 'voice' features (Lombardi 2001), because 'place' and 'voice' are not primitives of the theory but rather language-specific categories. Instead, it *is* possible to state general conditions on how (any) two features may interact. In that sense, substance-free phonology undoubtedly 'overgenerates' the set of conceivable descriptive patterns. However, since the patterns are contingent not just on the phonological computation but also on other factors, minimalist phonological computations are not directly comparable with the more substance-found analyses common in the literature. Rather, conventional grammars with an expansionist role for phonology should be compared with comprehensive accounts covering all of the factors behind the attestation of surface patterns, and traditional factorial typology is clearly only a part of this enterprise. The importance of such holistic modelling is particularly highlighted by Morley (2015), who demonstrates that even apparently well-defined phonological frameworks found in the literature still suffer from significant underdetermination. While the present work is by necessity somewhat exploratory in nature, I take Morley's result to mean that it would not necessarily be fair to dismiss the substance-free approach simply because it does not make easy, cut-and-dried typological predictions.

The approach advocated here, which seeks to distribute the explanatory burden of accounting for cross-linguistic variation across several contributing components, is a common denominator for otherwise quite different conceptions of 'substance-free' phonology. It is found in work by the 'Concordia school' (Hale and Reiss 2000a; Hale et al. 2007; Reiss 2007; Hale and Reiss 2008), extensively argued for by Samuels (2011), and used in what we might call Radical Substance-Free Phonology (Odden 2010, 2013; Blaho 2008).

Dresher (2014) expresses reservations about this scattering of explanations, arguing that the emphasis on extraphonological accounts of variation effectively relieves formal phonology of any explanatory responsibility (see also Hall 2011, 2014). Whether such criticisms are justified can sometimes only be decided with reference to a particular theory. An example is Samuels's (2011) extended argument against the necessity of the syllable, which assigns to extraphonological factors the responsibility for some of the phenomena traditionally accounted for using the syllable: Samuels may or may not be correct about this, but this is effectively an empirical question. However, the formal machinery of substance-free phonology – certainly as it is envisaged here – is not entirely devoid of explanatory burden. The focus in much of this book is on feature theory, and features are indispensable for the formalisation of phonological distinctions (both in underlying and surface representations), class behaviour, and interactions between classes. The next chapter in particular discusses how even a substance-free theory of features can impose non-trivial restrictions on the form of contrast, both through representational devices such as geometry and through relevant additional theories, such as the theory of contrast; I refer to Cowper and Hall (2014) in particular for discussion of the centrality of features to any theory of linguistic distinctions.

To sum up, to the extent we can speak of a Universal Grammar in a substance-free framework, it is envisaged as a set of principles underlying the construction and manipulation of phonological structure. This structure, once constructed, certainly does influence other aspects of linguistic behaviour, and imposes certain restrictions on them, for instance via the Interface Interpretation Principle. To be sure, other aspects of this behaviour are explained by factors that do not have anything to do with the phonological grammar, and in that sense phonology has 'less to do' in this framework. Yet this question is ultimately an empirical one, and answering it requires constructing an explicit theory. This is exactly what this book sets out to do.

2.6 Summary and outlook

In this chapter I have presented some very general outlines of the research programme of substance-free phonology. I have argued that there are several important consequences to the idea of phonology as a separate module. In particular, phonology is *autonomous*: there exist domain-specific representational and computational systems. Several corollaries follow from this idea, of which the following are of greatest importance:

- The autonomy of phonological representations: phonological representations are always language-specific, cannot be unambiguously recovered from the signal, and are evidenced by language-internal facts rather than aprioristic assumptions about the phonology–phonetics mapping.
- The autonomy of phonological computation: the principles of phonological computation make no reference to functional grounding, but are domain-specific. The fact that typological distributions closely follow functional bases is not an *explanandum* only for the theory of phonological computation, but also follows from considerations related to language acquisition and language change.
- The complexity of interfaces: interfaces effect the translation between different domains in complex ways, as relatively autonomous modules rather than deterministic transducers. However, there are some conditions on the functioning of the interfaces: in particular, they cannot collapse or introduce arbitrary contrasts present in the input.

These principles will be put to the test in a comprehensive analysis of the phonology of a Breton dialect in later chapters. To conclude this introduction, however, it is useful to identify some remaining issues.

The most important promissory note issued in this book has to do with acquisition and learning. A substance-free theory of phonology has to tread a narrow path between its commitment to the existence and important role of formal structure and the important role of statistical learning. Frameworks that rely on formal structure, such as mainstream generative phonology, often tend to rely on it as a kind of bootstrapping device, one that is always available to the learner and absolves them of the necessity to acquire it. For instance, van 't Veer (2015) offers a model of phonological acquisition where the features themselves are innate, and learning consists of the assignment of these features to segments and of the construction of relevant constraints. In a substance-free model, these latter steps must *also* be preceded by a process that extracts categories from the ambient data and assigns a label to them. This process must by necessity involve quite powerful statistical learning mechanisms, and the question arises whether such powerful mechanisms do not obviate the formal structure. There are some proposals in the literature for the learning of categories, with some of them incorporating both bottom-up and top-down mechanisms – see, for instance, Boersma et al. (2003); Escudero and Boersma (2003); van de Vijver and Baer-Henney (2014); and especially Gorman (2013) for a robust criticism of statistical inference from attested surface forms as the sole acquisition device – but the question is clearly very much open.

Similarly, we must leave open the question of how exactly language-specific phonological patterns feed into the distribution and labelling of phonological categories. Some very recent work in learning shows promising results in the acquisition of various phonological patterns, including 'allophony', i.e. patterns that create predictable surface distributions (Peperkamp et al. 2006; Dillon et al. 2012), and morphophonological alternations (Calamaro and Jarosz 2014), but a full theory of learning and labelling remains elusive. This has to be left for future work, although constructing a plausible theory of acquisition is clearly crucial to the entire substance-free enterprise.

The main aim of this book is to contribute to building an explicit substance-free theory of phonology in order to enable a proper comparison with other available proposals. By demonstrating the feasibility of a substance-free analytic approach, I hope to convince the reader that it would be worthwhile to develop further aspects of the theory, culminating eventually in the creation of an explicit computational model.

Notes

1. Interestingly, such cases still provide evidence for a non-universal mapping between surface phonology and phonetics. A classic case of such an unattested contrast is the one between palatalised dorsals and palatals in the SPE system: both are defined as [–ant –cor +hi –bk]. Although the prediction regarding the lack of contrast between these two categories *in a single language* appears to be correct, phonetically palatalised dorsals (as in, for example, Russian) are quite distinct from palatals (as in, for example, Hungarian), as demonstrated by Keating & Lahiri (1993). It seems difficult to formalise these facts without language-specific statements of how a particular phonological representation should be interpreted phonetically.
2. Note that [g] is exempt but [ɣ] is not. This is not necessarily a problem if we analyse stops and fricatives as using different sets of laryngeal features (Rice 1994).
3. Note, however, that the architecture of OT requires that the class in this case should be formed by the non-undergoing segments, because the constraint must have something to refer to in order to be active; in other words, the undergoing segments are not those that contain an active feature, but rather those that fail to resist the process. This is not a problem in a framework with binary features, because the existence of a constraint against any value of a feature presupposes the existence of that feature, but in a privative approach this requires that, say, in Navajo, it is the coronal fricatives that bear some features for markedness constraints to react to. Again, this is a difficulty

for Mielke's (2007) approach which relies on broad comparison, because it makes the precise identification of natural classes more difficult.
4. 'Distinktive Funktion kann [...] einer Lauteigenschaft nur insofern zukommen, als sie einer anderen Lauteigenschaft gegenübergestellt wird' (Trubetzkoy 1939: 30)
5. Cohn (1998) calls these situations 'phonetic doublets'.
6. For a discussion of the computational difficulties with formulating hypotheses for statistical learning (albeit in the context of PAC (probably approximately correct) learning rather than the Bayesian approaches common in linguistic work), see Aaronson (2013: §7.1), according to whom 'induction *cannot* be merely a matter of seeing enough data and then "generalizing" from it, because immense computations might be needed to *find* a suitable generalisation'.
7. For similar approaches in cognitive science, see Bever (1992) and especially Coltheart (1999).
8. Of course, production and perception can be two different interface modules; this is immaterial here. Here I focus mostly on the production direction of the phonetics–phonology interface.
9. The question of whether phonological grammar can access the morphological affiliation of phonological material is a vexed one. Proponents of modularity appear to agree that even if it is to be allowed, it has to be severely restricted, for instance by limiting it to alignment constraints (Bermúdez-Otero 2012) or via Coloured Containment (van Oostendorp 2007; Trommer & Zimmermann 2014), which limits the amount of information available.
10. Of course, such interface solutions clearly cannot resolve *all* cases of absolute neutralisation or opacity, but can only help with those where the absolute neutralisation or the opacifying rule come last in the derivation.
11. Also relevant here is Mihm's (2007) description of the status of final devoicing in German. He shows that it is a prescriptive norm with a somewhat shaky status in practice, only inconsistently applied even when speaking 'Standard' German, depending on the speaker's dialect background.
12. Discounting cases of imperfect production: we are interested in controlled aspects of the implementation here.
13. The notation is borrowed from semantics, where ⟦x⟧ stands for 'the meaning of x', and reflects the suggestion that the phonetic form is the result of an *interpretation* of the phonological expression in terms of physical events (Pierrehumbert 1990) and in parallel to the treatment of the representational system and computational system as the 'syntax of phonology' by Blaho (2008). In addition, the double-bracket notation is less conspicuous than 'human-figure' brackets, used for essentially the same purpose by Hale & Reiss (2008).
14. Note, however, that additional cues may serve to disambiguate the categories: while formant values show significant overlap or even full merger in both the Ulster English MEAT-MATE merger and Utah English FULL-FOOL

merger, the categories might still be disambiguated by the presence of a glide and creaky phonation respectively (Milroy & Harris 1980; Di Paolo & Faber 1990).
15. Of course, not all merger reversals proceed via this route (Maguire 2008).
16. The direct application of some of these techniques in the domain of phonology has been controversial: see Hay & Bauer (2007), Atkinson (2011), and Wichmann, Rama & Holman (2011) for proposals; and Donohue & Nichols (2011), and Moran, McCloy & Wright (2012) for critical discussion. However, this work focuses largely on phoneme inventories, which are only a small part of a complete phonological description of a language (as emphasised in section 2.2.3).
17. Similar sentiments are expressed by Nevins (2009) in his reaction to Evans & Levinson's (2009) rejection of abstract analysis, and by Reiss (2003), and Hale & Reiss (2008).

3

Representational assumptions

This chapter lays out the representational system used in the book, which is a version of the Parallel Structures Model (PSM) of feature geometry (Morén 2003, 2006, 2007; Krämer 2009; Youssef 2010, 2015; Iosad 2012a; Uffmann 2013) that incorporates the insights of Modified Contrastive Specification (e.g. Dresher et al. 1994; Dyck 1995; Ghini 2001a, 2001b; Dresher 2003, 2009; Hall 2007; Mackenzie 2013). More specifically, I use the PSM, which is based on privative features, and adapt it to the Successive Division Algorithm (SDA). Dresher (2009) concentrates on a version of the SDA with binary features, but see Ghini (2001a, 2001b), Hall (2007), and Cowper and Hall (2014) for applications of the SDA to privative features. I show that this version of the PSM combines the advantages of classic feature geometry (correct grouping of features that behave as a unit, explicit tier structure), language-specific contrastive specification (adherence to the Contrastivist Hypothesis), privative features (economy, non-stipulative expression of markedness relationships), and binary features (surface ternarity in phonology).

3.1 The Parallel Structures Model

The Parallel Structures Model of feature geometry, proposed originally by Morén (2003), is based on unary features and an elaborate geometric structure that builds on the achievements of several previous theories. In its consistently privative approach to featural structure, the PSM is related to Particle Phonology (Schane 1984), Dependency Phonology (Anderson and Ewen 1987; Ewen 1995), and Element Theory (e.g. Harris 1994; Harris and Lindsey 1995; Backley 2011). The recursion of organising nodes and the overall outlines of the treatment of place are inherited from Unified Feature Theory (Clements 1991a, 1991b; Clements and Hume 1995), while the treatment of manner has important points of contact with work such as that by Lombardi (1990) and Steriade (1993).

The organising principle of the PSM is *economy*. It is a minimalist theory, relying on a very small number of architectural assumptions to derive universals of subsegmental organisation, such as tier organisation,

Representational assumptions 37

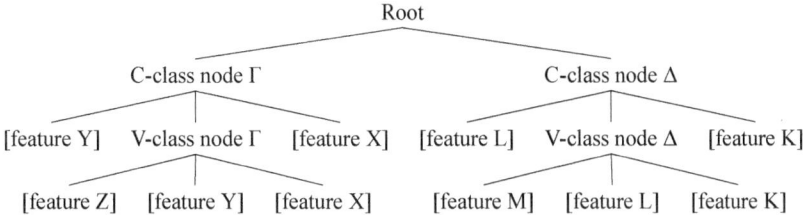

Figure 3.1 Example PSM representation

node recursion, and a small number of privative features. As discussed in section 2.5, this has the consequence that the number of such universals is rather small in a substance-free theory, since the phonetic realisation of PSM structures is not the job of the phonology. Nevertheless, the PSM does disallow some non-trivial classes of potential interactions between phonological objects.

An important characteristic of the PSM is that features never depend directly on the root node: all features must be dominated by a class node, unlike some other proposals which treat at least major class features as dependents of root nodes (Sagey 1986; McCarthy 1988; Halle 1995). However, in the version of PSM I use here, the reverse does not hold: class nodes *can* be terminal. Nevertheless, there is still a distinction between class nodes and features: the SDA prevents class nodes from implementing lexical contrast in the absence of features. This makes the present version of PSM different from frameworks such as Element Theory and the proposal of Blaho (2008), which dispense with class nodes altogether and assume that features may simply depend on other features.

An example PSM representation is shown in Figure 3.1, and explained in more detail in the following sections.

3.2 Tier organisation

An important feature of the Parallel Structure Model of feature geometry is its commitment to tier structure. While SPE-style feature theories usually view segments as unordered bundles of feature values, in the PSM tiers are no less important than features, especially in the present version embracing the contrastive hierarchy. Tiers play two important roles in this model, both of which have to do with restricting possible types of feature interaction: they sort features and they establish autosegmental domains.

3.2.1 *Tier structure in the PSM*

As noted above, all features in PSM representations must be dominated by a class node. A language can have several different types of nodes.

Although in principle the labels associated with class nodes and features are arbitrary, for convenience I will use familiar labels such as Place, Manner, and Laryngeal, rather than, say A, B, or Γ. This is because in the data under scrutiny here interactions between features can be described along these dimensions, although a single feature can have phonetic correlates along more than one of them.

A given feature can only depend on a class node belonging to a single type: a feature cannot reassociate from, say, Manner to Place in the course of the derivation.[1] This is a restriction on GEN: since GEN only produces licit PSM representations (Morén 2006, 2007; Uffmann 2007), the computation cannot enforce such a reassociation.

Another important aspect of tier structure in PSM is recursion. Class nodes, but not features, may dominate nodes of the same type: a Manner node can dominate a Manner node (but not a Place node), while feature nodes are always terminal. Following standard PSM practice, I will refer to nodes dominated by the root node as C-nodes and to those dominated by a C-node as V-nodes. It must be emphasised, however, that this is purely a matter of convenience: there is nothing preventing consonants from having V-features, or vowels from having C-features: the affiliation of features depends on their phonological behaviour. It must also be noted that even though I only make reference to one level of recursion here, i.e. there are no class nodes dominated by V-nodes, there is nothing in the representational system that prohibits their existence. They may well be required for some languages.

3.2.2 Feature typing

When features are unordered bundles, there is in principle no restriction on how they may interact in phonological processes. In a geometrical theory, there are representational restrictions on which features go under which tiers: for instance, there is widespread agreement that features such as [coronal] do not depend on class nodes such as Aperture or Manner. As discussed above, such restrictions are very strong in the PSM, since tier affiliation is essentially part of a feature's definition.

Assigning a type to every feature has a number of important consequences for restrictions on possible feature interactions. Consider a situation where a class node spreads from one segment to another, but some aspect of the language's grammar disallows the recipient to be or to become associated with the feature that this node dominates. In the PSM, there are only two solutions to this conundrum: either the ban is ignored or the spreading fails. In a representational theory without strong feature typing, a third solution is to spread the offending feature to a different class node. The PSM predicts such processes to be impossible.

Importantly, it is only the *type* of the class node that matters here, not its status as a C- or a V-node. It *is* possible for a feature to reassociate from a C-node to a V-node or vice versa, as long as its type remains the same; for specific proposals to this effect, see Clements (1991a), Youssef (2015), and section 11.3.3.2.

Strong typing also does not mean that features of different types cannot interact at all. They may, of course, interact with each other, but the interaction is always mediated by their common mother node – most frequently the root node; cf. the discussion of *{|A|, |B|} constraints by Blaho (2008: §2.5) and see section 4.2.4 for the implementation. It is possible for feature co-occurrence constraints, for instance, to mention both Place and Manner: however, they must formally refer to a node that dominates both of the relevant features. On the other hand, it is not possible for the presence or absence of, say, a Manner node to 'count' when determining whether any potential targets have been skipped in a process involving a Place feature, which is a type of interaction that does not involve the root node. Again, this puts some non-trivial (and falsifiable) restrictions on GEN.

3.2.3 Locality

Another task assigned to class nodes in classic autosegmental phonology is the determination of locality domains (e.g. Avery and Rice 1989; Odden 1994): for instance, a segment lacking a Place node cannot be involved in a process spreading a Place feature, because such a segment is invisible on the Place tier. Similarly, it is commonly assumed that autosegmental spreading cannot skip eligible targets, with tier structure used to determine whether a segment should be treated as such a target. The PSM inherits all these assumptions.

3.3 Featural structure

Just like tier labels, featural labels are in principle arbitrary, although in practice more or less 'phonetic' labels are used, for instance [coronal], [labial], and [dorsal] in the case of Place. Note that there is nothing in the theory to prevent us from incorporating other approaches to Place, such as [peripheral], should that be needed for some language, or even phonetically arbitrary 'abstract' features.

The main function of features is implementing lexical contrast, in line with the Contrastivist Hypothesis. In this section I discuss the issue of featural economy and the unification between the PSM and the contrastive hierarchy that I use heavily in this book.

3.3.1 Feature geometry and the contrastive hierarchy

It is commonly claimed that combining privative features with feature geometry weakens the predictions of privative feature theory, in that it allows for surface ternary contrasts. Specifically, binary features allow [ØF], [+F], and [–F]; purely privative theories allow only Ø and [F]; but a privative theory with bare nodes sides with the apparently less restrictive binary approach by allowing ⟨×⟩, ⟨×, Node⟩, and ⟨×, Node, [F]⟩. This is assumed to be a major weakness of geometric approaches, and consequently many authors stipulate that bare nodes are not possible in the representational system (e.g. Lombardi 1995a), ostensibly because representations such as ⟨×⟩ and ⟨×, Node⟩ never contrast with one another in a single language.

In this book, I question this assumption and embrace the possibility of ternarity inherent in the system, for the simple reason that ternarity appears to be empirically necessary. This is, in principle, not a new argument. Many arguments for ternarity, however, rely on the connection between *input* underspecification and the possibility of alternations and lexical exceptions (Krämer 2012: §4.6), phenomena for which alternative accounts are available: input ternary contrasts are a (contested) analytic device, not direct empirical evidence, in particular since relevant analyses aim to collapse them into binary distinctions in surface forms.

A more convincing argument for the necessity of ternary representations is the existence of cases of *surface ternarity* (see also Strycharczuk 2012; Sen 2015), which appear to falsify the strictly privative approach. In Chapter 11 I analyse just such a case of surface ternarity from Breton, arguing that previous accounts of the relevant phenomena (Krämer 2000; Hall 2009), which employ mapping a ternary contrast in the input to a binary one on the surface, are inadequate. Following Ghini (2001a, 2001b), I treat representations with bare nodes as the result of contrastive non-specification for a privative feature. I demonstrate that while this approach is less restrictive (but more empirically adequate) than one based on unary features only, it is *more* restrictive than a binary-feature framework.

3.3.2 Bare nodes as contrastive non-specification

The version of the PSM used in this book allows bare nodes both in input and output representations. The difference between featureless representations with and without bare nodes is related to contrast.

I suggest that learners are biased to posit inventories that are consistent with a contrastive hierarchy as built up by the SDA (Dresher 2009: §7.8). I use a version of the SDA similar to that proposed by Ghini (2001a, 2001b) but adapted to PSM representations. In 'orthodox' binary-features SDA, feature specification proceeds by a recursive division of an inventory into two subinventories by assigning a + or − value of some feature to each subinventory, stopping when a resulting subinventory consists of a single segment. In the version of the SDA used here, at each cut one subinventory becomes associated with a feature, and therefore – given the architecture of the PSM – also with a class node. The complement of this subinventory set receives the bare class node.

A toy example of this procedure is shown in Figure 3.2. The three-vowel inventory /i u a/ can be classified in a number of ways. For the sake of the argument, I use a contrastive hierarchy that puts V-manner[closed] (or, more traditionally, [(±)high]) above V-place[coronal] ([coronal] or perhaps [(±)back]). Under this contrastive hierarchy, /i/ is treated as {V-pl[cor], C-man[cl]}, /u/ is C-man[cl], and /a/ remains featureless. However, contrastive non-specification is also reflected by tier structure: despite being featureless, /a/ does bear an empty V-manner node, and /u/ bears an empty V-place node. However, /a/ does not bear a V-place node, because it does not contrast for V-place features.

Thus, tier structure essentially recapitulates the key insight of underspecification theory: a distinction between lack of featural specification due to a lack of contrast and lack of specification as the absence of (the marked value of) a *contrastive* feature. This distinction is very easy to express using binary features as one between [±F] and ∅, but it is unavailable in theories using privative features. However, there are several additional implications of this approach that are not expressible in theories using multiply valued features.

Crucially, the presence of a class node signifies the *existence of contrast* along some dimension, while its absence signifies lack of contrast along that dimension. At the same time nodes alone cannot be used to implement lexical contrasts, because, per the algorithm, a class node can

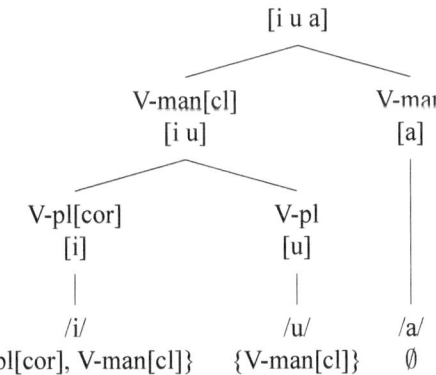

Figure 3.2 Example of successive division with PSM representations

only appear in the representation if required by the assignment of some feature.

The presence or absence of structure can be due both to the properties of lexical entries and to the computation. For instance, since class nodes and features are similar phonological objects, we can posit that markedness constraints of the *[F] family may target both of them. Thus, a constraint *V-place can be used to neutralise all V-place contrasts by enforcing (given the correct ranking) the deletion of the V-place node and thus all its dependent features (cf. Ghini 2001b). Importantly, since the computation is free to manipulate phonological representations without reference to properties of the input, it can also *create* output structures that are not needed for lexical contrast or not consistent with a contrastive hierarchy. Thus, in Chapter 11 I argue that although only two classes of obstruents are required for lexical contrast in Bothoa Breton, the computation creates a third class of 'delaryngealised' obstruents, which are identical to laryngeally specified obstruents except in lacking a C-laryngeal node.

This autonomy of computation, i.e. its relative freedom to manipulate phonological representations, is a major source of cross-linguistic variation, alongside universal and language-specific representation assumptions. It also shows that the differences in contrastive hierarchies, despite their important role, cannot be the only source of variation in phonological patterning across languages (cf. Hall 2007; Mackenzie 2013). In particular, the computation may introduce structures that are at odds with the contrastive hierarchy. The hierarchy is essentially a bootstrapping device, which allows the learner to introduce order into the system of phonological contrasts by breaking the phonological space down into more manageable subinventories. In that sense, it serves purposes that are highly similar to those claimed for the concept of feature economy (e.g. Clements 2003).

This view of the contrastive hierarchy allows us to reject the conclusion by Hall (2007) that it is incompatible with an OT approach, specifically with Richness of the Base. Even if the learner converges on a lexicon where all entries consist of segments that can be arranged into a contrastive hierarchy, it is still incumbent on the computation to map 'deviant' inputs to allowable outputs. Since the contrastive hierarchy is *not* construed as a restriction on possible inputs (unlike the principles of the representational system, i.e. the PSM), a restricted version of Richness of the Base is still upheld.

3.3.3 Empty segments and hierarchy subversion

One apparently undesirable feature of marrying the contrastive hierarchy with a privative approach is that a privative version of the SDA will always designate one segment as being featureless (Hall 2007; Blaho 2008), as is the case with /a/ in Figure 3.2. However, I suggest this is not necessarily a fatal problem. The solution to this issue is partly representational and partly computational.

Representationally, there is no logical requirement for empty root nodes to be impossible segments. Empty root nodes are possible in surface representations in a variety of theories, most prominently in versions of CVCV phonology (e.g. Kaye 1990; Lowenstamm 1996; Scheer 2004), although they are also found in other frameworks. We even find proposals for featureless root nodes that are *pronounced*, for instance as a schwa (e.g. van Oostendorp 2000; Nesset 2002). Thus, the existence of a featureless segment might in fact be a desirable prediction for some languages.

From the computational viewpoint, the contrastive hierarchy serves as a device to construct plausible inputs, not the full set of allowed outputs. It is entirely possible for the computation to map an input empty segment to something else, especially if there is some evidence for that in the patterns of alternation (we shall see some evidence for that in Breton in section 11.3.3). In this case, the existence of the featureless segment in the input to the phonology (perhaps provided by the rich base), or the potential for it being created by the computation, has no significant consequences for the surface inventory, as long as it maps to a non-empty output.

This possibility forces us to confront the issue of whether phonological evidence can lead the learner to construct inventories that are not fully in line with the restrictions on inventories available in the input (as argued by Blaho 2008; Krämer 2009). I suggest the answer is positive: the contrastive hierarchy as construed here is a bootstrapping device or a bias to organise the system of contrast, not an absolute restriction on inputs. Given the autonomy of computation, it should not be problematic for some features or feature configurations to be preserved on the surface despite not fitting in with the hierarchy.

However, accepting this conclusion has potentially grave consequences for the Contrastivist Hypothesis: how do we define what is 'contrastive' if restrictions on the input are not available as a criterion? Here, I assume the following hypothesis: a feature is 'contrastive' if there exists a contrastive hierarchy that is consistent with the data where that feature is used to make at least one distinction.

Since cuts in a contrastive hierarchy constructed using the SDA never introduce redundant distinctions, the requirement of non-redundancy is still met; at the same time this requirement prevents using the empty segment 'loophole' to introduce redundant features. The contrastive hierarchy constructed for Bothoa Breton in section 7.4 exemplifies this kind of analysis: there, I argue that the place of the empty segment in the contrastive hierarchy is occupied by the segment [h], consisting of the feature C-laryngeal[voiceless]. This feature is not redundant in the language at large, since it is *also* used to distinguish the two series of obstruents. For more discussion of the condition, see Iosad (2015a).

3.3.4 Further consequences of gradualness

The contrastive hierarchy as a way of organising the system of contrast is an alternative to Morén's (2003, 2006, 2007) proposals regarding the gradual structure of representations. He suggests that learnability requires all complex featural structures allowed in a language to be divisible into two allowed simple structures. A corollary of this principle is that all features possible in simpler structures should have a 'unit segment', i.e. a segment consisting just of that feature, because a complex structure {|A|, |B|} must by this hypothesis be divisible into {|A|} and {|B|} (see Blaho 2008 for extensive discussion). An inventory such as that shown in Figure 3.2 should be impossible in this version of the PSM, since V-place[coronal] does not have a unit segment in this toy example.

I suggest that the contrastive hierarchy offers an alternative to this conception of gradualness, since it also makes it possible to build up bigger structures from smaller ones. In practice most features will still have unit segments, because the privative version of the SDA always specifies one segment in each (sub)inventory as featureless. Once a feature is used to make a cut in the inventory, there will exist a segment which possesses that feature but no others.

A further restriction on the shape of inventories, noted by Blaho (2008) and true for the version of PSM proposed here, is that the gradual build-up of contrastive structure is reflected in dependency relations between phonological elements. In PSM terms this means that when, say, a Manner feature is used to divide a set of segments that have not yet been specified for Manner, the resulting node will always be C-manner. On the other hand, if the relevant segments have already received a Manner node at a previous iteration, the relevant feature can be added either to the existing C-manner node or to a recursive, i.e. V-manner node. Thus, if a language makes use of a C- and a V-tier for some dimension, at least one C-feature must be higher than all V-features of the same type on the contrastive hierarchy.

Note

1. Yip (2005) proposes that such reassociation should be possible, but her argument relies on cross-linguistic comparison of the behaviour of the feature [lateral]. In the present framework, features in different languages are not comparable even if they have similar phonetic expression.

4

Computational assumptions

Although the present book mostly focuses on highlighting the role of phonological representations in accounting for cross-linguistic variation, it is also important to recognise the power of phonological computation. Representations alone are not sufficient either to provide an explicit analysis or, more importantly, to establish the falsifiability of the proposal.

In this chapter I describe some general properties of the computational system in substance-free phonology, provide some discussion of constraint schemata and in particular the augmentation schema, and conclude by sketching the stratal approach I use to account for morphology–phonology interactions.

4.1 The power of computation

As discussed in Chapter 2, computation is free to manipulate the representations fed into the phonological module in a manner unconstrained by non-phonological considerations. It can ensure that certain surface structures or input–output mappings are excluded from the phonological grammar.

In Optimality Theory, the postulate of Richness of the Base (Prince and Smolensky 1993; McCarthy 2005) makes it possible to derive differences among inventories solely by computational means, i.e. by the reranking of the universal constraint set CON (e.g. Kirchner 1997; Flemming 2005). This has contributed to another swing of Anderson's (1985) representation/computation pendulum towards a more or less explicit assumption that phonological representations are trivial. In other words, in many OT approaches representation does not play any explanatory role in accounting for cross-linguistic variation in sound patterns (as Scheer 2010: 385 puts it, it has no 'sovereign arbitral award').

In a substance-free theory, the language-specificity and learned character of the interface between phonetics and phonology precludes such a total computational reorientation. However, the substance-free approach also recognises the importance of computation, in contrast to declarative formalisms (e.g. Bird and Klein 1994; Bird 1995; Scobbie et al. 1996;

Scobbie 1997; Coleman 1998; Lodge 2009), where computation boils down to the very simple unification procedure, with no cross-linguistic variation. Phonology, in the substance-free view, has both a 'semantics' (Pierrehumbert 1990) and a 'syntax' (Blaho 2008), and both can vary non-trivially across languages.

In this book I use a stratal version of a fairly orthodox variety of Optimality Theory (with a substance-free twist in CON). Specifically, I use a correspondence rather than containment approach to input–output faithfulness (i.e. MAX and DEP rather than PARSE and FILL). I also do not use the different constraint families proposed to deal with the issue of opacity, such as output–output correspondence constraints. When I do analyse opaque mappings, I rely mostly on level ordering, and I will show in Chapter 10 that the data I consider provide strong support for the cyclic model of morphology–phonology interactions over approaches based on correspondence between surface forms. The advantage of using a stratal approach is thus not only conceptual – it is more parsimonious to derive the interactions from level ordering, which is supported on independent grounds (Bermúdez-Otero 2011, 2012) – but also empirical.

4.2 Towards a substance-free computation

Computation in a substance-free phonological theory is encapsulated and thus free of non-phonological concerns. In practice, most non-phonological factors encountered in OT-based literature either are based on 'functional' considerations (reflecting some properties of the human vocal tract, perceptual system, and so on) or are used to transfer morphosyntactic information that may be relevant for the phonology. In this section I concentrate on the former type of phonological non-autonomy.

Functional biases can be introduced into an OT computation in two different ways: via constraint formulations and via constraint rankings. I suggest that neither of these devices is in line with a substance-free approach: all rankings are in principle free, and there are no substantive restrictions on the make-up of the set CON.

4.2.1 No fixed rankings

Fixed rankings, such as the peak and margin hierarchies of Prince and Smolensky (1993) or their ranking metacondition FAITH(Root) » FAITH(Affix), are used to make sure that certain structures are always preferred over others. For instance, they can be deployed to make sure that, *ceteris paribus*, a higher-sonority nucleus is preferred to a low-sonority one, or that 'less marked' places of articulation are preferred as outcomes of neutralisation to more marked ones. There are two types of objections to this approach.

One, argued in detail by de Lacy (2006: §§5.2.2, 5.4, 6.2.3), concerns the fact that fixed rankings cannot derive certain attested patterns of markedness conflation, and are therefore inferior to an approach relying on stringent sets of constraint violations. This is a valid argument, as long as the alternative theory can reproduce the markedness hierarchy effects demonstrated by de Lacy (2006). As I discuss in section 4.2.3, the PSM-based approach defended here is able to do so, despite the differences in formalism.

Another argument arises from the architecture of substance-free phonology. A universal fixed ranking can only exist if it is possible to compare constraints across languages. Since constraints inevitably refer to representations, they are not directly comparable in this manner, because the representations they mention are contentless labels: there is nothing that guarantees a '[coronal]' feature in language L_1 to be in any sense 'the same' as a '[coronal]' feature in language L_2. Consequently, the only way to establish fixed rankings would be through substance, by stating them in a way that requires a constraint C_1 referring to a structure *implemented* in a particular way to always dominate a similar constraint C_2 referring to a structure implemented in another way. Since implementation is not part of the phonology under a substance-free approach, and referring to non-phonological realities is a violation of modularity, fixed rankings cannot be part of the substance-free computational machinery.

4.2.2 *The importance of constraint schemata*

Another way of restricting the computational possibilities of an OT grammar is ensuring that certain 'unmotivated' types of constraints are absent from the universal set CON. Since, by hypothesis, the set CON is universal, a candidate can be excluded if CON does not include a constraint that favours that candidate. The question, then, is the internal organisation of CON.

Can there be any principled substantive restrictions on the structure of constraints? Consider the question of the existence of final obstruent voicing (Blevins 2004; Yu 2004; de Lacy 2006; Kiparsky 2006, 2008a). It is commonly agreed that this process is either very rare (Blevins 2004; Yu 2004) or impossible (Kiparsky 2008a), at least as the result of a phonological pattern enforcing obligatory neutralisation of laryngeal contrasts in word-final position. It can then be hypothesised that word-final laryngeal neutralisation is due to a constraint of the form *[F].[1] The non-existence of final voicing is then explained by the fact that CON contains an appropriate constraint *[+voice] but not *[−voice].[2] This 'constraint-tailoring' approach, however, raises two questions.

First, since features are not comparable across languages, it is probably not possible to formulate such a restriction in any case in a substance-free framework. Second, consider the case of 'final devoicing' in German. Normally seen as a relatively trivial devoicing process, it has been argued (e.g. by Iverson and Salmons 2007) to represent the addition of a [spread glottis] laryngeal feature at the right edge of words. If this analysis is correct, CON should provide for some device (in all probability a constraint, call it ADD) promoting the appearance of [spread glottis] at word edges. If such a type of constraint is available, it is not clear why a similar constraint cannot exist for [voice] rather than [spread glottis].

'Explanations' proposed for the non-existence of *[–voice]$_{Wd}$ and ADD([voice]) are usually functional or historical: voiced obstruents are poorly perceptible in word-final position (e.g. Steriade 1997), and the addition of glottal spreading is a grammaticalisation of utterance- or phrase-final glottaling (Hock 1999). However, these explanations are not valid in substance-free phonology: there is nothing in the theory to exclude the existence of the 'incorrect' constraints.

Following Pulleyblank (2006) and Morén (2007), I suggest that this is not necessarily undesirable. The computation provides the resources for constraint construction in the form of *constraint schemata*: the existence of concrete instantiations of these schemata is a matter of learning. (Like Pulleyblank 2006, I remain non-committal on whether the schemata are part of language-specific knowledge, i.e. Universal Grammar, or emerge from more general learning mechanisms.) In other words, if good evidence exists for a constraint *schema*, then the learner is free to produce more constraints of the same form, filling in the slots as required by the ambient data. Considerations of functional utility or factorial typology do not come into the equation.

This amounts, of course, to a denial of the universality of CON: it is not true that all languages have the same constraints, since the representations over which these constraints hold are not comparable in any case. The universality of the set of schemata is also an open question.[3]

The question thus becomes one of the constraint formalism, which is what establishes the schemata. Normally, constraints are stated in some variety of first-order predicate logic. At the same time they are often not very explicit about the type of representations used. In this book, I will use a variety of model theory as applied to OT by Potts and Pullum (2002), extending their proposal (as they suggest) by the use of hybrid logic (Blackburn 2000; Areces and Blackburn 2001).

4.2.3 *Non-exhaustive markedness*

One important issue in a privative representational theory based on underspecification is the interpretation of constraints that only refer to a subset of some structure. Consider a PSM structure ⟨x, C-laryngeal, [voice]⟩. Assume that we also have markedness constraints of the very general form *[F], with the schema given in (2) (cf. Potts and Pullum 2002).

(2) |*F|:=*output*→ ¬F

'It is false that [F] is true at an output node'[4]

Given such a definition of *[F], it is obvious that a constraint *C-laryngeal, formulated as in (3), is violated by the structure ⟨x, C-laryngeal, [voice]⟩, or indeed by any structure which contains the C-laryngeal node, such as ⟨x, C-lar⟩.

(3)   *|C-lar|:=*output*→ ¬C-lar

'It is false that C-lar is true at an output node'

This result is in line with the standard interpretation of markedness constraints on complex structures (cf., for instance, Causley 1999). However, it has been suggested (e.g. by Morén 2007) that it might be desirable to interpret such markedness constraints exhaustively. It is in fact possible to formulate such a constraint in the present framework, as shown in (4) (the predicate T is true at every node); to distinguish such constraints from *[F], I will use the ad hoc notation **[F].

(4) |**C-lar|:=*output* → ¬(C-lar∧ (¬⟨↓⟩T))

'It is false that a C-lar output node dominates no nodes'

Such exhaustive interpretation of markedness constraints presents a specifically phonological problem: it allows the computation to single out smaller structures as being more highly marked. Consider the tableau in (5), which uses non-exhaustive evaluation.

(5)   Stringent violation sets

		*Rt	*C-lar	*[voice]
(a)	⟨x⟩	*		
(b)	⟨x, C-lar⟩	*	*	
(c)	⟨x, C-lar, [voice]⟩	*	*	*

Under this interpretation, the subset relations of the structures are directly reflected in the subset relations of the violation sets. In other words, this interpretation allows us to use geometric structure to reproduce quite directly the stringent violation sets of de Lacy (2002, 2004, 2006). This is not at all surprising, since in de Lacy's system the stringent violation sets emerge from the same kind of subset relations, with the difference that they arise from multiple-valued phonological features such as Place (what he calls the *xo* Theory of markedness).

The advantage of this approach is that no markedness constraint instantiating the *[F] schema of (2) can favour a bigger structure over a smaller one: unless factors such as more complex markedness constraints or faithfulness are taken into account, ⟨x, C-lar⟩ will be preferred over ⟨x, C-lar, [voice]⟩ under any ranking of the *[F] constraints. Thus, structure size translates directly into markedness relationships as defined by the constraint set, in line with the results of Causley (1999) and Rice (2003). Consequently, in this book I will use the term 'marked' to refer to bigger structures, rather than to any other sense of 'markedness' current in the literature. I will call the cluster of properties associated with these bigger structures (Rice 2003; de Lacy 2006) 'markedness-related behaviour'. For more discussion of these issues, see Chapter 5.[5]

These results are subverted by the exhaustive interpretation (i.e. the **[F]) constraints. The tableau in (6) shows how **C-lar can choose ⟨x, C-lar, [voice]⟩ over a smaller structure.

(6) Exhaustive evaluation subverts markedness

		**Rt	**C-lar	*[voice]	**[voice]	*C-lar	*Root
(a)	⟨x⟩	*!					*
(b)	⟨x, C-lar⟩		*!			*	*
(c) ☞	⟨x, C-lar, [voice]⟩			*	*	*	*

I hypothesise that this particular situation should be impossible, and that constraints of the form **[F] are not part of CON.

4.2.4 Complex structure faithfulness

Another issue related to constraints on complex structure is the interpretation of structures that do not stand in a subset/superset relationship. Specifically, I suggest that if feature co-occurrence constraints are to be admitted into CON in one guise or another, there is nothing to prevent us from introducing faithfulness constraints demanding the preservation of all parts of a complex structure. The existence of such constraints, while not always accepted – see Wolf (2007a), in reply to Crowhurst and Hewitt (1997) – has important repercussions for the structure of inventories.

Any OT framework with Richness of the Base faces the necessity of excluding some combinations of features, and normally this is done using (unviolated) feature co-occurrence constraints, although this is not necessary: Morén (2006, 2007) shows extended examples using local constraint conjunction. In the formalism adopted here, a constraint that bans the co-occurrence of features [F] and [G] cannot be expressed using simple logical conjunction, because a node in the model cannot be simultaneously [F] and [G]. Therefore, the proper formulation of the constraint is that shown in (7), which uses the $\downarrow$ relation (corresponding to autosegmental domination) proposed by Potts and Pullum (2002). In this respect, the model used here differs from that of Potts and Pullum (2002), where features are seen as predicates holding directly of root nodes.

(7) $*[F, G]|:=(output \wedge Root) \rightarrow \neg(\langle\downarrow\rangle F \wedge \langle\downarrow\rangle G)$

'An output root node cannot simultaneously dominate a node where [F] is true and a node where [G] is true'

Note that this sort of definition makes a 'feature co-occurrence' constraint essentially indistinguishable from a locally conjoined constraint: it must mention the domain (here, the root node), and the consequent contains the conjunction operator $\wedge$. I suggest that (7) represents a constraint schema that can be freely used to ban combinations of an arbitrary number of features within a domain.[6] In the analyses that follow, I will simply refer to 'feature co-occurrence constraints', without prejudice with respect to the status of local conjunction.

If a constraint schema of this sort exists for markedness, we face the question of whether a parallel argument can be made for faithfulness. Consider the formalisation of the simple constraint MAX([F]) in (8), adapted from Potts and Pullum (2002).[7]

(8) $|MAX([F])|:=(input \wedge F \rightarrow (\langle\mathbf{io}\rangle)F)$

'If [F] is true at an input node, then that node has an output correspondent where [F] is true'

It is also possible to give a schema producing constraints such as those in (9).

(9) $MAX([F, G])|:=(input \wedge Root \wedge \langle\downarrow\rangle F \wedge \langle\downarrow\rangle G) \rightarrow (\langle\mathbf{io}\rangle\langle\downarrow\rangle F \wedge \langle\mathbf{io}\rangle\langle\downarrow\rangle G)$

'If an input root node dominates both [F] and [G], then its output correspondent dominates both [F] and [G]'

The schema is entirely parallel to the schema used to produce feature co-occurrence constraints, except that creating the new constraint requires adding a clause not just to the consequent but also to the antecedent. It would thus seem that there is no principled way of prohibiting the existence of such 'multiple faithfulness' constraints. I will therefore assume this is a possible constraint schema.

Note that Crowhurst and Hewitt (1997) make a similar proposal, but derive the schema from an implication relation between independently existing faithfulness constraints (similar to constraint conjunction). However, Wolf (2007a) argues that admitting implication into the inventory of constraint connectives produces undesirable results, since some of the types of constraints formed by material implication turn out to be neither faithfulness nor markedness constraints according to the definitions of Moreton (2004), with far-reaching computational consequences.

In the present proposal, multiple faithfulness constraints do not require any status for material implication, since they are in no sense built out of pre-existing constraints: they are just another constraint schema. They are also licit faithfulness constraints, since they do not assign any violation marks to the fully faithful candidate. Thus, I will assume this constraint schema is possible.

The existence of multiple faithfulness constraints has the important consequence that relatively large structures can be singled out of preservation when structures that are their subsets are militated against by a highly ranked constraint. Basically, a ranking MAX([F, G, H]) » *[F, G] » MAX([F]) predicts an inventory which includes [F, G, H] but not [F, G], *pace* the proposals of Morén (2003, 2007). Nevertheless, the existence of such a pattern is not unexpected if we accept that more marked (i.e. larger) structures can be singled out by faithfulness constraints; cf. de Lacy's (2006) 'Preservation of the Marked'. For a specific example of the operation of multiple faithfulness, see section 9.1.

4.2.5 *The augmentation constraint schema*

In this section I argue for a relatively unrestricted schema of augmentation (licensing, enhancement) constraints that favour certain types of larger (more marked) structures over smaller (less marked) ones. Such constraints are sometimes treated with caution in phonological theory, but I suggest that they are relatively harmless conceptually, and will therefore make liberal use of such constraints in the analysis.

The notions of 'licensing', 'enhancement', or 'augmentation' have a long history in phonological theory. However, their use is often wound up with non-phonological, functional concerns. The idea of licensing is often specifically associated with a requirement to associate some sort of 'marked' (understood as 'generally dispreferred') structure to a 'better' (i.e. 'more prominent') position, as in work by Zoll (2004) and Walker (2000, 2011). 'Enhancement' is usually understood to increase the (phonetic) salience of certain contrasts (Stevens and Keyser 1989, 2010; Avery and Idsardi 2001; Keyser and Stevens 2006; Hall 2011). A less functional approach is seen in work related to 'augmentation' constraints, understood to increase the complexity of more prominent ('head') elements; as Teeple (2009) notes, augmentation constraints can be *monoconditional*, taking into account only the properties of the head as such (e.g. Smith 2002), or *biconditional*, comparing the properties of heads and non-heads (e.g. Dresher and van der Hulst 1998).

From a formal perspective, of course, the only difference between a markedness constraint (such as that in (3)) and an augmentation constraint is the absence of the negation in the latter. Consider, as a random example, the (slightly simplified) constraint from Walker (2005) shown in (10).

(10) LICENSE([+high], σ́)

'[+high] [...] must be associated with a stressed syllable'

In the model-theoretic framework, this could be reformulated as in (11).

(11) |LICENSE([+high], σ́)|:=(output∧[+high]) → ⟨↑⟩*stress*

'If [+high] is true at an output node, that node is dominated by one where the predicate *stress* is true'

There would seem to be nothing in the formalism to prevent us from having both traditional markedness constraints (with a negation in the consequent) and constraints which require the *presence* of some structure. In fact, quite apart from licensing, enhancement, and augmentation, orthodox OT approaches are rife with constraints that must be formalised with the simple schema $A \to B$ (rather than $A \to \neg B$). Particularly frequent are structure-building constraints in prosody, such as PARSE ('a segment must be dominated by a prosodic node'), ONSET ('a syllable must dominate an onset', although see Smith 2012), FOOT BINARITY ('a foot must have two syllabic or moraic dependents'), or WEIGHT BY POSITION ('a node dominated by a coda node must be dominated by a mora node'). Some alignment constraints can also be construed as requiring the presence of certain elements in certain contexts. Another possible application of this augmentation schema could be found in a hypothetical OT implementation of Nevins's (2010) theory of harmony, where agreement is triggered by the requirement for 'needy' vowels to receive a specification for some feature.

Many objections to 'positive' constraints focus on issues such as factorial typology and the prediction of functionally implausible patterns, which I have argued to be of limited relevance. However, augmentation constraints do have a property worthy of investigation, and that is their ability to enforce neutralisation towards a more marked structure (noted, for instance, by Morén 2001). This prediction seems to run counter to the suggestion made in section 4.2.3 that markedness constraints do not favour more marked structures over less complex ones.

However, there are some important differences. The existence of neutralisation processes that create more or less marked structures depending on the context cannot be doubted (cf. the notion of 'markedness hierarchy conflict' in de Lacy 2006): some neutralisation towards larger structures should be inevitable. The important difference between an exhaustively interpreted markedness constraint and an augmentation constraint is that the latter is satisfied by a more restricted set of candidates. An exhaustively interpreted markedness constraint (4) simply militates against the appearance of some structure, and can be satisfied either by deletion of that structure or by an arbitrary increase in markedness: the hypothetical constraint **C-lar is satisfied by the candidates ⟨×⟩, ⟨×, C-lar, [voice]⟩, and ⟨×, C-lar, [spread glottis]⟩. On the contrary, an augmentation constraint – say, one that requires C-lar to be augmented ('enhanced') by a [spread glottis] feature (perhaps in some contexts) – can be satisfied either by deletion or by inserting *just* the element required by the constraint.[8] The augmentation constraints are thus not equivalent to exhaustively interpreted markedness constraints (which I assume not to exist), although their effects are rather similar.

4.2.6 *The role of* MAXLINK *and* DEPLINK

The constraints MAXLINK and DEPLINK, specific to versions of OT making use of Correspondence, demand the preservation of autosegmental associations in input–output mappings. They require that elements that stand in an input–output correspondence relationship also preserve (i.e. do not add or remove) associations to other elements; for extensive discussion, see Morén (2001).

We can formulate these constraints using *hybrid logic*, an extension of modal logic that introduces *nominals* (predicates that are only true at one node of the model) and *satisfaction statements*. A satisfaction statement $@_i \phi$ means 'ϕ is true relative to the state referenced by i', making it possible to describe individual nodes rather than an entire set of nodes that satisfy some condition.

A possible hybrid-logic version of MAXLINK is given in (12).

(12) |MAXLINK[a]-b|:=(*input*∧ a∧ ⟨↓⟩ b∧ ⟨io⟩i)→ $@_i$⟨↓⟩ b

'If a node where *a* is true has an output correspondent *i* and dominates a node where *b* is true, then *i* also dominates a node where *b* is true'

Computational assumptions   55

This is a relatively weak version of MAXLINK, since it does not require that the nodes where the predicate b is true in the input and output stand in correspondence to each other, merely that they both be associated with the relevant version of a and both have property b.[9] For our purposes, this definition is sufficient, although it is not difficult to give stronger versions.

Formulated as in (12), MAXLINK is very similar to the traditional IDENT-IO, as well as to Blaho's (2008) IDENT, in that it enforces a faithfulness requirement relative to a specific node rather than merely requiring the existence of correspondence. In particular, it is vacuously satisfied by deletion: if the relevant node has no output correspondent, the last clause of the antecedent is false. I will therefore use MAXLINK constraints in this book in lieu of IDENT-IO.

Formally, the constraint DEPLINK has a very similar definition, the only difference being the use of the relation of output–input correspondence rather than vice versa. The importance of this constraint for our purposes lies in the fact that it can be used to derive subtraction as an epiphenomenon of additive morphology, in line with Generalised Nonlinear Affixation (e.g. Saba Kirchner 2010; Bye and Svenonius 2012; Bermúdez-Otero 2012; Trommer and Zimmermann 2014).

The basic autosegmental mechanism is shown in Figure 4.1. Assume that a feature [b], associated with class node A, is deleted in some process. We can derive this by postulating a floating A node that must be realised in the presence of a ban on floating features.[10] Faithfulness compels a coalescence of the two nodes present in the input; however, this would create a violation of DEPLINK[A]-b. If that constraint is ranked over MAX(b), deletion of [b] ensues. The OT mechanism is shown in the tableau in (13).

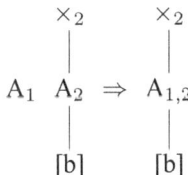

Figure 4.1 Subtraction as an additive phenomenon

(13) Subtraction as an epiphenomenon of floating element prefixation

	$A_1 + \langle x, A_2, b \rangle$	*FLOAT	MAX(A)	DEPLINK[A]-b	MAX([b])	UNIFORMITY
(a)	$A_1 + \langle x, A_2, b \rangle$	*!				
(b)	$\langle x, A_1, b \rangle$		*!	*		

(c)	⟨x, A$_{1,2}$, b⟩		*!		*
(d)	⟨x, A$_1$⟩	*!		*	
(e) ☞	⟨x, A$_{1,2}$⟩			*	*

This solution has a number of advantages. First, it is able to derive subtraction as an additive process without recourse to any special mechanisms, rendering it epiphenomenal. A DEPLINK solution is similar in spirit to that proposed by Bye and Svenonius (2012), as it also involves the ranking of a faithfulness constraint over MAX to derive subtraction; however, their approach requires the postulating of uninterpretable features which never appear on the surface, while the present solution uses only well-established mechanisms without too much abstraction.[11]

Another advantage of this mechanism is that the floating element docks to a host thanks to completely standard MAX constraints. An alternative approach could enforce it by way of a MAXFLOAT constraint, which singles out floating features for preservation (Wolf 2005, 2007b). However, MAXFLOAT has at least two less desirable properties. First, it is, by itself, not sufficient to enforce the docking for floating features to a root node. If it is to be a faithfulness constraint (Moreton 2004), it must assign zero violation marks to the fully faithful candidate, and therefore it must be satisfied by candidates with surface floating features. Thus, it can only enforce docking in concert with *FLOAT – clearly a more complex construction than the one proposed in (13), which also needs *FLOAT but does not introduce new constraint types. Second, MAXFLOAT predicts that some features can only be allowed in surface forms if they are floating (or come from a floating source) under the ranking MAXFLOAT([F]) » *[F] » MAX([F]). The mechanism proposed here can derive the behaviour of floating features, whether it involves addition or deletion of elements, using standard faithfulness constraints, and thus MAXFLOAT may be unnecessary as a constraint schema.

This concludes the discussion of some constraint families and patterns of constraint interaction that will be important for the analyses presented below. In the remainder of this chapter I sketch the stratal approach to phonological computation that I will use in this book.

4.3 Stratal aspects of the computation

I use a broadly stratal approach, which seeks to recapitulate the insights of Lexical Phonology and Morphology (e.g. Kiparsky 1982, 1985; Mohanan 1986; McMahon 2000) in an OT-based computational system (e.g. Kiparsky 2000, 2008b; Bermúdez-Otero 1999, 2003, 2006, 2011,

2012).[12] Stratal frameworks provide a particularly good fit to some of the data that I deal with; see in particular Chapter 10. I take no position on the general applicability of alternative theories here (although in at least one instance I show that output–output correspondence appears unable to derive the facts). In particular, I do not attempt a comparison between the present approach and frameworks where the gradual derivation proceeds not by morphosyntactically derived levels but by local unfaithful mappings, such as OT–CC (McCarthy 2007; Wolf 2008) and Harmonic Serialism (e.g. McCarthy and Pater 2016), leaving this task to future research.

For concreteness, I will follow the lead of Bermúdez-Otero (2011, 2012) in the main aspects of the architecture. Although the sort of fine-grained data that are often used in stratal reasoning are not available at this point, I will argue that at least in broad outline the data considered in the following chapters are consistent with this approach. For the present purposes, the following aspects of the stratal architecture are of greatest relevance:

- tri-stratal organisation
- the stem-level syndrome
- stratal restrictions on Richness of the Base.

4.3.1 Tri-stratal organisation

The most important aspect of stratal architecture is the assumption that the phonological computation over a single word proceeds in three passes, depending on its morphosyntactic structure, with the output of each stratum being fed as (part of) the input to the next one. Bermúdez-Otero summarises the approach thus:

> the attachment of an affix to a root necessarily produces a stem-level category; the attachment of an affix to a stem may produce a stem-level or word-level category depending on the idiosyncratic affiliation of the affix [...] In contrast, full grammatical words trigger word-level cycles and complete utterances trigger phrase-level cycles. (Bermúdez-Otero 2011: 2023)

The stratal affiliation of each process is contingent on independent factors, namely the morphosyntactic status of the nodes participating in the spell-out as roots, stems, full words, or utterances. This is crucial because the architecture compels the existence of the three levels in all cases, irrespective of the vagaries of the lexicon and the structure of the paradigms, which play in important role in approaches based on output–output correspondence or paradigm uniformity (Bermúdez-Otero 2011, 2012).

The tri-stratal hypothesis furnishes two important analytic tools. Reranking across strata largely captures opaque rule orderings, allowing us to account for why certain processes happen or fail in certain morphological contexts (see in particular section 10.2) without recourse to constraint indexation, cophonologies, sympathy, and the like. The availability of faithfulness at later levels contributes to accounting for a wide range of effects. In this book we will most be concerned with faithfulness to prosodic structure: since the output of the previous stratum is used as the input at any given level, inputs at later levels contain significant amounts of prosodic structure, unlike the stem level, where prosodic structure can only come from the lexicon (and is rare).

4.3.2 The stem-level syndrome

Stem-level derivations possess some exceptional properties that are not found in the case of word- and phrase-level phonology. Specifically, they give rise to 'cyclic' reapplication, i.e. a case can be made for cyclic processes applying more than once in the derivation of a given word; such reapplication is usually not assumed to be possible for word- and phrase-level derivations (Scheer 2010: §4.3). Stem-level processes also exhibit particular patterns of non-application, such as outright exceptionality and sensitivity to token frequency (see in particular Collie 2007).

Bermúdez-Otero (2012) provides a comprehensive survey of this 'stem-level syndrome' (see also the overview by Kaisse and McMahon 2011) and broaches some possibilities for deriving the unique properties of stem-level rules from architectural considerations (specifically mechanisms of lexical storage and retrieval). Again, some of the data analysed here support his approach to cyclicity, in that they obey the expected generalisations with respect to the stem-level syndrome; a particularly clear case is found in coronal palatalisation (section 10.1.2).

4.3.3 Stratal aspects of Richness of the Base

Another feature of stratal approaches is that they put an important restriction on Richness of the Base. Although I assume that Richness of the Base per se is a feature of OT-based computation at all levels, its effects become weakened at relatively shallow strata (cf. Kiparsky 2008b, 2011; Bermúdez-Otero 2007b). Normally, the fact that some theory predicts inputs of a particular shape to map to a deviant output is seen as a weakness of that theory, since it essentially relies on stipulations regarding inputs to derive the correct grammar. However, in stratal approaches such less desirable rankings can be allowed at shallow levels if it can be shown that the preceding level will never produce the structure that proves problematic when fed as the input to further computation. An example of this is seen with the analysis of 'devoicing sandhi' in Breton (section 11.3.3.3). The analysis crucially relies on certain features of the input (the absence of a C-lar specification of word-final obstruents) which are nevertheless invariably present due to the operation of word-level phonology.

Notes

1. I ignore the precise mechanism used to restrict the neutralisation to word-final position.
2. The example is purely illustrative. See de Lacy (2006) for a possible analysis of final voicing in terms of a sonority increase driven by moraicity.
3. In practice, the commitment to the universality of CON is not always upheld, in particular with reference to morphological phenomena, such as Kurisu's (2001) REALISEMORPHEME or Pater's (2009) 'constraint cloning'. Such constraints must make reference to blatantly language-specific categories, and are in essence indistinguishable from constraint schemata. A schematic approach to CON is also explored by Smith (2004).
4. Note that 'node' is here used in the model-theoretic sense, not to refer specifically to autosegmental nodes.
5. I also use the term 'markedness constraint' in the commonly accepted way, for lack of a widespread alternative.
6. A potential objection is that such a constraint schema can of course produce wildly implausible constraints such as 'a word cannot contain both a consonant and a vowel'. However, I agree with Potts & Pullum (2002: fn. 12) who are 'extremely skeptical of the idea that formalisms exist that correspond exactly to what linguists wish to say'.
7. Note that this formulation simply requires the existence of an output correspondent, without putting additional restrictions such as the preservation of associations or the number of correspondents. In this respect, it is highly similar to the 'existential faithfulness' constraints proposed by Struijke (2000).
8. Formally, exhaustive markedness constraints contain the consequent $\langle\downarrow\rangle$T 'dominates some element', while in augmentation constraints the predicate is more specific.
9. Compare the definition of constraints such as MAXLINK-µ[V] by Morén (2001), which requires that, say, a vowel associated with a mora in the input be also associated with *a* mora in the output, not that it be associated with the output correspondent of *the same* mora.
10. Note that such a ban can also be construed as an augmentation constraint, requiring the presence of a root node.
11. Of course, nothing in a substance-free approach prevents us from postulating such uninterpretable features: since all features are abstract, the learner might be free to postulate unpronounceable features if the pattern requires it.

Therefore, I cannot rule out that Bye & Svenonius's (2012) mechanism might in fact be required for some languages, e.g. because it can be established on independent grounds that DepLink is ranked in a way that disallows its use for subtraction.

12. Another multiple-level version of OT is Derivational OT (e.g. Rubach 2000, 2005), which, however, suffers from the lack of an explicit theory of levels.

5

Complexity and markedness in substance-free phonology

5.1 Structural markedness: a review

In section 4.2.3 I discussed the fact that a geometric theory, such as the version of the PSM presented here, generates stringent violation sets for markedness constraints similar to those suggested by de Lacy (2002, 2004, 2006). However, the substance-free approach appears less restrictive than de Lacy's, because the markedness hierarchies only follow from the structure of representations, while he also connects them very tightly to phonetic substance. In this section I will argue, following Rice (2007, 2009, 2011), that a structural approach taking cognisance of contrast correctly predicts that the markedness-related behaviour of segments *in a given language* can be accounted for purely by reference to the structure of representations. At the same time these predictions do not have to be too closely tied to phonetic substance.

De Lacy (2006) proposes a theory of markedness that rests on the existence of markedness hierarchies, defined using stringent violation sets. The basic idea is that if a structure S violates some markedness constraint C, then all structures that are more marked than S along the relevant dimension also violate C, as shown in (14) for place features. A markedness constraint can never single out less marked structures: no ranking of the markedness constraints of the type *[place feature] can make sure that [dorsal] is preferred to [glottal], because surface instances of [dorsal] violate all the same constraints that surface instances of [glottal] do and then some others.

(14) Stringent violation sets according to de Lacy (2006)

		*{dors}	*{dors, lab}	*{dors, lab, cor}	*{dors, lab, cor, gl}
(a)	[ʔ]				*
(b)	[t]			*	*

| (c) | [p] | | * | | * | | * | |
| (d) | [k] | * | * | | * | | * | |

The existence of these markedness hierarchies has important advantages for deriving markedness-related behaviour, specifically with reference to the phenomena de Lacy (2006) calls markedness reduction, Preservation of the Marked, and markedness conflation. I will not review these advantages here, but they are real enough (see also Causley 1999; Rice 2003).

As shown in section 4.2.3, the geometric structure of the PSM allows us to derive the stringent violation sets, and thus the OT account of markedness-related behaviour, directly from the subset relations in the structure, à la Causley (1999). In fact, de Lacy (2006) derives the stringent violation sets in a similar way, using what he calls the *xo* Theory of markedness: features entering markedness relationships are multivalued, and violations emerge from subset relations among multiple values. Thus, the hierarchy [dors] » [lab] » [cor] » [gl] is in reality a hierarchy that goes from [*xxx*Place] to [*ooo*Place], where a constraint such as *[*xx*Place] is violated by all [Place] values containing *xx*, i.e. [*xxo* Place] and [*xxx*Place]. Thus, de Lacy's (2006) theory is, from a formal perspective, also a structural markedness theory like the one proposed here.

However, there are two important differences between the two approaches. First, a substance-free approach is incompatible with de Lacy's (2006) second major hypothesis, namely that the mapping between the multivalued *xo* features and phonetic substance is part of Universal Grammar.[1] Second, if markedness is derived from structural size rather than strings of the *xo* type, then markedness 'ties' are possible: in *xo* Theory, the markedness ordering is total, whereas in PSM it is partial. That is, in de Lacy's system [labial] is always more marked than [coronal], since no ranking of *[Place] constraints can prefer the latter, whereas in PSM C-place[coronal] and C-place[labial] are of the same size, and thus their relative markedness has to be determined by the constraint ranking. In other words, in both cases the predictions of de Lacy (2006) are narrower. Nevertheless, I suggest that his approach is *too* restrictive.

5.2 Markedness and contrast

In an OT-based framework of structural markedness, the only logically necessary universals are those that emerge from the interaction of the constraint set CON and the types of structures admitted by the representational system. For instance, it is possible to derive the fact that bigger (more marked) structures are preferred as triggers of assimilation, or that they resist assimilation more easily. This is due to Preservation of the Marked (Rice 2003; de Lacy 2006), which is itself made possible by the fact that faithfulness constraints can protect bigger structures to the exclusion of smaller ones. Similarly, neutralisation, when driven by constraints of the form *[F], will always result in structures of smaller size.

On the other hand, the mapping from structure size to substance is arbitrary in a substance-free approach, so at first blush it would seem that nothing prevents the substance-free theory from generating many patterns that de Lacy (2006) argues to be impossible, such as neutralisation of place contrasts to [dorsal]. I would suggest, however, that this is not necessarily a bad result.

As pointed out by Rice (2009), generalisations about markedness-related behaviour often only come into their own when there is a contrast to be made. That is, in positions where the phonology allows several elements, markedness relationships tend to exhibit hierarchical structures along the lines identified in research on typological markedness. However, when the contrasts are neutralised, the outcome of neutralisation is less predictable, with many different possibilities attested cross-linguistically.

Consider a situation where, say, consonant place contrasts are neutralised in some position (e.g. word-finally). The natural OT account is to assume that this is an instance of markedness reduction: *[F] constraints ensure that all place features are removed, but the C-place node remains intact. That is, the phonology will output a bare C-place node in the relevant position. In terms of realisation, however, the expression of this C-place node depends on the system of contrasts in the language: phonologically placeless segments can be glottal in one language, dorsal in another, and coronal in a third one, depending on the markedness patterns seen in alternations in the language at large.

When neutralisation is avoided, the learner will have additional evidence to set up the markedness hierarchies. As discussed in Chapter 2, these hierarchies will be shaped by extrinsic factors such as diachrony and acquisition, and there the functional tendencies underlying the expression of markedness, à la Steriade (1994, 1997, 2001), will make themselves felt. Therefore, in the presence of contrast the effect of substance will be much more pronounced (Rice 2009), although the ultimate explanation for this fact is not within the purview of the theory of phonology.

The key point here is the arbitrariness of the phonetic expression of unmarked structures, argued for extensively by Rice (2003, 2007, 2009, 2011) but rejected by de Lacy (2006), for whom all such differences are to be compelled by hierarchy conflict. Here, I side with Rice (2011) in assuming that the arbitrariness is indeed greater than prescribed by the narrow predictions of de Lacy (2006). In particular, in Chapter 11 I will provide extensive arguments for an analysis of Bothoa Breton that treats voiceless obstruents as more marked than voiced ones, contrary to the frequent assumption that [+voice] obstruents are relatively marked. Importantly for the general theoretical context of this section, I argue that even if the precise PSM analysis of the Breton pattern is rejected, the relevant markedness relationship can still be established in Breton – indeed that it has been done, if implicitly, in the existing literature. This argument provides support for the position that while markedness relationships *within a language* exhibit the kind of behaviour exhaustively analysed by de Lacy (2006), the cross-linguistic validity of the relationships between markedness hierarchies and substance is less secure.

5.3 Geometry and markedness

Another potential advantage of the geometrical approach is that it not only derives phonological behaviour related to markedness hierarchies but also offers solutions to issues of locality.

It has been recognised in the autosegmental literature (e.g. Avery and Rice 1989; Piggott 1992; Odden 1994) that processes such as spreading interact closely with tier structure, and in particular that spreading processes involving some element x that is autosegmentally dominated by A ignore elements which do not bear A; similarly, spreading of x can be blocked depending on the presence of some structure also dominated by A. These insights translate naturally into the PSM (cf. in particular Youssef 2010).

The version of the PSM proposed in Chapters 3 and 4 has the property of expressing notions such as 'contrastive' and 'marked' via feature geometry: segments that are contrastively specified for a feature $A[x]$ are those that bear a (possibly bare) instance of A, and 'more marked' segments are characterised by additional structure, making them likely blockers. Segments that are unmarked for a dimension will not bear the tier node for that dimension, due to the lack of contrastive specification.

The same tripartite division of unmarked vs contrastively specified vs marked feature values appears in work on vowel harmony by Nevins (2010). Working in a principles-and-parameters framework, he argues that 'Search' processes responsible for harmony may target (or be blocked by) all values of a feature, contrastive ones or marked ones. This is particularly important for the typology of blocking and transparency – the bread and butter of autosegmental theory. Crucially, however, in the present version of the PSM the status of certain structures as contrastively specified or marked is not a diacritic associated with each value by an extrinsic algorithm, but rather emerges from the operation of the contrastive hierarchy. Although the empirical coverage of this book does not extend to long-distance processes such as harmony, the availability or otherwise of tier nodes plays a crucial role in the account of the interaction between consonant mutation and external sandhi in section 11.3.3.3.

5.4 Partial markedness orders and augmentation

Another difference of the present proposal vis-à-vis de Lacy's (2006) is the possibility of partial markedness orders: in the present framework, the relative markedness of two structures of equal size is defined by the constraint ranking rather than representationally. This has some consequences for the treatment of hierarchy conflicts.

De Lacy (2006) does not allow markedness reversals: if an element that is more marked along some hierarchy H is preferred to a less marked element in cases of neutralisation, this must be due to the existence of some other markedness hierarchy that prevails over H in a particular context. In the present theory, apparent markedness reversals have two potential sources. One of them, predicted to be impossible by de Lacy (2006), is representational: differences in the mapping between phonological structure and substance that go against well-established patterns. In Chapter 11, I argue in detail that just such a situation arises in Bothoa Breton where, I suggest, voiceless (unaspirated) obstruents are phonologically more marked than voiced ones, contrary to the normal assumption of [+voice] as the more marked value in systems not using aspiration (e.g. Honeybone 2005a; Petrova et al. 2006; Harris 2009). Another type of neutralisation to the more marked value can be driven by augmentation constraints. This type of neutralisation is apparently inevitable in theories based on privative features: if some instances of neutralisation involve reduction in structural size (e.g. Harris 1997), and languages may possess neutralisation processes that, depending on the context, may proceed in both directions along a given hierarchy (de Lacy 2006), then it is inevitable that some neutralisation processes should be represented as addition of structure.

Thus, augmentation constraints are merely a formalisation of contextual markedness hierarchies that impel neutralisation in directions opposite to those required by context-free markedness constraints. This is, in fact, a desirable result in view of the fact that augmentation constraints, when formulated in the metalanguage used here, always mention a context in which the augmentation is required. Therefore, a total ranking of such augmentation constraints will always define a totally ordered markedness hierarchy, just as required by the *xo* Theory. This shows an important difference between augmentation constraints and exhaustively interpreted markedness constraints, which can be satisfied by the addition of *some* structure to the element they militate (section 4.2.5). Augmentation constraints always require the addition of some specific structure, correctly reproducing the effects of de Lacy's (2006) *xo* Theory, whereas exhaustive markedness constraints do not express quite the same insights with respect to markedness hierarchies. For this reason, I will assume that exhaustive markedness constraints should not be part of CON.

Once again, careful comparison of the narrow predictions of de Lacy (2006) and the more permissive approach to hierarchies espoused here in the spirit of Rice (2003, 2007) lies outside the scope of this book. In order to demonstrate the viability of the framework, however, in the following chapters I will proceed to apply the theoretical framework to a detailed analysis of the sound patterns of the Breton dialect of Bothoa.

Note

1. Although de Lacy concedes that at least in one case phonetic substance is phonologically ambiguous, as in the case of place neutralisation of nasals to [ŋ], which he assumes to be phonologically [glottal] (2006: §2.2.1.1.1).

6

The Breton language

The Breton language belongs to the Brythonic subdivision of the Celtic group of the Indo-European language family. It is spoken in Brittany, a peninsula in the west of present-day France, where it was brought by settlers from Britain in the fifth century AD. Historically, it has been spoken in Lower Brittany (French *Basse-Bretagne*; Breton *Breizh-Isel*), i.e. in the western part of the historic Duchy of Brittany. Today, native speakers are mostly spread throughout rural Brittany, and the language is severely endangered.[1]

6.1 Dialectal divisions

Traditionally, Breton is divided into four major dialect groups, on the basis of the old diocesan borders. These are as follows:

- Cornouaillais (*Kerneveg*), the dialect of Cornouaille, the biggest of the dioceses covering the south-west corner of Lower Brittany and most of its inland region. The traditional centre of the diocese is the city of Quimper (*Kemper*); today it covers the southern part of the *département* of Finistère (*Penn-ar-Bed*), and also includes some regions in the south of the *département* of Côtes d'Armor (*Aodoù-an-Arvor*) and in the north-west of Morbihan (*Mor-Bihan*).
- Léonais (*Leoneg*) is the dialect of Léon, the diocese in the north-west of Brittany centred around Saint-Pol-de-Léon (*Kastell-Paol*); today the northern part of Finistère.
- Trégorrois (*Tregereg*), in the north-east of Brittany, and in today's *département* of Côtes-d'Armor. This also includes the dialects of Goëlo, a small area in the extreme north-east of the Breton-speaking region, which belongs to the otherwise entirely Romance-speaking traditional diocese of Saint Brieuc (*Sant-Brieg*).
- Vannetais (*Gwenedeg*), spoken in the south-eastern part of Brittany, in the traditional diocese of Vannes (*Gwened*).

It is often claimed in the literature that the first three dialects are relatively homogeneous, and they are sometimes referred to together as a single dialect grouping called KLT, which is opposed to the Vannetais dialect. The basis for this division is partly philological and partly sociolinguistic. Philologically, Vannetais presents striking differences with respect to the other dialects. Most prominently, it has final stress where other Brythonic varieties show penultimate stress (although it is not universally agreed whether this is a shared innovation or a retention); on the other hand, Vannetais dialects show the sound change of proto-Brythonic *θ to [h]. From a sociolinguistic perspective, Vannetais has had a literary tradition separate from the other Breton dialects (Guillevic and Le Goff 1902).

Nevertheless, these distinctions are not as clear-cut as the above picture suggests. As discussed by Jackson (1967: §§23–7), it may be more accurate to describe Léonais and Vannetais as genuine dialect groupings (though with significant internal diversity), whereas Trégorrois and Cornouaillais are best described as a more or less homogeneous single 'central' dialect. Trégorrois is said to have undergone significant influence from Upper (i.e. Eastern) Léonais, whereas Cornouaillais, according to Jackson (1967), is an area characterised merely by not having some features distinguishing Léonais on the one hand and Vannetais on the other; Hewitt (1973) aptly calls it 'a dialect by default'.

6.2 The dialects and the written language

The situation of written Breton is quite precarious, since it is very little used by native speakers and in addition suffers from the existence of competing orthographic standards (Wmffre 2007a, 2007b); for a general overview, see e.g. Hewitt (1973); Jones (1995). The written standard(s) are, for historical and political reasons, in important respects based on the dialect of Léon. Especially in terms of representing the sound system, the prevalent orthography (the so-called *orthographie unifiée*) in some respects sacrifices consistency in the name of providing a single norm for all dialects (Hewitt 1973; Wmffre 2007a, 2007b; Madeg 2010). I will sidestep the orthographic issues, and, where I give the written form, I will follow the relevant source, even if it may differ from the dialect form at hand in some phonological or morphological details.[2]

The relationship between the dialects and the standard language, which exists in written form and is also used in schools (including Breton-medium schools), is fraught (e.g. Le Pipec 2013). Opinions are frequently expressed in the literature to the effect that the standard language is too far removed from the living language, with accusations that it is oriented too much towards the French norm, either in that it is strongly influenced by French (e.g. in phonetics) or shows signs of self-conscious hypercorrection and purism in an effort to underscore 'non-Frenchness', for instance in aspects of syntax and notably in the lexicon (e.g. Hewitt 1973; Jones 1995; Le Dû 1997; Wmffre 2007b; see also Adkins 2013 for critical discussion of 'authenticity' in the Breton context). To some extent these reports rely on anecdotal evidence, although see, for instance, Kennard (2014).

Although my sights in this book are firmly trained on the traditional dialects, this gap between them and revived Breton is worth keeping in mind. It is particularly relevant in view of the fact that a significant proportion of the available 'descriptive' literature – and in particular of that available in English – focuses on the standard language, or at least on a constructed 'representative' variety (and may in fact be prescriptive – this is particularly true of many available dictionaries) rather than on the dialects. This is pertinent given that a significant proportion of the literature in theoretical linguistics that engages with Breton data relies on precisely this kind of source. In the next section, however, I offer a brief overview of the available sources.

6.3 Sources

6.3.1 General descriptions

As noted above, most existing general overviews of Breton focus on the standard language, with only occasional and unsystematic remarks regarding the living dialects. This is particularly true of reference grammars, of which Hemon (1940), Kervella (1946), Trépos (1966), and Press (1986) are perhaps the most comprehensive. An exception is the grammar of Favereau (2001), which often presents a pandialectal, descriptive perspective (albeit with little reference to phonetics and phonology). Shorter overviews of varying depth are provided by Stephens (1993), Press (2004), and Ternes (1993, 2011).

With respect to dialectology, a very important source is the *Atlas linguistique de la Basse-Bretagne*, or ALBB (Le Roux 1924–63), based on data gathered in the period between 1911 and 1920.[3] It has served as a source of primary data for much subsequent work. A newer dialectological atlas is Le Dû (2001).

Two other important works must be mentioned. Jackson (1967) presents a comprehensive historical phonology of Breton. It is very useful not only in diachronic terms, but also as an important compendium of data that are otherwise scattered in disparate and often obscure sources. It should be noted, however, that there were relatively few comprehensive dialect descriptions available when this work was published, and this was especially true of Cornouaillais varieties (the biggest dialect area), a situation that has improved since then. Nevertheless, it remains a very important source.

A comprehensive overview of the dialect situation (with a diachronic outlook) was presented in several versions by François Falc'hun in several publications culminating in Falc'hun (1981). He uses ALBB data to argue for a particular version of the history of Breton, making important contributions to systematic dialectology in the process.

For earlier stages of the language, the most important sources remain Fleuriot (1964) for Old Breton, Lewis and Piette (1962) for Middle Breton, and Hemon (1975) for a historical perspective on morphosyntax; see also Schrijver (2011a, 2011b) for shorter summaries.

6.3.2 Sources: dialect descriptions

Coverage of the Breton-speaking area by systematic phonetic and/or phonological descriptions is quite uneven, as the following list (which is, however, far from exhaustive) demonstrates:

- For Léonais, Sommerfelt (1978) (first published in 1922) is a study of the dialect of Saint-Pol-de-Léon, the original centre of the diocese. A milestone in Breton phonology is the study by Falc'hun (1951), who concentrated on the contrast between *fortes* and *lenes* which has a played a central role in much diachronic and synchronic literature on Breton. Falc'hun (1951) focused on his native dialect of Le Bourg Blanc (*Ar Vourc'h-Wenn*); however, his reliance on his own speech for his recordings may give cause for scepticism. Within the generative phonology tradition, Carlyle (1988) presents a study of some aspects of the phonology of the dialect of Lanhouarneau.
- For Trégorrois, apart from the early Le Gall (1903) and Le Clerc (1908), important sources are Jackson (1960) and Le Dû (1978, 2012), which treat the dialect of the peninsula of Plougrescant, close to the major town of Lannion. Jackson (1960) presents a relatively short descriptive study, without a consistent phonological approach. On the other hand, Le Dû (1978, 2012), drawing on his knowledge as a native speaker and on extensive fieldwork, presents a comprehensive account of the phonology, morphology, and lexicon of this variety of Breton, but he pays relatively little attention to phonetics and uses a structuralist phonemic notation which may or may not gloss over some phonetic details. Other, more cursory descriptions are found in Sommerfelt (1962) (Plouézoc'h) and Dressler (1973) (Buhulien).
- The Vannetais area is relatively well served by comprehensive descriptions: these include Ternes (1970) for Île de Groix, McKenna (1988) for Guéméné-sur-Scorff, Le Pipec (2000, 2008) for Malguénac, Cheveau (2006, 2007) for Grand-Lorient, and Crahé (2013) for Languidic. Shorter descriptions include Thibault (1914) for Cléguérec and Hammer (1969) for Plouharnel.

- There are also several major studies of Cornouaillais, although they are often concerned with 'peripheral' or 'transitional' varieties. An important work is the phonetic study by Bothorel (1982) for Argol in the Crozon peninsula; other works on 'core' Cornouaillais dialects include Dressler and Hufgard (1980) and Sinou (1999, 2000) for the extreme south-west; Denez (1977) for Douarnenez; and Timm (1984), Favereau (1984), and Wmffre (1999) for the environs of Carhaix. For transitional zones, we find Ploneis (1983) for Berrien on the border with Léon, Humphreys (1972, 1995) for Bothoa in the far north-east, and Evenou (1987), with a short French summary in Evenou (1989), for Lanvénégen on the border with Vannetais.

In addition to this selection of sources, information on the phonetic and phonological make-up of the relevant dialects can sometimes be gleaned from the numerous publications describing the dialectal lexicon (though these often use the orthography), and from sound materials published by organisations such as *Dastum* dedicated to preserving the sound heritage of Brittany.

6.3.3 Theoretical studies

Breton phonology has not been the subject of great attention from theoretical phonologists working in the generative tradition. Moreover, the existing body of literature is heavily biased towards issues related to initial consonant mutation. Breton mutations are often considered together with those of other Celtic languages, in particular the closely related Welsh; some examples here are Willis (1986), Pyatt (1997), and Green (2006, 2007). Stump (1987, 1988) deals with both phonological and morphological aspects of mutation, while prosodic conditioning of some Breton mutations is considered by Pyatt (2003). Wolf (2005, 2007b) proposes an account of some phonological aspects of the mutation system.

Outside of the mutation system, the amount of attention paid to Breton in the theoretical phonological literature is small. Anderson (1981) considers the complicated behaviour of vowel quantity and quality in Léonais, based on Falc'hun's (1951) description. Some of the same facts, along with a range of other phenomena, are treated in a non-linear framework by Carlyle (1988), also on Léonais, but based on original fieldwork. Dressler (1973) and Dressler and Hufgard (1980) consider Breton data in the context of speech rate-related phonological subsystems in a Natural Phonology framework. Krämer (2000) and Hall (2009) propose OT accounts of some sandhi phenomena in Breton, based on the description of Île de Groix Breton by Ternes (1970); I return to these works in section 11.5.

6.4 The dialect of Bothoa

In this book I explore the sound system of the Breton dialect of Bothoa (Breton *Botoha*, locally [bʊtəˈhaː]), a village in the *commune* of Saint-Nicolas-du-Pélem (Breton *Sant-Nikolaz-ar-Pelem*, locally [zaj̃kɔˈlaːz̺]), located in the eastern part of Cornouaille (the south-west of the modern *département* of Côtes-d'Armor), in the traditional region of Fañch.

The main source for the description is the monographic description by Humphreys (1995), which is an edition of the author's doctoral thesis defended at the University of Western Brittany in Brest in 1985. The thesis, but not the published version of the book, includes a glossary, which I have also consulted. To check the attestation of phonological patterns, a corpus of all forms found in the body text of Humphreys (1995) was constructed, coupled with custom query tools written in Common Lisp; both are publicly available at https://github.com/anghyflawn/bothoa-corpus. I also used other publications by the author dealing with the Bothoa dialect (Humphreys 1972, 1990). In addition to these sources, I used recordings of Humphreys' principal informant for the study, Françoise Le Provost, which were collected for the *Nouvel Atlas Linguistique de la Basse-Bretagne* (Le Dû 2001), and have been made available online through the *Corpus de la parole* project at http://corpusdelaparole.huma-num.fr/spip.php.

Technically, the dialect of Bothoa belongs to the (vaguely defined) Cornouaillais group, but it is in many respects divergent from the 'average' Cornouallais type. Humphreys (1995) describes it as belonging to the Vannetais-influenced area of eastern Cornouaille and southern Trégor. Phonologically, the most important signs of this influence is the stress system (see Chapter 8), which may represent a historical development of the Vannetais type (cf. Plourin 1985), and the breakdown of the relationship between vowel length and consonant quality that is otherwise so characteristic of the Brythonic languages (Falc'hun 1951; Jackson 1967; Wells 1979; Anderson 1981; George 1999; Iosad 2015a). Some features of the dialect, such as the wide use of the suffix [o] to form verbal nouns, are characteristic of an even narrower 'centre-east' area. In other respects, however, notably laryngeal phonology, the dialect is representative of Breton-wide patterns.

Notes

1. Apart from varieties of Standard French, the local Gallo-Romance variety, called *gallo*, is also spoken in Upper Brittany.
2. For Breton orthographic forms, I have used the dictionaries by Hemon & Huon (2005) and Cornillet (2006). I have also used Favereau (1997), which is a descriptive work incorporating dialect forms, often containing forms

not shown in the standard-oriented dictionaries but attested in the variety at hand; crucially, however, different editions of that dictionary use different orthographies.
3. These dates are significant; before World War I, much of Lower Brittany remained primarily Breton-speaking, whereas wartime service provided the impetus for a very large proportion of the population to learn French (Broudic 1995).

7

Segments and representations

In this chapter I lay out the vowel and consonant inventories of Bothoa Breton and discuss the most important aspects of variation in their phonetic realisation. I also present the proposed featural specifications for these segments that will be used in the following analysis chapters.

7.1 Vowel inventory

The inventory of the Bothoa dialect includes long and short oral vowels, as well as several nasal vowels and oral diphthongs. The system of the oral monophthongs is fairly symmetric, with a two-way backness contrast, a symmetrical distinction in length, and two front rounded qualities; its main unusual feature is the apparent presence of three height classes in 'mid' vowels. In line with typological expectations, the nasal vowel system is smaller than the oral one, and there is only a very limited length contrast among the nasal vowels. The diphthongs also present a relatively unremarkable system: they are all falling diphthongs with high vowels as non-syllable elements. I consider the three subsystems in turn.

7.1.1 *Oral monophthongs*

The oral monophthongs are shown in Table 7.1; I refer to Humphreys (1995) for exhaustive (albeit impressionistic) descriptions of their phonetic realisation. Here I concentrate on two aspects of the system that deserve further comment: the mid vowel system and the status of the [ə]/[ø] distinction.

7.1.1.1 Mid vowels
In the mid vowel region, there is a three-way height contrast for both front unrounded and back rounded vowels. Humphreys (1995) uses the French-based convention of using accents to distinguish among the three heights; I silently retranscribe his symbols as shown in Table 7.2.

Table 7.1 The oral monophthong inventory of Bothoa Breton

Height	Front		Central	Back
	Unrounded	Rounded		
High	i iː	y yː		u uː
Mid-high	e eː			o oː
Mid	ɛ ɛː	ø øː	(ə)	ɔ ɔː
Mid-low	æ æː			ɒ ɒː
Low			a aː	

Table 7.2 Mid vowel transcription

Humphreys (1995)	This book	Humphreys (1995)	This book
é	[e]	ó	[o]
e	[ɛ]	o	[ɔ]
è	[æ]	ò	[ɒ]

Minimal or near-minimal pairs for height contrasts among front vowels are shown in (15). (See section 7.3.2 for explanation of the notation for final obstruents.)[1]

(15) Minimal pairs for mid vowels
    (a) ['biː]   *bioù*   'cows'
    (b) ['beː]   *bez*   'grave, tomb'
    (c) ['meːz̪] *mezh* 'shame, disgrace'
    (d) ['mɛːz̪] *maez* 'outside'
    (e) ['lɛːr]   *lêr*   'leather'
    (f) ['læːr] *laer* 'thief, robber'

This three-way distinction is characteristic of many Breton varieties. Cf. also Falc'hun (1951), with a generative analysis in Anderson (1981), and Le Dû (1978, 2012) and Le Gall (1903) for Tréguier.

The contrast between the mid vowels [ɛ ɔ] and mid-low vowels [æ ɒ] appears unstable. According to Humphreys (1995: 97), 'cases where both heights are admissible are not rare, which tends to obscure the phonemic boundaries'.[2] In many cases either mid-low or mid vowels are apparently admissible.

(16) Variation in mid vowels
    (a) ['frɛːr] *frer* 'monk'
    (b) ['fræːr]

(c) [ˈkãːnɛ]   kane   '(s)he sang'
(d) [ˈkãːnæ]

From Humphreys' description it appears that the distribution of such variability is primarily lexical, i.e. the merger[3] is a lexically diffusing change. Specifically, the marginal contrast between mid and mid-low vowels in Bothoa represents the last stages of an ongoing merger, in line with the general principle enunciated by Labov (1994: ch. 12). Alternatively, we may be dealing with a near-merger, i.e. the auditory neutralisation recorded by Humphreys (1995) does not necessarily mean there is a phonological neutralisation between the two classes. It is of course impossible to provide a full picture of such a complicated situation, but for the purposes of phonological analysis I will assume that the Bothoa dialect contrasts six peripheral mid vowels.

7.1.1.2 The schwa

Humphreys (1995) uses a phoneme-based approach with special attention to complementary distributions. This is particularly relevant to the status of the phoneme /ə/, which is not found in stressed syllables, and conversely of the phoneme /ø/, which is never found in unstressed position. Given this complementary distribution, Humphreys (1995) interprets the two segments as representing the same phoneme.

In the substance-free framework, this complementary distribution criterion is not sufficient to establish whether the two segments represent different phonological symbols or a single one. This is because it must first be confirmed that the difference between [ə] and [ø] is in fact visible to the phonology. This evidence could come from alternations or at least from data showing phonetic categoricity.

The former criterion, alternations, does not furnish strong evidence in Bothoa Breton. In this respect, it contrasts with some other dialects. In Vannetais varieties, for instance, stress is consistently word-final, and stress shift under suffixation can feed neutralisation to schwa, as in the example in (17) from the dialect of Languidic (Crahé 2013).

(17) Vowel reduction in Languidic
 (a) [aˈvaːl]   aval   'apple'
 (b) [ˌavəˈlœɥ] avaloù 'apples'

In Bothoa, such alternations are much restricted in scope (see section 9.1), and hence alternation evidence is difficult to come by. In the absence of reliable phonetic data, we are left with two possibilities:

- There is a single phonological symbol corresponding to the (perceptual) categories ⟦ə⟧ and ⟦ø⟧, and no phonological operations creating

two distinct symbols in the phonological grammar. The complementary distribution is an artefact of the skewed distributions of phonetic tokens across the stressed vs unstressed context, e.g. due to undershoot.
- The phonology of the language makes reference to both [ø] and [ə] as phonological symbols and (to satisfy Richness of the Base) includes a mapping whereby an input unstressed /ø/ reduces to [ə] and an input stressed /ə/ is enhanced to [ø].[4]

In the absence of secure phonetic data, it is currently impossible to make this determination. For concreteness, I will adopt the latter hypothesis throughout this book.

The unstressed schwa is frequently shortened in certain positions, or even absent from the phonetic record. This phenomenon affects initial position (18) and what I will call the 'trough' position, i.e. the second syllable in trisyllabic words with initial stress. Some variants are shown in (18).

(18) Schwa deletion in initial position
    (a) [(ə̃)'veʒəw]   *a-wechoù*   'sometimes'
    (b) [(ə̃)'hasə]   *ac'halese*   'yonder'

Schwa deletion in medial position
    (a) ['haːdərəʒ]   *haderezh*   'sowing season'
    (b) ['haːdrəʒ]
    (c) ['tapəfæ]   *tapfe*   '[if] [(s)he] took'
    (d) ['tapfæ]

If the dropped schwa is adjacent to a sonorant, that sonorant may either be lengthened (when it precedes the schwa) or assume a syllabic quality if it follows, as shown in (19).

(19) Medial schwa and sonorants
    (a) ['mãnə̃gə̃n]   *maneg*   'glove'
    (b) ['mãnːgə̃n]
    (c) ['ʃaːdə̃nə̯w]   *chadennoù*   'chains'
    (d) ['ʃaːdn̩əw]

In section 8.3.2 I argue that this variable realisation of the schwa is phonologically irrelevant and that the output of the phonological grammar always contains the [ə] in these cases.

Long [eː] and [oː] are slightly diphthongised, but, as (20) shows, they contrast with the diphthongs [ɛĭ] and [əŭ]. An exception is the position before [r], where [eː] – but not [oː] – is a monophthong.

(20) Long vowels and diphthongs
 (a) [ˈɛĭzəd] *eizhvet* 'eighth'
 (b) [ˈeĭzəd] *aezet* 'easy'
 (c) [ˈgəŭ] *gaou* 'lie, untruth'
 (d) [ˈgoᵘ] *goz* 'mole'

7.1.2 Nasal vowels

The dialect of Bothoa has six nasal vowels. According to Humphreys (1995), they are phonetically distinct from contingently nasalised vowels, which realise phonologically oral vowels adjacent to nasal consonants; presumably this corresponds to something like the difference between nasal vowels in French and nasalised vowels in English (Cohn 1990, 1993).

All nasal vowels except /ã/ do not enter into length contrasts. The low front nasal vowel [æ̃] corresponds to the modern French pronunciation of the vowel in words such as *bain*. It is overwhelmingly attested in borrowings from French such as [ˈtræ̃] 'train' (French *train*).

The low nasal vowel /ã/ is amply attested not only in roots, but in a number of productively used suffixes, and accounts for the vast majority of nasal vowel tokens. It is described as the nasalised correspondent of the back low unrounded vowel [ɑ].

(21) Examples of [ã]
 (a) [ˈmãm] *mamm* 'mother'
 (b) [ˈbrasã] *brasañ* 'biggest'

The low vowel is the only nasal vowel to enter a length contrast, as the example in (22) demonstrates.

(22) Length contrast in nasal vowels
 (a) [ˈlãn] *lann* 'gorse bush'
 b) [ˈlãːn] *leun* 'full'

7.1.3 Diphthongs

Humphreys (1995) identifies the following diphthongs in the Bothoa dialect: [ɛĭ], [əy̆], [əŭ] or [æŭ] (depending on the speaker), [aŭ], and [ãw̃]. These are exemplified in (23).

(23) Diphthong examples
 (a) [ˈsɛĭz̺] *seizh* 'seven'
 (b) [ˈəy̆n] *evn* 'bird'[5]
 (c) [ˈdəŭ] *daou* 'two (masc.)'

(d) [ˈdæŭ]
(e) [ˈdaŭr]   *dour*   'water'
(f) [ˈdã̰w̃ʒər]   *tavañjer*   'apron'

The non-nucleus part of the diphthong can only contain high vowels, which I propose below to be mannerless. While this is not necessarily significant in view of the typological frequency of such a pattern, it might also be taken as additional evidence for the status of high vowels as mannerless segments, as this restriction receives a straightforward featural basis: no V-manner features are allowed in the non-head portion of a diphthong.

As for the nuclear portion, there is evidence for just one contrast in nucleus quality: that of [əw] (which is ⟦æw⟧ for some speakers) versus [aw]. I suggest that phonologically the possible diphthongal nuclei are [ə] (V-manner[lax]) and [a] (V-manner[open]), with no V-place features, or more generally complex segments, allowed in diphthong nuclei. If this generalisation is correct, it provides some evidence for [ə] and [a] as segments that consist solely of V-manner features (called 'unit segments' in some of the PSM literature). I will therefore use the phonological notation for diphthongs as shown in Table 7.3. I use the symbol [w] rather than [u] for the diphthongal glide for consistency with [ãw̃].

7.2 Consonants

The consonant inventory of the dialect of Bothoa is shown in Table 7.4.

The table shows a phonological analysis rather than a phonetic description of the facts; I refer to Humphreys (1995) for the phonetic description of relatively straightforward phonetics–phonology mappings. However, some aspects of phonetic implementation deserve comment.

7.2.1 Laryngeal contrasts

The stops [p t k] and [b d g] and the affricate pair [tʃ dʒ] are distinguished by voicing; the voiceless stops are said to lack noticeable aspiration (*sans*

Table 7.3 The phonological interpretation of diphthongs

Phonetic notation	Surface phonology
[ɛĭ]	[əi]
[əy̆]	[əy]
[əŭ]/[æŭ]	[əw]
[aŭ]	[aw]
[áŭ]	[ãw̃]

80   A Substance-free Framework for Phonology

Table 7.4 The consonant inventory of Bothoa Breton

Manner	Labial	Coronal	Postalveolar	Palatal-labial	Palatal	Dorsal	Glottal
Stops	p b	t d				k g	
Affricates			tʃ dʒ				
Fricatives	f v	s z	ʃ ʒ				h
Nasals	m hm	n hn			j̃		
Laterals		l hl					
Rhotics		r hr					
Approximants	w hw			ɥ hɥ	j hj		

aspiration notable), while the voiceless stops are described by Humphreys as fully voiced. This kind of laryngeal system seems to be common across the Breton-speaking area, and the instrumental study of the dialect of Argol in the Crozon peninsula in the far west of the area conducted by Bothorel (1982) confirms its existence in that variety. Le Dû (1978) also claims that this is the case for Plougrescant on the basis of instrumental data. Nevertheless, there are some references to aspiration of stops of the [p t k] series in some varieties, even if it is sometimes described as quite weak; examples are Falc'hun (1951) for Le Bourg Blanc, Ternes (1970) for Île de Groix, McKenna (1988) for Guéméné-sur-Scorff, and Le Pipec (2008) for Malguénac. The latter three are all Vannetais varieties, and the latter two in particular are spoken in the north of Vannetais territory, not too far from the Pays Fañch where Bothoa is located, so relying on descriptions of other Cornouaillais dialects such as that of Argol could be risky.

Nevertheless, Humphreys' description of the nature of laryngeal contrast in Bothoa Breton can be verified with reference to the recordings of the Bothoa speaker made for the NALBB dialect atlas project (Le Dû 2001) and available via the *Collections de corpus oraux numériques* project (http://cocoon.huma-num.fr).[6] While the recording quality makes precise quantitative analysis difficult,[7] a typical fortis stop can be seen in Figure 7.1, with a short burst and no extended voice onset time (only 27 ms in this example). This is consistent with Humphreys' description of fortis stops in Bothoa Breton as 'unaspirated'. In general, only a targeted instrumental study (such as that conducted by Bothorel 1982) can confirm whether the descriptions of 'aspiration' in Breton varieties truly refer to fortis stops with relatively long voice onset times or to the short-lag VOT found in fortis stops in 'voice' languages such as French or Russian (Petrova et al. 2006; Beckman et al. 2013).

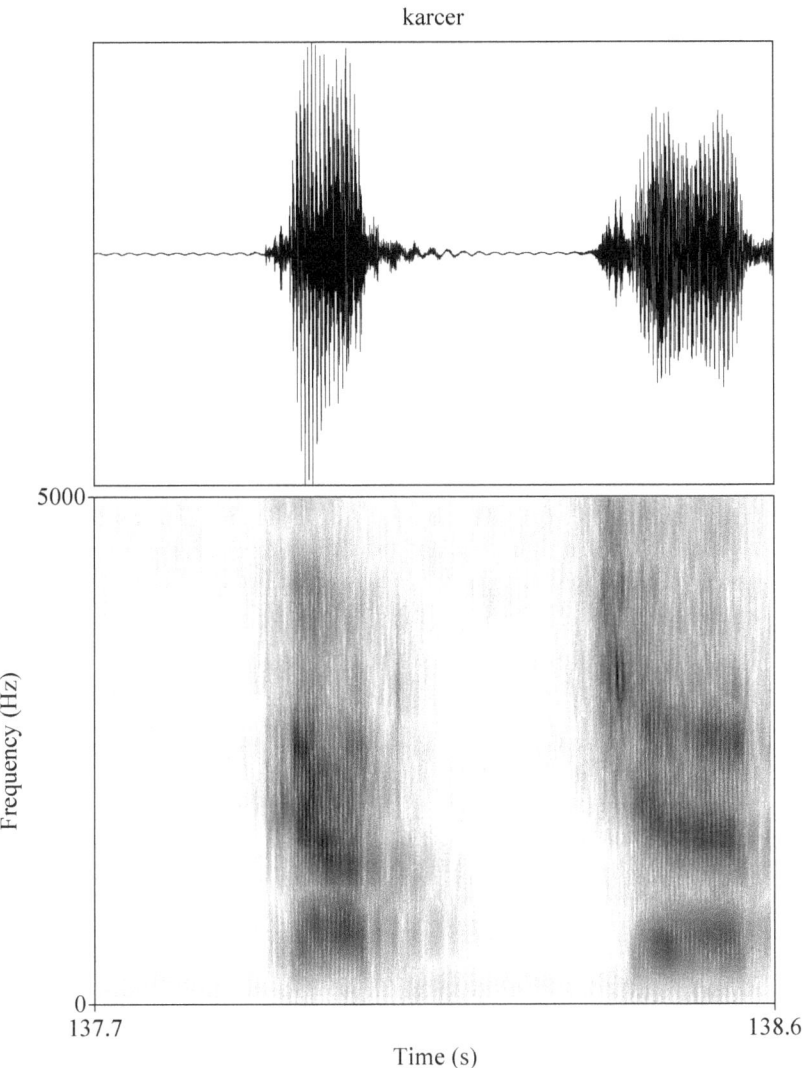

Figure 7.1 Waveform and spectrogram of [ˈkartʃər] 'quarter'

7.2.2 Velar palatalisation

The velar stops [k g] have fronted allophones, which Humphreys (1995) writes as [c ɟ] and describes as 'mediopalatal'. These are found before the segment [i]. I assume they represent the same phonological segment as [k] and [g] and thus will transcribe them as [kʲ gʲ]. The main reason for this is that there no evidence for a phonological distinction between [k g]

82   *A Substance-free Framework for Phonology*

and [kʲ gʲ]. In addition, nasals are realised as [[ŋ]] and not [[ɲ]] before these segments, which presumably means that they have a velar rather than palatal articulation. Given the clear phonetic rationale and lack of strong phonological evidence for the distinction, I assume that these segments are produced outside of the phonology at the phonetic implementation level, and hence that there are no distinct phonological symbols corresponding to [[kʲ gʲ]].

(24)   Palatalised velars
    (a)   [ˈlakʲiãm]   *lakiamp*   'we will put'
    (b)   [akʲ i ˈziː]   *hag he zi*   'and her house'
    (c)   [ˈvrãŋkʲiz]   *frankiz*   'open space, the outdoors'
    (d)   [ˈklɒːgʲiad̪]   *klogiad*   'ladleful'

7.2.3 Coronal palatalisation and overlap

Segments acoustically similar to [[t͡ʃ]] and [[d͡ʒ]] may also appear as the extremes of a continuum of variable realisations corresponding to the sequence of a coronal stop and the vowel [i] before another vowel, as in (25).

(25)   Coronal stops before [i] in hiatus
    (a)   [ˈbɒrd̪]   *bord*   'side'
    (b)   [ˈbɒrd͡ʒəw]   *bordoù*   'sides'
    (c)   [ˈbɒrdiəw]
    (d)   [ˈkon̪ˌtɛl]   *kontel*   'knife'
    (e)   [ˈkontiəw]   *kontilli*   'knives'
    (f)   [ˈkontjəw]
    (g)   [ˈkont͡ʃəw]

The fricatives [ʃ] and [ʒ] do not appear to participate in variation with coronal fricatives parallel to that shown in (25).

(26)   Coronal fricatives before [i] in hiatus
    (a)   [ˈmɒrˌzɛl]   *morzhol*   'hammer'
    (b)   [ˈmɒrziəw]   *morzholioù*   'hammers'
    (c)   [ˈmɒrzjəw]
    (d)   *[ˈmɒrʒəw]

The segment that Humphreys (1995) interprets as a palatal nasal phoneme /ɲ/ is only realised as [[ɲ]] word-medially following [r] and [j]; in all other contexts, it is realised as a nasalised palatal glide [[j̃]], and these two segments are in free variation following [w]. Neither is found word-initially.

(27) Realisation of /ɲ/
    (a) [ˈpwiːj̃al]   *poaniañ*   'to upset'
    (b) [ˈkɛjnəw]   *keinioù*   'backs'
    (c) [ˈtõj̃əw]   *tonioù*   'tunes'
    (d) [ˈhãwɲo]   *anvel*   'to call, name'
    (e) [ˈhãwj̃o]

However, a segment resembling 〚ɲ〛 can appear as the member of a continuum of possible realisations, from [ni] through [nj] and [nʲ] to [ɲ], as shown in (28).

(28) The coronal nasal before [i] in hiatus
    (a) [ˈbiːniəd̥]   *benniget*   'blessed'
    (b) [ˈbiːnĩəd̥]
    (c) [ˈbiːnjəd̥]
    (d) [ˈbiːɲəd̥]

The high front vowels /i y/ 'freely alternate' with the glide 〚j〛 before a vowel in an unstressed syllable, as shown in (29); however, they can also be syllabic, and in this case they are said to be 'very short'. Again, there appears to be a range of possible realisations.

(29) Variable gliding of high vowels
    (a) [ˈbaːdĩo]   *badeziñ*   'baptise'
    (b) [ˈbaːdjo]
    (c) [ˈlaːrỹən]   *Larruen*   placename (French *Lanrivain*)
    (d) [ˈlaːrjən]

I take the description of the variability in the realisation of high vowels in a C_V context to reflect the presence of a gradient, phonetic process along the lines described for English postlexical palatalisation (as in *miss you*) by Zsiga (1995, 2000). Specifically, this variation reflects the partial (but occasionally full) overlap between the consonantal and the vowel gestures, rather than a phonological process that manipulates symbolic representations; in section 10.1 we shall see that such a process also exists in Breton, but creates categorical outcomes that are different from the phenomenon described here. As far as the phonological analysis is concerned, I will treat the relevant forms as containing a nuclear high vowel in hiatus: [ˈbiːniəd̥] 'blessed', [ˈbaːdio] 'baptise', etc.

7.2.4 The 'glottal' fricative

In preconsonantal contexts, /s/ (or /z/) may alternate with [h] (phonetically normally 〚ɦ〛 in this position). This is especially frequent with the prefix /diz-/.

(30) The /s/ ~ /h/ alternation
    (a) [ˌdisˈliːvo]   *dislivañ*   'discolour'
    (b) [ˌdihˈliːvo]
    (c) [ˈdihmãnt]   *dismantrañ*   'waste'
    (d) [ˈdismãnt]

The alternation does not appear to be systematic, but is lexicalised in at least one case.

(31) The lexicalised /z/ ~ /h/ alternation
    (a) [ˈhraːz̞]   *razh*   'rat'
    (b) [ˈhraːhəd̞]   *razhed*   'rats'

The fricative that Humphreys (1995) transcribes phonologically as /h/ has a number of realisations. The voiceless glottal phonation ⟦h⟧ is found word-initially, word-medially following [l r], and immediately before the vowel bearing the main stress. The breathy voiced phonation ⟦ɦ⟧ is normally found intervocalically, and occasionally word-initially. The voiceless velar fricative ⟦x⟧ is found utterance-finally and before a voiceless consonant, while its voiceless correspondent ⟦ɣ⟧ is a rare variant noted word-finally in sandhi before [m v]. Finally, the pharyngeal ⟦ħ⟧ is the most common preconsonantal variant, alternating 'freely' with ⟦x⟧ and ⟦ɣ⟧.

(32) Realisations of /h/
    (a) [ˈhɛɪ]   *heiz*   'barley'
    (b) [ˈmarhəw]   *marc'hoù*   'stallions'
    (c) [ˈzɛɦo]   *sec'hañ*   'to dry'
    (d) [o ˈzaːɦ e]   *ur sac'h eo*   '(it) is a bag'
    (e) [o ˈplaːx]   *ur plac'h*   'a girl'
    (f) [o ˌplaːx ˈpəʊr]   *ur plac'h paour*   'a poor girl'
    (g) [ə ˈvjɒɣmə]   *ar vuoc'h-mañ*   'this cow'
    (h) [dæħˈmaːt]   *dalc'hmat*   'always'
    (i) [o ˌvjɒħ ˈlart]   *ur vuoc'h lart*   'a fat cow'

Most of this allophony is described as variable, and so in the absence of strong evidence to the contrary I shall assume that all of these phonetic realisations correspond to a single phonological symbol [h].

'Occasionally' this fricative may also alternate with [s] (the precise nature of the variation is not described). The pattern is reminiscent of that described above for [s] and [z], as in (33).

(33) The /h/ ~ /s/ alternation
    (a) [ˈzɛːx]   *sec'h*   'dry'
    (b) [ˈzɛstər]   *sec'hder*   'dryness'

(c) ['zɛhtər]
(d) [ˌdɛstəˈnoːs]   dec'h-da-noz   'tonight'
(e) [dɛːx]   dec'h   'today'

7.2.5 Voiceless sonorants

Finally, Bothoa Breton possesses a set of voiceless sonorants [m̥ n̥ l̥ r̥ w̥ ů]. In addition, [ç], as we shall see below, stands in the same relationship to [j] as voiceless sonorants do to voiced ones. The phonetic realisation of these segments was studied by Humphreys (1972). He found that [m̥], [n̥], and [l̥] can be broken up into a voiceless and a voiced portion: [m̥m], [n̥n], and [l̥l]. The palatal-labial voiceless glide [ů] is extremely rare; the voiceless palatal [ç] is described as similar to the German *ich-Laut*, and [w̥] is said to be similar to the [ʍ] of certain English dialects. Finally, the realisation of [r̥] varies: some speakers have a voiceless tap or trill [r̥] similar to Welsh *rh*, and others have a uvular fricative [χ].

Humphreys (1995) treats these voiceless sonorants as (tautosyllabic) clusters of [h] and the respective sonorant, citing phonological evidence, especially from initial consonant mutation. I agree with this analysis and adopt such representations for these segments. For particularly compelling evidence to this effect, see section 11.3.2.

7.3 Sandhi

The realisation of consonants, and especially obstruents, in phrasal contexts is often different from that found in lexical contexts; this is particularly true in utterance-final position. The phonetic alternations can be broadly classified into two groups: lack of release and loss of laryngeal specification.

7.3.1 Lack of release

Word-final stops, whether before a pause or before another consonant, are often unreleased, which can even lead to confusion as to the place of the stop.

(34) Place of word-final stops
(a) [ˈdib̚]   dibr   'saddle'
(b) [o ˈhad̚]   ur c'had   'a hare'
(c) [ˈgwaːg̚]   gwak   'weak'
(d) [ˈhriːdəg̚]   redek   'run'
(e) [ˈhriːdəd̚]

In word-final nasal-stop sequences, not only can the stop remain unreleased, but also the nasal may be realised with greater duration. If an underlyingly voiceless stop is deleted or obscured in this manner, the nasal is also often, though not necessarily, voiceless (except before a voiced segment). The appearance of stops is especially disfavoured before another consonant.

(35) Word-final nasal-stop sequences
    (a) [o ˈpont]   *ur pont*   'a bridge'
    (b) [o ˈpont̚]
    (c) [o ˈpon̥]
    (d) [o ˈpoṉː]
    (e) [o ˌpoṉː ˈkoːẓ]   *ur pont kozh*   'an old bridge'
    (f) [o ˌpon ˈkoːẓ]
    (g) [ˈdɛnt]   *dent*   'teeth'
    (h) [ˌdɛn ˈbraː]   *dent brav*   'good teeth'
    (i) [ˌdɛnː ˈbraː]
    (j) [on ˈdãnd al]   *un dant all*   'another tooth'
    (k) [on ˈdãnː al]

A similar phenomenon involving the loss of the stop articulation and a lengthening of the preceding consonant is found in obstruent sequences, in practice limited to sequences of [s] and a stop.

(36) Word-final fricative-stop sequences
    (a) [ˈtrist e]   *trist eo*   '[it] is sad'
    (b) [ˌlɒst ˈhiːr]   *lost hir*   'a long tail'
    (c) [ˌlɒsː ˈhiːr]
    (d) [ˌlɒs ˈhiːr]
    (e) [ˈʒist]   *chistr*   'cider'
    (f) [ˈʒisː]
    (g) [ˈʒisː ˈkaləd̥]   *chistr kalet*   'hard cider'
    (h) [ˈʒis ˈkaləd̥]

Final coronal stops may disappear from the acoustic record before another consonant: this is said to be obligatory in unstressed syllables, as in (37), and 'sporadic' in stressed ones, as in (38).

(37) Final coronal stops in unstressed syllables
    (a) [vid̥]   *evit*   'for, in order to'
    (b) [miːrəd̥]   *mirout*   'keep, look after'
    (c) [vi ˌmiːrə ˈbwid̥]   *evit mirout boued*   'in order to watch the food'

(38) Final coronal stops in stressed syllables
    (a) [ˈkwɛd̥]   *koad*   'forest'
    (b) [ˌkwɛ logəˈtaːz̥]   *koad Lokeltaz*   'the forest of Locqueltas'

When two identical consonants straddle a word boundary, the result is a 'slightly geminated' articulation when both consonants belong to stressed syllables; in other positions the result is said to be indistinguishable from a single consonant.

(39) Identical consonants across a word boundary
    (a) /kwæd/   *koad*   'wood'
    (b) [ˌkwædˈdær]   *koad derv*   'oak'
    (c) /paruz/   *parrez*   'parish'
    (d) [əˈbarusə]   *ar barrez-se*   'this parish'

7.3.2 *Laryngeal phenomena*

Word-finally, the contrast between voiced and voiceless obstruents is suspended. However, the outcome of this suspension depends on the phonetic context.

I use the term 'final laryngeal neutralisation' (see Iverson and Salmons 2011) to refer to the fact that both voiced and voiceless obstruents exhibit what Humphreys (1995: 190) calls the 'voiceless realisation' before a pause (i.e. phrase-finally). Fully voiced obstruents are entirely absent from this position. However, according to Humphreys (1995), the actual realisation is not necessarily identical to that of true voiceless obstruents:

> It should be pointed out that the alternation between voiced and voiceless segments, which represents the most important category of these [sandhi] modifications, is, from the phonetic point of view, not a simple binary choice: quite often one encounters not just voiceless lenes, but also consonants with a decrease in voicing. The faster the speech rate and the more relaxed the articulation, the more pronounced are the assimilations.[8] (Humphreys 1995: 190)

In effect, Humphreys appears to be describing word-final sandhi as involving *incomplete neutralisation* of the laryngeal contrast (e.g. Slowiaczek and Dinnsen 1985; Charles-Luce and Dinnsen 1987; Ernestus and Baayen 2006; van Oostendorp 2008; Dmitrieva et al. 2010). He is also not alone in claiming that the obstruents produced in sandhi neutralisation in Breton are not identical to their underlyingly voiced or voiceless congeners. For instance, Wmffre (1999: 5) says that 'this variation due to sandhi before a pause [i.e. final devoicing] is less systematic than certain linguistic descriptions [...] have led readers to believe [...].'

'Variation' in the realisation of underlyingly voiced stops is also noted by Sommerfelt (1978: §154): 'There is variation in the treatment of word-final stops that follow a long vowel in a monosyllables. One hears sometimes [kēt], sometimes [kēd], or even sometimes a voiceless [d].'[9] Consequently, I use the devoicing diacritic for prepausal obstruents in both phonetic and surface-phonological transcription. (Phonological arguments for a distinction are provided below.) Two examples are shown in (40), together with forms without neutralisation which demonstrate the underlying laryngeal specification.

(40) Final laryngeal specification
    (a) ['kɔg̊]   kog   'rooster'
    (b) ['kɔgəw]   kogoù   'forests'
    (c) ['tɔg̊]   tog   'hat'
    (d) ['tɔkəw]   togoù   'hats'

When an obstruent is not final in the phrase and is followed by a sonorant, a vowel, or a voiced obstruent, it is generally realised with voicing irrespective of its underlying laryngeal specification.

(41) Voicing assimilation in sandhi
    (a) [kɔg̊]   kog   'rooster'
    (b) [o ˌhɔk ˈtrøt]   ur c'hog treut   'a skinny rooster'
    (c) [ˌkɔg izˈmaːj]   kog If-Mai   'Yves-Marie's rooster'
    (d) [tɔg̊]   tog   'hat'
    (e) [on ˌtɔk ˈʃik]   un tog chik   'a chic hat'
    (f) [on ˈtɔg ˌal]   un tog all   'another hat'
    (g) [ˌtɔg ˈʒãː]   tog Yann   'Jean's hat'

'Quite often' the underlying voiceless fricatives /f/, /s/, and /ʃ/, when preceded by short vowels, resist the voicing in the relevant context. It is not clear whether this resistance is a property of lexical items or whether the same lexical item can appear in both forms. Humphreys (1995) says that examples like those in (42) 'coexist' with those in (43) (all the relevant words end in lexical voiceless obstruents).

(42) Assimilation of voiceless fricatives
    (a) [o ˈprøz wæ]   ur pres a oa   'it was a cupboard'
    (b) [o ˈpeʒ laˈpiːnəd̥]   ur pech lapined   'a rabbit trap'

(43) Non-assimilation of voiceless fricatives
    (a) [on ˈtas wæ]   un tas a oa   'it was a cup'
    (b) [on ˈhaʃ ˈlem]   un hach lem   'a well-sharpened axe'

As for final consonant sequences, Humphreys (1995: 196) distinguishes three types of realisations before vowels:

- If the first element is a liquid, word-final obstruents behave exactly as if they followed a vowel.
- In the case of sequences of the type 'nasal + stop', the situation is complicated by the fact that, as discussed above, these tend to undergo some sort of progressive assimilation in terms of nasality, losing the burst. Nevertheless, as that example shows, if the stop is not deleted or obscured in such sequences, it can be realised with voicing.
- In sequences of the type '/s/ + stop' (where the majority are of the form /st/), dropping of the final consonant is common (especially before a consonant, as is the case for stops generally). Interestingly, even if the stop disappears from the acoustic record, pre-sonorant (or at least prevocalic) voicing of such sequences is uncommon: while realisations like that in ['ʒiz al] 'another cider' compared with [ʒis] in isolation do exist, Humphreys (1995) attributes them to restructuring of the underlying form (so that e.g. 'cider' is underlyingly /ʒis/ rather than /ʒist/). However, voicing assimilation is possible before obstruents. The segment [h] inhibits pre-sonorant voicing.

(44) Sandhi phenomena in fricative-stop clusters
    (a) ['lɒst]   lost   'tail'
    (b) ['lɒst ˈhiːr]   lost hir   'long tail'
    (c) ['lɒsː ˈhiːr]
    (d) [o ˌlɒzd ˈbɛːr]   ul lost berr 'a short tail'
    (e) [o ˌlɒzː ˈbɛːr]
    (f) [o ˌlɒz ˈbɛːr]
    (g) ['ʒist]   chistr   'cider'
    (h) ['ʒisː]
    (i) [ˌʒis ˈkalət]   chistr kalet 'strong cider'
    (j) [ˌʒisː ˈkalət]
    (k) ['ʒiz ˈal]   chistr all   'another cider'
    (l) ['trist]   trist   'sad'
    (m) ['trist e]   trist eo   '[it] is sad'

In section 11.1 I offer a phonological interpretation of word-final sandhi phenomena as stemming from the lack of any laryngeal specification in word-final obstruents.

7.4 Featural representations

As discussed in Chapter 3, in this book I use a version of the Parallel Structures Model of feature geometry, where segmental representations are preferentially arrived at using a variation on the Successive Division Algorithm of Dresher (2003). In Figure 7.2 I propose a complete contrastive hierarchy for the phonological segments of Bothoa Breton.

The same specifications are shown in tabular form in Table 7.5 for consonants; see Chapter 9 for vowels.

7.4.1 Laryngeal contrast

I argue that laryngeal contrast in obstruents in Bothoa Breton is implemented using a feature I call C-laryngeal[voiceless], associated to the 'fortis' series of stops, affricates, and fricatives. In principle, an analysis of a laryngeal contrast system whereby it is the fortis obstruents that are relatively more marked compared with the lenis counterparts is not unprecedented (Avery 1996; Avery and Idsardi 2001; Jessen and Ringen 2002; Honeybone 2002, 2005a, 2012; Petrova et al. 2006; Helgason and Ringen 2008; Beckman et al. 2013). It has been argued, however (Honeybone 2005a; Beckman et al. 2013), that when the *phonology* of the language requires such an analysis, it is unavoidably tied up with a particular *phonetic* realisation: namely, that fortis stops in such systems should be pronounced with long-lag VOT (at least in prosodically 'strong' positions such as foot-initially). We have seen that Bothoa Breton appears to belong to a different type, normally associated with a phonological system where the 'lenis' ('voiced') obstruents are marked.

I submit, however, that the phonological arguments adduced in Chapter 11 are sufficient to adopt a [voiceless] analysis, despite the phonetic appearances. This is, after all, the essence of the substance-free approach: the mapping between phonology and phonetics is not direct, so there is no *logical* reason for 'laryngeal realism' – the idea that languages differ in how they represent the contrast between obstruent series – to uncritically adopt the tight phonology–phonetics coupling. The existence of the Breton system is a strong argument for a substance-free theory of the phonetics–phonology interface.

7.4.2 Manner contrasts

The contrast between stops (and affricates) and fricatives is implemented by the use of the feature C-manner[open] for the latter, and no manner feature for the former. The argument here is primarily phonological: the processes analysed in section 10.1 involve a neutralisation of the manner contrast, with the fricatives being its outcome. Since the neutralisation is driven purely by considerations of markedness (i.e. the neutralisation is not positional or assimilatory as far as manner changes go), we are led

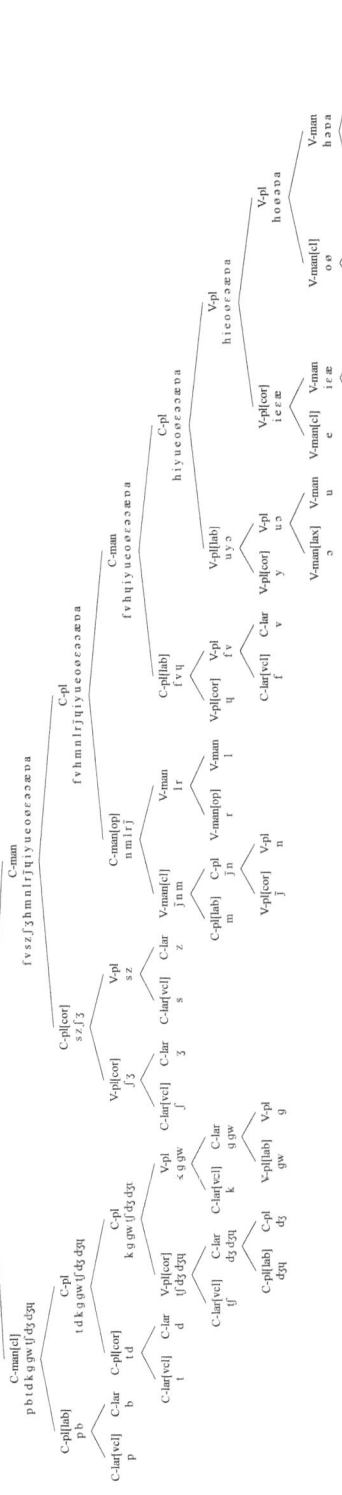

Figure 7.2 A contrastive hierarchy for Bothoa Breton

Table 7.5 Featural specifications of Bothoa Breton consonants

	Segment	C-place [labial]	C-place [coronal]	V-place [coronal]	V-place [labial]	C-manner [open]	C-manner [closed]	V-manner [open]	V-manner [closed]	C-laryngeal [voiceless]
Stops	/p/	✓					✓			✓
	/b/	✓					✓			
	/t/		✓				✓			✓
	/d/		✓				✓			
	/k/						✓			✓
	/g/						✓			
	/gw/				✓		✓			
	/tʃ/		✓	✓			✓			✓
	/dʒ/		✓	✓			✓			
	/dʒɥ/		✓	✓			✓			
Fricatives	/f/	✓				✓				✓
	/v/	✓				✓				
	/s/		✓			✓				✓
	/z/		✓			✓				
	/ʃ/		✓	✓		✓				✓
	/ʒ/		✓	✓		✓				
Sonorants	/h/									✓
	/ɥ/	✓						✓		
	/n/		✓						✓	
	/m/	✓							✓	
	/j/			✓					✓	
	/l/									
	/r/									

to conclude that fricatives are unmarked in manner in Bothoa Breton compared with stops. Similarly, in the analysis of mutation in section 11.3.1 stops are seen to undergo spirantisation, which can be analysed as a subtractive process, and given the mechanism I offer for subtraction (see section 4.2.6) this also requires that stops bear some manner feature. Given the minimalist, contrastivist nature of the feature assignment mechanism, then, and in the absence of positive evidence for a manner feature in fricatives, they remain mannerless in the phonological specification.

Again, this result may appear slightly surprising in view of the commonly held belief that stops are less marked than fricatives, derived from typological facts about consonant inventories (Hyman 2008). Even in a substance-free framework, Morén (2006) suggests that mannerless segments are, in some ways, not prototypical (for instance, they may have a restricted distribution), tying this fact to the fact that manner determines a segment's sonority and therefore its phonotactic patterning. Here, I take a more strongly substance-free position, where tier labels like 'Manner' do not have any substantive content. Given this principle, and in the absence of direct evidence for the relevant specification in fricatives, I adopt the analysis in Table 7.5.

7.4.3 Nasal vowels

I do not discuss the nasal vowels at length, for lack of reliable data. Here, I note two particular properties that would need to be discussed in a fuller account of Bothoa Breton phonology.

First, there is suggestive evidence for treating nasal vowels as representationally related to the coronal nasal [n]. The clearest evidence is provided by alternations such as those shown in (45).

(45) Nasal vowel alternations
    (a) [ˈpon̪d̪]   *pont*   'bridge'
    (b) [ˈpõːʃəw]   *pontioù* 'bridges'

Here, the nasal does not appear because of a restriction on homorganic nasal–fricative sequences which appears to be exceptionless in Bothoa Breton.[10] Instead, the nasal coalesces with the preceding vowel, which suggests that nasalisation and the nasal segment are representationally similar. However, the data in (45) are potentially also amenable to an analysis where the nasal vowel in (45b) is in fact the result of a gestural overlap rather than the outcome of a phonological rule. I will therefore not offer an analysis of this aspect of the system for lack of reliable data.

Notes

1. As discussed above, orthographic forms are given following published dictionaries (Favereau 1997; Hemon & Huon 2005; Cornillet 2006). They use the so-called *peurunvan* ('unified') orthography.
2. '[L]es cas où les deux apertures sont admises ne sont pas rares, ce qui tend à obscurcir les limites phonématiques.'
3. Diachronically, the source of the contrast in Bothoa is the incompleteness of the merger of the diphthongs [aɛ̯] and [aɔ̯] (proto-Brythonic **ai* and **au*) with the 'low mid' vowels [ɛ ɔ], which is otherwise characteristic of many Breton dialects (Jackson 1967: §§253, 353).
4. See Iosad (2015a) for a specific OT implementation of a similar asymmetry in Welsh.
5. This word, along with its plural [ˈəy̑nəɖ], is the only example of this diphthong in the dialect (Humphreys 1995: 120).
6. The digitisation of the recordings was completed by the LACITO laboratory (*Langues et civilisations à traditions orales* UMR 7107) and Michel Jacobson at the *Laboratoire ligérien de linguistique* (UMR 7270).
7. The original recordings are fairly noisy, making the identification of periodicity (especially in low-amplitude signals such as those associated with stop voicing) difficult.
8. 'Il faut se rappeler [...] que l'alternance sourde/sonore, qui représente la catégorie plus importante de ces modifications, n'est pas, sur le plan phonétique, un simple choix binaire: on rencontre assez souvent, non seulement des sourdes douces, mais aussi des consonnes à sonorité décroissante. Plus le débit rapide et l'articulation relâchée, plus les assimilations sont poussées.'
9. 'Il y a flottement en ce qui concerne le traitement en fin de mots des occlusives qui suivent la voyelle longue d'un monosyllable. On entend tantôt [kēt], tantôt [kēd], ou même quelquefois un [d] sourd [...].'
10. Non-homorganic sequences are allowed: [ˈamzər] 'weather', [ˈpinviʧaɖ] 'enrich oneself'.

8

Suprasegmental phonology

In this chapter I offer an analysis of some aspects of suprasegmental phonology in Bothoa Breton. I focus on three issues:

- Stress placement. Unlike most other Brythonic varieties, stress in Bothoa Breton is to a certain extent lexical and therefore unpredictable. However, some non-trivial generalisations regarding its placement can still be extracted, and they provide some important insights into the stratal model of morphology–phonology interactions in the language. I also propose that a system that appears to be potentially analysable as a 'pitch accent' pattern in fact derives from differences in metrical structure.
- The role of syllable structure in phonotactic restrictions. As I show in this chapter, an explicit understanding of syllabic structures that are (dis)allowed in the language offers diagnostics for the phonological status of some important patterns.
- The interaction between consonant quality and vowel length. Here, again, Bothoa Breton differs from most other Brythonic varieties, and this difference will play an important role in the analysis of laryngeal phonology in Chapter 11.

8.1 Stress

The stress system of Bothoa Breton differs significantly from that of other varieties of Brythonic Celtic. In Welsh (and Cornish) and most varieties of Breton, stress falls regularly on the penultimate syllable, and (barring a handful of modern borrowings) is in any case restricted to a two-syllable window at the right edge of a word. In south-eastern (Vannetais) varieties of Breton, on the other hand, stress regularly falls on the final syllable; there is no agreement in the literature on whether this represents a retention of the Old Brythonic pattern of final stress or an innovation, possibly induced through contact with French. The dialect of Bothoa, which Humphreys (1995) classes as a Cornouaillais variety, also shares a number of features with Vannetais, which is unsurprising given its location. One of the ways in which this Vannetais presence in manifested is the stress system, which it shares with some other varieties in the region (Plourin 1985). In addition, some of the characteristics of its prosodic system are quite unusual even within the wider Brythonic context.

8.1.1 Types of stress

According to Humphreys (1995), stressed vowels are characterised by greater intensity, greater duration and rising pitch (this latter especially pronounced on final syllables).

There is one type of word where the realisation of stress is not entirely straightforward. According to Humphreys (1995), there is a marked difference between two classes of disyllabic words, exemplified in (46).

(46) Two types of stress
    (a) [ˈpærson]   *person*   'parson'
    (b) [ˈdaˌvad̪]   *dañvad*   'ewe'

If Humphreys' description is correct, in words of the first type intensity, length, and pitch peaks all converge on the initial syllable. In words of the second type, however, both syllables are of the same duration. Moreover, final syllables in these words bear an especially abrupt rise in pitch, with the result that the accentuation of a word such as [ˈdaˌvad̪] 'ewe' 'rather strikingly resembles Welsh accentuation' (Humphreys 1995: 68).[1]

Humphreys (1995) interprets this additional prominence on final syllables as secondary stress. He notes, however, that the ordering of the main and secondary stress in disyllabic forms such as [ˈdaˌvad̪] can be difficult to determine: they may also surface with the second syllable more prominent than the first one, or with both syllables equally prominent. Humphreys (1995) entertains an account where the contrast between the two types of words shown in (46) is really a contrast between words with one stress (ˈσ) and words with two stresses (ˈσˈσ). In this section I argue that this interpretation is correct.

Apart from this special case, Humphreys (1995) also recognises the existence of a more orthodox type of secondary stress. Its placement is generally unpredictable, so it is marked in the transcription. Humphreys (1995) also describes a 'tertiary stress', said to fall on peripheral syllables where they are separated from main stress by one or more unstressed syllables. Tertiary stress is 'almost as perceptible as secondary stress' (Humphreys 1995: 68). It is not marked in Humphreys' transcriptions, but I will suggest that it may also be treated as phonological.

8.1.2 Stress placement

I propose that stress placement in Bothoa Breton is lexical, with several qualifications:

- Long vowels are always stressed.
- Where possible, the stress foot is a moraic trochee.
- If there are several feet in the word, the rightmost one bears the main stress.

In words with only short vowels, stress can in principle fall on any syllable, with the exception of disyllables: as described above, possible patterns are L̇L and LL̇, where the latter has a range of possible realisations. Humphreys (1995) gives a few examples of LL̇ forms, but since this pattern is also said to be a possible realisation of 'L̇L̇', it is not entirely clear that tokens of LL̇ are not in fact instances of 'double-stressed' words for which L̇L̇ variants have not been recorded as a matter of accident.

(47) Two syllables
Initial stress
  (a) [ˈmɛlən]   *melen*   'yellow'
  (b) [ˈdiskɔlb̥] *diskolp* 'rude'

Two stresses
  (c) [ˈdaˌvad̥] *dañvad* 'ewe'
  (d) [ˈlaˌɡad̥] *lagad*   'eye'

(48) Three syllables
Initial stress
  (a) [ˈɡløskərəd̥] *gleskered* 'frogs'
  (b) [ˈparuʒəw]   *parrezioù* 'parishes'
  (c) [ˈskwarnətad̥] *skournata* 'to slap'

Penultimate stress
  (d) [ãnˈkwɛjyz̥] *ankouaus* 'forgetful'
  (e) [liˈbærte]   'freedom' (French *liberté*)

Double stress
  (f) [ˌasˈtʃɛləw] *eskell*   'wings'
  (g) [ˌlaˈɡadən] *lagadenn* 'bud'

Final stress
  (h) [kariˈtʃɛl] *karrigell* 'wheelbarrow'
  (i) [tʃilɔˈmɛd̥] *kilometr*   'kilometre'

(49) Four syllables and more
Initial stress
(a) [ˈdɔrnərəzəw] *dornerezhoù* 'threshings'
(b) [ˈtʃɛzəkənəĝ] *kazekenned* 'mares'

Variable stress
(c) [ˈpɔʃənadəw] *pochennadoù* 'many bags'
(d) [pɔʃəˈnadəw]

Other patterns
(e) [sigaˈrɛtən] *sigaretenn* 'cigarette'
(f) [sigaˈrɛtənəw] *sigaretennoù* 'cigarettes'
(g) [digɔməˈradən] *degemeradenn* 'reception'
(h) [digɔməˈradənəw] *degemeradennoù* 'receptions'

Long oral vowels generally attract stress. In particular, long vowels in final syllables always bear main stress (secondary stress is sometimes possible on an initial syllable with a short vowel, with an unclear distribution).

(50) Stress on final heavy syllables
Two syllables
(a) [boˈneːl] *banal* 'broom (plant sp.)'
(b) [ˌskaˈriːn] *skarin* 'severe cold'

Three syllables
(c) [tʃimiˈnɛːr] *kemener* 'tailor'
(d) [baraˈdoːz̧] *baradoz* 'paradise'

Long vowels in non-final syllables also generally attract stress.

(51) Long vowels in non-final syllables
Two syllables
(a) [ˈlaːbor] *labour* 'work'
(b) [ˈdɛːbo] *debriñ* 'eat'

Three syllables
(c) [ˈhaːdərəʒ] *haderezh* 'sowing season'
(d) [byˈgaːle] *bugale* 'children'

Four syllables and more
(e) [ˈdɛːvəʒərəz] *devezhierez* 'day labourer (f.)'
(f) [ˈdɛːvəʒərəzəḑ] *devezhierezed* 'day labourers (f.)'
(g) [tʃiˈdʒiːənəw] *kegined* 'jays'
(h) [tʃimiˈnɛːrəzəḑ] *kemenerezed* 'dressmakers'

If more than one long vowel is found in the word (a relatively rare occurrence), the last one bears main stress, while the first one bears secondary stress.[2]

(52) More than one heavy syllable
    (a) [ˌhyː'aːl]   *hual*   'hindrance'
    (b) [ˌziːjaˈtyːr]   *sinatur*   'signature'
    (c) [ˌtʃɒːˈdiːʒən]   *teod-ejen*   'plantain'
    (d) [ˌbyːˈeːəw]   *buheziou*   'lives (n.)'

The diphthongs do not appear to pattern with long vowels, in that they may be unstressed: they do not attract stress from short vowels and they do not receive secondary stress when a long vowel is present.

(53) Diphthongs are metrically light
    (a) [pəiˈzãntəd̪]   *peizanted*   'peasants'
    (b) [hrəiˈtaːl]   *raktal*   'suddenly'

While the attraction of stress to long vowels can be ascribed to phonological factors, as argued below, the unpredictability of stress in words with only short vowels appears to indicate a lexical specification. That the position of the stress is also associated with the morpheme rather than with the prosodic structure of the word as a whole is confirmed by the fact that stress remains immovable in most cases of suffixation. However, the placement of stress can also be influenced by morphological factors. I turn to these in the next section.

8.1.3 *Morphological factors in stress placement*

Humphreys (1995) distinguishes between three types of affixes with respect to their stress-related behaviour: he calls the three classes 'unstressable', 'stressable', and 'stressed'. 'Unstressable' affixes simply do not influence the stress placement and are apparently indistinguishable from any other unstressed syllable; since Bothoa Breton does not mandate a stress window like some other Brythonic varieties, these morphemes simply surface without stress.

The difference between 'stressable' and 'stressed' affixes[3] lies in their behaviour in word-final position: the former only appear as stressed when another affix follows (as in (54)), but the latter always attract main stress.

(54) Stressable affixes
    (a) [ˈlærːəw]   *loeroù*   'pair of stockings'
    (b) [ˌlæːˈrəwjər]   *loereier*   'pairs of stockings'

(c) ['dɒrnaɖ]   dornad   'handful'
(d) [ˌdɒr'nadəw]   dornadoù   'handfuls'

(55) Stressed affixes
(a) ['ʃyːbaɖ]   skubañ   'to sweep'
(b) [ˌʃyːˈbadər]   skubadur   'swept rubbish'
(c) ['desko]   deskiñ   'study'
(d) [ˌdesˈkadəræʒ] deskadurezh 'teaching'

Humphreys (1995) casts the contrast between the two types in lexical terms. However, Table 8.1 shows that for the most part it can be explained with reference to the prosodic structure of the relevant morpheme.

With the exception of the past-participle suffix /-əid/, all 'stressed' elements either have a long stressed vowel or contain more than one syllable following the stress (or both). I suggest that this represents the true difference between these two classes: 'stressable' suffixes bear lexical stress, just like the 'stressed' ones, but this stress cannot surface as the main stress in final position because of constraints on foot structure (though it can surface as secondary stress). Moreover, the equivalence of two syllables with short vowels and of syllables with long vowels suggests that the foot type in Bothoa Breton is the moraic trochee.

8.1.4 Multiple stressed elements

So far we have seen two types of elements that may bear (main or secondary) stress: these are lexically stressed syllables and syllables with long vowels. In this section I consider their interaction. As already pointed

Table 8.1 Stressed and stressable elements

Stressable	Stressed	
/ˈɒd/	/Vː/ in a final syllable	
/ˈæd/	/ˈiːãm/	/ˈuːr/
/ˈɛl/	/ˈiːaj̃/	/ˈadən/
/ˈin/	/əid/	/ˈadər/
/ˈəw/	/ˈãnte/	/ˈadəræz/
/ˈard/	/ˈãːs/	/aˈdyːræz/
/ˈãnt/	/ˈɛːr/	/ˈasən/
/əˈmãnt/	/ˈɛːrəz/	/ˈiːʒən/
/ˈad/	/ˈærte/	/ˈaːb/
/ˈaz/	/ˈætən/	
/ˈyz/	/əˈriː/	

out (see (52)), in words with more than one long vowel main stress falls on the rightmost one. The same rule applies in other cases of more than stressed element in a word.

This is most clearly seen when a stressed affix is added to stems with a long vowel. In these cases main stress falls on the rightmost element, i.e. on the suffix, while the long vowel receives secondary stress.

(56) Long vowels and stressed affixes
    (a) [ˌʃyːˈbadər]   *skubadur*   'swept rubbish'
    (b) [ˌluːˈdadər]   *louedadur*   'mould'
    (c) [ˌgwiːˈladən]   *goueladenn*   'outbreak of tears'
    (d) [ˌlyːˈnɛdəw]   *lunedoù*   'spectacles'

Similarly, stressed prefixes also receive secondary stress but do not attract main stress in words longer than two syllables.

(57) Main stress right
    (a) [ˌdisˌlaːˈradən]   *dislavaradenn*   'forfeit'
    (b) [ˌdisˌliːˈvadən]   *dislivadenn*   'discoloured patch'

Finally, the same right alignment of main stress is in evidence when disyllabic words with the 'double accent' (i.e. with the structure σ́σ̀~σ̀σ́) receive additional suffixes. In these cases main stress moves to the right, creating a stress flip within the paradigm.

(58) 'Stress flip' in double-stressed words
    (a) [ˈdaˌvaḍ]   *dañvad*   'ewe'
    (b) [ˌdaˈvadəw]   *deñved*   'sheep'
    (c) [ˈlaˌgaḍ]   *lagad*   'eye'
    (d) [ˌlaˈgadən]   *lagadenn*   'bud'

I conclude that in Bothoa Breton lexical stress may fall on any syllable in the word, but is dispreferred on final light syllables. Long vowels (but not diphthongs) always attract stress. When there is more than one stress-bearing element (a lexically stressed syllable or a long vowel) in a word, main stress falls on the rightmost of these; the exception is found in disyllables with only short vowels, where the realisation is the more complicated 'pitch-accent' pattern.

For the sake of completeness, there are a few instances of stress-and-length alternations similar to those found in other Brythonic varieties.

(59) Length and stress alternations
    (a) [ˈfæːb̥]   'weak' (French *faible*)
    (b) [fɛˈbliːʒən]   *feblijenn*   'failure'

(c) [ˈgliːʑ]   *glizh*   'dew'
(d) [gliˈzætən] *glizhetenn* 'drizzle'

However, these appear to be irregular and isolated, and also demonstrate unstressed vowel shortening, which is otherwise uncharacteristic of Bothoa Breton: instead, as we have seen, a long vowel that does not bear main stress keeps secondary stress and does not shorten. These examples are perhaps best treated as lexicalised remains of the system that is characteristic of other varieties, or perhaps borrowings from such varieties.

8.2 Foot structure

In this section I argue that the stress facts discussed above are best treated in terms of a parse utilising the moraic trochee, i.e. a bimoraic foot (with morae licensed almost exclusively by vowels). Additionally, word-final (and possibly word-initial) light syllables also form (degenerate) feet. The head foot of the word is the rightmost non-degenerate foot, and lexical factors may also influence foot formation.

8.2.1 *The generalisations*

To recap, the basic generalisations regarding stress placement in Bothoa Breton are as follows; I exclude 'double-stressed' words from consideration at this point:

- The presence of tautosyllabic consonants following vowels generally has no effect on stress placement.
- Long vowels are always stressed; certain suffixes – all of them at least bimoraic in length – also attract stress (I will henceforth call long vowels and sufficiently long suffixes *dominant* stressed elements).
- If there is more than one dominant stressed element in the word, main stress falls on the rightmost of these; those that do not receive main stress carry secondary stress.
- If there are no dominant stressed elements, stress may fall on any syllable in the word. It remains immobile if unstressed suffixes are added.

I suggest that, in very general outlines, the stress system of Bothoa Breton exemplifies a default-to-opposite pattern: it is rightmost in words with multiple bimoraic feet and leftmost otherwise, similar to the pattern in Eastern Mongolian in Walker (2000), albeit without non-finality. However, there are added complications, including interaction with lexical stress specification and cyclic preservation effects.

Since there is no consensus in the literature on the proper analysis of default-to-opposite stress systems (Zoll 1997; Walker 2000; Baković

2004; Hyde 2006), or indeed on their very existence (Gordon 2000), for reasons of focus (and lack of completely reliable data) I do not offer a detailed theoretical analysis here. Nevertheless, in this section I will discuss the foot structures that can be found in the data, setting the scene for a formal analysis that must be left for the future.

8.2.2 Stress on dominant elements

If the word contains one or more long vowel or bimoraic lexically stressed suffix, main stress falls on the rightmost of these (vacuously so if the dominant stressed element is the only one), as in the footings in (60).

(60) Footing in forms with long vowels and stressed suffixes
    (a) [bo('neː$_{\mu\mu}$l)]   *banal*   'broom (plant sp.)'
    (b) [('lɛː$_{\mu\mu}$)rən]   *lerenn*   'strap'
    (c) [by('gaː$_{\mu\mu}$)le]   *bugale*   'children'
    (d) [des('ka$_\mu$də$_\mu$)(ˌræẓ)] *deskadurezh* 'teaching'
    (e) [(ˌtʃɒː$_{\mu\mu}$)('diː$_{\mu\mu}$)ʒən] *teod-ejen* 'plantain'
    (f) [(ˌgwiː$_{\mu\mu}$)('la$_\mu$də$_\mu$n)] *goueladenn* 'burst of tears'

The presence of stress (i.e. foot structure) on long vowels is usually accounted for via a WEIGHT-TO-STRESS constraint (Prince 1992; Prince and Smolensky 1993).

As for dominant suffixes, I have argued that they are lexically stressed suffixes with enough segmental material to build a bimoraic foot. The nature of this marking is not entirely clear. One way would be to suggest that they actually are stored with the entire foot structure in place, so that bimoraic feet are part of the input to the phonology. However, as we shall see below, this approach begets problems when we consider lexically stressed monomoraic syllables. An arguably more insightful account requires the lexically stressed syllable to be somehow marked as a foot head, leaving it to the computation to decide whether a bimoraic foot can be built.

8.2.3 Stress with no dominant elements

In words with no dominant elements, stress may fall on any syllable, and it remains immobile throughout the paradigm if no stress-influencing morphemes are added.

(61) Stress in forms with no dominant elements
    (a) [siga('rɛ$_\mu$tə$_\mu$n)]   *sigaretenn*   'cigarette'
    (b) [siga('rɛ$_\mu$tə$_\mu$)(ˌnə$_\mu$w)] *sigaretennoù* 'cigarettes'
    (c) [(ˌka$_\mu$ri$_\mu$)('tʃɛ$_\mu$l)]   *karrigell*   'cart'

(d) [(ˌkaₘriₘ)(ˈtʃɛₘlaₘd)]   karrigellad   'to cart'
(e) [(ˈpaₘruₘz̥)]   parrez   'parish'
(f) [(ˈpaₘruₘ)(ˌʒəₘw)]   parrezioù   'parishes'

One apparent restriction is that LL words never have the structure LĹ: they are either orthodox (ĹL) trochees or 'doubly stressed' (Ĺ)(L̀) words. However, in longer words final stress is apparently allowed. This is consistent either with a pure default-to-opposite system or with a default right-aligned trochee (possibly with extrametricality) similar to Welsh and some other Breton varieties (see Iosad forthcoming b for discussion). The latter option is attractive in that it does not postulate a default-to-opposite system, but consistently aligns main stress to the right in words with and without dominant elements. However, it also predicts the existence of Welsh-like alternations where suffixation draws stress further towards the right (as in (59)), which I have suggested to be absent from the synchronic grammar in Bothoa Breton. Thus, it would seem that stress in such words is leftmost unless compelled to be placed elsewhere by faithfulness.

A minor point in this connection is that prefixes do not count for the purposes of leftmost stress. However, productive prefixes in Bothoa Breton are themselves stressed (although, given that they precede the necessarily stressed stem–suffix complex, this stress is always secondary), which suggests they may be separate phonological words. As we shall see in section 11.2.2.3, there is also evidence to this effect from segmental phonology.

8.2.4 Doubly stressed words

As I suggested in section 8.1.1, disyllabic words transcribed by Humphreys (1995) with the pattern L̀L̀ are best treated as being underlyingly parsed into two degenerate feet.

(62) Single-stressed words
  (a) [(ˈpaₘruₘz̥)]   parrez   'parish'
  (b) [(ˈpaₘruₘ)(ˌʒəₘw)]   parrezioù   'parishes'

(63) Double-stressed words
  (a) [(ˈdaₘ)(ˌvaₘd̥)]   dañvad   'ewe'
  (b) [(ˌdaₘ)(ˈvaₘdəₘw)]   deñved   'sheep (pl.)'

Alternations such as those in (63) are particularly important for the analysis, as they show the connection between the 'double-stress' pattern in disyllabic words and foot structure that becomes more apparent under suffixation. Specifically, the fact that suffixation in a form such as (63b) is accompanied by preservation of the stress on the second syllable establishes a contrast with forms such as those in (62), which exemplify the pattern found when there is no underlying stress on the stem's second syllable.

As described by Humphreys (1995), one of the ways in which the difference between the two types of words is expressed is in the pitch contours. Thus, Bothoa Breton is a potential example of a 'tonal accent' language, where laryngeal mechanisms such as pitch or glottal occlusion are used to express the boundaries of metrical constituents, in this case foot structure. Similar analyses of 'tonal accent' systems are provided by Morén-Duolljá (2013) for North Germanic, Köhnlein (2016) for West Germanic, and Iosad (2015b) for Scottish Gaelic (this latter also contains further discussion of the Bothoa Breton situation). For the purposes of the present analysis, the postulation of underlying feet in forms in (63) is sufficient.

8.2.5 Stratal aspects of Bothoa Breton stress

In the previous section, I suggested that some suffixes in Bothoa Breton are underlyingly stressed, and hence can attract main stress away from a stem. However, this proposal encounters problems with 'stressable' suffixes such as /-ad/ and /-əw/. These are able to attract stress, as seen under conditions of suffixation (hyphens show morpheme boundaries).

(64) Suffixes are stressed when followed by a suffix
  (a) [(ˌdɒ$_μ$r)(ˈn-a$_μ$d-ə$_μ$w)]   *dornadoù*   'handfuls'
  (b) [(ˌbɒ$_μ$)(ˈt-ə$_μ$w-jə$_μ$r)]   *boteier*   'pairs of shoes'

However, when these suffixes are not followed by another morpheme, the 'double-stress' pattern, which we would expect given two adjacent underlying stressed syllables, fails to appear.

(65) No double-stress pattern in the absence of following suffix
  (a) [ˈdɒrnad̥]   *dornad*   'handful'
  (b) [ˈbɒtəw]   *botoù*   'pair of shoes'

I suggest that this difference is best explained in a stratal model of phonological computation. The important generalisation, which is not stated explicitly by Humphreys (1995) but emerges from the corpus, is that most 'double-stressed' words are monomorphemic. The exceptions are a few compounds and prefixed forms ([ˈpæmˌtʃəs] 'five times', [ˈseisˌtʃəs] 'seven times', [ˈdiˌʃɒːl] 'sunset'), which can reasonably be assumed to contain more than one phonological word, and the word [ʃyːˈbɛl] 'broom', which, however, seems to derive from a *bound* root /ʃyːb/. (See below for 'past participles' in [-əid̪].)

Since the double-stress pattern relies on the possibility of preserving underlying degenerate feet, we can conclude that such preservation of underlying stress is allowed at the stem level, at the point of root-to-stem derivation. This suggestion is confirmed by the fact that the (rare) instances of final stress in all-light-syllable words such as [kariˈtʃɛl] 'cart' are also found only in morphologically underived forms.

However, degenerate feet then cannot be created at the word level. They *can*, however, be preserved when part of the input, due to high-ranked faithfulness. This means that word-level derivational suffixes (such as /-ad/) and inflectional morphemes (such as the plural /-əw/) can only be stressed if a binary foot can be built with material introduced at this level. Thus, an underlying /(ˈbɔt)ˈəw/ 'pair of shoes' loses the stress on the suffix, since it cannot be parsed into a binary foot. An underlying /(ˈbɔt)ˈəwjər/ 'pairs of shoes' does retain this stress, since the word-level material is sufficient to build a binary foot.

The strong prediction made here is that if an underlyingly stressed suffix consists of a single light syllable but still surfaces with stress in a final syllable, then it must be stem-level, as otherwise that stress could not be preserved. Hence, the appearance of stress on degenerate feet must be driven by morphosyntactic properties of the affix. This prediction is confirmed by the existence of the stressed monosyllabic suffix /-əid/ used to form past participles.

(66) Double stress in [-əid̪] past participles
    (a) [ˌɛsˈtəid̪]   *esaed*   'tried'
    (b) [ˌbraˈsəid̪]   *brasaed*   'increased'

Morphosyntactically, the passive participle suffix (which has two allomorphs, the other one being /-əd/) attaches to verbal stems to derive adjectival forms.[4] That these participles are derived specifically from verbal stems rather than directly from roots is confirmed by forms such as [ˌkoˈsəid̪] 'aged', where the suffix attaches not to the root /koːz/ ([ˈkoːz̩] 'old', [ˈkoːzəni] 'old age') but to the specifically verbal stem /kos-/ as in [ˈkosad̪] 'to get old', derived from the root by morphological provection (section 11.2.1). I propose that this categorial change provides evidence for the participle suffixes triggering a stem-level cycle (stem-to-stem derivation). The prediction is thereby confirmed.[5] Still, further work on the morphosyntactic properties of the affixes listed in Table 8.2 is needed to reach a fuller understanding of the issues involved.

The classification of stressed suffixes is summarised in Table 8.2. The phonological difference between the stem level and the word level lies in the possibility of constructing degenerate feet (or at least monosyllabic

Table 8.2 The behaviour of underlyingly stressed suffixes in Bothoa Breton

Size	Stem-level	Word-level
Monomoraic	Stressed	Unstressed
	[ˌkoˈsəid]	[ˈdʊrnad]
Bimoraic		Stressed
		[desˈkadəræz]

feet with a short vowel), which, in a stratal model, must be explained by reranking. In the next section I present evidence that such feet are again made possible at the postlexical level.

8.2.6 Edgemost degenerate feet: lapses and segmental structure

Finally, I adduce evidence that monosyllabic (probably degenerate) feet can be built at word edges, presumably to avoid lapses. This follows from Humphreys' (1995) description. He claims that final syllables that are separated from the main stress by at least another syllable bear 'tertiary' stress, even when they are light.

(67) Example of 'tertiary' stress
    (a) [(ˈpa$_\mu$ru$_\mu$)(ˌʒə$_\mu$w)]   *parrezioù*   'parishes'
    (b) [des(ˈka$_\mu$də$_\mu$)(ˌræ$_\mu$z̸)]   *deskadurezh*   'teaching'

In (67), I write these final syllables as heading their own degenerate feet. These footings are confirmed by circumstantial segmental evidence. Unstressed final syllables license the full range of segmental contrasts. At the same time, as discussed in section 9.3, the second syllable in words of the form LLL and HLL is a weak position: it demonstrates both reduced duration and (*modulo* cyclic effects) a reduced range of segmental contrasts; for instance, it disallows the low peripheral vowels [æ] and [ʊ]. At the same time the final syllable in these words does not show phonetic shortening and freely allows the full range of vocalic segments. This can be accounted for if we assume the parses (L̇L)(L) and (H)L(L) for the relevant structures; the weak position can then be succinctly described as any position other than the head of a foot.

The degenerate status of these word-final feet follows from the fact that they do not attract main stress from preceding binary feet. This can be due either to a complexity requirement à la Dresher and van der Hulst (1998), prohibiting that the words be headed by a non-branching foot in the presence of a branching one, or to a reranking between strata, so that these degenerate feet are built to ensure lack of lapses but the stress system stops enforcing rightmost stress. A more precise analysis would require more data than is available.

The lack of data also prevents making any pronouncements on the exhaustivity of parsing. The appearance of degenerate feet in forms such as (ĹL)(L̀) could, in principle, be due to *LAPSE. However, Humphreys (1995) also states that tertiary stress is found on *final* syllables separated from the main stress by *two* syllables, implying foot parses such as (ĹL) L(L̀) which do not optimise rhythm.

Another option is a prohibition on unparsed syllables. However, 'tertiary stress' is not described for non-peripheral syllables, and thus in principle we could also be dealing with the effects of a constraint requiring that all word edges coincide with the edges of some foot. Humphreys (1995) does not describe any iterative stress, though this is perhaps understandable given that longer words are not very numerous in Bothoa Breton. Thus, the question of whether all syllables in Bothoa Breton are parsed into feet or if some syllables are outside the metrical system cannot be settled at this point. I leave these questions for further research.

The stratal differences in Bothoa Breton foot structure are summarised in Table 8.3. In the next section I consider syllable-internal structure in more detail.

8.3 Syllabic structure and phonotactics

In this section I consider issues related to syllable structure, in particular with reference to syllable size restrictions, the interpretation of 'disallowed' consonant sequences, and the distribution of vowel qualities.

8.3.1 Syllable size restrictions

An important descriptive generalisation regarding Bothoa Breton phonotactics is the following: long vowels rarely precede consonant sequences, and never precede sequences of obstruents. In this and the next section I provide evidence for a strong form of this generalisation, formulated as follows:

> **The syllable size restriction (SSR):** All Bothoa Breton syllables are of the form C^*VX, i.e. the syllable rhyme contains either a long vowel or a long vowel and a single consonant, but never both.

8.3.1.1 Data

Descriptively, the SSR is violated in final syllables: words in Bothoa Breton may end in consonant sequences (subject to sonority constraints)

Table 8.3 Stratal aspects of Bothoa Breton foot structure

Level	Process	SHEEP	SHEEP-PL	HANDFUL	HANDFUL-PL	PARISH	PARISH-PL	AGE-PASS. PART
Stem	Insertion	('da)(ˌvad)	('da)(ˌvad)	dɔrn		paruz		kos
	Foot construction[a]			('dɔrn)		(ˈparuz)		(ˈkos)
	Insertion			('dɔrn)				(ˈkos)(ˈeid)
	Foot construction[a]							(ˈko)(ˈseid)
Word	Insertion		('da)(ˌvad)ˈəw	('dɔrn)ˈad	('dɔrn)ˈadˈəw		(ˈparuz)ˈəw	(ˈko)(ˈseid)
	Foot construction[b]	(ˈda)(ˌvad)	(ˌda)(ˈvadəw)	(ˈdɔrnad)	(ˌdɔr)(ˈnadəw)		(ˈparu)zəw	(ˌko)(ˈseid)
							(ˈparu)(ˌzəw)	
Postlexical	Lapse elimination[c]							
Output		[ˈda ˌvad̥]	[ˌda ˈvadəw]	[ˈdɔrnad̥]	[ˌdɔrˈnadəw]	[ˈparuz̥]	[ˈparuˌzəw]	[ˌkoˈseid̥]

[a] Binary feet built, degenerate feet allowed if compelled by faithfulness (or under minimality restrictions, see section 8.3.5).
[b] Binary feet built, degenerate feet allowed if compelled by faithfulness; main stress assigned to the rightmost foot.
[c] Or another constraint building peripheral feet; main stress cannot move.

and in a single consonant preceded by a long vowel (though long vowels before more than one consonant are still excluded). Such stems, however, provide the most direct evidence for the SSR: when they are suffixed with consonant-initial morphemes, the long vowels are shortened, demonstrating the SSR's force as an active synchronic restriction.

(68) Shortening before consonant clusters
    (a) [ˈvyːr]   *fur*   'sage'
    (b) [ˈvyrnəz]   *furnez*   'wisdom'
    (c) [ˈbraːz̹]   *bras*   'big'
    (d) [ˈbrastər]   *braster*   'size'

Another type of violation of the weak generalisation is seen when a long vowel precedes a *muta cum liquida* sequence. These structures are allowed in Bothoa Breton: all instances of this pattern found in Humphreys (1995) are shown in (69). Interestingly, all of them appear to be Romance borrowings; I give the corresponding Standard French form for reference, though the source is likely to be local *gallo* varieties.

(69) Long vowels before rising-sonority clusters
    (a) [ˈduːblo]   *doublañ*   'to line (cloth)'   *doubler*[6]
    (b) [ˈpaːtron]   *patrom*   'spitting image'   *patron*
    (c) [maˈnøːvro]   *maneuriñ*   'to manoeuvre'   *manœuvrer*
    (d) [ˈhræːglən]   'rule'   *règle*
    (e) [ˈtaːblən]   'table'   *table*
    (f) [ˈaːdrəz]   *adres*   'address'   *adresse*

The position before a *muta cum liquida* sequence does allow for a vowel length contrast, in inherited words as well as borrowings.

(70) Short vowels before rising-sonority clusters
    (a) [ˈzɛblãɖ]   *seblant*   'omen'
    (b) [ˈpɔtrəɖ]   *paotred*   'boys'
    (c) [ˈzakriz̹ɖ]   *sakrist*   'sexton'

These facts are of course unproblematic if we assume that correct analysis of these sequences involves prosodic structure, specifically syllable divisions: the long vowels in (69) stand before a branching onset; in (simplified) OT terms, NoCoda in Bothoa Breton dominates *ComplexOnset, ensuring onset maximisation *modulo* phonotactic constraints. The relevant constraints can be formulated as follows, assuming the predicates *Coda* and *Onset* are available in the metalanguage.

Suprasegmental phonology 111

(71) |NoCoda|:=$(output \land \langle\uparrow\rangle\sigma) \rightarrow \neg\, Coda$

'If a node is dominated directly by a syllable node, it is not a coda'

(72) |*ComplexOnset|:=$(output \land Onset \land \langle\downarrow\rangle i \land \langle\downarrow\rangle j) \rightarrow @_i j$

'If an Onset node dominates two nodes, then they are the same node'

Moreover, MaxLink-µ[V] dominates constraints penalising long vowels (such as *µµ), ensuring that input vowels are never shortened.

(73) Preference for open syllables: [ˈzɛblanḓ] 'omen', [ˈduːblo] 'to line'⁷

		Parse-(Seg)	Max-Link-µ[V]	No Coda	*[µµ]_σ	*Complex-Onset
(a) /zɛblant/ ☞	[ˈzɛ_µ.blanḓ]					*
(b)	[ˈz(ɛb)_µ.lanḓ]			*!		
(c)	[(ˈze_µ)_σ b(l(an)_µ)_σ ḓ]	*!				
(d) /duːblo/	[ˈdu_µ.blo]		*!			*
(e)	[ˈd(ub)_µ.lo]		*!	*		
(f) ☞	[ˈduː_µµ.blo]				*	*
(g)	[ˈdu_µ(ub)_µ.lo]			*!	*	
(h)	[(ˈduː_µµ)_σ b(lo_µ)_σ]	*!			*	

In the next section I propose to derive the SSR from the interplay of restrictions on branching complexity in syllables and moraicity.

8.3.1.2 Analysis

I suggest that syllables in Bothoa Breton are never larger than two morae, with possible branching of the first mora in a syllable. Following standard assumptions, I propose the stress-attracting elements (which in Bothoa Breton are long vowels) must be represented as a single root node attached to two morae. For the sake of concreteness, I also place the morae under a syllable constituent, and ignore feet for now. I take no position on the exact representation of onsets and simply adjoin them to the syllable node.

112   *A Substance-free Framework for Phonology*

(74)   Bimoraic long vowel: [ˈbiː] 'cows'

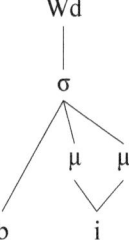

We also find situations where the initial, head mora in a bimoraic syllable branches (but the dependent one does not). This representation is found in the case of diphthongs. As discussed above, diphthongs behave like short vowels for the purposes of stress placement, and hence they are monomoraic: they do not necessarily attract stress and may precede tautosyllabic consonants. The representation of coda consonants following diphthongs is difficult to determine. If they are moraic, as in (75), the prediction is that such syllables will always attract stress. It appears to be borne out, but the number of examples is too small to draw any definite conclusions.[8]

(75)   Diphthong before a tautosyllabic consonant: [ˈdrəistã] 'over him'.

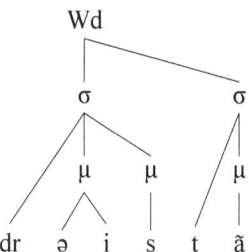

In this context, the moraic coda is allowed under pressure from PARSE-Seg which requires all segments to be dominated by a syllable node. Normally, if syllable structure places consonants in a coda, they are adjoined to the nuclear mora (hence creating a monomoraic syllable), but since this solution is unavailable in cases such as (75), the consonant projects a mora instead.

(76)   Bimoraicity compelled by PARSE[9]

/drəistã/		PARSE(Seg)	SYLSTRUC	*μ[C]
(a)	[(dr(əi)$_\mu$)$_\sigma$(sta$_\mu$)$_\sigma$]		*!	

(b)	[(dr(ə$_μ$)(is$_μ$))$_σ$(ta$_μ$)$_σ$]		*!	
(c)	[(dr(əi)$_μ$)$_σ$s(ta$_μ$)$_σ$]	*!		
(d) ☞	[(dr(əi)$_μ$s$_μ$)$_σ$(ta$_μ$)$_σ$]			*

In the next section I consider another important class of apparent exceptions to the SSR.

8.3.2 *The trough pattern*

In Bothoa Breton, a penultimate unstressed syllable immediately following a stressed syllable is 'weak', both phonetically and phonologically. Phonologically, I will argue in section 9.1 that it is the locus of vowel reduction. Here, I concentrate on its 'phonetic' weakness. Specifically, I argue that the vowel [ə] output by the phonological computation in this position is subject to phonetic shortening, possibly due to the overlap of consonantal gestures (Browman and Goldstein 1990). This can lead to its total disappearance from the acoustic record. I suggest, nevertheless, that this process is part of phonetic implementation and does not create exceptions to the phonological SSR.

As argued above, the final syllable in words with antepenultimate stress forms a degenerate foot; the correct parses for HLL and LLL words with initial stress are (H)L(L) and (L̇L)(L); the medial syllable is never the head of a foot. A surface [ə] in this position can be shortened or even entirely dropped.

(77) Variable deletion of [ə] in a medial syllable
    (a) [['jiːrəzəd]]   *yerezed*   'chickens'
    (b) [['jiːrzəd]]
    (c) [['tapəfæ]]   *tapfe*   '[if] [(s)he] took'
    (d) [['tapfæ]]
    (e) [['mãnəgən]]   *manegenn*   'glove'
    (f) [['mãngən]]
    (g) *[['mãŋgən]]

This 'dropping' of the schwa can violate otherwise exceptionless phonological generalisations, specifically the SSR and phonotactic constraints. The latter case is illustrated by (77b), where a long vowel appears to precede a consonant sequence that is not a possible complex onset. Even more blatant violations are found in the case of conditional formation, such as that exemplified by (77d), where the resulting sequence appears to be generally disallowed outside the context of the conditional. In fact, the structure of the conditional merits additional discussion.

Humphreys (1995) gives the form of the conditional suffix as /-Vf/, and morphologically this suffix is always followed by the person-number suffixes of the 'habitual imperfect', which all contain at least one vowel. Thus, normally a conditional form is at least trisyllabic, containing the verbal root, the /-Vf/ suffix, and a person-number suffix. However, four verbs possess stems with no vowels. In this case, the vowel of the conditional suffix is a stressed [æ].

(78) Disyllabic conditional forms
    (a) [ma ˈhræfæ]   *ma rafe*   'if [(s)he] did'
    (b) [ma ˈhræfæ]   *ma rofe*   'if [(s)he] gave'
    (c) [ma ˈtæfæ]   *ma teufe*   'if [(s)he] came'
    (d) [ma ˈhæfæ]   *ma afe*   'if [(s)he] went'

With longer stems, the vowel either is realised as [ə] or disappears completely. Humphreys (1995) presents this as a lexical distribution, saying that some stems take the vowel-less form, some take the /-əf/ form, and a small minority exhibit free variation. However, he also notes (somewhat contradicting himself) that the vowel-less forms 'never seem to be obligatory variants' (1995: 372) of those containing [əf].[10] The vowel-less forms can violate both the SSR and generalisations regarding possible consonant sequences.

(79) Long vowels before heterosyllabic clusters
    (a) ⟦ˈpaːlfæ⟧   *palfe*   '[if] [(s)he] dug'
    (b) ⟦ˈluːd̪fæ⟧   *louedfe*   '[if] [it] went mouldy'

(80) Otherwise impossible sequences
    (a) ⟦ˈfankfæ⟧   *fankfe*   '[if] [(s)he] neglected'
    (b) ⟦ˈstaːgfæ⟧   *stagfe*   '[if] [(s)he] tied'

These examples also show the behaviour of voiced obstruents before the conditional suffix. According to Humphreys (1995), they do not undergo complete devoicing (as would be expected otherwise; see section 11.2.2), but are realised as either 'voiceless lenes' (*sourde[s] douce[s]*) or as 'lenes with decreasing voicing' (*douce[s] à sonorité décroissante*); Humphreys (1995) explicitly compares their realisations with the voicing found in sandhi contexts.

I suggest that the apparent dropping of the schwa in these circumstances is a phonetic process rather than the effect of a phonological rule. In other words, the phonetics–phonology interface allows a continuum of realisations for the phonological segment [ə] in this position, but this does not change the phonological representation. If the proposal is correct, the forms cited in (79) and (80) do not violate either the SSR or the language's phonotactics. Moreover, if schwa deletion is not phonological but rather driven by phonetic considerations,[11] the variation found in the majority of these cases is only to be expected.

However, the issue of variation is not quite as simple. Humphreys (1995) only notes variation for those forms where he has actually encountered it; when he has not heard a particular type of realisation, he does not write it, and for this reason many of the distributions are stated in lexical terms, as we have seen with the conditional. Yet categorical behaviour does not necessarily mean categorical representation: since the forces behind the variation are functional, we can only expect the functionally beneficial variant to be over-represented in the corpus. I will therefore assume that if there are good reasons to suppose that a form recorded without variation actually may contain the [ə] vowel in the 'trough' position, then surface-phonological representations with a schwa may be hypothesised unless there is specific evidence to the contrary.

8.3.3 Consonant sequences

The phonotactics of Bothoa Breton are relatively simple. We have already discussed the syllable size restriction. In terms of sonority and possible consonant sequences, the language presents a familiar picture. Complex onsets are of the familiar type (s)C(R(G)), where C is any consonant, R is a sonorant and G is a glide: the largest possible onset is found in [skrwẽːʒal] 'screech' (*skrijal*). There are also familiar sub-restrictions such as the absence of [tl] and [dl] onsets; and nasals are almost never found in complex onsets (the only exception is [mn]).

In closed syllables, more than one consonant following the (necessarily short) vowel is only allowed word-finally (and then the final sequences must still be of falling sonority). Heterosyllabic sequences of more than two consonants are only allowed if they can be syllabified in accordance with these principles: thus [mpl] is an allowed sequence, as in [imˈpliːo] 'employ' (*implijout*), but, say, *[rpf] is not (though it may appear due to phonetic schwa deletion, as in [ˈharpfæ] '[if] [(s)he] leant' (*harpfe*)). All these restrictions can be derived from the SSR coupled with familiar restrictions on sonority in onsets. Since the issues here are not significantly different from other well-studied systems, I do not offer a detailed analysis here.

8.3.4 The distribution of vowel length

In most varieties of Brythonic Celtic, the length of stressed vowels depends in nontrivial ways on the nature of the following consonant. A common system in Breton is one where stressed vowels are long before voiced obstruents and short before voiceless ones (at least in penultimate syllables), with a lexical contrast before at least some sonorants. Examples of such systems in Breton are Le Bourg Blanc (Falc'hun 1951), Plougrescant (Le Dû 1978), Berrien (Ploneis 1983), Léchiagat (Sinou 1999), and Lanhouarneau (Carlyle 1988). Similar systems are found in Welsh (Awbery 1984) and Cornish (George 1999). Analyses of these patterns in generative phonological terms are offered for Breton by Anderson (1981) and Carlyle (1988), and for Welsh by Awbery (1986) and Iosad (2012b).

In Bothoa Breton, however, this system appears to have largely broken down. (This is perhaps not surprising, as the Brythonic stress system has done likewise.) The distribution of length in 'VCV sequences is shown in Table 8.4, essentially reproduced from Humphreys (1995: 92). A plus sign means that the relevant vowel is attested before the relevant consonant, a minus sign means a lack of attestation, and (+) is reserved for long vowels before [f], which in most if not all cases represent merely the optional realisation of a V(ː)ə sequence found in conditional forms of verbs with final-vowel roots, as in (81). I have also excluded nasal vowels, since they generally do not participate in length contrasts.

(81) Long vowels in the conditional
   (a) [ˈpɛːfæ]   paefe   '(if) [(s)he] paid'
   (b) [ˈpɛəfæ]
   (c) [ˈzaːfæ]   savfe   '(if) [(s)]he raised'
   (d) [ˈzaːəfæ]

Shading is used in Table 8.4 to highlight those cases where the distribution of length is unexpected under traditional assumptions, i.e. long vowels before voiceless obstruents and [m], short vowels before voiced obstruents, as well as the absence of the reverse pattern (long vowel before a voiced obstruent; short vowel before a voiceless obstruent or [m]).

The table shows that Bothoa Breton does not conform to the traditional picture regarding the relationship between vowel length and laryngeal features in Breton dialects; both cases of a short vowel followed by a voiced obstruent and of a long vowel followed by a voiceless obstruent are attested in this dialect.

(82) Long vowel before a voiceless obstruent
   (a) [ˈgleːpã]   glepañ   'wettest'
   (b) [ˈglepã]
   (c) [hrɛzoˈnaːpᵔh]   'more reasonable' (French *raisonnable*)
   (d) [ˈjɒːtən]   geotenn   'blade of grass'
   (e) [ˈjɒtən]
   (f) [ˈfɔːtən]   faot   'mistake'
   (g) [ˈnaːtyr]   natur   'nature'

Table 8.4 Vowel length and quality of following consonant in Bothoa Breton

		b	p	d	t	dʒ	tʃ	g	k	v	f	z	s	ʒ	ʃ	h	m	n	ɲ	l	r	w	ɥ	j
i	Long	+	-	+	-	+	-	-	-	+	(+)	+	-	+	-	-	+	+	-	+	+	-	-	-
	Short	-	+	+	+	-	+	+	+	+	+	+	+	-	+	+	-	-	-	+	+	-	-	+
e	Long	+	-	+	-	+	-	-	-	+	(+)	+	-	+	+	-	-	+	-	+	+	-	-	-
	Short	-	+	-	+	-	+	+	+	-	-	-	+	+	-	-	+	+	-	-	+	-	-	+
ɛ	Long	+	-	+	-	+	-	-	-	+	(+)	+	-	+	+	-	-	+	-	+	+	-	-	-
	Short	-	+	-	+	-	+	+	+	-	-	-	+	-	-	-	+	+	-	+	+	-	-	+
æ	Long	+	-	+	-	+	-	-	-	+	-	+	-	+	-	-	-	+	-	+	+	-	-	-
	Short	-	-	-	-	-	-	-	-	-	-	-	-	-	-	-	-	-	-	-	+	+	-	-
y	Long	+	-	+	-	+	-	-	-	+	(+)	+	-	+	-	-	-	+	-	+	+	-	-	-
	Short	-	+	-	+	-	+	+	+	-	-	-	+	-	+	-	+	+	-	+	+	-	-	+
ø	Long	+	-	+	-	+	-	-	-	+	(+)	+	-	+	+	-	-	+	-	+	+	-	-	-
	Short	-	+	+	+	-	+	+	+	-	-	-	+	-	-	-	+	-	-	+	-	-	-	+
u	Long	+	-	+	-	+	-	+	-	+	(+)	+	-	+	-	-	-	-	+	+	+	-	-	-
	Short	-	+	-	+	-	+	-	+	-	-	+	+	-	+	-	+	-	-	+	-	-	-	+
o	Long	+	-	+	-	+	-	-	-	-	-	+	(+)	+	-	-	-	+	-	+	-	-	-	+
	Short	-	+	+	+	-	+	-	+	-	-	+	+	-	+	+	+	-	-	-	+	-	-	-
ɔ	Long	+	-	+	-	+	-	+	-	-	(+)	+	+	+	+	+	-	-	-	-	-	-	-	+
	Short	-	-	+	+	-	-	+	+	-	-	+	-	-	-	-	-	-	-	-	-	-	-	-
ɒ	Long	+	-	+	-	-	-	+	+	+	(+)	+	-	-	-	+	-	+	-	+	+	+	-	+
	Short	-	-	-	-	-	-	-	-	-	-	-	-	-	-	-	-	-	-	-	-	-	-	-
a	Long	-	+	+	+	+	+	+	+	+	+	+	+	+	+	+	+	+	-	+	+	-	-	+

(83) Short vowel before a voiced obstruent
    (a) [ˈkogəw]   *kogoù*   'roosters'
    (b) [ˈivul]   *eoul*   'oil'
    (c) [ˈlɒgɒd̥]   *logod*   'mice'
    (d) [ˈgɔdəl]   *godell*   'pocket'

The pattern shown in (82) is the less widespread of the two. Its most prominent source appears to be the failure of (morphologically induced) vowel shortening in comparative and superlative forms of adjectives: as discussed in section 11.2.1, these forms involve regular devoicing of voiced obstruents and (less regular) shortening of the vowel; when the shortening fails, the anomalous pattern emerges. Another source of the pattern is Romance borrowings; cf. the last two examples in (83) with French *faute, nature*.

As for the reverse pattern, Humphreys (1995) calls many of the examples 'isolated'; nevertheless, some generalisations can also be extracted. For instance, many of these short vowels before voiced obstruents involve the segment [v] originally inserted to avoid hiatus.

(84) Short vowels before historical hiatus
    (a) [ˈivul]   *eoul*   'oil'
    (b) [ˈdyvyn]   *dihuniñ*   'to dream'
    (c) [ˈʒævyẓ]   *joaius*   'cheerful'

Unfortunately, Humphreys (1995) does not expand on the nature of this hiatus-breaking in detail. Hiatus is not systematically avoided in the dialect; most examples of hiatus-breaking [v] appear before a high rounded vowel, but (at least historically) it is also compatible with both non-high round vowels and preceding long vowels, as in [ˈhraːvon] 'Rennes' (*Roazhon*).[12]

Another set of cases involves disyllabic words with identical vowels in both syllables, as in (85).

(85) Short vowels before an identical vowel
    (a) [ˈmyzyl]   *muzul*   'measure'
    (b) [ˈgrizi]   *grizilh*   'hail'
    (c) [ˈlɒgɒd̥]   *logod*   'mice'

However, examples of similar words obeying the expected generalisations also exist.

(86) Long vowels before an identical vowel
    (a) [ˈziːbi]   *sivi*   'strawberries'
    (b) [ˈdʒɥiːzi]   *gwizi*   'sows'
    (c) [ˈiːliz]   *iliz*   'church'

Prominent examples of the pattern are the productive derivational suffixes /-adən/ and /-adər/.

(87) Examples in suffixes
    (a) [ˌkonˈtadən]   *kontadenn*   'tale'
    (b) [ˌhriːˈdadən]   *redadenn*   'running'
    (c) [ˌhweˈːzadər]   *c'hwezenn*   'sweat'
    (d) [ˌpliːˈʒadər]   *plijadur*   'pleasure'

On the whole, however, Bothoa Breton does not exhibit any special relationship between vowel length and laryngeal features: long and short vowels and voiced and voiceless obstruents freely co-occur in all combinations; where such interactions do exist, as discussed in section 11.2.1, they are treated as indicative of morphologically restricted processes rather than general properties of the language's phonology.

In theoretical terms, the important feature of Bothoa Breton compared with other Brythonic varieties is the status of underlying vowel length. For languages such as Welsh or Léonais Breton, it can be argued that underlyingly long vowels can be shortened in certain positions, because constraints such as syllable extrametricality and stress alignment impose a certain prosodic structure which disallows long vowels outside a two-syllable window at the right edge of the word. In Bothoa Breton, on the other hand, vowel length surfaces faithfully, and the prosodic system follows from constraints such as WEIGHT-TO-STRESS. This means that MAXLINK-μ (prohibiting, among other things, vowel shortening) and WEIGHT-TO-STRESS dominate well-formedness constraints militating against bimoraic syllables and non-peripheral feet.

(88) Faithfulness to underlying length: [ˈhaːdərəz] 'sowing season'

/haːμμdərəz/		MAXLINK[V]	WSP	*[μμ]σ	ALIGN-R(Hd, Wd)
(a) ☞	[(ˈhaːμμ)dərəʐ]			*	**
(b)	[haːμμ(ˈdərəz)]		*!	*	
(c)	[(ˈhaμdə)rəz]	*!			**

Similarly, where other Brythonic languages enforce vowel lengthening to impose the necessary prosodic structure via STRESS-TO-WEIGHT or similar constraints, Bothoa Breton is very judicious in deploying lengthening, with the result that underlying length and shortness are reproduced quite faithfully in surface representations. These issues are the subject of the next section.

8.3.5 Extrametricality and (sub)minimality

In this section I conclude the discussion of Bothoa Breton suprasegmental phonology by treating the relaxation of syllable structure constraints in word-final position. In this position, both consonant sequences ([ˈarhãn̥d̥] 'money') and long vowels before a consonant ([ˈfæːb̥] 'weak') are allowed. This can be accounted for if the final consonant is parsed outside the syllable and thus cannot influence its structure. To formalise this special status of word-final consonants, I suggest that they are allowed to be adjoined to the higher-level word node.

(89) Word-final extrametricality

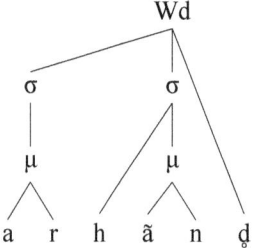

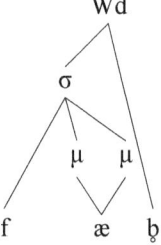

The status of final consonants in monosyllabic words with short vowels like [ˈtɔg̊] 'hat' is more complicated, hinging on both extrametricality and word minimality. The first issue is whether extrametricality in Bothoa Breton is actively enforced by a constraint requiring it, or only used as a last resort to rescue unparsable segments. The second issue is whether CVC forms are bimoraic (violating constraints against consonant moraicity) or subminimal.

In principle, subminimality in Bothoa Breton can be repaired by vowel lengthening. This is demonstrated by the alternations in (90), which show the neutralisation of underlying length contrasts in the context of stressed monosyllables.

(90) Underlying short vowels: lengthening
    (a) [ˈbroː]   *bro*   'country'
    (b) [ˈbrojəw]   *broioù*   'countries'

(91) Underlying long vowels: faithful mapping
    (a) [ˈtiː]   *ti*   'house'
    (b) [ˈtiːər]   *tier*   'houses'

The issue, then, is why the vowel does not lengthen in forms such as [ˈtɔĝ] 'hat'. I suggest that these forms are in fact subminimal, because PARSE(Seg,σ) and *μ[C] outrank FTBIN and SEGMENT EXTRAMETRICALITY. This also means that extrametricality in (89) is enforced by PARSE(Seg), i.e. a constraint requiring that segments be parsed into any sort of prosodic structure (rather than specifically a syllable) outranking whatever constraint prohibits extrametrical segments.

The constraints can be formulated as shown in (92).

(92) |SEGMENT EXTRAMETRICALITY|:=(*output* ∧ *Root* ∧ ⟨↑⟩i ∧ @$_i$ *Wd* ∧ ¬⟨r⟩ ⟨↑⟩i) → ¬(⟨↑⟩μ)

'A word-final segment is not dominated by a mora'

(93) |PARSE(Seg)|:=(*output* ∧ *Root*) → ⟨↑⟩T

'A root node is dominated by some segment'

(94) |*μ[F]|:=(*output* ∧ *Root* ∧ [F]) → ¬(⟨↑⟩μ ∧ *head*)

'An output root node with the features [F] is not the head of a mora'

The rankings can be summarised as shown in (95).

(95) Lengthening only in open stressed monosyllables[13]

		MAX LINK-μ	PARSE (Seg)	PARSE (Seg, σ)	*μ[C]	FTBIN	SEG-XM	*[μμ]$_σ$
(a) /fæːb/	☞ [(ˈfæː$_{μμ}$)<b>]			*				*
(b)	[(ˈfæː$_{μμ}$)b]		*!	*				*
(c)	[(ˈfæ$_μ$b$_μ$)]	*!			*		*	
(d)	[ˈf(æb)$_μ$]	*!				*	*	
(e) /bro/	[(ˈbro$_μ$)]					*!		
(f)	☞ [(ˈbroː$_{μμ}$)]							*
(g) /tɔg/	[(ˈtɔ$_μ$ĝ$_μ$)]				*!		*	

(h)	[(ˈtɔːμμ)<ǵ>]		*!			*
(i)	[(ˈtɔːμμ)ǵ]		*!	*		*
(j)	☞ [ˈt(ɔǵ)μ]				*	*

Notes

1. For discussion of the relationship between stress and pitch in Welsh, see Thomas (1967); Williams (1999); Cooper (2015).
2. The only exception appears to be [zuːbəˈnɛːr] 'soup lover', from [ˈzuːbən] 'soup'. Given that the /-ɛːr/ suffix appears to permit secondary stress elsewhere in the word, as in [ˌniːʒəˈtɛːr] 'nest-hunter', the omission of the stress mark could be simply a mistake.
3. Or rather elements: Humphreys (1995) includes submorphemic segment sequences in this class.
4. Past participles are morphosyntactically adjectives: this is confirmed by their ability to take comparative inflection: [aˈvãːsəd̥] 'advanced', [aˈvãːsətɒh] 'more advanced'.
5. Another option is to assume that participles in /-əid/ are exceptional and thus the relevant forms are stored, allowing them to bypass regular phonology via blocking. This is consistent with the fact that the distribution of /-əid/ is severely restricted, and the regular participle suffix is /-əd/ (Humphreys 1995: 351ff.). However, in the context of the proposals by Bermúdez-Otero (2012) this still requires participles to be stem-level constructs, because storage of exceptional prosodic structure ('nonanalytic listing') is only available at the stem level, and thus the basic stratal insight remains the same.
6. And [ˌduːˈblaðər] 'lining' (*doubladur*).
7. Only violations of NoCoda in the relevant syllable are shown in (73).
8. The only instance where a diphthong undoubtedly precedes a tautosyllabic consonant (i.e. a consonant sequence other than *muta cum liquida* or a word-final consonant sequence) is found in forms of the preposition [ˈdrəist] 'over, above'. In all these forms the diphthong appears to be stressed, which might be significant given the fact that the person and number suffixes associated with this preposition normally bear stress when attached to other prepositions.
9. For the sake of the argument, I assume that syllable structure constraints treat [st] as an illicit onset, even though [st] happens to be possible word-initially. However, given the cross-linguistically frequent aberrant status of such sequences, the argument is not very strong. In addition, underlyingly long vowels shorten before [st] sequences: [ˈbraːz̥] 'big' but [ˈbrastər] 'size'. As noted in the text, there are no examples with *prima facie* illicit onsets such as *[drəilta], but the prediction is that these should also be parsed with a moraic coda in the first syllable.

10. 'Malgré sa grande frequence, /-f-/ ne semble jamais être une variante obligatoire et /-əf-/ est capable de le remplacer après n'importe quelle finale' (Humphreys 1995: 372).
11. I do not go into detail on what exactly these 'phonetic' considerations are. The phonology–phonetics interface allows schwa deletion in this position: I take no stance on whether this deletion is controlled (e.g. depending on speech rate) or completely automatic (e.g. due to the aerodynamic properties and elasticity of the organs of speech), or (most likely) both.
12. The atlas of Le Roux (1924–63) (map 544) shows forms with hiatus such as [Rãõn] (point 21, Lohuec, around 30 km NW of Bothoa); at point 34 (Pemeurit-Quintin, 9 km NW of Bothoa in the same *canton* of St-Nicolas-du-Pélêm) the form is given as [Rãːʷõn], still with a long vowel.
13. I use the notation ⟨segment⟩ for extrametrical segments (i.e. those adjoined to the word node) and no bracketing for completely unparsed segments.

9

The phonology of vowels

In this chapter I show how the representations proposed for Bothoa Breton vowels in section 7.4 are consistent with the morphophonological alternations observed in the language (with the exception of consonant–vowel interactions, for which see the following chapter). The featural representations that follow from the contrastive hierarchy in Figure 7.2 are reproduced in Table 9.1.

9.1 Stress-related alternations

The most widespread alternations involving vowels are those involving stress mobility. However, as I described in detail in section 8.1, stress mobility in Bothoa Breton is quite limited: stress mostly stays immobile within a paradigm or across morphologically related items, and where it does move, some form of secondary stress normally remains. Nevertheless, a few alternations can be found.

Table 9.1 Featural specifications of Bothoa Breton vowels

	V-place		V-manner		
Segment	[cor]	[lab]	[op]	[cl]	[lax]
/i/	✓				
/u/		✓			
/y/	✓	✓			
/e/	✓			✓	
/o/				✓	
/ø/				✓	✓
/ɛ/	✓				✓
/ɔ/		✓			✓
/ə/					✓
/æ/	✓		✓		✓
/ɒ/			✓		✓
/a/			✓		

9.1.1 Data

As described by Humphreys (1995), the plural suffixes /-ən/ and /-jən/ cause the stress to shift from a short vowel to the vowel preceding the suffix.[61] These plural suffixes are strongly associated with the agentive derivational suffixes /-ər/ and /-ɛːr/. In the case of the former, the stress shift leads to an alternation between [ə] and [æ], as shown in (96).

(96) Alternation between [ə] and [æ]
    (a) [maˈsõːnər]   *masoner*   'mason'
    (b) [masoˈnærjən]   *masonerion*   'masons'
    (c) [ˈtoːər]   *toer*   'roofer'
    (d) [toˈærjən]   *toerion*   'roofers'
    (e) [ˈtoːərjən]

The alternation between [æ] and [ə] also appears in the conditional suffix /-æf/. This morpheme appears most often as [ə], since it normally attaches to a stem that is (at least) monosyllabic (and normally stressed) and is followed by another syllable in the person and number suffix, and hence the vowel ends up in the trough position. As seen in section 8.3.2, that position is the locus of another [æ]-[ə] alternation.

(97) The conditional suffix
    (a) [ma ˈt-æf-æ]   *ma teufe*   'if [(s)he] came'
    (b) [ma ˈpaːl-əf-æ]   *ma palfe*   'if [(s)he] dug'

In general, the vowels [æ], [ɒ], and [a] in the 'trough' position all can alternate with the schwa. The examples in (98) show this for [ɒ] and [a].

(98) Reduction in the trough position
    (a) [ˈlɒgɒd̪]   *logod*   'mice'
    (b) [ˈlɒgətad̪]   *logota*   'catch mice'
    (c) [ˈtɒhad̪]   *toc'had*   'ear (of corn, wheat, etc.)'
    (d) [ˈtɒhətad̪]   *toc'hata*   'gather, harvest'

However, both these examples involve derivational rather than inflectional morphology. If the trough pattern is created by the addition of inflectional suffixes, the low vowels may remain intact, as seen in (99) with the singulative suffix /-ən/ and plural /-əw/.

(99) Preservation of low vowels
    (a) [ˈlɒgɒd-ən]   *logodenn*   'mouse'
    (b) [ˈgɒlɒz-əw]   *golvizhier*   'beaters'
    (c) [ˈdɒrn-əræz-əw]   *dornerezhoù*   'threshings'

In addition, [a] in the trough position can also be preserved in derivational morphology.

(100) Preservation of [a] in derivation
    (a) ['bɒlhaḍ]   *golc'hed*   'duvet'
    (b) ['bɒlhadaḍ]   *golc'hedad* 'duvet contents'

However, the suffix /-ad/ in (100) can be ascribed to the word level (this is confirmed by the stress data discussed in section 8.2.5), whereas the examples with reduction in (98) all involve part-of-speech-changing derivations, which trigger stem-level phonology. It thus appears possible, although not certain, that vowel reduction (at least of [a]) is restricted to the stem level.

It is also possible that the mid vowels [ɛ] and [ɔ] are subject to reduction to schwa in at least some positions. There is evidence for this in the case of [ɛ]. Both [ə] and [ɛ], when found in the trough position before a [j] derived from [l] via a palatalisation process (see section 10.1.2), undergo coalescence with it to surface as [i].

(101) Reduction of [ə] and [ɛ]
    (a) ['mɒrzəl]   *morzhol*   'hammer'
    (b) ['mɒrziəw]   *morzholioù* 'hammers'
    (c) ['hras‿tɛl]   *rastell*   'rake'
    (d) ['hrastiəw]   *rastelloù* 'rakes'

This is perhaps best analysed as involving reduction from [ɛ] to [ə] in the trough position that feeds coalescence (see section 10.1.2.2 for an explicit account). This approach allows us to unify the behaviour of the two vowels. In addition, [ɛ] is almost never found in the trough position otherwise.[62]

In fact, neither [ɛ] nor [ɔ] is very frequent in 'weak' positions, i.e. those other than the main stressed syllable and the final syllable. Neither vowel is found in the trough position at all in the corpus. While they may appear in other unstressed syllables, it is overwhelmingly either the initial syllable or in inflected forms with stress shifts (as in [dɛˈvɒtɒh] 'more pious', from [ˈdɛvɒḍ] 'pious'), where lack of reduction could be cyclic (see section 11.2.1 for an account of this stress shift). Thus, it is not inconceivable that at least [ɛ], and possibly also [ɔ], might undergo reduction to [ə] in some positions, though alternation evidence for [ɔ] is lacking.

Finally, the complementary distribution between [ø] in stressed syllables and unstressed [ə] must also be derived by the grammar somehow; although alternations seem rare, I will assume that unstressed [ø] and stressed [ə], when provided by the rich base, map to the other member of this pair, which can also be analysed as vowel reduction.

9.1.2 Analysis

In terms of the featural specifications shown in Table 9.1, reduction of [æ], [ɒ], and [ɛ] (and potentially [ɔ]) can be represented as the delinking of a V-manner[open] specification in weak positions. In the case of [ɒ], this creates [ə] directly; in the case of [ɒ], the expected segment is {V-man[lax],V-pl[cor]}, i.e. the vowel [ɛ], which is also disallowed in this position and further reduces to [ə]. The relevant autosegmental diagrams are shown in (102) and (103).

(102) Reduction of [æ]: autosegmental account

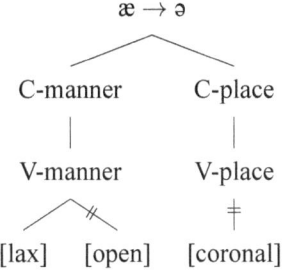

(103) Reduction of [ɒ]: autosegmental account

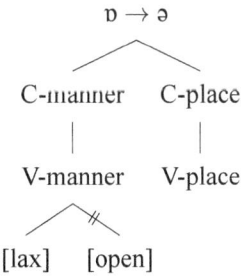

Of the mid vowels [ɛ] and [ɔ] also reduce to schwa in weak positions. Both reduction processes can be treated as the delinking of the relevant V-place feature (note that [ə] has a V-place node according to the contrastive hierarchy). This is shown in (104).

(104) Reduction of [ɛ] and [ɔ]

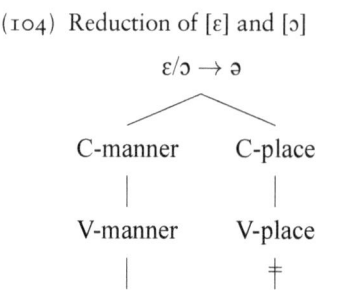

Computationally, this alternation is a straightforward instance of the reduction of subsegmental complexity in non-head position, in line with other privative approaches such as those of Harris (1997, 2005). I will assume a positional-faithfulness approach (e.g. Beckman 1998; Alderete 1999), although nothing in particular hinges on this in Breton. The rankings are shown in (106). The basic idea is that constraints against complex structures (such as *{V-man[lax], V-man[op], V-pl[cor]}, which corresponds to *[æ], and *{V-man[lax], V-man[op]}, i.e. *[ɒ]) dominate general Max constraints (which effects vowel reduction) but not Max_Hd constraints (which blocks reduction in foot heads).

(105) Vowel reduction in Bothoa Breton

			Max_Hd (V-pl[cor])	Max_Hd (V-man[op])	Max (V-man[lax])	*{V-man[lax], V-man[op], V-pl[cor]}	*{V-man[lax], V-pl[cor]}	*{V-man[lax], V-man[op]}	Max (V-man[op])	Max (V-pl[cor])
/toːær/	(a)	[(ˈtoː)ær]				*!	*	*		
	(b)	[(ˈtoː)ɛr]					*!		*	
	(c)	[(ˈtoː)ɒr]						*!		*
	(d)	[(ˈtoː)ar]			*!				*	*
	(e)	[(ˈtoː)ir]			*!				*	
	(f) ☞	[(ˈtoː)ər]							*	*
/toærjən/ (g) ☞		[to(ˈærjən)]				*	*	*		
	(h)	[to(ˈɛrjən)]			*!		*			
	(i)	[to(ˈɒrjən)]	*!						*	*
	(j)	[to(ˈarjən)]	*!		*				*	*
	(k)	[to(ˈirjən)]		*!	*				*	
	(l)	[to(ˈørjən)]	*!		*				*	*

The complementary distribution between {V-man[lax]} [ø] and {V-man[lax], V-man[closed]} [ə] requires an account of both reduction in unstressed position – analysed as loss of V-man[cl] – but also enhancement of a smaller segment in a prominent position. This can be accounted for by a ranking in which preservation of the complex structure is enforced not by a specific faithfulness constraint but by the enhancement constraint that only applies in stressed position.

(106) Complementary distribution between [ø] and [ə]

			*V-man [lax]	Stress ⇒ V-man[cl]	*{V-man [lax], V-man[cl]}	Dep (V-man [cl])	Max (V-man [cl])
/ø/	(a)	[ø]	*		*!		
	(b) ☞	[ə]	*				*
/'ə/	(c) ☞	['ø]	*		*	*	
	(d)	['ə]	*	*!			

In this section I assumed that vowel reduction is in fact a phonological process, possibly with lexical or stratal restrictions. There are some indications that this assumption may be incorrect and that at least in some cases the vowel written [ə] in the trough position might in fact be a phonological [æ], meaning that the ⟦ə⟧ is an artefact of phonetic interpretation (cf. Barnes 2007; Iosad 2012a). The evidence is provided by the fact that there are some examples of the [æ] in the conditional suffix /-æf/ surfacing in a medial syllable, indicating the variable character of this reduction. One example is [ˈøːrəʒæfæ] '([s]he) would marry'. Note that the [æ] is not properly in the trough position as defined above, although the form does alternate with [ˈøːrəʒfæ]. Another example is [ˌkusˈkæfæ] '([s]he) would sleep', which coexists with [ˈkuskfæ]. Both examples are noted for one speaker, and are described as 'sporadic variants'. The issue can only be resolved by empirical study, however.

9.2 Vowel raising

Short unstressed [e] productively alternates with [i] in hiatus (recall that phonetically this [i] may be realised as a non-syllabic glide). This [i] can be preceded by dorsal stops.

(107) Raising in hiatus
    (a) [ˈalve]   *alc'hwez*   'key'
    (b) [ˈalviəw]   *alc'hwezioù*   'keys'
    (c) [ˈklɔːge]   *kloge*   'ladle'

(d)	[ˈklɔːgiəw]	klogeoù	'ladles'
(e)	[ˈʃaːre]	charre	'scythe handle'
(f)	[ˈʃaːriaḍ]	charread	'forceful blow'
(g)	[ˈbøːre]	beure	'morning'
(h)	[ˈbøːriʋh]	beureoc'h	'earlier in the morning'

However the raising is motivated (note that in all cases it happens in the trough position, since an unstressed [e] is in these cases preceded by a stressed syllable and necessarily followed by another syllable), in autosegmental terms it is easily understood as the delinking of a V-manner[closed] feature, as seen in (108).

(108) Raising of [e] via delinking

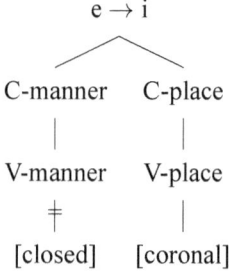

9.3 Diphthongs

As discussed in section 7.1.3, the diphthongs of Bothoa Breton are [əi], [əy], [əw], [aw], and [ãw̃]. The non-nucleus part of the diphthong can only contain mannerless segments (i.e. the high vowels). While this is not necessarily significant in view of the typological frequency of such a pattern, it might also be taken as additional evidence for the status of high vowels as mannerless segments, as this restriction receives a straightforward featural basis: no V-manner nodes are allowed in the non-head portion of a diphthong.

9.4 Morphologically conditioned alternations

Finally, some vowel changes visible in inflection appear to be driven by morphology or even triggered on a word-by-word basis.

The back vowels [a], [ɔ] and [ã] are fronted to [i] by the plural suffix /-i/, but this suffix is unproductive and extremely rare. Instances for [i] that appear in this formation trigger palatalisation of dorsal stops to postalveolar affricates.

(109) Morphologically conditioned alternations
    (a) ['kɔg̊]   *kog*   'rooster'
    (b) ['ʧiːdʒi]   *kegi*   'roosters'
    (c) ['pɔːləz̥]   *polez*   'chicken'
    (d) ['piləzi]   *polezi*   'chickens'
    (e) ['gast]   *gast*   'bitch'
    (f) ['dʒisti]   *gisti*   'bitches'
    (g) ['brãːn]   *bran*   'crow'
    (h) ['briːni]   *brini*   'crows'

There is a very small class of nouns forming plurals purely by vowel change, such as [ˈmiːn] 'stone' (*maen*), plural [ˈməin] (*mein*); I do not have much to say about these alternations here.

9.5 Summary: vowels

Despite having a relatively large vowel inventory, Bothoa Breton does not exhibit many vocalic alternations that would give evidence for the representations. Consequently, the evidence for some of the specifications I propose is rather inconclusive; in some cases, as in the case of [o], the assignment of features has to be relatively arbitrary. However, this system allows us to give an account of such facts as can be gleaned from Humphreys' (1995) description. A fuller account is of course possible, but it requires a better understanding of the possible alternations and their conditioning, as well as of the interaction between prosody and segmental phonology, than is available at the moment.

Notes

1. Humphreys (1995: 247) says that the stress shift happens 'sometimes'; however, his examples of lack of shift are either words with monosyllabic bases (where the shift applies vacuously) or bases with long vowels, where the shift is blocked for phonological reasons.
2. There is one example, [ˈtãnɛrɒh] 'softer' (*teneroc'h*), but it appears anomalous, in that the [ɛ] is the product of an otherwise irregular stress shift ([tãˈnɛːr] 'tender'), so there is clearly some exceptionality involved.

10

The phonology of consonants: palatalisation and gliding

In this chapter I offer an analysis of a nexus of phenomena that all revolve around the behaviour of the high front vowels /i y/ and their make-up as bearers of the feature V-place[coronal]. I demonstrate how this feature is involved in a range of palatalisation processes and propose an OT analysis making use of the relevant PSM representations. I also identify a range of exceptions from the palatalisation process, and argue that while some of these are motivated phonologically, others demonstrate a non-trivial type of underapplication opacity, where the opaque form surfaces exceptionlessly throughout the paradigm. This phenomenon presents a challenge to several OT approaches to opacity but is predicted by a stratal approach (see Bobaljik 2008; Bermúdez-Otero 2012; Trommer 2013); I conclude therefore that Bothoa Breton offers a strong empirical argument in favour of the latter.

10.1 Palatalisation

Bothoa Breton shows two distinct palatalisation processes: the palatalisation of dorsals by following high front vowels and the palatalisation of coronals and dorsals due to coalescence with an onset [i]. I discuss them in order.

10.1.1 Velar palatalisation

The postalveolar affricates [tʃ] and [dʒ] appear in many contexts where there is no evidence for deriving them from other segments: they contrast with dorsal stops, fail to alternate with them, and the context is not a priori conducive to palatalisation, as in the examples in (110).

(110) (a) [ˈstʃøːl]   *skeul*   'ladder'
     (b) [ˈkøwəd̥]   *kavout*   'find'
     (c) [ˈtʃevələġ]   *kefeleg*   'woodcock'
     (d) [kazəˈkɛnəġ]   *kazekenned*   'mares'
     (e) [ˈtʃahəd̥]   *kerzhet*   'to walk'
     (f) [ˈkaləd̥]   *kalet*   'hard'

The phonology of consonants: palatalisation and gliding 133

This demonstrates that [tʃ] and [dʒ] are part of the inventory of underlying segments. Nevertheless, there is also evidence that at least some instances of [tʃ] and [dʒ] are derived from dorsal stops.

10.1.1.1 Data
First, sequences of dorsal stops [k g] (phonetically ⟦kʲ gʲ⟧ in this position) followed by high front vowels [i y] are relatively rare in the language. The sequence [ky] appears not to be found at all, while [gy] is only attested in the clearly borrowed name [ɔgysˈtiːn] 'Augustine' (moreover, this is an underived form, known to commonly sustain exceptions). As for [ki] and [gi], they are found in the contexts shown in (111).

(111) Postlexically
    (a) [ak i ˈziː]   *hag he zi*   'and her 'house'
    (b) [ag ˈivul]   *hag eoul*   'and oil'

(112) Before the future suffixes /-id̥/ (2nd person plural), /-iːãmp/ (1st person plural), /-iːajtʃ/ (2nd person plural).
    (a) [ˈlakiãmb̥]   *lakiamp*   'we will put'
    (b) [ˈpleːgid̥]   *plegit*   'you (pl.) will fold'

(113) Before certain derivational suffixes:[1]
    (a) [ˈvrãŋkiz̥]   *frankiz*   'open space, the outdoors'
    (b) [ˈbegiʃad̥]   *begisat*   'to chatter'

(114) Before instances of [i] derived by raising (section 9.2):
    [ˈklɒːgiəw]   *klogeoù*   'ladles'

Alternations between dorsal stops and affricates are few and far between. They are found with the plural suffix /-i/, which also causes the otherwise irregular overwriting of the root vowel with an [i(ː)]. This high vowel in the root also causes the alternation.[2]

(115) Velar palatalisation in inflection
    (a) [ˈkɔg̊]   *kog*   'rooster'
    (b) [ˈtʃiːdʒi]   *kegi*   'roosters'
    (c) [ˈgast]   *gast*   'bitch'
    (d) [ˈdʒisti]   *gisti*   'bitches'

I suggest that the fact that [k] and [g] are all but impossible before high front vowels morpheme-internally indicates that the phonological computation maps the dorsal stops [k] and [g] to [tʃ] and [dʒ] in this context. I will refer to this alternation as *velar palatalisation*. It happens only at the stem level, explaining the paucity of alternations, as well as the fact that the alternation is blocked before [i] derived by raising: below I show that raising belongs to the word level, which explains the counterfeeding relationship between palatalisation and raising. The stem-level affiliation of velar palatalisation is supported by the fact that clearly inflectional suffixes, which attach at the word level, do not trigger it.[3]

Moreover, at least in the case of [tʃ] there is evidence from initial consonant mutations that some tokens of word-initial affricates are derived from underlying dorsal stops followed by [j]. Specifically, the so-called spirantisation (see section 11.3.1) involves a change from [k] to [h]. Moreover, when the [k] precedes a sonorant, the result is the so-called voiceless sonorant (this provides important evidence for representing voiceless sonorants as [h]-sonorant sequences).

(116) Spirantisation of /k/
    (a) ['kaːz̥]   *kazh*   'cat'
    (b) [mə 'haːz̥]   *ma c'hazh*   'my cat'
    (c) ['kriːb̥]   *krib*   'comb'
    (d) [mə 'hriːb̥]   *ma c'hrib*   'my comb'

The outcome of the spirantisation of [tʃ] in the sequence [tʃɥ] is the same as that of [k] before sonorants.

(117) Spirantisation of [tʃɥ]
    (a) ['tʃɥiːzin]   *kegin*   'kitchen'
    (b) [i 'hɥiːzin]   *he c'hegin*   'her kitchen'

This behaviour is consistent with the word for 'kitchen' being underlyingly represented as /kɥiːzin/.

Similarly, [tʃ] before a high front vowel is spirantised to [h], which could be derived if the [tʃ] corresponded to underlying /k/.

(118) Spirantisation of /k/: underlying /ki(ː)/
    (a) ['tʃiː]   *ki*   'dog'
    (b) [ə 'hiː]   *ar c'hi*   'the dog'

Thus, the spirantisation facts are at least consistent with positing underlying forms such as /ki(ː)/ for 'dog', with velar palatalisation in the unmutated form and spirantisation of [k] in the mutated forms. This is important, since such forms are provided by OT's rich base, and they must be made to conform to the patterns of behaviour otherwise attested in the language.

No such argument from mutation can be made for [dʒ]. If words such as [dʒiːr] 'word' (*ger*) had an underlying dorsal stop, we would expect that stop to become [h] in the course of lenition (section 11.3.3). However, this does not happen, and [dʒ] remains unchanged.

(119) No [dʒ] from underlying /g/
    (a)   ['gɔˌdɛl]   *godell*   'pocket'
    (b)   [i 'hɔˌdɛl]   *e c'hodell* 'his pocket'
    (c)   ['dʒiːr]   *ger*   'word'
    (d)   [i 'dʒiːr]   *e c'her*   'his word'
    (e)   *[i 'hiːr]

As detailed in section 11.3.3.5, however, this asymmetry between the two affricates receives a principled explanation: once the stratal affiliation of the different mutation-inducing morphemes is taken into account, an underlying /#gi/ sequence is predicted to surface as /dʒi/ in both lenition and non-lenition contexts. Taken together with the circumstantial evidence for a /g/ → /dʒ/ mapping before high front vowels in forms such as ['dʒisti] (as the plural of ['gast]), this indicates that the data are consistent with a stem-level process of velar palatalisation.

10.1.1.2 An aside: the evidence from article allomorphy

Humphreys (1995) discusses another kind of evidence for a distinction between underived and derived instances of [tʃ dʒ]. Like other varieties of the language, Bothoa Breton distinguishes between two allomorphs of the definite and indefinite articles, which are sensitive to the phonology of the following word. Of particular interest here is the distinction between following coronals and non-coronals: [ən 'dɒrʐ] 'the bread roll' (*an dorzh*) with a nasal before the word-initial coronal but [ə 'gəw] 'the lie' (*ar gaou*). In the case of [tʃ] and [dʒ], the article allomorphy reproduces the diachronic origin of the affricate: [n]-ful forms are chosen before affricates descending from **tj* and **dj* ([ən 'dʒəwl] 'the devil', cf. Welsh *diawl*) but [n]-less forms are used before those going back to dorsals ([ə 'dʒiːr] 'the word', cf. Welsh *gair*). Similarly, initial /h/ is associated with [n]-ful forms ([ən 'hãw̃n] 'the name') but [h] derived from /tʃ/ (and ultimately [k]) takes [n]-less forms, like dorsals ([ə 'hiː] 'the dog', cf. Welsh *cî*). This may suggest that the article allomorphy is somehow sensitive to whether a surface postalveolar affricate is underlyingly a dorsal stop or not.

However, I suggest that the article allomorphy cannot be used to diagnose the phonological make-up of words. First, it is also sensitive to etymological differences that are not recoverable from synchronic alternations. A case in point is initial [hw], with [n]-ful forms before **huV* and [n]-less forms before **xw*: [on 'hwarn] 'an iron' (Welsh *haiarn*) but [o 'hwarz] 'a laugh' (Welsh *chwerthin*). This indicates that at least some arbitrary subcategorisation must be involved.

Second, the class of onsets selecting for [n]-ful forms ([t d ∅ h w]) does not seem to be motivated by the featural structure of the language otherwise. Finally, if the selection of the article allomorphs were driven by the phonology, it would have to be sensitive to the featural make-up of the initial consonant *before* the application of the velar palatalisation rule. However, palatalisation belongs to the stem level, whereas the article is clearly a separate lexical item. This creates an ordering paradox: one would expect insertion of the article to follow the entire cycle of the phonological derivation in the noun. While this may appear less of an issue in fully parallel frameworks, one would still have to deploy whatever machinery one uses to deal with counterbleeding opacity in this case. Moreover, this example demonstrates the greater restrictiveness of stratal models: while fully parallel frameworks and some current versions of serial OT allow the interaction of any two processes (e.g. via PREC constraints), stratal models impose more restrictive global conditions on rule ordering, and they predict such an interaction to be impossible.

10.1.1.3 Analysis

In featural terms, velar palatalisation is represented as a straightforward process of the spreading of V-pl[coronal] from [i] and [y] to the placeless dorsal stops. Note that although dorsal stops are placeless in the sense that they do not bear any C-place or V-place *features*, they are assumed to bear a V-place *node*, since they are contrastively specified for V-place[coronal] (see section 3.3.1.2); hence, the spreading happens entirely on the V-place tier.

(120) Velar palatalisation: /ki/ → [tʃi]

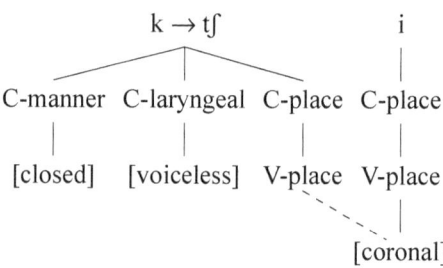

Velar palatalisation thus provides evidence both for the featural specification of [i] and [y] as V-place[coronal] vowels and for the markedness relationships and place specifications for the nonanterior stops. Such relationships, with dorsals unmarked for place and easily susceptible to place changes, are of course not uncommon, as documented by Rice (1996, 2003).

There are two further remarks that must be made here. First, I assume that spreading is triggered only by [i] and [y] that are parsed as nuclei; see the next section for discussion of onset [i] and [y]. Second, spreading is triggered only by those V-place[coronal] vowels that do not bear any

V-manner features. I suggest that both these restrictions can be expressed as restrictions on domain heads (Kenstowicz 1997; Morén 2001; de Lacy 2002, 2006; Jurgec 2010).

In OT terms, this requires that some constraint driving spreading dominate DEPLINK(V-pl[cor]), although it is in turn dominated by constraints on domain heads. In this instance, we require the following constraints, using the notation Δ_F to mean 'head (or 'designated terminal element') of the domain of [F]'. (Following Jurgec 2010, I assume that Δ-constraints only apply to heads of branching domains, i.e. that they are not the same as feature co-occurrence restrictions or moraic enhancement constraints.)

(121) *$\Delta_{\text{V-pl[cor]}}$V-man[lax]/[cl]: 'assign a violation mark for each head of a V-pl[cor] domain that also bears a V-man[lax]/V-man[cl] feature.'[4]

(122) HAVE-µ/$\Delta_{\text{V-pl[cor]}}$: 'assign a violation mark for each head of a branching V-pl[cor] domain that does not also head a moraic domain'.
This constraint ensures that spreading of V-pl[cor] only happens from nuclear positions.

Since the architecture of spreading is not the focus of this study, I use the non-committal constraint schema SHARE to account for spreading despite some of its typological problems. The ranking is shown in (123), using [ˈtʃiː] 'dog' to demonstrate palatalisation and [ˈklɒːge] 'ladle' to show lack of spreading from complex segments. I also show the result for an underlying /kiɛzeg/ 'horses', where, under the ranking given in (123), palatalisation fails because the high front vowel is parsed as an onset, so the output at the stem level is [kjɛzəg]. This form ultimately surfaces as [ˈtʃɛzəg̊], as discussed below. To save space, I do not show the constraint MAX(V-man[cl]), which ensures that this feature is not deleted to satisfy *$\Delta_{\text{V-pl[cor]}}$/V-man[lax], as in [ˈklɒːdʒi] for /klɒːge/. A more nuanced description of the constraint UNIFORMITY also follows below.

(123) Velar palatalisation

		UNIFORMITY	HAVE-µ/ $\Delta_{\text{V-pl[cor]}}$	*$\Delta_{\text{V-pl[cor]}}$ {V-man[cl], V-man[lax]}	ONSET	SHARE (V-pl [cor])	DEPLINK (V-pl [cor])	*COMPLEX ONSET
/ki/	(a) [k(iːµµ) V-pl[cor]]				*!			
	(b) ☞ [(tʃiːµµ) V-pl[cor]]						*	
/klɒːge/	(c) ☞ [ˈklɒːg(eµ) V-pl[cor]]					*		

	(d)	[ˈklɒː(dʒeμ) V-pl[cor]]			*!		*
/kiɛzəg/	(e)	[k(iμ) V-pl[cor]* εμzəg]			*!	*	
	(f)	[(tʃiμ) V-pl[cor]* εμzəg]				*!	*
	(g) ☞	[k(j)_V-pl[cor] εμzəg]					*	*
	(h)	[(tʃj)_V-pl[cor] εμzəg]		*!			*	*
	(i)	[(tʃ)_V-pl[cor] εμzəg]	*!					

This concludes the analysis of velar palatalisation, and we proceed to the other palatalisation process.

10.1.2 Coronal palatalisation

Unlike velar palatalisation, coronal palatalisation does not produce post-alveolar affricates except in a very restricted class of cases, and in fact it does not affect dorsal stops at all. Also unlike velar palatalisation, there is robust alternation evidence for this phenomenon in Bothoa Breton. This allows us to form a better picture of what triggers this process.

10.1.2.1 Data

In the case of coronal obstruents, coalescence produces postalveolar fricatives [ʃ] and [ʒ], except in the case of the sequence [st], in which case the outcome is [stʃ].

(124) [d] → [ʒ]
    (a) [ˈpraːd̥]   *prad*   'prayer'
    (b) [ˈpraːʒəw]   *pradoù*   'prayers'
    (c) [ˈøːrəd̥]   *eured*   'marriage'
    (d) [ˈøːrəʒo]   *eurediñ*   'marry'

(125) [t] → [ʃ]
    (a) [ˈpond̥]   *pont*   'bridge'
    (b) [ˈpõːʃəw]   *pontioù*   'bridges'

(126) /z/ → [ʒ]
    (a) [ˈmiːz̥]   *miz*   'month'
    (b) [ˈmiːʒəw]   *mizioù*   'months'

The phonology of consonants: palatalisation and gliding 139

	(c)	['temʑ]	*temz*	'manure'
	(d)	['temʒo]	*temzañ*	'fertilise with manure'

(127) [s] → [ʃ]
    (a)   ['plaʑ]   *plas*   'place'
    (b)   ['plaʃəw]   *plasoù*   'places'

(128) [st] → [stʃ]
    (a)   ['lɒst]   *lost*   'tail'
    (b)   ['lɒstʃəw]   *lostoù*   'tails'

(129) [n] → /ɲ̃/ (phonetically [ɲ] or [j̃])
    (a)   ['pwi:n]   *poan*   'pain'
    (b)   ['pwi:j̃əw]   *poanioù*   'pains'
    (c)   ['tʃærn]   *korn*   'horn'
    (d)   ['tʃærɲəw]   *kornioù*   'horns'

(130) [l] → [j]
    (a)   ['pɑ:l]   *pal*   'shovel'
    (b)   ['pɑ:jəw]   *palioù*   'shovels'

(131) [ˌɛl], [əl] → [i]
    (a)   ['mɒrˌzɛl]   *morzhol*   'hammer'
    (b)   ['mɒrziəw]   *morzholioù*   'hammers'

I interpret this phenomenon as involving coalescence with an onset [i]. That at least some relevant suffixes do contain this segment in their segmental representations is demonstrated by the examples in (132) and (133).

(132) The plural suffixes /-iəw/ and /-iən/
    (a)   ['bro:]   *bro*   'country'
    (b)   ['brojəw]   *broioù*   'countries'
    (c)   ['lɛvəɹ]   *levr*   'book'
    (d)   ['lɛvərjəw]   *levrioù*   'books'
    (e)   ['ɛskɔb̪]   *eskob*   'bishop'
    (f)   [ɛs'kɔbjən]   *eskibien*   'bishops'

(133) The derivational suffix /-iad/
    (a)   [ɔ'tɔ:]   *oto*   'car'
    (b)   [ɔ'tɔjad̪]   *otoiad*   'contents of a car'
    (c)   ['lwɛ:r]   *loar*   'moon'
    (d)   ['lwɛ:rjad̪]   *loariad*   'lunar month'

Importantly, this explicit [j] appears following exactly those segments that do not undergo coronal palatalisation, i.e. vowels, labials, and [r].

As for dorsals before onset [i], the evidence is somewhat ambiguous. Historically, *kj tended to give ʃ and *gj could yield either ʒ or j (Jackson 1967: §585). In the case of kj gj → ʃ ʒ, this means that the treatment of dorsals is identical to the treatment of coronal stops, although not in the case of *gj → j.

Examples with suffixation are not abundant, but it is at least possible for sequences of a dorsal stop and [j] to coalesce into affricates.

(134) Coronal palatalisation and velars
    (a) [ˌlasˈtikən]   'rubber band' (French *élastique*)
    (b) [ˈlastitʃəw]   'rubber bands'

There is also some evidence for palatalisation-as-spirantisation in Bothoa Breton from initial mutations. As discussed in section 10.1.1, initial [tʃ] derived from [k] undergoes spirantisation to [h]. However, initial [tʃ] before vowels other than [i y], i.e. in positions where it cannot be derived from /k/, spirantises to ⟦ç⟧, phonologically [hj].

(135) Spirantisation of [tʃ]
    (a) [ˈtʃɛzəɡ̊]   *kazegennoù*   'horses'
    (b) [mə ˈhjɛzəɡ̊]   *ma c'hazegennoù*   'my horses'

This can be explained if the underlying form of the word is /kiɛzəɡ/, and [k] coalesces with the [i] to create [tʃ]; cf. the tableau in (123). This example, however, is less relevant to coronal palatalisation given the difference in the morphophonological context.

The evidence for the treatment of /gj/ as [j] is sparse, but it is seen in the example in (136).

(136) Palatalisation of /g/
    (a) [ˈbɛːləɡ̊]   *beleg*   'priest'
    (b) [ˈbɛːliən]   *belegion*   'priests'

As discussed in section 10.2.2.3, [ˈbɛːliən] can be derived from an intermediate [ˈbɛːləiən].[5] Nevertheless, it appears this pattern is not regular in Bothoa Breton, so I will assume it is an exception from a synchronic perspective, and that the alternation between the velar stop and the post-alveolar affricate is the phonologically regular pattern. A possible argument in favour of this conclusion is the fact that coalescence as seen in (130) applies to what is clearly a recent borrowing, whereas the mapping from /gj/ to [j] is necessarily an older process which may have already lost its productivity.

The initial [i] of a suffix, whether part of the suffix itself or produced by palatalisation from [l], can also create the variable palatalisation phenomena discussed in section 7.1.

10.1.2.2 Analysis

The analysis of coalescence with coronal obstruents does not present significant complications. Coronal stops (*modulo* laryngeal features) are specified as {C-manner[closed], C-place[coronal]}, while the outcome of palatalisation, i.e. the fricatives [ʃ] and [ʒ], is {C-place[coronal],V-place[coronal]}. Simple merger of coronal stops with the {V-place[coronal]} segment is impossible due to feature co-occurrence constraints, and the C-manner specification is sacrificed to satisfy these latter, as shown in (137). Since in all cases of coalescence the sequence is followed by a vowel, I assume that coalescence is driven by the combined power of ONSET and *COMPLEXONSET (recall from (123) that the former dominates the latter).

(137) Coronal palatalisation: /dj/ → [ʒ]

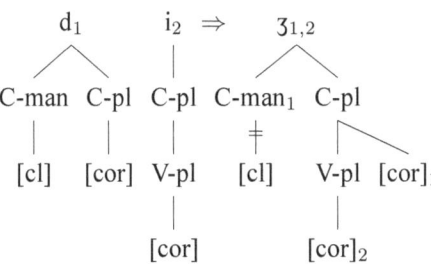

In the case of the coronal fricatives, the situation is all but identical: the only difference is that the fricatives do not have a C-manner feature to begin with, so there is simply full coalescence.

The sequence [st] presents a somewhat different outcome,[6] but one that is straightforwardly predicted by the current proposal. Rather than the expected *[sʃ], the result of coronal palatalisation is [stʃ]. In featural terms, this means that the stop's C-manner[closed] feature is preserved at the expense of its C-place[coronal] specification. The reason for this is presumably a phonotactic constraint against [sʃ] sequences, which are indeed unattested in the language. The derivation is shown in (138).[7]

(138) Coronal palatalisation: /st/ → [stʃ]

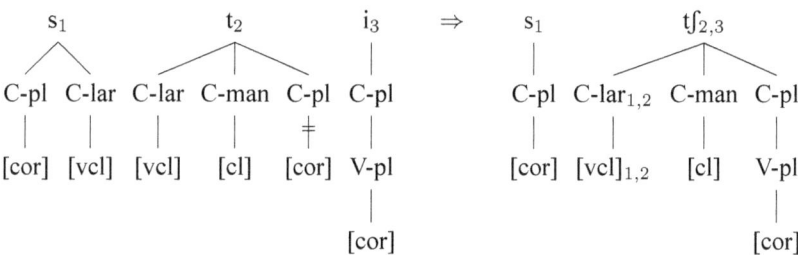

The combined tableau for coronal obstruents is shown in (139). Note that *COMPLEXONSET (and by extension ONSET) have to dominate UNIFORMITY in order to produce coalescence. To save space, I do not show candidates which delete the feature V-place[coronal]. I also do not show candidates where an input root node does not have a correspondent, assuming unviolated MAX(Root).[8]

(139) Palatalisation of coronal obstruents: [ˈpraːʒəw] 'prayers', [ˈlɒstʃəw] 'tails', [ˈtemʒɒ] 'to fertilise with manure'

		*{C-man[cl], C-pl[cor], V-pl[cor]}	*[ʃ]	ONSET	*COMPLEX ONSET	UNIFOR- MITY	MAX (C-pl [cor])	MAX (C-pl [cor])
/praːd₁i₂əw/	(a)	[ˈpraː.d₁i₂.əw]		*!				
	(b)	[ˈpraː.d₁j₂əw]				*!		
	(c)	[ˈpraː.{C-man[cl], C-pl[cor], V-pl[cor]}₁,₂əw]	*!				*	
	(d)	[ˈpraː.dʒ₁,₂əw]					*	*!
	(e)	[ˈpraː.j₁,₂əw]					*	*!	*
	(f) ☞	[ˈpraː.ʒ₁,₂əw]					*		*
/lɒst₁i₂əw/	(g)	[ˈlɒs.t₁i₂.əw]		*!				
	(h)	[ˈlɒs.t₁j₂əw]				*!		
	(i)	[ˈlɒs.{C-man[cl], C-pl[cor], V-pl[cor], C-lar[vcl]}₁,₂əw]	*!				*	

The phonology of consonants: palatalisation and gliding   143

	(j) ☞	['lɒs.tʃ₁,₂əw]				*	*	
	(k)	['lɒs.ʃ₁,₂əw]	*!			*		*
	(l)	['lɒs.j₁,₂əw]				*	*	*!
/temz₁i₂o/	(m)	['tem.z₁i₂.o]		*!				
	(n)	['tem.z₁j₂o]			*!			
	(o) ☞	[tem.ʒ₁,₂o]				*		
	(p)	[tem.j₁,₂o]				*	*!	

Among the other phonetic coronals, /l/ surfaces as [j], because coalescence results in the delinking of the C-manner node of the [l] due to feature co-occurrence constraints. In the case of [n], however, coalescence does create a licit segment.

(140) /nj/ → [ɲ̃]

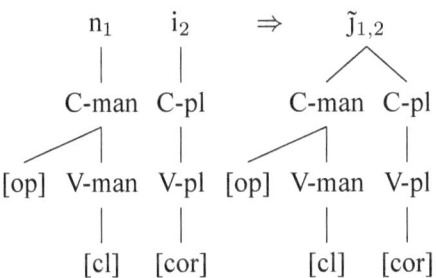

(141) /lj/ → [i]

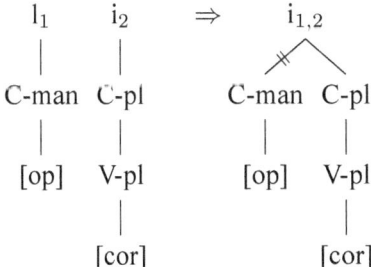

The tableaux for coronal sonorants are given in (142) and (143). The interesting constraint in both cases is *{C-man[op], V-pl[cor]}. In the case of /lj/ sequences, it is ranked sufficiently high to prevent the appearance of an otherwise unattested segment consisting of these two features, and the response of the computation is to delete C-man[op] to yield an onset [i].[9] In the case of /nj/, however, this constraint is violated by the winner, as the outcome of coalescence is the segment /ɲ/, consisting of the features {C-man[op], V-man[cl], V-pl[cor]}. In this case, deletion of C-man[op] is expected to create a licit segment; however, this segment is the vowel [e]. It cannot be parsed either as a nucleus (since this violates ONSET) or as an onset (since this parse is completely impossible for this segment in the language), and therefore candidate (c) is the winner.[10]

(142) Coalescence with sonorants: [ˈpwiːɲəw] 'pains', [ˈpaːjəw] 'shovels'

		SYL-STRUC	ONSET	MAX (V-man [cl])	*COMPLEX ONSET	*{C-man [op], V-pl[cor]}	UNI-FORMITY	MAX (C-man [op])
/pwiːn₁i₂əw/	(a) [ˈpwiː.n₁i₂.əw]			*!				
	(b) [ˈpwiː.n₁j₂əw]				*!			
	(c) ☞ [ˈpwiː.ɲ₁,₂əw]					*	*	
	(d) [ˈpwiː.e₁,₂əw]			*!			*	*
	(e) [ˈpwiː.e₁,₂əw]	*!					*	*
	(f) [ˈpwiː.j₁,₂əw]				*!		*	*
/ˈpaːl₁i₂.əw/	(g) [ˈpaː.l₁i₂.əw]			*!				
	(h) [ˈpaː.l₁j₂əw]				*!			
	(i) [ˈpaː.{C-man[op], V-pl[cor]}₁,₂əw]					*!	*	
	(j) [ˈpaː.j₁,₂əw]						*	*

In the case of [r], both coalescence and the deletion of C-man[op] create illicit segments containing {V-man[op], V-pl[cor]}, and faithfulness blocks the deletion of V-pl[cor]. With all segmental options exhausted, the derivation settles on a violation of *COMPLEXONSET. Note that the relative ranking of *{V-man[op], V-pl[cor]} and MAX constraints is immaterial here, although the lack of the relevant segment in the surface inventory indicates that the markedness constraint dominates at least one of the MAX constraints. Note, however, that *{V-man[op], V-pl[cor]} must be outranked by a faithfulness constraint protecting larger structures (section 4.2.4): this is needed for underlying /æ/ ({V-man[op], V-pl[cor], V-man[lax]}) to surface, at least in foot head position, despite containing the offending feature pair. Note also that forms such as [ˈlwɛːrjaḓ] clearly

The phonology of consonants: palatalisation and gliding   145

contain complex onsets, because the sequence [rj] is preceded by a long vowel (section 8.3.1).

(143) Coalescence blocked, complex onset results: [ˈlwɛːrjaɖ] 'lunar month'

	/lwɛːr₁i₂aɖ/	*{V-man [op], V-pl[cor]}	Max (V-pl [cor])	Onset	Max (V-man [op])	*Complex Onset	*{C-man [op], V-pl [cor]	Uni- formity	Max (C-man [op])
(a)	[ˈlwɛː.r₁i₂.aɖ]			*!					
(b) ☞	[ˈlwɛː.r₁j₂aɖ]					*			
(c)	[ˈlwɛː. {C-man[op] V-man[op] V-pl[cor]}₁,₂aɖ]	*!					*	*	
(d)	[ˈlwɛː.r₁,₂.aɖ]		*!					*	
(e)	[ˈlwɛː. {V-man[op], V-pl[cor]}₁,₂aɖ]	*!						*	*
(f)	[ˈlwɛː. {C-man[op], V-pl[cor]}₁,₂aɖ]			*!			*	*	
(g)	[ˈlwɛː.j₁,₂aɖ]				*!			*	*
(h)	[ˈlwɛː.l₁,₂aɖ]		*!			*		*	

All labials (both obstruents and the sonorant [m]) do not undergo coalescence with [j]; the mechanism is similar to that seen with [r]: Max(C-pl[lab]) and Max(V-pl[cor]) prevent deletion and feature co-occurrence blocks coalescence, ensuring violation of *ComplexOnset (see tableau (146)). As concerns the placeless stops (phonetic dorsals), the prediction is that they undergo a process similar to that shown for the stop in [st] sequences and will surface as [tʃ] resp. [dʒ], as shown in (144).

(144) Coalescence of placeless stops with [j]

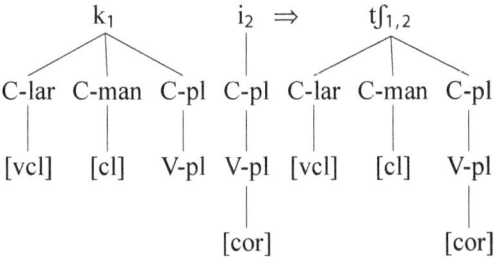

This is exactly what happens with word-initial [tʃ] before a vowel other than [i] or [y], as discussed above.

Although the analyses presented in this section successfully derive the patterns of coronal palatalisation, they are at odds with those offered in the preceding section for *velar* palatalisation. Specifically, coalescence requires *COMPLEXONSET to dominate UNIFORMITY, which is at odds with the ranking established in (127). I suggest that this contradiction should be reconciled by adopting a stratal model of phonological architecture. In the next section I present a detailed analysis of stratal differences in the behaviour of high vowels, and relate these facts to the different types of palatalisation.

10.2 Gliding

In this section I consider the status of the glides [w j ɥ] and their relationship to the high vowels [u i y]. I argue that [w] and [j] can be considered to be non-nuclear realisations of [u] and [i], whereas [ɥ] is best treated as a separate segment.

Humphreys (1995: 166) discusses these matters, albeit in little detail. He claims that glides and high vowels are in all but complementary distribution, driven by position within the syllable. A few exceptions do exist and will be discussed below. Moreover, he notes that syllabic pronunciations are very occasionally heard for what are normally [w] and [j], so ⟦biˈɔ̃ːn⟧ and ⟦luˈarn⟧ for [ˈbjɔ̃ːn] 'fast' (*buan*) and [ˈlwarn] 'fox' (*louarn*). However, he does not discuss the phonological evidence at length. In this section I consider the three potential glides in order.

10.2.1 *The back rounded vowel*

On the surface, [w] and [u] stand in complementary distribution: no instances of short [u] are found prevocalically, and [w] is never found before consonants (with the exception of [w] as the second part of a diphthong). There are, however, no alternations that would confirm the phonological identity of these segments. Thus, it seems safe to conclude that [w] and [u] represent the same phonological segment in non-nuclear and nuclear position respectively. This analysis is further buttressed by the proposed analysis of the lenition of [gw], for which see section 11.3.3.

10.2.2 *The front unrounded vowel*

The situation with [i] is more complex, since there is more evidence for a distinction between [i] and [j], which comes from palatalisation processes. Specifically, [j], but not [i], triggers coronal palatalisation. On the other hand, both trigger velar palatalisation (in certain conditions). To

The phonology of consonants: palatalisation and gliding 147

disentangle the behaviour of [i] and [j], we need a closer analysis of the interaction between morphology and phonology.

As discussed above, there is evidence for at least one level distinction: some [i]-initial suffixes (for instance, the future inflection suffixes) fail to trigger velar palatalisation, while it is all but exceptionless morpheme-internally, as well as across stem-level boundaries. In addition, [i] derived from [e] via raising is also not a spreading trigger. In this section I consider further evidence for phonological levels.[11]

10.2.2.1 The stem level: gliding

At the stem level, an input [i] before another vowel undergoes gliding by being parsed into a non-nuclear syllabic constituent. This is seen most clearly in the existence of morpheme-internal sequences of a labial followed by [j], because these sequences are not fed into further alternations in later cycles.

(145) Gliding of [i] in tautomorphemic contexts
    (a) [ˈbjan]   *bihan*   'small'
    (b) [ˈpjɒh]   *peoc'h*   'peace'
    (c) [ˈmjãːwal]   *miaoual*   'meow'

As discussed in section 10.1.1, this is due to ONSET and faithfulness constraints dominating *COMPLEXONSET. Another dominated constraint is HAVE-μ[V] which requires vowels to project a mora.

(146) Gliding at the stem level: [ˈbjan] 'small'

	/b$_1$i$_2$an/	*{C-pl[lab], V-pl-cor]}	MAX (V-pl[cor])	MAX (C-pl[lab])	ONSET	*COMPLEX ONSET
(a)	[b$_1$i$_2$.an]				*!	
(b) ☞	[ˈb$_1$j$_2$an]					*
(c)	[ˈ{C-pl[lab], C-man[cl], V-pl[cor]}$_{1,2}$an]	*!				
(d)	[ˈb$_{1,2}$an]		*!			
(e)	[ˈdʒ$_{1,2}$an]			*!		

As for sequences of non-labials followed by [i] and a vowel, more discussion of the role of UNIFORMITY is in order. In (123), I assumed that UNIFORMITY is ranked high enough to prevent coalescence, at least in the case of /kj/, where it cannot be blocked by feature co-occurrence as in (146).

In 10.1.1.3 I assumed without argument that /kiV/ sequences (at the stem level) are mapped to [kjV] rather than [tʃV]. The evidence for this comes mainly from initial consonant mutation. Recall that initial [tʃ] before a non-high vowel undergoes spirantisation to [hj] ([ɕ]), in parallel with single /k/ spirantising to [h]. However, if we assumed that the coalescence of the two onset segments happened at the stem level, we would run into an ordering paradox: unless the mutation-triggering autosegment is also present at the stem level, it cannot rescue the underlying [k] from coalescence and turn it into [h].

Below I will provide evidence that the trigger of the relevant mutation ('spirantisation') is an agreement morpheme belonging to the word level, which means that the distinction between underlying /tʃ/ and /ki/ must be preserved until at least the input to the word level. If this is so, it is possible to analyse the derivation of [tʃɛzə̃ɡ̊] 'horse' from /kiɛzəɡ/ without running into these problems. Specifically, if [i] is parsed into the onset at the stem level, we can unify this coalescence with 'coronal palatalisation': both are triggered at the word level by onset [i]. Thus, assuming that [i]-gliding is operative at the stem level provides us with an account of dorsal-[j] coalescence that does not run into ordering issues.

However, the ranking which ensures the lack of coalescence in (123) also predicts the blocking of coalescence following coronals, and it is not obvious that this prediction is borne out. In the absence of alternations, it is difficult to ascertain whether the stem level allows complex onsets consisting of a coronal and [i]. There are a few examples that could be interpreted in this way, but the number of these is not very large. Some examples are given in (147).

(147) Failure of gliding in underived contexts
    (a) [pasiˈãnto]   *pasiantaat*   'wait'
         *[paˈʃãnto]
    (b) [komprəˈnasion]   *komprenasion*   'understanding'
         *[komprəˈnaʃon]

Many of these words appear to be Romance borrowings; in particular, the suffix /-sion/ is always borrowed in this form, although it is difficult to say whether such words are treated as monomorphemic or derived in Breton. There are a few exceptions to this generalisation, but they are always morphologically non-trivial, involving, for instance, what appears to be bound allomorphs.

(148) Failure of gliding in derived contexts
    (a) [haˈnaːo]   *anavout*   'to know'
    (b) [ˈhãndiæz]   *anaoudegezh*   'knowledge'

The phonology of consonants: palatalisation and gliding   149

(c) ['talo]   talvout   'to earn'
(d) ['talfiæz̪]   talvoudegezh   'value'

In principle, this could be consistent with either hypothesis. We could take the existence of forms such as [kɔmprə'nasiɔn] and ['talfiæz̪] as evidence for the admissibility of such complex onsets at the stem level in Bothoa Breton, which would allow for uniform behaviour of [i] following all consonants. On the other hand, the relative peripherality of such sequences could be treated as evidence for their exceptional status: stem-level rules (such as coalescence would have to be) are known to sustain lexical exceptions. A third alternative is to assume that forms such as [kɔmprə'nasiɔn] and ['hãndiæz̪] are exceptional in that they contain onsetless syllables because the instances of [i] are underlyingly moraic, and this is faithfully reproduced by the stem-level phonology. In this case, we could assume that an input nonmoraic [i] is allowed to coalesce with preceding coronals, explaining the lack of unambiguous examples of complex [Cj] onsets with coronals.[12]

I would suggest that this last alternative is in fact the most appealing one. However, if coalescence with coronals is a live rule, we have to explain why it is allowed in this context (*COMPLEXONSET » UNIFORMITY) but blocked in the case of [kj] onsets (UNIFORMITY » *COMPLEXONSET). A possible solution is assuming that coalescence with coronals is disallowed not by the general UNIFORMITY constraint but by a locally conjoined constraint [*{C-man[cl], V-pl[cor]}&UNIFORMITY]$_{Seg}$, which prohibits coalescence from producing [tʃ dʒ] but not [ʃ ʒ ɲ j]. As tableau (149) shows, there is one undesirable prediction, in that it is assumed that underlying /stiV/ sequences can surface as [stjV], and such sequences are unattested. Nevertheless, this is a relatively minor overgeneration issue.

(149) Coalescence cannot produce [tʃ]

			*[sʃ]	[*{C-man[cl] V-pl[cor]}& UNIFORMITY] Seg	*COMPLEX ONSET	UNIFORMITY
/k₁i₂V/	(a) ☞	[k₁j₂V]			*	
	(b)	[tʃ₁₋₂V]		*!		*
/t₁i₂V/	(c)	[t₁j₂V]			*	
	(d) ☞	[ʃ₁₋₂V]				*
/st₁i₂V/	(e) ☞	[s.t₁j₂V]			*	

(f)	[s.ʃ₁₋₂V]	*!		*
(g)	[s.tʃ₁₋₂V]		*!	*

However, given the unclear status of exceptional forms, I leave the ultimate resolution of this issue for future work.

10.2.2.2 The word level

At the word level, gliding is also active, and it is also supplemented by coalescence. At the same time 'velar' palatalisation is switched off at this level. Consider the forms in (150), where hyphens mark morpheme boundaries.

(150) No gliding in word-level suffixes
    (a) /pwiːn-iəw/   poanioù   'sorrows'
         [ˈpwiːȷ̃əw]
    (b) /kwæd-iəw/   koadioù   'forests'
         [ˈkwæʒəw]

The stratal model can also explain why [i] derived by raising from [e] fails to be reparsed into the onset, and does not trigger coalescence, as seen in forms such as [ˈklɒːgiaɖ] 'ladleful' (*[ˈklɒːdʒaɖ]), from [ˈklɒːge]. At the stem level, the vowel [e] is parsed as a nucleus, and while the word-level ranking allows raising, it blocks changes in the prosodic parse due to faithfulness. Thus, the [i] remains nuclear even when that creates a hiatus.

Similarly, when an underlying [i] is parsed as a nucleus at the stem level, adding a vowel-initial suffix does not lead to gliding, with faithfulness compelling a violation of ONSET. This explains the only minimal pair given for the [i] ~ [j] contrast by Humphreys (1995: 166).

(151) Underapplication of gliding by cyclic transfer
    (a) [ˈtʃɛːr]   kêr   'village'
    (b) [ˈtʃɛːrjəw]   kêrioù   'villages'
    (c) [ˈtʃɛːri]   kevre   'string'
    (d) [ˈtʃɛːriəw]   kevrioù   'strings'

The difference between the two forms is that the [i] has no prosodic parse in the input in [tʃɛːrjəw], being introduced as part of the word-level suffix, and so it is glided to avoid hiatus. On the other hand, in [ˈtʃɛːriəw] the [i] is moraic in the input to the word level, since it receives a mora via normal syllabification processes at the stem level. The ranking is shown in (152). I assume that the operative constraint here is MAXLINK-µ[V]. Note that MAXLINK can be vacuously satisfied via deletion, so MAX(V-pl[cor]) is necessary to prevent this.

(152) Faithfulness blocks gliding

			MaxLink-µ[V]	Max (V-pl[cor])	Onset	*Complex Onset
/tʃɛːμμriəw/	(a)	[ˈtʃɛːμμriμ.əμw]			*!	
	(b) ☞	[ˈtʃɛːμμrjəμw]				*
	(c)	[ˈtʃɛːμμrəμw]		*!		
/ˈtʃɛːμμriμəw/	(d) ☞	[ˈtʃɛːμμriμ.əμw]		*		
	(e)	[ˈtʃɛːμμrjəμw]	*!			*
	(f)	[ˈtʃɛːμμrəμw]	*!			

The same principle is at work in cases of the failure of gliding or coalescence that are abundantly attested across the boundary between the verbal stem and vowel-initial verbal inflections.

(153) Failure of gliding and coalescence
    (a) [ˈbiːni-o] *bennigañ* 'bless'
        *[ˈbiːɟo]
    (b) [ˈbaːdi-o] *badeziñ* 'baptise'
        *[ˈbaːʒo]

Finally, there are (at least) two exceptions to the generalisation: gliding fails to apply in the forms [ˈbʊrdiəw] 'tables' and [avɔˈkadiən] 'lawyers'. It is clear that it cannot be blocked by phonotactic considerations: the expected forms *[bʊrʒəw] and *[avɔˈkaʒən] are by no means exceptional.

These forms may be problematic for Bermúdez-Otero's (2012) conception of lexical listing. He proposes that exceptional word-level constructs (which these plural forms seem to be) are stored analytically, i.e. as strings of underlying *segmental* representations. This is opposed to nonanalytic listing, which involves *fully prosodified* representations, but is only available at the stem level. Since the exceptional status of forms such as [avɔˈkadiən] is related to their prosodic structure rather than segmental make-up, analytic listing would be insufficient to derive the exceptionality.

However, Bermúdez-Otero (2011, 2012) also proposes that word-level suffixes may exceptionally attach to bare roots rather than stems, and in these cases the phonology treats them as if they were stem-level (cf. section 10.1.1). Thus, the exceptionality of [ˈbʊrdiəw] and [avɔˈkadiən] lies in their morphosyntactic structure: the plural suffix attaches to the bare root rather than to the stem. This triggers a stem-level phonological cycle, which has access to the nonanalytically listed exceptional forms and faithfully reproduces them on the surface.[13]

Apart from an increased role for faithfulness, there is at least one reranking in the word-level phonology: coalescence may apply to onset [ki] sequences at this level, producing [tʃ]. This applies both to [kj] onsets created by stem-level cycles (as in [ˈtʃɛzəɡ̊] 'horses') and to those created by concatenation at the word level (as in [ˈlastitʃəw] 'rubber bands').

10.2.2.3 Later levels

There is another instance of the underapplication of coalescence due to constraint reranking between levels. As we saw in section 10.1.2, coronal palatalisation of [l] produces [i], normally glided to [j], as in [ˈstʃøːjəw] 'ladders' from /stʃøːliəw/. If the [l] is preceded by an unstressed [ə] or [ɛ], however, the outcome is a non-glided [i] (i.e. a nucleus [i] that does not trigger coronal palatalisation).[14]

(154) No gliding of coalesced /lj/
    (a) [ˈmɒrˌzɛl]   *morzhol*   'hammer'
    (b) [ˈmɒrziəw]   *morzholioù*   'hammers'
    (c) *[mɒrʒəw]
    (d) [ˈøbəl]   *ebeul*   'foal'
    (e) [ˈøbiən]   *ebeulien*   'foals'
    (f) *[ˈøbjən]

As discussed in section 9.1, I assume the patterning of [ɛ] and [ə] reflects a vowel reduction process. The motivation for the pattern whereby [əi] is realised as [i] is not entirely clear from the data. We could speculate that, for instance, the sequence [ə.jV] is dispreferred because the less sonorous vowel [ə] projects a mora whereas [i] does not.

In any case, it appears to be true of the language that short [ə] never precedes a hiatus. Thus, while the word-level phonology outputs the plural of 'hammer' as [mɒrzəiəw] (ignoring prosodic structure for the moment), at a later (phrasal) level the [əi] sequence is realised as a (nuclear) [i]. However, consonant-[i] coalescence is inactive at that level.

This can be accounted for via a reranking on the postlexical level, whereby both UNIFORMITY and whatever constraints conspire to ban the [əi] sequence are promoted above ONSET. This is shown in (155). The postlexical computation takes the output of the word level as input, which means that [i] is not moraic. I assume that it becomes moraic and that the preceding vowel is deleted, requiring a violation of the constraint DEPLINK-μ, which prohibits moraic reassociation.

The phonology of consonants: palatalisation and gliding 153

(155) No coalescence at the postlexical level: [ˈbrøziəw] 'wars'

/brøz₁ə₂ᵤjəᵤw/	Uniformity	*[əi]	Max (V-pl[cor])	Onset	Max (V-man [lax])	DepLink-µ
(a) [ˈbrøz₁ə₂ᵤjəᵤw]		*!				
(b) [ˈbrøz₁ə₂ᵤəᵤw]			*!	*		
(c) ☞ [ˈbrøz₁i₂ᵤəᵤw]				*	*	*
(d) [ˈbrøʒ₁,₂ᵤəᵤw]	*!				*	

The hypothesis that the word-level phonology outputs forms with the [Vj] is supported by examples such as those in (156), with variant forms with and without secondary stress on the vowel before the /lj/ sequence. Secondary stress can block vowel reduction, which, in turn, blocks further coalescence and allows the [j] to surface intact after the unreduced vowel. When secondary stress is absent, however, the entire sequence undergoes coalescence to [i].

(156) Variant forms with /Vlj/ coalescence
    (a) [ˈkonˌtɛl]   *kontel*   'knife'
    (b) [ˌkonˈtɛjəw]   *kontilli* 'knives'
    (c) [ˈkontiəw]

The nature of the variation is not noted; however, it is commonly acknowledged that the variable application of rules (in this case the deletion of the second foot) is often associated with the postlexical level, further supporting the stratal affiliation of the relevant processes.

Similarly, coalescence is inactive before the future suffixes /-iːamp/ and /-iːaȷ̑tʃ/. The [iː] in these suffixes is underlyingly long, which is seen when they attach to stems that do not contain a syllable nucleus: [ˈgr̩ːiːamb̥] 'we will do'. However, with other stems the [i] can shorten, albeit without causing coronal palatalisation.

(157) No coalescence with future suffixes
    (a) [ˈlɛniamb̥]   *leniamp* 'we will read'
    (b) [ˌlɛˈniːamb̥]
    (c) *[ˈlɛȷ̑amb̥]

The shortening in these cases is also variable, so perhaps we would be justified in treating it as a variably applied postlexical rule (although it is not clear to what extent the process is morpheme-specific, which would be incompatible with postlexical status). This would mean that the suffix vowels are long at the word level, and since long vowels are always faithfully parsed as bimoraic nuclei, the lack of coalescence in (157) follows straightforwardly.

The proposal for the phonological behaviour of [i]/[j] at various levels is summarised in Table 10.1. I show processes within each level for ease of exposition, without implying within-level ordering. Nuclei are given in [square brackets]. The symbol SP stands for the trigger of spirantisation, to be discussed in more detail in section 11.3.1.

As discussed in section 7.2.3, surface nuclear [i] in hiatus is phonetically often realised as a glide. This means that Bothoa Breton has two separate gliding phenomena: one that is a phonological process operating on the stem level and one that is a phonetic process that is still not part of the computation, a representative case of rule scattering (Bermúdez-Otero 2015).[15] Its existence provides further corroboration of the modular architecture of grammar and a distinction between phonetics and phonology.

10.2.3 The front rounded vowel

Unlike the other two high vowels, I propose that the vowel [y] and the glide [ɥ] are different phonological segments.

Descriptively, they almost stand in complementary distribution: short [y] is almost never followed by a vowel, and preconsonantal [ɥ] only appears as part of the diphthong [əɥ]. There are a couple of exceptions, such as [ˈlaːryən] 'Lanrivain (placename)' (*Larruen*) and [ˈdaːryo] 'to mature' (*dareviñ*), but both of these are explainable in a stratal model: the first is monomorphemic and thus possibly exceptional, in the second the [y] is parsed as a nucleus at the stem level (cf. [ˈdaːry] 'ripe, mature').

However, [ɥ] has an important property that makes it very different from [w] and [j]: it can never form a syllable onset on its own. This is especially visible in the lenition mutation: while initial [gw] maps to [w] (which I analyse as an instance of [u]), initial [dʒɥ] maps not to [ɥ] but to [v]: [i ˈveːle] 'his bed' from [dʒɥeːle] 'bed'. However, [ɥ] is retained in the spirantisation of [tʃɥ] to [hɥ] ([ə ˈhɥiːzin] 'the kitchen', from [ˈtʃɥiːzin]), since it can remain a part of the complex onset. In addition, [ɥ] is not attested as a single onset in non-derived environments either: it is always part of an onset cluster.[16] I suggest that this behaviour is due to the segment [ɥ] bearing a C-place[labial] rather than a V-place feature, since this allows for a simple account of the alternation with [v].

The prosodically driven alternation between [ɥ] and [y] can be analysed as reassociation of [labial] between the C- and V-place tiers (Clements 1991a; Youssef 2015). A word like [ˈdʒɥeːle] 'bed' could be /gyeːle/ underlyingly. At the stem level, the prosodic parse pushes the second segment into the onset to avoid hiatus; however, since [y] (the segment

Table 10.1 The stratal analysis of high vowels and glides

Level	Process	HORSE	SP+HORSE	DOG	LADLEFUL	FOREST-PL	HAMMER-PL	READ-FUT.1PL
Stem	Prosodic parse	kiɛzæg	kiɛzæg	ki	klɒ:ge	kwæd	mɒrzɛl	lɛn
		(ki[ɛ])σzæg	(ki[ɛ])σzæg	(k[i])σ	klɒ:(g[e])σ	(kw[æ]d)σ	mɒr(z[ɛ]l)σ	(l[ɛ]n)σ
	Velar palatalisation	–	–	(tʃ[i])σ	–	–	–	–
Word	Affixation	–	SP-(ki[ɛ])σzæg	–	klɒ:(g[e])σad	(kw[æ]d)σiəw	mɒr(z[ɛ]l)σiəw	(l[ɛ]n)σi:amp
	Spirantisation	–	(hi[ɛ])σɡæz	–	–	–	–	–
	Prosodic parse	–	–	–	klɒ:(g[e])σ([a]d)σ	(kw[æ])σ(di[əw])σ	mɒr(z[ɛ])σ(li[əw])σ	(l[ɛ])σ(n[i:])σamp
	Raising	–	–	–	klɒ:(g[i])σ([a]d)σ	–	–	–
	Vowel reduction	–	–	–	–	–	mɒr(z[ɛ])σ([ə]w])σ	([w]e[i])σ([e]z])σ
	Coronal palatalisation	(tʃ[ɛ⁻])σzəg)	–	–	–	(kw[æ])σ(ʒ[əw])σ	mɒr(z[ɛ])σ(i[əw])σ	–
Phrase	[ə]-[i] fusion	–	–	–	–	–	mɒr(z[i])σ([əw])σ	–
	Shortening	–	–	–	–	–	–	(l[ɛ])σ(n[i])σamp
Output		tʃɛzæɡ̊	hjɛzæɡ̊	tʃi:	klɒ:giad	kwæʒəw	mɒrziəw	lɛniambə̥

{V-pl[lab], V-pl[cor]}) is disallowed in the onset, the [labial] feature reassociates to the C-place node, as shown in (158).

(158) Reassociation of [labial]

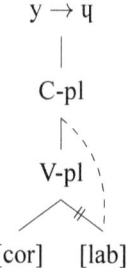

In OT terms, this is achieved by ranking ONSET above constraints which prohibit the reassociation of the [labial] feature, as in (159). In the case of [i], ONSET is satisfied by pushing the /i/ into a complex onset, but I assume syllable structure constraints disallow this for [y] (perhaps because it is a relatively complex segment), so instead reassociation creates an allowed onset segment. Note that spreading of V-pl[cor] and coalescence are not viable options at the stem level, as shown in (123), so I do not show relevant candidates in (159).

(159) The gliding of [y] as a featural change

		/gye:le/	ONSET	SYLSTRUC	MAX(V-pl[lab])	DEPLINK (C-pl) ([lab])	MAXLINK (V-pl) ([lab])
(a)		[gy_μ.e:_μμle]	*!				
(b)		[gye:_μμ.le]		*!			
(c)		[gje:_μμ.le]			*!		
(d)	☞	[gɥe:le]				*	*

Once this segment is in place at the word level, it can coalesce with a preceding dorsal stop to produce what I interpret as a [dʒɥ] segment (I discuss other aspects of this segment's behaviour, including the rationale for treating it as a segment and not a sequence, in section 11.3.3), as shown in (160). The ranking does not present significant problems, as *COMPLEXONSET outranks UNIFORMITY at the word level and featurally the coalescence is unproblematic. Note that this scenario also explains the absence of [ky] and [kɥ] sequences in Bothoa Breton surface forms.

(160) Coalescence of dorsals with [ɥ]

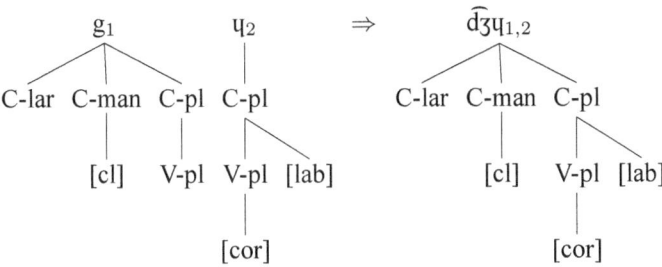

10.3 Discussion: the case for cyclicity

In this section I discuss the theoretical importance of the analysis offered here, focusing in particular on the behaviour of [i]. The stratal framework, coupled with an explicit representational system, provides a full account of its prosodic and segmental patterning in Bothoa Breton. Particularly important for the analysis is faithfulness to prosodic structure, which allows moraic status to persist across strata and prevent gliding or coalescence from applying to instances of [i] that are moraic either underlyingly or due to prosodic parses at earlier levels. In this section I argue that this analysis outperforms a whole range of solutions to the opacity problem that do not rely on a cyclic architecture.

10.3.1 Parallel approaches with Free Base Priority

A notable feature of the stratal analysis of the Bothoa Breton facts is the independence of phonological opacity from the availability of free-standing reference forms. The high vowel remains moraic in forms such as [ˈtʃɛːriəw] 'strings', [ˈbiːniəɟ] 'blessed', and [ˈbaːdio] 'to baptise' by virtue of its final position in a stem-level domain, not because a bare form of the right prosodic shape is available. In contrast, approaches to opacity based on transderivational identity (e.g. Kenstowicz 1996; Benua 1997; Kager 1999) rely on establishing a correspondence relation between a surface form where the relevant phenomenon is phonologically transparent and one where the pattern is opaque. This has been referred to as the Free Base Generalisation, which states that opacity can only exist with reference to such a free-standing form.

As discussed above, free-standing reference forms with a final vowel are not available for verbs such as [ˈbaːdio] in the Bothoa dialect. In other Breton varieties unsuffixed verbal stems are found as imperatives and 3sg present tense forms; however, the Bothoa dialect uses the (suffixed) 2nd person present form ([ˈbiːniəɟ]) to express the imperative meaning and a suffix [-a] for 3sg present (['biːnia]). In fact, all verbal suffixes in Bothoa Breton are vowel-initial, which could lead us to expect that a stem-final [i] should be glided or coalesced with the preceding consonant across the paradigm.

A comparison with other Breton dialects is instructive here. For instance, the dialect of Plougrescant (Jackson 1960, 1972; Le Dû 1978, 2012) also demonstrates an opaque interaction between rules regulating the prosodic parse of high front vowels; however, Plougrescant Breton data submit both to a cyclic analysis and to a base-priority approach.

The Plougrescant data are not directly compatible with those from Bothoa, because in the latter forms with underapplication of gliding, such as [ˈbiːnio] 'to bless', result historically from the loss of intervocalic consonants that are often preserved at Plougrescant[17] ([biˈnijã] 'to bless', [biˈnijəd] 'blessed'); even when the consonant is not preserved, the vowel is often not high ([baˈdɛːĩ] 'to baptise', [baˈdeːəd] 'baptised'). However, the facts of word-level coalescence in Plougrescant are largely comparable to those in Bothoa.

(161) Surface [j] in Plougrescant plurals
    (a) [ˈbroː]   *bro*   'country'
    (b) [ˈbroːjo]   *broioù*   'countries'

(162) Coalescence in Plougrescant plurals
    (a) [ˈpraːd]   *prad*   'meadow'
    (b) [ˈpraːɟo]   *pradioù*   'meadows'

Another aspect of the Plougrescant pattern has no direct correspondent in Bothoa. Stress in Plougrescant Breton is overwhelmingly penultimate, which creates paradigmatic alternations between [i] and [j] of the type that the Bothoa variety lacks. Specifically, when /i/ is the penultimate vowel in a word, it becomes a syllable nucleus even in a C_V context. In paradigmatically related words, this /i/ does not coalesce with the preceding consonant even if unstressed.

(163) Underapplication of coalescence in Plougrescant
    (a) [itaˈliːən]   *italien*   'Italian'
    (b) [italˈjãːnəd]   *italianed*   'Italians'
    (c) [farmaˈsiːən]   *farmasien*   'pharmacist'
    (d) [farmasˈjãːnəd] *farmasianed* 'pharmacists'

In Bothoa Breton, cognate forms do not show stress shift and are recorded with a vowel throughout the paradigm, which I analysed as due to faithfulness to an input moraic [i].[18]

(164) No alternation in Bothoa
  (a) [itali'ãn]   italien   'Italian'
  (b) [itali'ã:nəz]   italianez   'Italian woman'

In a stratal approach, the Plougrescant data can be accounted for thanks to the availability of faithfulness. We can assume that the stem-level prosodification pattern assigns a mora to the high vowel in a form such as /italiɲ/. In an unsuffixed form, the moraic [i] surfaces as a long vowel (for independent reasons). When a word-level suffix is added to the stem, the stress moves further to the right, but coalescence is prevented by a faithfulness constraint which protects segments that head some prosodic domain (in this case the mora) in the input.[19]

Crucially, the Plougrescant data are equally amenable to an analysis in parallel approaches with base priority, with the singular treated as the reference form and highly ranked OO-IDENT constraints preventing moraicity alternations. The data from Bothoa, on the other hand, do not show this analytic underdetermination, showing clearly the advantage of a stratal account.

10.3.2 Optimal Paradigms

A different parallel approach is Optimal Paradigms (OP) (Cable 2004; McCarthy 2004), which eschews Base Priority in favour of evaluating entire paradigms. Paradigmatic uniformity is ensured by OP-IDENT constraints that prohibit certain types of alternations in related forms. In this approach, the moraic status of the word-final [i] in ['tʃɛːri] 'string' is carried over to prevocalic [i] in the plural [tʃɛːriəw] (in violation of ONSET) because of a constraint OP-MAXLINK-μ, as shown in the tableau in (165).

(165) Optimal Paradigms with free-standing bases

		/tʃɛːri/+/∅/, /əw/	SYLSTRUC	OP-MAXLINK-μ	ONSET
(a)	☞	['tʃɛːri], [tʃɛːriəw]			*
(b)		['tʃɛːri], ['tʃɛːrjəw]		*!	
(c)		['tʃɛrj], ['tʃɛːrjəw]	*!		

This approach does not need to rely exclusively on free-standing forms to subvert phonological generalisations. In the case of [baːdio] 'to baptise', where we find no alternations in moraicity, the data can be accounted for by assuming that the relevant stems are stored in the lexicon with a moraic /i$_\mu$/; this achieves the correct result even without recourse to OP constraints.

(166) Hiatus via faithfulness in Optimal Paradigms

		MaxLink-μ	OP-MaxLink-μ	Onset
/baːdi$_\mu$/+/a/, /o/...				
(a)	☞ ['baːdia], ['baːdio]...			**...
(b)	['baːdja], ['baːdjo]...	**!		

Although the rich base also supplies stems such as /baːdi/ with a nonmoraic [i], the grammar (in view of the existence of palatalisation-related alternations) will map this stem to [baːʒ] before a vowel, so by Lexicon Optimisation (Prince and Smolensky 1993; Itô et al. 1995; Krämer 2012) such stems are not expected to be found in the language.

However, the Optimal Paradigms approach entails a significant loss of generalisation compared with the stratal analysis. In the latter, the exceptional non-gliding in ['baːdio] and the paradigmatically conditioned non-gliding in ['tʃɛːriəw] have a single source: the final position of the vowel in a stem-level domain. In the former, while simple faithfulness can cope with the case of ['baːdio], it is insufficient to cope with ['tʃɛːriəw]. Although one could assume that ['tʃɛːri] 'string' was stored as /'tʃɛːri$_\mu$/, the rich base still supplies the input /'tʃɛːri/, and without the OP constraint the prediction is a paradigm ['tʃɛːri], pl. ['tʃɛːrjəw], which is not attested. Thus, the explanation for what is essentially the same pattern has to be split in two, while the stratal approach provides a unified account.

To conclude, Bothoa Breton offers strong evidence for the correctness of the stratal, cyclic approach to opacity. In this framework, the loci of opacity emerge from an interplay of morphosyntactic structure and phonological restrictions on faithfulness. Thus, opacity is not left at the mercy of accidents of morphology or sound change. The comparison with Plougrescant Breton shows that the non-availability of free-standing bases in [i]-final verbs is due to a rather trivial morphological change whereby the unsuffixed imperative is replaced by the indicative form. An OO-correspondence approach makes the strong prediction that such a morphological change should inevitably lead to a loss of opacity, yet this has not happened. In this sense the Breton case is similar to the Albanian situation discussed by Trommer (2013), where opacity persists despite morphological 'accidents' such as paradigm defectivity and deponence. This principled connection between the (non-)application of

The phonology of consonants: palatalisation and gliding 161

phonological rules and morphosyntactic structure is an important advantage of the stratal approach.

Notes

1. There also exists a derivational suffix /-yz/, but there appear to be no relevant examples.
2. There is also at least one instance of velar palatalisation in an irregular plural before a non-high front vowel: [ˈdʒɛvər] 'goats' (*gevr*), cf. singular [ˈgawr].
3. Note, however, that the inflectional suffix /-i/ also triggers this alternation in [ˈtʃiːdʒi] 'roosters', singular [ˈkɔğ]. Following Bermúdez-Otero (2012), I suggest that this form is an irregular root-based formation rather than one where the inflectional suffix is added to the stem. Root-based formations undergo stem-level rather than word-level phonology, allowing velar palatalisation to go through. This structure is supported by the bound status of the root allomorph [ˈtʃiːdʒ].
4. It is not enough to ban the presence of a V-manner node with the feature set proposed in section 7.4, because [i] and/or [y] always have to be specified for V-manner to distinguish them from other V-pl[cor] segments.
5. There are several examples of this paradigm in Middle Breton (Lewis & Piette 1962; Schrijver 2011a): *b(a)elec* 'priest', plural *baeleyen, beleien* (but also *beleguyen* with [gj]); *marchec* 'horse rider', plural *mareien*; *benhuec* 'tool', plural *binhuyoud*; *guynieyer* 'vineyards', Modern Breton *gwinieg*. Favereau (2001: §54) notes: 'Words in -*eg* [...] have a slightly irregular plural in -*eien* or -*eion* (although local usage has sometimes preserved -*egion* [in Vannetais], or -*ejen* ← -*egien*).' He also notes doublets such as *kregier* or *krejer* for 'fangs' (*krog*), and *ste(g)ier* or *stejer* for 'strings' (*stag*).
6. Since there are no [zd] sequences, the result for them is unknown.
7. It is also possible that the C-place node also undergoes coalescence, in which case the first segment is phonologically a [ʃ] (recall that phonetically the sequence is realised as ⟦ɕtɕ⟧). In any case, there is no contrast between mannerless {C-pl[cor], C-lar[vcl]} segments before [tʃ].
8. Note that in cases where the coalescing sequence is preceded by a short vowel, as in [ˈøːrəʒo] 'to get married' from /øːrədio/, *ComplexOnset can be repaired by building a closed syllable: [ˈøːrəd.jo]. However, as discussed in section 8.3.4, I assume NoCoda dominates *ComplexOnset, so this candidate is not viable.
9. In other Breton dialects, the inventory includes the palatal lateral [ʎ], which is also the outcome of palatalisation, e.g. at Plougrescant (Le Dû 1978). The difference between these dialects and Bothoa Breton is easily derived via reranking of *{C-man[op], V-pl[cor]} and Max(C-man[op]), assuming the featural representations are comparable.
10. This account is reminiscent of the analysis of labial epenthesis in Serbian by Morén (2006), where sequences of a labial and floating V-place[coronal]

surface as [pʎ] etc., even though [ʎ] in Serbian is also a relatively complex segment and alternatives with less subsegmental structure are available for epenthesis. For instance, for underlying /kap͡iɛ/ '(it) drips' (where ͡i is the floating feature) the winning form is [ˈkapʎɛ] with {C-man[cl], V-man[cl], V-pl[cor]} [ʎ] rather than, say, {V-pl[cor], V-man[cl]} [ɛ]. The reason, Morén (2006) suggests, is top-down conditioning of prosodic structure, which treats the candidate [kapʎɛ] as preferable to *[kapɛɛ].

11. I thank Ricardo Bermúdez-Otero for discussion of several issues treated in this section.
12. The key question here is the status of forms such as *komprenasion*: Humphreys (1995) writes them as <kómprenasjon>, but given that in all cases [i] is unstressed, the 'gliding' might just be an effect of shortness.
13. Note that nonanalytic listing with faithfulness, being accessible at the stem level, would also be required to derive the exceptions from coalescence in underived forms.
14. There are (isolated) examples with other vowels or consonants, e.g. [ˈmyzio] 'to measure' from [ˈmyzyl] 'measure' and [ˈbɛːliən] 'priests', singular [ˈbɛːləĝ]. Humphreys (1995) also notes variation between [ˈpapərjəw] and [ˈpapriəw] as the plural of [ˈpapər] 'paper', with the second explainable as due to an intermediate [paprəiəw] with metathesis.
15. In line with the theory of the life cycle, the phonetic gliding process appears to be making inroads into the phonology: Humphreys (1995) cites a form [ˈlyːdʒənad] 'burn a fire until only ashes are left', clearly related to [ˈlyːdy] 'ashes' (*ludu*) and derived from what would normally be predicted to surface as [ˈlyːdyənad], with no gliding due to stem-level syllabification. Note that [d] alternates with [dʒ] rather than with [ʒ], as it normally does in coronal palatalisation, confirming that the processes are distinct.
16. With the exception of [tʃɥ] and [dʒɥ], which are historically derived from [kw] and [gw] before front vowels, other examples of onset [ɥ] involve French borrowings, but the contrast between [w] and [ɥ] is said to be robust (Humphreys 1995: 167).
17. All Plougrescant forms are given following Le Dû (2012), retranscribed into IPA.
18. Incidentally, the ascription of the moraicity of [i] in /itali$_μ$an/ to the lexicon in Bothoa (as opposed to the stem level in Plougrescant) is fully in line with the conception of domain narrowing and the life cycle of phonological processes (Bermúdez-Otero 2007a, 2015; Ramsammy 2015): since the application of the stem-level phonology consistently results in the assignment of the mora to the [i] vowel, speakers assume this [i] must be lexically moraic.
19. Similar constraints are employed by Kiparsky (2011) and Bermúdez-Otero (2013) to account for the blocking of the deletion of vowels that are stressed in the input to a stratum but unstressed in its output in Maltese and Spanish respectively.

11

Laryngeal phonology

In this chapter I consider a range of phenomena involving the laryngeal contrast between obstruents in Bothoa Breton. These phenomena provide the strongest support for a substance-free model of the relationship between phonological representations and their phonetic realisation. In section 7.2.1, we saw that the phonetic realisation of the contrast between [p t k] and [b d g] in Bothoa Breton agrees with languages such as French or Russian, in that the 'fortis' series of stops is realised with short-lag VOT (as 'voiceless unaspirated' stops), while the 'lenis' series is realised with full voicing. It has been proposed in the literature (e.g. Honeybone 2005a; Petrova et al. 2006; Beckman et al. 2013) that in such languages the 'lenis' series always shows the hallmarks of greater markedness, since it is these segments that bear a laryngeal feature whilst the 'fortis' ones remain unspecified. In this chapter I argue that this precisely not the case in Bothoa Breton, and that instead it is the 'fortis', short-lag VOT stops (and fricatives) that are the more marked series, on the basis of their phonological behaviour. I examine three areas of Bothoa Breton phonology to provide this evidence:

- final laryngeal neutralisation ('final devoicing')
- 'provection', i.e. adjacency-driven devoicing
- initial consonant mutations and laryngeal sandhi.

11.1 Final laryngeal neutralisation

As discussed in section 7.3.2, the laryngeal contrast in Bothoa Breton is suspended word-finally, with both fortis and lenis stops being realised in ways that largely depend on the context. Several types of realisations were identified:

- voiceless realisations (phrase-final and adjacent to voiceless consonants)
- voiced realisations (before voiced consonants)
- unreleased (after a nasal and before consonants, especially homorganic ones).

I analyse this neutralisation as complete suspension of laryngeal contrast in non-onset position. I formalise it as deletion of the C-laryngeal node with preservation of other features. In other words, there are *three* possible types of laryngeal specification available in surface representations. Bothoa Breton is therefore a counterexample to Lombardi's (1995a: 28) dictum: 'There is no phonological contrast between a representation with a bare Laryngeal node and no Laryngeal node at all.'

11.1.1 *The ternary contrast on the surface*

I use the term 'final laryngeal neutralisation' (see Iverson and Salmons 2011) rather than 'final devoicing' to emphasise that in Breton the process is not one of mapping one class of segments (the voiced obstruents) onto another class (the voiceless obstruents), where the latter surfaces unchanged in the relevant position; rather, it represents complete suspension of contrast (Steriade 1997) between the two classes of segments. The phonetic realisation of the outcome of this neutralisation, however, is variable.

I suggest that, given surface underspecification (Pierrehumbert and Beckman 1988; Keating 1988a, 1990b, 1996; Jansen 2007a; Colina 2009; Strycharczuk et al. 2014), those aspects of the phonetic implementation that are normally co-opted to realise laryngeal contrast are relatively free to vary contextually. The concept of 'freedom' is best understood in terms of Keating's (1988b, 1990a, 1996) window model of coarticulation, where more freedom corresponds to a wider window.

This freedom is often taken to mean that surface underspecification necessarily implies that the unspecified element is realised by interpolating between the target values of the flanking specified elements (Pierrehumbert and Beckman 1988; Cohn 1993; Hsu 1998; Colina 2009), although recent work, discussed in more detail below, shows that this view must be nuanced.

In any case, Humphreys' (1995) description of word-final obstruents as 'consonants with decreasing voicing' appears compatible with the supposition that voicing in positions of neutralisation in Breton is gradient rather than categorical. As Westbury and Keating (1986) and Jansen (2004) discuss in detail, variable voicing can be accounted for through the overspill of vocal fold vibration in the absence of an active devoicing gesture. In phrase-final position, this overspill is inhibited by the lack of a following voiced segment as an interpolation target, the lower pressure differential across the larynx due to lower respiratory effort, and possibly to enhancement at domain boundaries via glottaling (Hock 1999; Blevins 2004; Iverson and Salmons 2007).

Further phonetic evidence for the ternary contrast is provided by what I called 'lack-of-release phenomena' in section 7.3.1; these involve progressive assimilation in terms of nasality, lack of burst (especially following fricatives), and sometimes deletion (which seems, at least in some cases, to be gestural overlap rather than a phonological deletion process). The fact that no such phenomena are described for other positions further suggests that the phonology outputs a third category of obstruents word-finally.

This approach further underscores the lack of a direct link between phonological dimensions and their phonetic implementation, and therefore the abstract nature of phonological features. While the variable voicing of delaryngealised obstruents could be construed as a matter of surface interpolation of laryngeal state, it is more difficult to ascribe the lack-of-release phenomena exclusively to laryngeal phonetics. However, lack of release does create additional indeterminacy in terms of the identification of the 'laryngeal' series, since it obscures potential cues such as burst strength and the duration of closure or frication. This demonstrates that the 'C-laryngeal' dimension in Bothoa Breton is in fact implemented by a multitude of covarying cues (Kingston and Diehl 1994; Kingston et al. 2008), which are *all* affected when a phonological operation affects the featural node.

Given all of the above, I suggest that the difference between obstruents voiced in sandhi and categorically voiced onset obstruents reflects a difference in the output of the phonological module. The phenomena of sandhi 'voicing' and 'devoicing' (Le Dû 1986) do not represent assimilation operations carried out by the phonological grammar: instead, they are phonetic interpretation phenomena. In the following sections I present phonological evidence for the existence of this ternary contrast.

11.1.2 *Geometric analysis*

The process of final laryngeal neutralisation in a word like /kɔg/ 'rooster' is shown in (167): the C-lar node is delinked from the word-final consonant, while the C-lar node in the onset (shaded) remains intact (cf. Hall 2009).

(167) Final laryngeal neutralisation: /kɔg/ → [kɔg̊]

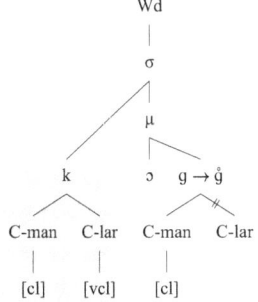

In a word with an underlying voiceless consonant such as /tɔk/ 'hat', also realised with a laryngeally unspecified final consonant, the only difference is the presence of a [voiceless] feature under the C-laryngeal node; the same process will apply in the case of a final sonorant–obstruent sequence.

One obvious exception to this generalisation is the behaviour of the segment [h]; if the C-laryngeal delinking rule were to apply, the outcome would be an empty root node (possibly with an empty place and/or manner node, depending on the contrastive hierarchy); however, underlying [h] in word-final position is realised either as ⟦x⟧ (phrase-finally) or as a range of dorsal, pharyngeal, and laryngeal sounds (⟦ħ⟧, ⟦ɣ⟧, ⟦ɦ⟧).

Conceptually there is nothing preventing us from treating these as the phonetic realisation of an empty root node. I suggest, however, that word-final underlying [h] is in fact realised faithfully. Phonetically, the possibility of voiced realisations in a phrasal context (despite the C-lar[voiceless] specification) should not be surprising. First, the window of allowed realisations for [h] can be wider because the segment does not contrast with one that only differs from it by a laryngeal feature; absence of contrast along a dimension is known to be able to lead to greater variability (e.g. Dyck 1996; van Alphen 2007). Second, voiceless [h] is known to be poorly perceptible in intervocalic position (Mielke 2003), so we would expect the use of such enhancement strategies if allowed by the phonetics–phonology interface of the language. Finally, the very fact that word-final [h] has essentially the same range of realisation as word-internal [h] suggests that they are the same segment, if we assume that the phonetics–phonology interface cannot completely neutralise output contrasts (the Interface Interpretation Principle, Chapter 2).

The contrastive hierarchy for Bothoa Breton given in Chapter 7 also provides a phonological argument. In this hierarchy, [h] is the segment that is assigned a default specification because it would otherwise be featureless. If the ban on empty root nodes is enforced across the board by the phonological grammar, we expect the output correspondent of a featureless node to be exactly [h] (see also section 11.3.3.2 for more evidence to this effect).

Thus, although there is no *conclusive* phonological evidence that would allow us to decide whether word-final [h] should be treated as an empty root node or as a surface [h], I adopt the latter solution as being consistent with both phonetic and phonological data.

Finally, some comment is in order on word-final obstruent sequences (⟦sp⟧, ⟦st⟧, and ⟦sk⟧ are possible in this position, but the absence of ⟦stʃ⟧ is an accident of history). According to Humphreys (1995), these are realised as voiceless phrase-finally and prevocalically, but are voiced before obstruents (irrespective of whether the final stop is released, though voiced pronunciations with a released stop, of the type ⟦ˌlɒzd ˈbɛːr⟧ 'short tail' are said to be extremely rare). The analysis for such words is given in (168). I am assuming a doubly linked instance of C-laryngeal[voiceless] in the underlying representation in line with standard approaches to Lexicon Optimisation (Prince and Smolensky 1993; Inkelas 1994): since there are no alternations which could show that the two consonants have separate instances of the feature, and below I argue that word-medially the outcome will be a doubly linked C-laryngeal [voiceless].

(168) Prosodic parse of /lɒst/ 'tail'

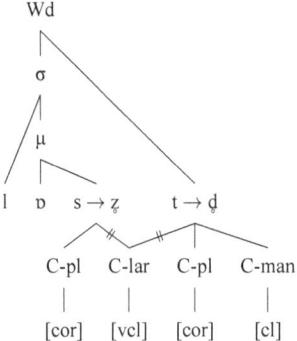

Despite being parsed into the syllable, the coda obstruent [z̥] still loses its laryngeal specification, as demonstrated by the possibility of a voiced pronunciation before a voiced obstruent. Before vowels, such sequences are described as normally voiceless in Bothoa Breton, with a voiced pronunciation said to be very rare. Long obstruent articulations normally inhibit 'passive' voicing (Ohala and Solé 2010), which is consistent with the lack of prevocalic voicing in this context; that obstruents do trigger (phonetic) regressive assimilation can be due to the fact that, unlike vowels and sonorants, they are actively voiced, and this gesture can trigger anticipatory voicing (Jansen 2004). Again, a fuller picture can only emerge given instrumental data, so the proposal must remain a hypothesis for now.

11.1.3 *OT analysis*

For the sake of concreteness, I suggest that final laryngeal neutralisation in Breton is driven by a ranking that protects C-laryngeal specification in syllable onsets but leaves them unlicensed in other positions (e.g. Bethin 1992; Beckman 1998; Lombardi 1999). This approach is clearly related to proposals that laryngeal contrasts are preserved before sonorants rather than specifically in an onset (Lombardi 1995a, 1995b; Rubach 2008; Beckman et al. 2009; Jurgec 2010), but below I discuss some evidence showing the importance of onsets rather than pre-sonorant position.

11.1.3.1 Final neutralisation

In the simplest case, final neutralisation is driven by the classic positional faithfulness ranking of MAX$_{Onset}$([F]) over *[F] over MAX([F]). In Bothoa Breton, both classes of obstruents undergo the neutralisation, meaning that *C-laryngeal outranks both MAX(C-lar) and MAX(C-lar[vcl]); in other words, there is no Preservation of the Marked (de Lacy 2006; see also Chapter 5).[1] In addition, it has to dominate a constraint which penalises segments that lack a C-laryngeal node; I write this augmentation constraint as HAVE(C-lar). The ranking is shown in (169). I ignore the violations of HAVE(C-lar) incurred by vowels, since candidates without these violations are knocked out by highly ranked co-occurrence constraints.

(169) Final laryngeal neutralisation: [ˈkwæḍ] 'forest' (plural [ˈkwæʒəw]), [ˈtɔġ] 'hat' (plural [ˈtɔkəw])

			MAX$_{Onset}$ (C-lar)	*C-lar	MAX (C-lar)	MAX (C-lar[vcl])	HAVE (C-lar)
/kwæd/	(a)		[ˈkwæd]		kd!			
	(b)	☞	[ˈkwæḍ]		k	ḍ		ḍ
	(c)		[ˈġwæd]	ġ!		ġḍ	ġ	ġḍ
/tɔk/	(d)		[ˈtɔk]		tk!			
	(e)		[ˈtɔg]		tg!		g	
	(f)	☞	[ˈtɔġ]		t	ġ	ġ	ġ
	(g)		[ˈḍɔġ]	ḍ!		ḍġ	ġ	ḍġ

This ranking ensures that C-lar nodes are deleted unless the segment is parsed as an onset. However, this ranking predicts that a non-onset [h] should map to an empty root node, which above I argued to be impossible on the surface. In principle, one could recruit the constraint HAVE(C-lar) to force a violation of *C-lar (with MAX(C-lar[vcl]) ensuring preservation of the feature), but the tableau in (169) shows that this solution is not viable. I suggest, therefore, that we need a constraint requiring that a root node dominate at least one feature, which I will call HAVE([F]). The existence of such a constraint further confirms the necessity for the representational metalanguage to distinguish between geometrical nodes and features. The constraint has to be formulated as shown in (170).

170   *A Substance-free Framework for Phonology*

(172) Onset enhancement: [ˈbroː] 'country' (hypothetical form), [ˈnɔː] 'nine', [ˈalve] 'key'

			Dep(Root)	*[n̥]	Align-L (σ- C-lar)	Dep (C-lar)	Dep(C-lar[vcl])
/b̥ro/	(a)		[ˈb̥roː]			*!		
	(b)	☞	[ˈbroː]				*	
	(c)		[ˈproː]				*	*!
/nɔː/	(d)	☞	[ˈnɔː]			*		
	(e)		[ˈn̥ɔː]		*!		*	
	(f)		[ˈnʰɔː]		*!		*	*
/alve/	(g)	☞	[ˈalve]			*		
	(h)		[ˈ⟨x, C-lar⟩alve]	*!			*	
	(i)		[ˈhalve]	*!			*	*

Due to the OT principle of minimum violation and to the subset relationships among featural structures (and thus violation sets), the ranking ensures that only the minimal amount of structure necessary to satisfy the constraint which enforces the unfaithful mapping is inserted in the surface representation. Thus, the proposal formulates in precise geometrical terms an insight that has been expressed by several authors previously, namely that *voiced obstruents are less marked than voiceless ones in Breton phonology*. I shall return to this issue in more detail in section 11.5.

The necessity of Align-L(σ, C-lar) happens to be confirmed not just by hypothetical considerations around Richness of the Base, but also by some facts of Breton phonology. As we shall see below, processes of consonant mutation mostly involve obstruents as both inputs and outputs. However, the lenition mutation creates an alternation between [m] and [v].

(173) Lenition of [m]
  (a) [ˈmaːb̥]   *mab*   'son'
  (b) [ˈdəw ˈvaːb̥]   *daou vab*   'two sons'
  (c) *[ˈdəw ˈɣaːb̥]

Under the representational assumptions of this book, the alternation creates a C-lar segment from one that has no laryngeal specification, and, if lenition is at all phonological, the appearance of the C-lar specification must be ascribed to a constraint militating against laryngeally unspecified obstruents in onset position. This is precisely the role of Align-L.

(170) |HAVE([F])|:=(output ∧ Root) → ⟨↓⟩ feature
'An output root node dominates a node which is a feature'

In the metalanguage, features are distinguished from nodes by having the predicate *feature*, which allows this constraint to be formulated.

The ranking ensuring preservation of non-onset [h] is shown in (171). Note that MAX(Root) must also dominate *C-lar to ensure that the latter constraint is not satisfied via deletion (Lombardi 2001).

(171) Preservation of non-onset [h]: [ˈzɛːh] 'dry'

/zɛːh/		MAX(Rt)	HAVE([F])	*C-lar	MAX (C-lar)	MAX (C-lar [vcl])
(a)	☞ [ˈzɛː⟨x, C-lar, [vcl]⟩]			*		
(b)	[ˈzɛː⟨x, C-lar⟩]		*!	*		*
(c)	[ˈzɛː⟨x⟩]		*!		*	*
(d)	[ˈzɛː]	*!			*	*

11.1.3.2 Onset enhancement

As discussed so far, laryngeally specified obstruents stand in complementary distribution with those lacking a C-laryngeal node: the former appear in onsets and the latter elsewhere. The tableaux in the preceding section show how this distribution is achieved for underlyingly specified obstruents. However, under Richness of the Base the ranking must also ensure the same result is achieved for input delaryngealised obstruents (Inkelas 1994). The ranking in (169) is not sufficient for this purpose: it ensures that input C-lar is preserved in the onset, but cannot force the insertion of C-lar in an onset when it is not present in the input.

I propose that the preservation of C-lar is due to a constraint ALIGN-L(σ, C-lar) which requires that left edges of syllables be marked with the presence of a laryngeal specification (cf. Krämer 2000). In other words, this constraint penalises delaryngealised segments at the left edge of a syllable. By forcing the epenthesis of a C-lar node, it contributes to ensuring the complementary distribution. This constraint has to be outranked by both DEP(Root) (to ensure that no other segment, such as [h], is epenthesised in onsetless syllables to satisfy ALIGN-L) and by feature co-occurrence constraints (to prohibit the epenthesis of C-laryngeal in vowels and sonorants, which I assume to be incompatible with C-lar). The ranking is shown in (172), which uses the symbol [ṇ] for a combination of the features of [n] and a C-laryngeal node and the symbol [nʰ] for a C-lar[vcl] [n].

Note that ALIGN-L can also be used to replace MAX$_{Onset}$ in (169). This might be desirable in view of the ambiguous status of onsets in prosodic theory (see Topintzi 2010: ch. 7). In the standard theory of positional faithfulness, constraints such as MAX$_{Onset}$, and others such as initial syllable faithfulness (Steriade 1994; Beckman 1998; Casali 1998; Barnes 2006; Becker et al. 2011; Becker et al. 2012), coexist with faithfulness relativised to head positions (e.g. Beckman 1998; Alderete 1999). Since onsets are seldom, if ever, viewed as heads,[2] this is a somewhat uneasy coexistence.

This is probably part of the reason for proposals to replace constraints such as MAX$_{Onset}$ with pre-vocalic or pre-sonorant faithfulness constraints (e.g. Rubach 2008; Beckman et al. 2009; Jurgec 2010), which at least have a clear functional grounding (Steriade 1994, 2001). However, translating the present proposal into a framework assuming a special status for the pre-sonorant position seems poorly motivated. In particular, pre-sonorant position in sandhi is *not* a locus of preservation of laryngeal features, which obviously complicates any account appealing to pre-sonorant faithfulness. Thus, although I do not exclude the possibility of removing it from the grammar altogether, here I prefer the account using MAX$_{Onset}$.

Finally, it must be noted that the grammar which ensures this onset enhancement may have to be excluded from the postlexical level. As detailed in section 11.5, some analyses of Breton voicing sandhi rely on word-final consonants being resyllabified into the onset in suitable phrasal contexts. Although I argue that the specific analyses are incorrect, the possibility of such postlexical resyllabification still remains. The present state of the data does not allow us to decide whether the word-final obstruent in [ˈmaːd̥ ɛː] *mat eo* 'it is good' is syllabified as an onset or not; however, if it is, it should still remain delaryngealised. This can only be achieved if the onset-enhancing ranking is inactive postlexically, which would require DEP to outrank ALIGN-L – the reverse of (172).

11.2 Provection

I use the convenient label 'provection' (cf. Jackson 1967: §§446–9 *et passim*) to designate an alternation whereby single voiced obstruents or clusters of obstruents (irrespective of their underlying laryngeal specification) become voiceless. This label covers two distinct phenomena in Bothoa Breton (cf. Greene 1967): one that appears morphologically induced but for which there is ample evidence, and one that is phonologically driven but for which the evidence is more equivocal.

11.2.1 *Morphologically restricted provection*

This type of provection is associated with a number of suffixes, most prominently the comparative /-ph/ and superlative /-ã/. Similar changes are associated with the formation of denominal and deadjectival verbs with the suffix /-aɟ/ in the verbal noun.

11.2.1.1 Adjectives

Provection in adjectives (and adverbs) is much more regular than that in verbs, perhaps because the relevant suffixes are much more productive than the verbal /-aɟ/ suffix. Following Humphreys (1995), I only give comparative forms, since superlative forms can be derived by substituting /-ã/ for /-ʋh/.

In terms of segmental changes, the comparative suffix does not exert any influence on the following segments and sequences of segments:

- (voiced) sonorants: [m n ɲ l r]
- long vowels (whether stressed or unstressed)
- the segment /h/
- voiceless obstruents: [p t tʃ k f s ʃ] (inasmuch as the laryngeal specification of stem-final obstruents can be determined)
- the sequences [st sk]
- the sequences [mp nt ŋk].

Some cases are shown in (174).

(174) Phonologically motivated absence of provection
    (a) [ˈpɛl]   pell   'far'
    (b) [ˈpɛlʋh]   pelloc'h   'further'
    (c) [ˈhwɛr]   c'hwerv   'bitter'
    (d) [ˈhwɛrʋh]   c'hwervoc'h   'more bitter'
    (e) [ˈbeː]   bev   'alive'
    (f) [ˈbeːʋh]   bevoc'h   'more alive'

In a very few cases (apparently lexically determined), vowel-final adjectives may have optional variants with a [h] before the comparative suffix.[3]

(175) Variable [h] in adjectives
    (a) [ˈskãː]   skañv   'light'
    (b) [ˈskãːhʋh]   skañvoc'h   'lighter'
    (c) [ˈskãːʋh]

All underlyingly voiced obstruents (there are no examples for [ʒ]) are subject to devoicing.

(176) Devoicing in adjectives
    (a) [zɛˈlaːb̥]   sellapl   'stingy'
    (b) [zɛˈlapʋh]   sellaploc'h   'stingier'

    (c) ['pinvid͡ʒ̊]   *pinvidik*   'rich'
    (d) ['pinvitʃɒh]   *pinvidikoc'h*   'richer'

Connected with devoicing is the shortening of long vowels in the syllable preceding the devoiced obstruent; according to Humphreys (1995: 267), the two processes are 'generally' associated.[4]

(177) Shortening with provection
    (a) ['fæːb̥]   'weak' (French *faible*)
    (b) ['fæpɒh]   'weaker'
    (c) ['zoːd̥]   *sod*   'mad'
    (d) ['zotɒh]   *sotoc'h*   'madder'
    (e) ['gwaːg̊]   *gwak*   'soft'
    (f) ['gwakɒh]   *gwakoc'h*   'softer'

When the comparative and superlative suffixes are added to adjectives which end in sonorants or /h/, the shortening is optional.

(178) Variable shortening with provection of sonorants
    (a) ['bɛːr]   *berr*   'short'
    (b) ['bɛːrɒh]   *berroc'h*   'shorter'
    (c) ['bɛrɒh]
    (d) ['viːl]   *vil*   'ugly'
    (e) ['viːlɒh]   *viloc'h*   'uglier'
    (f) ['vilɒh]

In the case of polysyllabic bases where the vowel in the second syllable is a schwa, the 'trough pattern' arises, with the usual phonetic shortening of the second syllable. There is at least one case where this syncope appears to have become phonologised.

(179) Provection and syncope
    (a) ['ɛːzəd̥]   *aezet*   'easy'
    (b) ['ɛstɒh]   *aezetoc'h*   'easier'

Note the shortening of the vowel in the first syllable, which is uncharacteristic of the 'trough pattern' generally but agrees with the restriction on long vowels in closed syllables, and this indicates that the form in (179b) is phonologically disyllabic.

Finally, in cases of adjectives formed using the obstruent-final suffixes /-uz/, /-yz/, /-ãnt/, /-idʒ/, as well as the suffix /-i/, the formation of the comparative is accompanied by a shift of stress to the presuffixal syllable.

(180) Stress shift associated with provection
    (a) [ˈspontid͡ʒ]   *spontik*   'timid'
    (b) [sponˈtitʃɒh]   *spontikoc'h*   'more timid'
    (c) [ˈdɛvɒd̪]   *devot*   'devout'
    (d) [dɛˈvɒtɒh]   *devotoc'h*   'more devout'

The comparative suffix also induces lengthening of a stem-final vowel, if there are no long vowels in the stem otherwise.

(181) Lengthening of stem-final vowels
    (a) [ˈneve]   *nevez*   'new'
    (b) [neˈveːɒh]   *nevesoc'h*   'newer'[5]
    (c) [ˈkasti]   *kastiz*   'lean'
    (d) [kasˈtiːɒh]   *kastisoc'h*   'leaner'

If the stem does contain a long vowel already, there is no lengthening.

(182) No lengthening of final vowels
    (a) [ˈdaːry]   *darev*   'ripe, mature'
    (b) [ˈdaːryɒh]   *darevoc'h*   'riper'
    (c) [ˈbøːre]   *beure*   'morning'
    (d) [ˈbøːriɒh]   *beuroc'h*   'earlier in the morning'

11.2.1.2 Verbs

A similar alternation is found with verbs and their derivatives. Humphreys (1995) presents these facts in terms of a provection-inducing verbal noun suffix /-ad/; in fact, however, the provection is carried over to the inflected forms of these verbs, as well as to agentive nouns formed from these bases using the suffix /-ɛːr/: in other words, provection is used to build the verbal stem. I only show the verbal nouns in this section.

Provection and vowel shortening seem to be quite regular when this suffix is added to bases of the right form, as the following examples show.

(183) Provection in verbs
    (a) [ˈkaːʐ]   *kazh*   'cat'
    (b) [ˈkasad̪]   *kazha*   'to be on heat (of cats)'
    (c) [mahaˈmaːd̪]   *marc'had-mat*   'bargain'
    (d) [mahaˈmatad̪]   *marc'hatad*   'get a bargain'

Vowel shortening appears to be absent in contexts where provection is inapplicable, i.e. where the pre-suffix consonant is a sonorant or absent altogether; it does seem to happen when the stem-final segment is /h/.

Laryngeal phonology 175

(184) Lack of provection in verbs
    (a) [ˈvyːr]   *fur*   'wise'
    (b) [ˈvyːrad̦] *furaat* 'become wise'
    (c) [ˈhryː]   *ruz*   'red'
    (d) [ˈhryːad̦] *rusaat* 'redden'
    (e) [ˈjaːh]   *yac'h*   'in good health'
    (f) [ˈjahad̦]   *yac'haat* 'heal'

11.2.1.3 Autosegmental analysis

I suggest that this morphologically triggered process provides important evidence for the phonological activity of the feature C-lar[voiceless]. I analyse it as the suffixation of a C-lar[voiceless] segment (i.e. [h]) underlyingly linked to a mora. Faithfulness to moraic structure prevents the [h] from surfacing in an onset, so that instead it coalesces with the preceding consonant if that is possible, creating an (exceptional) moraic coda.

In the case of voiced obstruents, this coalescence leads to devoicing, since structurally voiceless obstruents are simply the union of their voiced counterparts and [h]. The surfacing of the suffixal mora creates prohibited trimoraic syllables, and so the second mora of the underlying vowel is delinked. The result is vowel shortening (cf. the analysis of shortening in Anywa by Trommer and Zimmermann 2014). The bimoraic status of the resulting syllable is confirmed by the fact the stress shift seen in polysyllabic stems, as in [ˈdɛvɒd̦] 'pious', [dɛˈvɒtɒh] 'more pious'.

(185) Morphological provection: autosegmental analysis

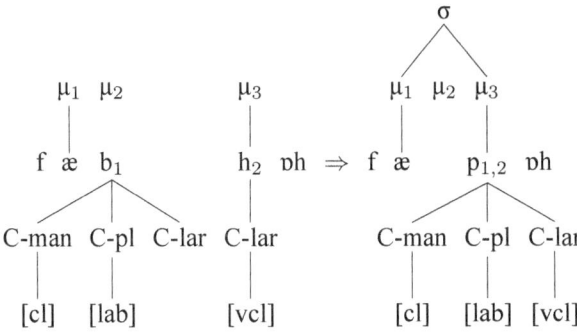

The nature of the vowel shortening as an *additive* process is emphasised by the lengthening of stem-final vowels, as in [kasˈtiːɒh] 'leaner' from [ˈkasti], which must come from the addition of the suffixal mora. Similarly, there is no vowel shortening in forms such as [ˈdyːɒh] 'blacker' from [ˈdyː] 'black'. Thus, the correct generalisation is *not* that the vowel shortens before a provecting suffix, but that it is shortened in this context only when followed by a consonant.

This is an important result, in that it slots into the Generalised Nonlinear Affixation programme (Saba Kirchner 2010; Bermúdez-Otero 2012; Bye and Svenonius 2012; Trommer 2011, 2014; Trommer and Zimmermann 2014; Zimmermann 2013a, 2013b), whereby all apparently destructive processes are derived in the phonological computation from the concatenation of pieces of phonological structure. The Breton case is particularly instructive, since the same morpheme is able to effect both structure building (lengthening) and apparent structure removal (shortening), confirming that morphologically the two operations are not distinct.

11.2.1.4 OT analysis

The ranking needed to derive devoicing in cases such as ['fæpɒh] is shown in (186). I suggest that the key constraint in the operation of provection is MAXLINK(C-lar[vcl])(μ), which requires that surface instances of C-lar[vcl] which are associated to a mora in the input are also associated with a mora in the output (i.e. head a moraic domain). In concert with MAX(C-lar[vcl]), this constraint ensures that both the mora and the feature are associated with a suitable consonant.

(186) Shortening as suffixation of a mora: ['fæpɒh] 'weaker'

/fæː$_{μ1μ2}$b + h$_{μ3}$ɒh/		SYLSTRUC	MAXLINK (C-lar[vcl]) (μ)	MAX(C-lar[vcl])	*μ[C]	MAX-μ	DEPLINK-μ
(a)	[fæː$_{μ1μ2}$bɒh]			*!		*	
(b)	[fæː$_{μ1μ2}$pɒh]		*!			*	
(c)	[fæː$_{μ1μ2}$p$_{μ3}$h]	*!			*		*
(d) ☞	[fæ$_{μ1}$p$_{μ3}$ɒh]				*	*	*
(e)	[fæ$_{μ1}$b.h$_{μ3}$ɒh]	*!			*	*	
(f)	[fæ$_{μ1}$b.hɒh]		*!			*	

In the case of sonorant-final stems, where vowel shortening is variable, C-lar[vcl] cannot associate to the stem-final consonant because of undominated feature co-occurrence restrictions. Therefore, the winning candidate must violate MAX(C-lar[vcl]). As the tableau in (187) shows, this means that the top stratum of the constraints cannot choose the winning candidate. I suggest that the variation observed in the output involves a candidate where the coalescence of the segments fails entirely, leading to deletion of the mora, and a candidate where the floating mora does attach to the coalesced segment, even though the C-lar[vcl] is lost. The variation depends on the ranking between *μ[C], which prohibits consonantal morae, and MAX(Rt), which can compel coalescence (with consequent preservation of the mora) even in the face of the deletion of some features.

(187) Variable shortening before sonorants: [ˈviː(ː)lɒh] 'uglier'

/viː$_{μ1μ2}$l$_a$ + h$_{bμ3}$ɒh/	*{C-man[op], C-lar[vcl]}	MaxLink (C-lar[vcl]) (μ)	Max(C-lar[vcl])	*μ[C]	Max(Rt)
(a) ☞ [viː$_{μ1μ2}$l$_a$ɒh]			*		*?
(b) [viː$_{μ1μ2}$l$^h_{a,b}$ɒh]	*!	*			*
(c) ☞ [vi$_{μ1}$l$_{a,bμ3}$ɒh]			*		*?
(d) [vi$_{μ1}$l$^h_{a,bμ3}$ɒh]	*!				*

Interestingly, stems ending in [h] present (across-speaker) variation in terms of vowel shortening. In terms of the current proposal this could be explained by a difference in whether C-lar[vcl] is allowed to dock vacuously to the [h]: see Wolf (2005, 2007b) for a discussion of constraints against vacuous association. If the constraint against vacuous docking is dominated by Max(Rt), then the feature can associate to stem-final consonant, bringing the mora with it and leading to shortening. However, if the constraint against vacuous docking prevents the surfacing of C-lar[vcl], the choice is passed on to the ranking in (187), which can produce both outcomes.

In general, however, moraic [h] seems to be dispreferred. In some cases, [h] does show the expected behaviour with shortening, as in [ˈbrahɒh] ~ [ˈbraːɒh] from [ˈbraː] 'beautiful'. In other cases, however, it is deleted entirely, whilst Max-μ compels the transfer of the mora to the vowel, as in (188).

(188) Mora suffixation leading to lengthening: [kasˈtiːɒh] 'leaner'

/kasti$_{μ1}$ + h$_{μ2}$ɒh/	*h$_μ$	Max (C lar[vcl])	Max-μ	*μμ
(a) [ˈkasti$_{μ1}$ɒh]		*	*!	
(b) [ˈkasti$_{μ1}$h$_{μ2}$ɒh]	*!			**
(c) ☞ [ˈkastiː$_{μ1μ2}$ɒh]		*		**

11.2.2 Phonological provection

In addition to the definition of 'provection' given in the previous section, the term can also refer to the distributional restrictions on obstruent clusters. I argue here that this restriction may reflect the outcome of a phonological process, giving further insight into the behaviour of laryngeal features.

11.2.2.1 Data

Obstruent sequences (in practice limited to two obstruents because of restrictions on syllable structure) are almost exclusively voiceless. Where stops are involved, there are just two exceptions: ⟦ɛgˈzamin⟧ 'examination' and ⟦ˌpazˈglãːn⟧ 'woolwork needle'. The first one appears to be a French borrowing, which means it is not necessarily indicative of the restrictions in the core vocabulary (it is also definitely monomorphemic, and so may be the locus of exceptions). The status of the second one is less clear. If it is not another exception, it could represent surface-phonological [ˌpazəˈglãːn] with phonetic dropping of the [ə] in the trough position. This is suggested by the form *pase-gloan* recorded by dictionaries (Favereau 1997; Hemon and Huon 2005). Alternatively, it may be a loose compound where the elements are treated as separate phonological words (see section 11.2.2.3). Under this interpretation, the ⟦z⟧ is word-final and is voiced via sandhi; phonologically the word might be [paːz̥ glãːn]. This suggestion can be supported by the cognate in the Plougrescant dialect, which Le Dû (2012 s. v. *gloan*) records as [paːz glãːn]: since Plougrescant Breton puts the same restrictions on syllable size as Bothoa Breton, the lack of vowel shortening in [paːz] before a cluster indicates that in the Plougrescant form the final consonant is word-final and thus extrametrical.

The best evidence for an active restriction on consonant sequences in Bothoa Breton comes from closely knit compounds, as seen in (189). According to Humphreys (1995: 202), these forms are 'tightly connected syntagms which could be considered compounds in the making'.[6] In many cases, they contrast with 'free' sequences of the same roots.

(189) Tightly knit compounds
    (a) /kaːz/   *kazh*   'cat'
    (b) [o ˌhasˈpjan]   *ur c'hazh-bihan*   'kitten'
    (c) [o ˈhaːz bjan]   *ur c'hazh bihan*   'a small cat'
    (d) /hweːz/   *c'hwezh*   'smell (n.)'
    (e) [ˈval]   *fall*   'bad'
    (f) [ˌhwesˈfal]   *c'hwezh-fall*   'stink'

Importantly, long vowels are shortened before consonant sequences that undergo provection, but not before those that are realised with voicing. The latter behaviour is characteristic of external sandhi, whereas vowel shortening is due to the syllable size restrictions in force at the word level. Morphosyntactically, the status of 'provecting' stem concatenations as compounds seems to be confirmed by the fact that they can serve as bases for further derivations.

(190) Derivation from tightly knit compounds
    (a) [ˈliːvəd̪]   *lived*   'pale'
    (b) [ˈval]   *fall*   'bad'
    (c) [ˌliːvəˈfal]   *lived-fall*   'pale'
    (d) [ˌliːvəˈfalad̪]   *lived-fallaat*   'to pale'

Important evidence is found in affixation. A key piece of data is the suffix /-dər/, which forms abstract nouns. The voicing specification of its first consonant is seen following sonorants.

(191) The abstract noun suffix /-dər/
    (a) [ˈhiːr]   *hir*   'long'
    (b) [ˈhirdər]   *hirder*   'length'
    (c) [ˈtom]   *tomm*   'warm'
    (d) [ˈtomdər]   *tommder*   'warmth'

When suffixed to obstruent-final bases, the resulting consonant cluster is always voiceless.

(192) Provection of underlyingly voiceless obstruents
    (a) [ãnˈwɛːzo]   *annoazhañ*   'offend'
    (b) [ãnˈwɛstər]   *annoazder*   'humiliation'

The examples in (192) show that even two underlyingly voiced obstruents become voiceless when adjacent.[7] This is characteristic of other Breton varieties too, as discussed by Falc'hun (1938), Jackson (1967), and Press (1986). Crucially, in Bothoa Breton the phonetic realisation of laryngeal contrasts makes it clear that these sequences can be neither ⟨x, C-lar⟩ (which would make them voiced) nor ⟨x⟩. In particular, in the latter case the obstruents would be expected to demonstrate the characteristics of delaryngealisation which are found in word-final sequences, such as lack of release for stops. Since this does not happen in word-internal 'voiceless' sequences, I conclude that word-internal and word-final obstruent sequences are distinct, providing further evidence that final laryngeal neutralisation in Breton is not simple 'devoicing'.

11.2.2.2 Analysis: laryngeal similation
Languages where all obstruent clusters have uniform laryngeal specification are usually analysed as showing voicing assimilation (e.g. Lombardi 1995a; Wetzels and Mascaró 2001). In Breton, however, as we have seen, there is an additional restriction on sequences of voiced obstruents,

which are (almost) always devoiced. To emphasise that the appearance of voicelessness is not always due to its presence on one of the segments in underlying representation (as in assimilation), I adopt Jurgec's (2010) useful term 'similation'.

Accounting for this phenomenon is especially important in view of the present featural proposal. The ban on what appears to be the spreading of a voicing feature (cf. for instance Uffmann 2005) but not of a voiceless one seems more consistent with a theory where voicing is the marked pole of the contrast: the alternations could be accounted for by a markedness constraint against double association of [voice] but not the Laryngeal node. The existence of a markedness constraint singling out a particular structure usually requires this structure to be bigger than those satisfying the constraint (see section 5.3).

The realisation of these word-internal sequences shows that they must bear the C-lar[vcl] feature; hence, there is a subversion of the 'default' Breton markedness hierarchy (where 'voiceless' is more marked than 'voiced') in the context of double linkage, exactly as described in Chapter 5. Specifically, when assimilations force the appearance of a doubly linked C-laryngeal node, a [voiceless] feature is epenthesised to license this double linkage. The autosegmental mechanism is shown in (193).

(193) Laryngeal similation: /ānwɛːzdər/ → [ānˈwɛstər]

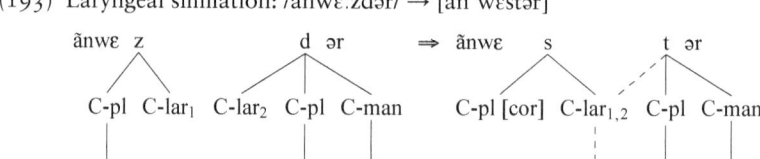

However, this process is blocked across certain boundaries. There are two productive obstruent-final prefixes in Bothoa Breton: the negative /diz-/ or /dis-/ and the repetitive /had-/. The latter provides almost no evidence for provection, because the behaviour of its final consonant is quite reminiscent of the behaviour of final [d] in external sandhi: it does not exert any influence on a following obstruent ([ˌhaˈdesko] 'relearn' (ad-deskiñ), from [ˈdesko] 'learn' (deskiñ)), and in fact normally disappears in preconsonantal position. When prefixed to another coronal stop, it can result in 'slight gemination', as in [[haˈtˑapo]] 'retake' (adtapout), again similar to external sandhi. The status of /had-/ as a separate (probably word-like) phonological domain is further suggested by the fact that it consistently bears (secondary) stress, despite consisting of just one light syllable. Tellingly, in the one (lexicalised) case where this prefix attracts main stress, the initial voiced obstruent also undergoes provection, which happens only inside the word-like domain: [ˈhatʃəʐ] 'once again' (ad-gwezh), from [ˈdʒøʐ] 'time, occasion' (gwezh),

Laryngeal phonology 181

indicating that this change of stress pattern involves the creation of a single word-level domain.

As for the prefixes /diz-/ and /dis-/, their behaviour is ambiguous. Their distribution is nearly complementary, but it cannot be derived from general principles of the phonology of the language. Since there is no intervocalic voicing in Bothoa Breton, the fact that /diz-/ appears prevocalically (as in [ˌdiˈzalve] 'place used to start opening something; keyhole', from [ˈalve] 'key') would seem to point to an underlying /z/. However, /dis-/ is found before [l] and [m] (but not [r]), and there does not seem to be a general restriction against the sequence [zl].[8]

In the context of provection, it is relevant that these prefixes (somewhat inconsistently) trigger lenition of the following verb stem (except in the case of [m]). In this case, the sequence [zv] can be created across the morpheme boundary.

(194) Lenition after prefixes
    (a) [ˈbaːdio]   *badeziñ*   'baptise'
    (b) [ˌdizˈvaːdio]   *divadeziñ*   'rename'
    (c) [ˈdzɥiːa̪d]   *gweañ*   'twist'
    (d) [ˌdizˌviːˈadən]   *disgweadenn*   'rotating, turning'

However, when lenition would normally be expected to create a voiced stop, it is blocked and the entire cluster is realised as a voiceless one.

(195) Lenition apparently blocked with voiceless stops
    (a) [ˈpako]   *pakañ*   'to pack'
    (b) [ˌdisˈpako]   *dispakañ*   'to unpack'
    (c) *[ˌdizˈbako]
    (d) [ˈkargo]   *kargañ*   'to load'
    (e) [ˌdisˈkargo]   *diskargañ*   'to unload'
    (f) *[ˌdizˈgargo]

At first blush, this seems paradoxical: the same boundary blocks similation when the second consonant is a voiced obstruent but not when it is voiceless. Spreading of C-lar[vcl] is in fact allowed across the prefix–stem boundary: [z] in the prefix /diz-/ is devoiced by following C-lar[vcl] fricatives (in practice this is only [h]): [ˌdishãˈnaː] 'unknown' ([hãˈnaːo] 'know') and [[ˌdiˈʃɒːl]] 'sunset', phonological [ˌdisˈhjɒːl] (cf. [hjɒːl] 'sun').

This paradox can be resolved thanks to feature geometry and the distinction between nodes and features. In the case of [ˌdizˈvaːdio], the similation constraint requires the sharing of C-laryngeal *nodes*, which the boundary blocks.

182   *A Substance-free Framework for Phonology*

(196) No spreading across a prefix-stem boundary

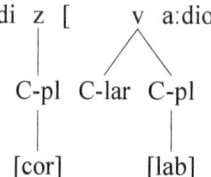

In the case of C-lar[vcl], it is the *feature* that spreads across the boundary rather than the node, and the requirement to spread the feature outranks the constraint that prohibits spreading across the boundary. Importantly, spreading requires the correct autosegmental domain, i.e. the two adjacent segments should both have a C-lar node. This could be problematic in light of the proposal that Bothoa Breton has coda delaryngealisation: since not all sequences straddling the prefix–stem boundary are licit onsets, one might expect the [z] in (196) to be delaryngealised.

I suggest that the answer is connected with the fact that the prefix /diz-/ triggers lenition. As I show in section 11.3.3, the trigger of lenition is a floating C-lar node. This node docks to the prefix-final obstruent, 'undoing' the effect of delaryngealisation; the specific context of this process is explored in the following section.

The same mechanism is responsible for the 'failure' of lenition seen when /diz-/ is prefixed to voiceless stops: the docking of the C-laryngeal node to the preceding segment creates the domain for [voiceless] spreading, as shown in (197).

(197) Spreading of [voiceless] across the prefix–stem boundary

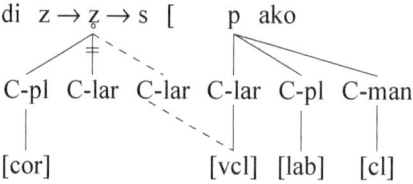

The ability of [vcl] to straddle a boundary to the exclusion of C-lar further confirms the fact that the former is structurally larger, and thus more marked, than the latter.

11.2.2.3 Boundary effects in provection

Provection, understood as sharing of a *C-laryngeal* specification, is allowed in compounds (or pseudo-compounds) such as [ˌkasˈpjan] 'kitten' but prohibited across a prefix–stem boundary (as in [ˌdizˈvaːdio]) 'rename'. On the other hand, the latter context does allow the spreading of the *feature* C-lar[vcl] if the correct domain is in place (as in

[ˌdisˈpako]) 'unpack'. The distinction between (pseudo-)compounds such as [ˌkasˈpjan], which pattern with unprefixed words in allowing provection, and prefixed forms such as [ˌdizˌviːˈadən], where provection is blocked, is somewhat problematic if we assume that the domain restrictions on provection were formulated in terms of prosodic constituency.

It might be reasonable to see the compounds as being formed of two (minimal) prosodic words, especially given examples such as [ˌkasˈpjan] with two stresses on light syllables. As we saw in section 8.2, stress on light syllables that does not obviously optimise rhythm usually emerges from high ranking of faithfulness to foot structure at the stem level.

I will assume the following analysis of compounds such as [ˌkasˈpjan]. The roots $\sqrt{kaːz}$ and $\sqrt{bjan}$ are prosodified in the course of root-to-stem derivation. (It is not clear whether prosodification at this level involves only foot structure or the construction of prosodic words as well.) The compounding itself triggers a second stem-level cycle, which takes as input the prosodified stems [(ˈkaːz)$_{Ft}$] and [(ˈbjan)$_{Ft}$], preserves the stresses but enforces unfaithful mappings, in particular provection and vowel shortening. If initial prosodification involves the construction of prosodic words, the second stem-level cycle might construct recursive prosodic words (in which case provection involves spreading across a minimal projection boundary) or it might simply leave the foot as the highest level of the prosodic hierarchy, for prosodic words to be built later.

Deciding whether the stem level derivation builds phonological words or only feet requires reference to many factors which I cannot discuss in detail here. The answer largely hinges not so much on provection as on the treatment of the final consonant of the first stem (here, /z/). In [ˈkaːẓ] 'cat', it is extrametrical, i.e. adjoined to the prosodic word node, but in [ˌkasˈpjan] this is clearly not so: the [s] must be adjoined to the nuclear mora. This could be either because extrametricality is only available for maximal projections of prosodic words, or because there is no prosodic word node at the first cycle and [z] is simply permitted to remain unparsed at the stem level, being adjoined to a mora later on.

(198) Adjunction to a recursive prosodic word at the stem level

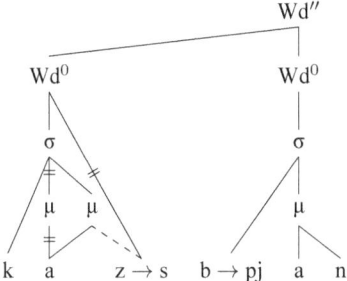

(199) Unparsed consonant, no recursion of prosodic words at the stem level

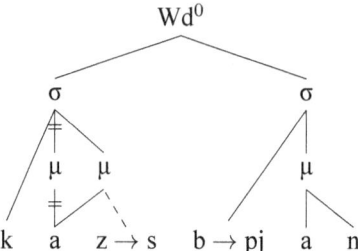

For concreteness, I will assume that provection in forms such as [ˌkasˈpjan] does not involve crossing a Wd⁰ boundary, because prosodic words are only built at the word level; this corresponds to the option shown in (199).

There is some morphosyntactic evidence that (pseudo-)compounds such as [ˌkasˈpjan] are stems, and hence that they undergo stem-level phonology. For instance, the morphosyntactic idiosyncrasies of the compound elements are invisible to inflectional categories: the comparative of [ˌmahaˈmaːɖ] 'cheap' is [ˌmahaˈmatɒh], even though the comparative of [ˈmaːɖ] 'good', which is the second part of the compound, is [ˈdʒɥɛlɒh]; this suggests that the compound stem is already unanalysable at the word level. Also, as noted above, these compounds can serve as inputs to what are clearly stem-building operations, as in the part-of-speech-changing derivation of [ˌliːvəˈfalaɖ] 'to pale' from the compound [ˌliːvəˈfal] 'pale'.

As for prefixed forms such as [ˌdizˈvaːdio] 'rename', I suggest for them the structure sketched in (200). Here, the (lexically stressed, i.e. foot-projecting) prefix /diz-/ is adjoined to a minimal projection of the prosodic word, with the result that the two adjacent obstruents cannot share a C-laryngeal specification, since they do not belong to the same minimal projection of a prosodic word node. Thus, the distinction between provection in [ˌkasˈpjan] and its lack in [ˌdizˈvaːdio] lies in the fact that in the former the construction of a prosodic word follows provection, whereas in the latter prosodic words boundaries are in place by the time the context for provection arises, thereby blocking it.

(200) Foot adjunction at the word level

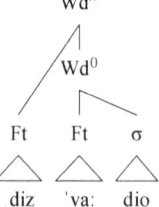

A final issue here is the surfacing of the floating C-lar node in the coda of /diz-/, which seems at odds with the analysis in section 11.1, which predicts codas to be unspecified for C-lar. However, this conundrum can be resolved in a stratal framework. Specifically, the analysis in (200) requires /diz-/ to be a word-level prefix. As discussed in section 8.1 with reference to stress, word-level morphemes undergo a cycle of stem-level computation before they enter the word-level computation. Given the syllabic analysis of final neutralisation in section 11.1, we expect the output of this stem-level cycle to be ['diẓ]. This output is fed into the word level, where it is concatenated with a floating C-lar node, normally expected to cause lenition of a following voiceless stop. As I argue in section 11.3.3.4, the surfacing of this floating node is driven by *FLOAT, a straightforward augmentation constraint requiring that class nodes be associated with root nodes.[9] In this case, it is always associated to the left, because the stem-level phonology provides it with a landing site that does not already bear a C-laryngeal node.

Crucially, we only need to consider the case of delaryngealised obstruents to the left of the floating node. The rich base certainly provides inputs where docking to the left would also create violations of UNIFORMITY, in which case the outcome would probably have been different from that observed in the language; however, there is a principled reason why such inputs are not found in actual forms: the stratal model predicts that only the input with a preceding delaryngealised obstruent is a possible one: all final consonants in such prefixes will have lost their C-lar specification at the stem level.

11.2.2.4 OT analysis

To analyse laryngeal similation, two kinds of unfaithful mappings must be accounted for. In the case of assimilation, as with the prefix /diz-/, some constraint must be invoked to account for the leftward spreading of C-lar[vcl] across the prefix–stem boundary. For the sake of concreteness, I shall use the non-committal formulation SHARE(C-lar), which requires that a C-lar specification be shared by two adjacent segments. In the model-theoretic framework used here, the constraint can be expressed as shown in (201).

(201) |SHARE(C-lar)|:= ($output \wedge Root \wedge \langle\downarrow\rangle i \wedge @_i C\text{-}lar \wedge \langle r\rangle j \rightarrow @_j \langle\downarrow\rangle i$)

'If a segment dominates a C-lar node i, then the adjacent segment to its right also dominates i'

This constraint is opposed by the markedness constraint *DOUBLE(C-lar), which penalises instances of C-lar linked to more than one root node.

(202) |*Double(C-lar)|:= (output ∧ C - lar ∧ ⟨↑⟩i ∧ ⟨↑⟩j) → @$_i$ j

'If a C-laryngeal is dominated by a node *i* and by a node *j*, then *i* and *j* are the same node'

Another constraint is needed to make sure that C-lar[vcl] specification is associated with obstruent clusters even when neither of the obstruents is underlyingly specified as C-lar[vcl]. To achieve this, I suggest the licensing constraint that targets doubly linked C-lar nodes in (203).

(203) HAVE([vcl])/Double:=(output ∧ C-lar ∧ ⟨↑⟩i ∧ ⟨↑⟩j ∧ @$_i$ ¬ j) → ⟨↓⟩ [voiceless]

'If a C-lar node is dominated by two different nodes, then it dominates an instance of [voiceless]'

This constraint may be compared to the constraint MULTILINK, used by Ringen (1999) and van Oostendorp (2003) to account for the fact that in Icelandic and Dutch respectively [spread glottis] (in certain contexts) can only appear when it is doubly linked. If this constraint together with the pro-assimilation SHARE dominates faithfulness constraints, then provection can be accounted for as shown in (204).

(204) The simple case of provection: [ãn'wɛstər] 'humiliation'

/ãnwɛ:zdər/		ALIGN-L (σ, C-lar)	SHARE (C-lar)	HAVE([vcl])/ Double)	*C-lar	DEP (C-lar[vcl])
(a)	[ãn'wɛ(z)$_{C-lar}$(d)$_{C-lar}$ər]		*!		**	
(b)	[ãn'wɛʑ.(d)$_{C-lar}$ər]		*!		*	
(c)	[ãn'wɛ(z.d)$_{C-lar}$ər]			*!	*	
(d)	[ãn'wɛʑ.ɖər]	*!				
(e) ☞	[ãn'wɛ(s.t)$_{C-lar}$ər]				*	*

The same ranking accounts straightforwardly for what looks like assimilation to C-lar[vcl], as in ['zɛhtər] 'dryness'.

For more complex cases, the set of constraints used in (204) must be supplemented with constraints regulating the spreading of C-laryngeal and C-laryngeal[voiceless] across various prosodic boundaries. These are often formulated in terms of CRISP EDGE constraints (e.g. Noske 1997; D'Imperio and Rosenthall 1999; Itô and Mester 1999), stating that certain domain boundaries should not be crossed by multiple-association lines. A less direct alternative is proposed by Bickmore (2000), who suggests formalising CRISP EDGE by requiring that two elements sharing some specification should also belong to the same higher-order prosodic constituent. Finally, these constraints may not be separate from those driving assimilation, if assimilation is due to alignment constraints which only require that a featural domain stretch to the edge of the relevant prosodic constituent (e.g. Jurgec 2010). For concreteness, I use the second approach, with a constraint schema CONTAIN([F])(Domain).

(205) |CONTAIN([F])(Domain)|:= (output ∧ [F] ∧ ⟨↑⟩i ∧ ⟨↑⟩j ∧ @$_i$ Root ∧ @$_j$ Root ∧ @$_i$ ¬j ∧ @$_i$ ⟨↑⟩k ∧ @$_k$ Domain) → @$_j$ ⟨↑⟩k

'If nodes i and j share a featural specification [F], they belong to the same prosodic domain k'

I suggest that such constraints can only refer to *prosodic* domains rather than morphosyntactic ones, for reasons of modularity. This means that any blocking of spreading by morphosyntactic boundaries should be mediated by prosodic constituents, stratal considerations, or both (Bermúdez-Otero and Luís 2009). As Bermúdez-Otero (2012) emphasises, the evaluation of such hypotheses requires attention not just to the phonological details but also to the morphosyntactic repercussions. Given the relatively meagre amount of available data, I will not discuss the analysis in depth. Nevertheless, some progress towards an analysis can be made. The ranking which blocks provection in this case is shown in (206).

(206) No provection across a Wd⁰ boundary

/diz(va:dio)$_{Wd}$/	SHARE (C-lar [vcl])	CONTAIN (C-lar) (Wd⁰)	CONTAIN (C-lar[vcl]) (Wd⁰)	SHARE (C-lar)
(a) ☞ Wd″ / Ft Wd⁰ / ˌdiz 'va:dio / C-lar C-lar				*
(b) Wd″ / Ft Wd⁰ / ˌdis 'faːdio / C-lar C-lar / [vcl]		*!	*	

In the prosodically identical case of [ˌdisˈpako] 'unpack', C-lar[vcl] is able to spread across a Wd⁰ boundary, because there is no conflict with CONTAIN(C-lar)(Wd⁰). The ranking is shown in (207).

(207) C-lar[vcl] assimilation across a Wd⁰ boundary

/diz + C-lar + (pako)_wd/	SHARE (C-lar [vcl])	CONTAIN (C-lar) (Wd⁰)	CONTAIN (C-lar[vcl]) (Wd⁰)	SHARE (C-lar)
(a) [structure: Wd″ → Ft, Wd⁰; ˌdiz ˈpako; C-lar C-lar; [vcl]]	*!			*
(b) [structure: Wd″ → Ft, Wd⁰; ˌdis ˈpako; C-lar⇠C-lar; [vcl]]		*!	*	
(c) ☞ [structure: Wd″ → Ft, Wd⁰; ˌdis ˈpako; C-lar C-lar; [vcl]]			*	*

To conclude, the behaviour of obstruent clusters in terms of their laryngeal specifications is heterogeneous. On the surface, at the word level, most of them share a C-lar[vcl] specification, but this behaviour has two sources. First, 'provection' may involve the sharing of a C-laryngeal node, which bears a [voiceless] feature to license this sharing. Second, a small number of cases involve the spreading of a [voiceless] feature across more than one C-laryngeal node. Crucially, the two processes interact differently with prosodic constituency: C-lar sharing cannot straddle the boundary of a minimal prosodic word, whilst [voiceless] sharing is allowed to do so. This behaviour emerges from the structural relationships between the two specifications:

C-laryngeal sharing implies sharing of [voiceless], whilst [voiceless] sharing does not imply sharing of C-laryngeal. This asymmetry provides further evidence for the central proposal of this chapter – that 'voiceless' obstruents in Bothoa Breton are structurally larger ('more marked') than voiced ones.

11.3 Initial consonant mutations

In traditional terminology (followed by Humphreys 1995), Bothoa Breton exhibits four types of consonant mutation: spirantisation, provection, lenition, and 'lenition-and-provection' ('mixed mutation'). Here I chiefly consider the phonological aspects of these alternations, although some discussion of morphosyntax is unavoidable.

11.3.1 Spirantisation

As the label implies, this mutation turns (voiceless) stops and affricates into fricatives, with additional voicing in the case of [t] and [p] and further modifications depending on the following segment. The changes are summarised in Table 11.1.

Table 11.1 The spirantisation mutation in Bothoa Breton

Process	Voicing		Fission		Spirantisation			
Unmutated	p	t	tʃ {ɛ, ø, a}	k	tʃ {i, y}	tʃɥ	kl	kr	kw
Spirantised, phonological	v	z	hj	h	h	hɥ	hl	hr	hw
Spirantised, phonetic	⟦v⟧	⟦z⟧	⟦ç⟧	⟦h⟧	⟦h⟧	⟦ɥ̊⟧	⟦l̥⟧	⟦r̥⟧	⟦w̥⟧

When segments that mutate to [h] before a vowel ([k] and [tʃ]) precede a sonorant in an unmutated form, the result is a voiceless sonorant, identical to that produced in the provection mutation.

(208) Spirantisation and provection
 (a) [ˈlɛːrənəw] *lerennoù* 'belts'
 (b) [ˈklɛːrənəw] *klerennoù* 'crosspieces'
 (c) ⟦o ˈl̥ɛːrənəw⟧ *ho lerennoù* 'your belts' (provection)
 (d) ⟦o ˈl̥ɛːrənəw⟧ *ho c'hlerennoù* 'their crosspieces' (spirantisation)

As discussed in Chapter 10, some unmutated instances of [tʃ] alternate with [hj] rather than [h], which is explained by spirantisation pre-empting coalescence at the word level; the phonological rationale of this is assimilated to that of the spirantisation of [k].

Spirantisation is triggered by a small set of proclitics, which never attach to verbs: [mə] 'my', [om] 'our', [o] 'their', and [i] 'her'.

Moreover, spirantisation is also caused by the definite and indefinite articles for words beginning with [k] and [tʃ] (and only these segments) in contexts where lenition is inapplicable (i.e. masculine singular, masculine plural inanimate, and feminine plural nouns).

(209) Spirantisation after the article
 (a) [ˈkaːz̺] *kazh* 'cat'
 (b) [ə ˈhaːz̺] *ar c'hazh* 'the cat'
 (c) [ˈtʃiːdʒi] *kegi* 'roosters'
 (d) [ə ˈhiːdʒi] *ar c'hegi* 'the roosters'

11.3.1.1 Analysis

I suggest that the traditional 'spirantisation' mutation is best analysed as consisting of two separate processes triggered in different contexts; I call them 'restricted' and 'full' spirantisation (cf. Timm 1985). As I discuss in this section (see also Iosad 2014), there is both phonological and morphosyntactic evidence to see the two processes as separate phenomena.

Restricted spirantisation refers to the mutation of [k] and [tʃ] following articles in certain morphosyntactic contexts. Within the featural system, it is analysable as the subtraction of the C-manner node. In the case of [k], deletion of the C-manner node is everything that is required.

We also need to analyse the spirantisation of [tʃ] to [h] before front vowels. Recall that in section 10.1.1 I considered the spreading of V-pl[cor] from nuclei to happen at the stem level. This means that when the spirantisation autosegment first becomes concatenated with the stop – at the word level – it is concatenated with a [tʃ]. In this case, the removal of the manner node creates an illicit segment, which is repaired by delinking of V-pl[cor].

(210) Restricted spirantisation as subtraction

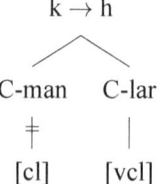

Laryngeal phonology 191

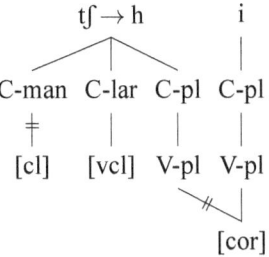

As discussed in section 4.2.6, I generally analyse subtraction as the coalescence of a floating node with an existing node. Thanks to the high rank of DEPLINK, this coalescence triggers the deletion of a feature attached to the coalesced node. The autosegmental mechanism is shown using [k] as an example; the pattern for [tʃ] is similar, except it also involves the deletion or delinking of V-pl[cor] due to feature co-occurrence constraints.

(211) Spirantisation of [k]: the coalescence mechanism

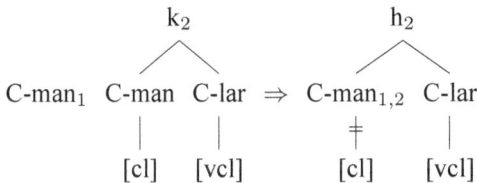

As discussed in section 10.2, the trigger of spirantisation must be present at the word level, since it 'sees' the contrast between [kj] and [tʃ] before it is obliterated by the word-level phonology. Therefore, despite being associated with the definite and indefinite article, the spirantisation trigger cannot be part of the lexical representation of the articles, as in that case it could only affect the initial consonant after word concatenation, i.e. in the postlexical phonology. Therefore, I suggest that the floating C-manner feature shown in (211) is associated with agreement for the feature DEFINITE, as well as for gender and number.

This agreement morpheme is inserted in certain contexts by input subcategorisation (Paster 2006; Bye 2007; Yu 2007), which also explains why segments other than [k] and [tʃ] are unaffected by restricted spirantisation: the mutation happens because the subcategorisation frame prevents the trigger from being inserted, as I discuss in more detail in Iosad (2014).

11.3.1.2 Full spirantisation

The term 'full spirantisation' refers to the entire gamut of changes shown in Table 11.1. It is triggered by an entirely different set of lexical items, namely by the possessive clitics ([mə] 'my', [om] 'our', [o] 'their', [i] 'her'). Interestingly, in the case of the former three it is also accompanied by a change from initial [hr] to [r].[10] However, a [hr] sequence *can* be created by the application of stop spirantisation to [k]; in other words, we are dealing with a chain shift.

(212) Chain shift in spirantisation
    (a) [ˈhrɔʃəd̥]   *roched*   'shirt'
    (b) [mə ˈrɔʃədəw]   *va rochedoù*   'my shirts'
    (c) [ˈkriːb̥]   *krib*   'comb'
    (d) [mə ˈhriːb̥]   *va c'hrib*   'my comb'

In the case of [p] and [t], spirantisation involves the removal of both C-manner[closed] and C-laryngeal[voiceless] specifications, which could be interpreted as shown in (213). Hereinafter I will use simple delinking to show subtraction in order to reduce clutter; the mechanism in all cases is the same as that in (210).

(213) Full spirantisation as subtraction

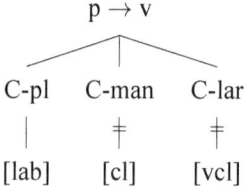

If the insertion of the mutation-triggering features is subject to subcategorisation requirements, as noted above, the fact that voiceless stops undergo spirantisation-cum-voicing but neither voiced stops nor voiceless fricatives undergo at least one part of this double process can be accounted for. The agreement morpheme which contains both the C-manner and C-laryngeal floating nodes only selects for segments that are *both* C-manner[closed] and C-laryngeal[voiceless]: hence, neither voiced stops nor voiceless fricatives undergo the mutation, since they are not concatenated with the right subsegmental material (Iosad 2014).

The proclitic [i] 'her' stands outside this system: unlike the other possessive proclitics treated here, it does not affect initial [hr]; in addition, as noted above, it prefixes [h] to vowels and sonorants (i.e. it has the form [ih], under the analysis in the following section). Thus, it is subject to very specific subcategorisation requirements, triggering a unique type of mutation that is similar but not identical to spirantisation; for a treatment of overlapping but distinct mutations as independent processes, cf. Ellis (1965). Still, the mechanisms involved are basically the same, so I do not discuss this lexical item further.

Although the same arguments regarding the word-level affiliation of the trigger apply in the case of full spirantisation (and in the case of the unnamed mutation caused by [i] 'her'), the agreeing features would have to be entirely different from those that need to be postulated for restricted spirantisation. All elements that trigger full spirantisation are possessive proclitics. Therefore, they represent possessive prefixes, with the noun agreeing with the determiner for number, gender, and person. Although it might seem uneconomical to postulate two different morphosyntactic processes with very similar phonological outcomes, the existence of this split can be sustained on independent grounds. Humphreys (1995) notes that restricted spirantisation ('spirantisation after the article') remains vital even in those dialects where other types of spirantisation are dying out (cf. also Hennessey 1990). If the proposal here is correct, then such dialects demonstrate obsolescence of possessive agreement but retain the agreement for definiteness and number.

11.3.2 Provection

A third use of the term 'provection' refers to a type of initial consonant mutation whereby all voiced segments (including sonorants) are devoiced, while vowels are prefixed with [h]. Voiceless obstruents and [hr] remain unaffected. The pattern of this mutation is shown in Table 11.2.

Provection is triggered for all the segments shown in Table 11.2 by the possessive proclitic [o] 'your (pl.)'. The proclitic [i] 'her', which triggers spirantisation of voiceless stops, also triggers the prefixation of [h] to vowels and the devoicing of sonorants. Examples of provection are shown in (214).

(214) Examples of the provection mutation
    (a) ['maːb̥]   *mab*   'son'
    (b) [o 'hmaːb̥]   *ho mab*   'your (pl.) son'
    (c) ['alve]   *alc'houez*   'key'
    (d) [o 'halve]   *hoc'h alc'houez*   'your (pl.) key'
    (e) ['brøːr]   *breur*   'brother'
    (f) [o 'prøːr]   *ho preur*   'your (pl.) brother'

11.3.2.1 Analysis: stops

A simple analysis of this pattern can be provided if the relevant clitics morphemes simply end in a [h] segment, which consists of just the C-laryngeal[voiceless] feature. Since nothing prevents the [h] from appearing before vowels, it is prefixed in this position. When it appears before an obstruent, it coalesces with the following segment; since all voiced obstruents have a C-laryngeal[voiceless] counterpart, devoicing is exactly the predicted outcome.

Table 11.2 The provection mutation in Bothoa Breton

	Devoicing									Prefixation of [h]				
Unmutated	b	d	dʒ	dʒɥ	g	gw	v	z	ʒ	V	j	w	l	m	n
Provected, phonetic	[p]	[t]	[tʃ]	[tʃɥ]	[k]	[kw]	[f]	[s]	[ʃ]	[hV]	[ç]	[w̥]	[l̥]	[m̥]	[n̥]
Provected, phonological	p	t	tʃ	tʃɥ	k	kw	f	s	ʃ	hV	hj	hw	hl	hm	hn

(215) Devoicing of obstruents by provection

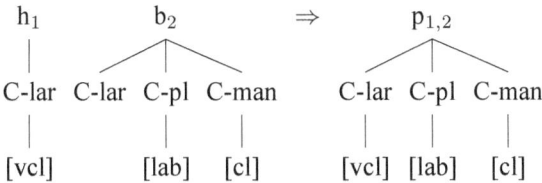

This behaviour of [h] contrasts with its patterning word-internally, where there is no coalescence in cases such as [ˈzɛħtər] 'dryness'. This difference can be accounted for via a distinction between the word level and the postlexical level. If the mutation trigger has the form /oh/, the mutation cannot happen before the postlexical level, because the conditions for it only arise following the concatenation of the target and the trigger. Then we can simply leverage the fact that C-lar[vcl] is dispreferred in non-syllable-initial positions, and rank the anti-coalescence constraint UNIFORMITY low enough. For the sake of the argument, I assume that the relevant constraint is *C-lar: coalescence is deployed to remove a violation of this constraint that is not neutralised by the higher-ranking ALIGN-L(σ, C-lar).

(216) Reranking of UNIFORMITY at the postlexical level: [ˈzɛħtər] 'dryness', [o ˈprøːr] 'your brother'

			UNIF$_{word}$	MAX (Seg)	*C-lar	UNIF$_{postlexical}$	Max(C-lar[vcl])
/zɛːh₁d₂ər/	(a)	☞ [ˈzɛh₁t₂ər]			***		
	(b)	[ˈzɛːt₁,₂ər]	*!		**		
	(c)	[ˈzɛːd₁,₂ər]	*!		**		*
	(d)	[ˈzɛːd₂ər]		*!	**		*
/oh₁ b₂røːr/	(e)	[oh₁ ˈp₂røːr]			**!		
	(f)	☞ [o ˈp₁,₂røːr]			*	*	
	(g)	[o ˈb₁,₂røːr]			*	*	*!
	(h)	[o ˈb₂røːr]	*!	*		*	

An unanswered question is why the coda [h] produced at the word level in [ˈzɛħtər] does not coalesce with the following [t] postlexically. The difference between the [h] in [oh] and the [h] in [ˈzɛħtər] at the postlexical level lies in their prosodic status in the input: since the latter is parsed into several layers of prosodic structure in the output of the word level, I assume it may be subject to faithfulness constraints that are not operative in the case of [oh] (which, being a clitic, is likely to not even be a prosodic word). Alternatively, the retention of the [h] in [ˈzɛħtər] has something to do with the fact that it forms part of a doubly linked structure (e.g. Hayes 1986; Kirchner 2000; Honeybone 2005b). For reasons of focus I leave this question for further research.

Finally, provection exemplifies Preservation of the Marked. Below we shall see that the ranking at the postlexical level requires that DEPLINK(C-lar)([vcl]) must outrank MAX([vcl]), because that ranking is required to effect the voicing that is part of the lenition mutation. The coalescence shown in (215) also violates DEPLINK(C-lar)([vcl]), so some other factor must make it possible. I suggest that the crucial constraint is MAXLINK(Rt)(C-lar[vcl]), which is inactive in the case of floating manner nodes, but preserves the link between a root node and the C-lar[vcl] feature when that link is present in the input, as in the case of [h]. Once again, structures that are bigger have the advantage of being able to be singled out by faithfulness constraints.

11.3.2.2 The status of voiceless sonorants

Humphreys (1972, 1995) analyses voiceless sonorants as tautosyllabic clusters consisting of a [h] and the relevant sonorant, and I follow this analysis here. He adduces two phonological arguments. First, such a treatment allows a unified treatment of provection as prefixation of [h] in both [o hmaːb̥] 'your son' and [o ˈhalve] 'your key'. Admittedly, this argument is not conclusive, since an alternative analysis, where voiceless sonorants are unitary phonemes, instead allows a unified analysis of provection for both obstruents and sonorants as coalescence.

Second, Humphreys (1995) draws attention to the fact that voiceless sonorants produced by provection are identical to those produced by spirantisation of [k] before a sonorant.[11] Here, the single-segment approach would require additional machinery to enforce coalescence.

Another relatively robust argument for the treatment of 'voiceless sonorants' as complex clusters lies in the existence of the (phonetic) segment [ɥ̥]: as discussed in section 10.2.3, the segment [ɥ] is only licensed in complex onsets, and alternates with [v] when a complex onset cannot be built. The fact that the sequence [tʃɥ] undergoes spirantisation to [hɥ] and not [f] might be taken as evidence for the status of the initial [hɥ] as a complex onset rather than as a unitary phoneme.

The onset-cluster analysis faces one potential problem. Initial mutations are able to single out the cluster/segment [hr]/[r̥], treating it differently from [h]; this type of non-local look-ahead could be theoretically problematic. Nevertheless, on balance the 'cluster' approach is simpler than the single-segment analysis, so I adopt the former here.

11.3.2.3 Sonorant provection: analysis

Once we accept that the 'voiceless sonorants' are onset clusters with [h], we can understand the reason for the resyllabification. If sonorants never bear a C-laryngeal node on the surface, parsing the [h] into the onset does not help with violations of the *C-lar constraint. I propose that resyllabification here is a strategy to satisfy ALIGN-L(σ, C-lar). The ranking is not different from that established at the word level.

(217) Provection as onset enhancement: [o ˈhmaːb̥] 'your son'

	/oh maːb̥/	ALIGN-L(σ, C-lar)	*C-lar	*COMPLEX ONSET	MAX (C-lar[vcl])	MAX(Seg)
(a)	[o .maːb̥]	*!			*	*
(b)	[oh .maːb̥]	*!	*			
(c) ☞	[o .hmaːb̥]		*	*		

As with the obstruents, the question is why [h.C] sequences persist outside mutation contexts. First, the answer might be the same to that eventually found for obstruents. Second, [h.C] sequences with sonorants are in fact very rare: according to Humphreys (1995: 173), they are found only in the word [dæhˈmaːd̥] 'always' and as allegro variants of the sequences '[s] + sonorant', themselves found only across a prefix–stem boundary. As we have seen, prefixes retain a degree of prosodic autonomy, which may prevent coalescence.[12]

11.3.2.4 The status of [hr]

The status of the voiceless sonorant [r̥] merits some more discussion. Together with [ç] and [w̥] (i.e. [hj] and [hw], which can be derived from underlying forms with unobjectionable /hi/ and /hu/ sequences), and unlike all other voiceless sonorants, it can be initial in unmutated words. In fact, initial [r] is completely excluded from word-initial position (*modulo* mutations), and only [r̥] is permitted. Similar developments are historically characteristic of Welsh, as well as many south-eastern Breton dialects, e.g. that of Grand-Lorient (Cheveau 2007). If this is a synchronic fact about Bothoa Breton phonology, it seems to require a fairly ad hoc constraint against word-initial [r] (which, however, has good phonetic motivation; Solé 2002), probably defeating a DEP constraint against insertion of root nodes. Alternatively, however, we could assume that this represents the addition of a C-lar[vcl] feature to [r] rather than insertion of a new segment, creating a unitary [r̥] – the only true voiceless sonorant in the system.

Moreover, as briefly discussed above, [r̥] exhibits special mutation behaviour which cannot be derived from the mutation behaviour of [h] alone, which also suggests that it may be a single segment, as otherwise these facts would require non-local reference in the choice of mutation allomorphs.

The problem with admitting [r̥] as a unitary segment lies in the fact that it breaks the parallelism between underived voiceless [r̥] as in [r̥ɔʃəd̥] 'shirt' and [r̥] as the outcome of spirantisation of [kr], as in [mə 'hri:b̥] 'my comb', which is clearly derived from a sequence of two root nodes (['kri:b̥] 'comb'). Of course, it might be the case that the neutralisation is not complete, in which case this is not a problem. However, if the two types of [r̥] are indeed the same phonological object, it appears additional computation is needed to enforce coalescence of [hr] to [r̥] in [mə 'r̥i:b̥], and neither possible motivation of coalescence discussed above is applicable in this case. An ad hoc constraint against [hr] onsets is possible, but not particularly insightful. I will therefore continue to treat [hr] as a cluster rather than a unitary segment.

11.3.3 Lenition

Lenition is by far the most productive mutation, appearing in the widest range of morphological contexts, and often said to be encroaching on the domain of other mutations (Hennessey 1990; Kennard and Lahiri forthcoming).

11.3.3.1 Data

The phonological rationale of lenition in shown in Table 11.3. It only affects obstruents, [m], and [hr]/[r̥].

Basically, voiced stops (and [tʃ]) undergo voicing in lenition contexts, as does [r̥]. The behaviour of voiced stops is heterogeneous: the labial stop (and [m], the only nasal to participate in mutation) is spirantised to [v]; the coronal stop (and the postalveolar affricate except before [ɥ]) is unaffected; and [g] is spirantised (losing its voice specification in the process) in most contexts but deleted before a [w]. In the sequence [dʒɥ], the affricate is deleted and the [ɥ] alternates with [v]. Other segments are unaffected.

Lenition is mostly triggered by specific lexical items.

(218) Lenition
[i] 'his'
(a) ['ti:]   ti   'house'
(b) [i 'di:]   e di   'his house'
    [də] 'to', [wa] 'on',
                      [diwa] 'from on'
(c) ['krɔiz̥]   kreiz   'middle'
(d) [wa ˌgrəiz an 'de:]   war greiz an dez   'in the open'

In some cases lenition is caused in concert by lexical and morphological factors; that is, certain lexical items trigger the mutation only in certain morphosyntactic contexts. Specifically, [o(n)] 'a(n)' and [ə(n)]

Table 11.3 The lenition mutation in Bothoa Breton

Process	Voicing				Spirantisation				Deletion				No change				
Unmutated	p	t	tʃ	k	r̥	b	m	g	gw	dʒɥ	d	dʒ	f	v	s	z	ʃ	ʒ	h	n
Lenited	b	d	dʒ	g	r	v	v	h	w	v	d	dʒ	f	v	s	z	ʃ	ʒ	h	n

'the' trigger lenition of feminine singular nouns; [oˈnōn] 'one' and [hāj] 'this' only trigger lenition if they refer to feminine singular nouns; and the definite article [ə(n)] triggers lenition of masculine plural animate nouns, unless they contain the suffix /-əw/.

11.3.3.2 Analysis

The changes involved in lenition can also be described as subtraction: voicing of voiceless stops and [hr] is represented as subtraction of a [voiceless] feature, while the spirantisation of stops and [m] represents deletion of C-manner features. As elsewhere in this chapter, I analyse this not as real subtraction but as the docking of a floating C-laryngeal *resp.* C-manner node with DEPLINK-driven deletion. As in the case of spirantisation, the different allomorphs of the mutation trigger are selected by a subcategorisation mechanism, depending on the consonant that follows.

The spirantisation of the voiced stop [b] is straightforwardly represented as the delinking of the C-man[cl] feature, with preservation of the C-laryngeal node and the place feature. In the case of [g], there is also a change in the laryngeal specification. I suggest this occurs because simple docking of the floating Manner node would otherwise create a featureless segment; this is repaired by epenthesising a [voiceless] feature on the Laryngeal node.

(219) Lenition of [b]

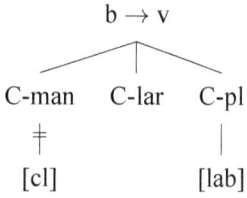

(220) Lenition of [g]

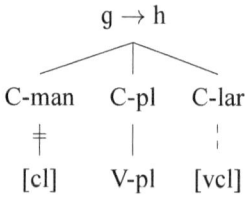

The ranking for the deletion of C-man[cl] in the case of [b] is similar to that discussed in section 4.2.6, so I do not show it here. The epenthesis of C-lar[vcl] in the case of [g] is shown in (221); this is another use for the constraint HAVE[F] prohibiting featureless segments.

Laryngeal phonology 201

(221) Epenthesis of C-lar[vcl] in lenition

	HAVE([F])	*DEP([vcl])	DEPLINK (C-lar)-[vcl]
g₂ ╱╲ C-man₁ C-man C-lar | [cl]			
(a) ☞ h₂ ╱╲ C-man₁,₂ C-lar | [vcl]		*	*
(b) ?₂ ╱╲ C-man₁,₂ C-lar	*!		

Note that this analysis does not hold before [gw]: rather than [hw], the result in this case is a [w]. This can be accounted for if [gw] is represented as a single segment bearing the feature V-place[labial]. The removal of the manner feature in this case does not create a featureless segment, but instead a V-pl[lab] segment. In addition, since the consonant is initially parsed as the onset, this segment retains this prosodic affiliation, and onset [u] is, as I argued in section 10.2.1, precisely ⟦w⟧.

(222) Lenition of [gw]

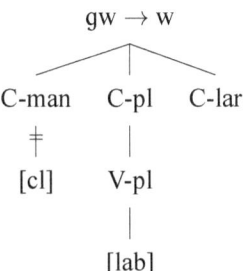

As for [dʒɥ], I suggest this segment cannot be a complex onset, since this would require lenition to operate non-locally, treating initial [dʒ] before a vowel differently from [dʒ] in a complex onset.[13] Instead, [dʒɥ]

202   *A Substance-free Framework for Phonology*

is a unitary segment {C-man[cl], C-pl[lab], V-pl[cor]}. The removal of the manner feature would normally produce the segment {C-pl[lab], V-pl[cor]}, which corresponds to [ɥ]. However, since [ɥ] is only licensed in complex onsets, the V-pl[cor] feature is also delinked, leaving just C-pl[lab], i.e. [v]: exactly the desired result.

(223) Lenition of [dʒɥ]

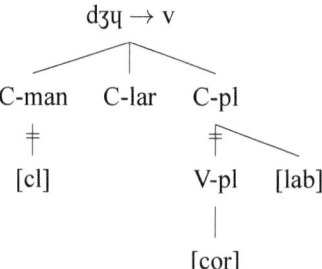

The basic ranking is shown in (224), although I do not expand on the nature of the constraint (or more likely ranking of multiple constraints) which prevents the appearance of the segment [ɥ] (but not its superset [dʒɥ]) as a simplex onset.

(224) Lenition of [dʒɥ]

C-man + {C-man[cl] C-pl[lab] V-pl[cor]}			Max(C-man)	*.ɥ	Max(C-pl[lab])	Max(V-pl[cor])	Max(C-man[cl])
(a)	{C-man[cl] C-pl[lab] V-pl[cor]}	[dʒɥ]	*!				
(b)	{C-pl[lab] V-pl[cor]}	[ɥ]		*!			
(c)	{C-man[cl] V-pl[cor]}	[dʒ]	*!				
(d)	{C-man[cl] C-pl[lab]}	[b]	*!			*	
(e) ☞	{C-pl[lab]}	[v]				*	*
(f)	{V-pl[cor]}	[i]		*!			*

The analysis of spirantisation in lenition as delinking of the manner node is directly applicable to nasals. Specifically, in the case of [m] delinking the C-manner node automatically leads to the deletion of all subsidiary nodes. The residue is precisely {C-pl[lab]}, corresponding to [v], as shown in (225). Note that if sonorants underlyingly lack a C-laryngeal node,

Laryngeal phonology 203

then this mutation should also involve the epenthesis of a C-lar node, forced by ALIGN-L(σ, C-lar) as discussed in section 11.1.3.2.

(225) Lenition of [m]

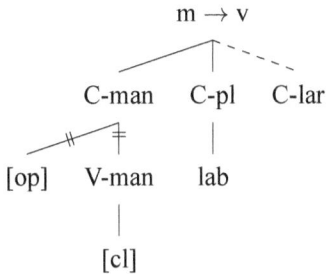

The voicing of stops is similarly analysed as the linking of a C-laryngeal node to a stop consonant to the exclusion of its underlying C-laryngeal specification, as shown in (226). The mechanics of the docking of C-lar are essentially the same, so I do not dwell on them further.

(226) Lenition of [p]

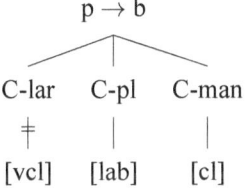

In all cases, this subtraction is achieved via the prefixation of a floating class node. As I demonstrate in the next section, postulating such a floating C-laryngeal node to account for subtraction of the [voiceless] feature has some highly desirable consequences.

11.3.3.3 The 'failure of lenition'

As discussed above, most of the time lenition is triggered by a combination of lexical and morphological factors. In one case, however, it also appears to interact with phonology. Specifically, feminine singular nouns and masculine plural animate nouns (these latter only if they contain the suffix /-əw/) also cause lenition of following adjectives, with an important exception: if the noun ends in any obstruent and the adjective starts with a voiceless stop (which would be expected to become voiced), the entire consonant sequence surfaces as voiceless. Lenition does happen if the adjective starts with a voiced stop (which undergoes spirantisation) or if the noun ends in a vowel or sonorant (in which case all adjectives may undergo mutation).

(227) Noun–adjective lenition
Sonorant + underlying voiceless obstruent: lenition (voicing of stops)
(a) [ˈpəwr]   *paour*   'poor'
(b) [ˈkoːz̥]   *kozh*   'old'
(c) [o ˌvroː ˈbəwr]   *ur vro baour*   'a poor country'
(d) [o ˌgaːdər ˈgoːz̥] *ur gador gozh* 'an old chair'

Obstruent + underlying voiceless obstruent: failure of lenition
(a) [o ˌrwek ˈpəwr]   *ur wreg paour* 'a poor woman'
     *[o ˌrweġ ˈbəwr]
(b) [on ˌiːlis ˈkoːz̥] *un iliz gozh*   'an old church'

Sonorant + underlying voiced obstruent: lenition (spirantisation of stops)
(a) [ˈbjan]   *bihan*   'small'
(b) [ˈdʒɥɛn]   *gwenn*   'white'
(c) [o ˌvroː ˈvjan] *ur vro vihan*   'a small country'
(d) [o ˌgaːdər ˈvɛn] *ur gador wenn* 'a white chair'

Obstruent + underlying voiced obstruent: lenition (spirantisation of stops)
(a) [o ˌrweg ˈvjan] *ur wreg vihan*   'a small woman'
(b) [on ˌiːliz ˈvɛn] *un iliz wenn*   'a white church'

At first blush, this is a problematic type of interaction between phonetics and phonology. Lenition, on the face of it, is at least partly morphologically conditioned, in that it appears to have access to proprietary morphosyntactic information such as the gender of the trigger or the presence of a particular allomorph of the plural suffix. At the same time its triggering seems to be sensitive to phonological information, namely the specification of the mutation target's initial consonant for manner and voicing. This seems to be an example of an interaction between modular components that is prohibited by the framework set out in Chapter 2.

In fact, however, this apparent failure of lenition receives a straightforward phonological analysis. As Jackson (1967: 350, n. 5) points out, the fact that the segmental restrictions in (227) only operate in noun–adjective syntagms is an accident. The correct generalisation is that lenition-as-voicing of stops fails after another obstruent: it simply happens to be the case that all closed-class triggers of lenition such as prepositions and articles are sonorant-final.

Once this is understood, the apparent failure of lenition for voiced but not voiceless stops can be analysed phonologically. The lenition of

Laryngeal phonology 205

voiced stops involves loss of a C-manner feature, and thus prefixation of a C-manner node. There are, as far as can be ascertained, no processes involving the interaction of C-manner nodes and a previous segment.

Lenition of voiceless stops, on the other hand, involves the subtraction of a C-laryngeal feature, and thus the prefixation of a C-laryngeal node. Thus, the expected sequence is 'noun + C-laryngeal + adjective'. Moreover, thanks to cyclicity, if the final consonant of the noun is an obstruent, it will invariably be delaryngealised, since the grammar described in section 11.1 is active at the word level. In these circumstances, the floating C-laryngeal node is able to spread leftwards to the delaryngealised obstruent, rather than rightwards to coalesce with the onset obstruent. Furthermore, the sequence of a C-laryngeal and a C-laryngeal[voiceless] obstruent is a domain for leftward spreading of [voiceless]. This is, in fact, exactly the same mechanism we encountered earlier in the analysis of lenition across a prefix–stem boundary.

(228) No lenition of voiceless stops after obstruents: [iːlis koːẓ] 'old church'

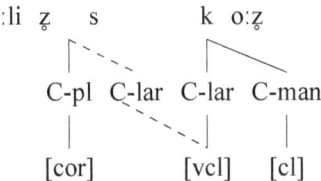

If the trigger (i.e. the noun) ends in a sonorant or a vowel, on the other hand, such leftward docking of C-laryngeal is impossible, because vowels and sonorants never bear a C-laryngeal specification, even a bare one.[14] Hence, C-laryngeal docks rightwards and produces lenition.

(229) Lenition of voiceless stops after sonorants: [kaːdər goːẓ] 'old chair'

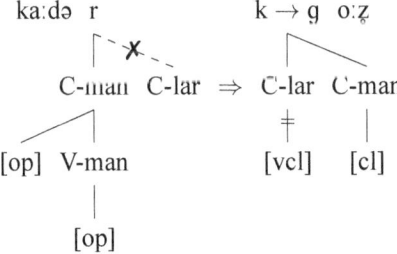

In the case of a voiced stop after an obstruent, the floating node is a C-manner node. These nodes obey a different phonological grammar, which always enforces docking to the right thanks to alignment requirements.

Hence, we find rightwards docking with delinking of the feature, irrespective of whether the preceding segment is mannerless or not.

(230) Lenition of voiced stops: [grweġ vjan] 'small woman'

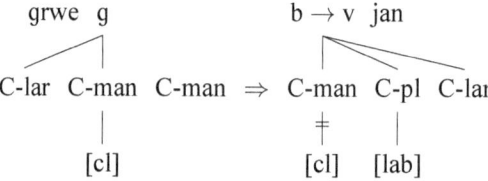

Thus, the phonological restrictions on lenition in noun–adjective syntagms do not require any cross-modular reference: the lenition trigger is always inserted in the right morphosyntactic circumstances, in a manner that is blind to the phonological context. The fact that it fails to exert a visible effect on the potential target is due solely to the workings of the phonological grammar, not to a phonologically driven lack of application.

11.3.3.4 OT analysis

I have discussed the OT aspects of subtraction above, so I do not dwell on them here. Nevertheless, we still require an analysis of directionality effects in lenition. These are as follows:

- Floating C-laryngeal can dock both leftwards and rightwards.
- Floating C-laryngeal docks leftwards if preceded by a delaryngealised obstruent and followed by a laryngeally specified one.
- Otherwise C-laryngeal docks rightwards.
- C-manner always docks rightwards.

This behaviour can be derived from the interaction of alignment constraints and constraints against coalescence. In the case of C-laryngeal, both leftward and rightward docking involve violation of DepLink(Root) (C-lar), but leftward docking makes it possible to avoid coalescence, i.e. violation of Uniformity. Leftward docking also means that the C-laryngeal associated to the word-final consonant is not aligned with the left edge of a word. The ranking in (231) demonstrates this.

(231) Lenition of voiceless stops

/iːliz$_1$ + C-lar$_2$ + k$_3$oːʑ/		Share (C-lar[vcl])	Max(C-lar)	DepLink(Rt, C-lar)	Uniformity
(a)	/iːliz$_1$ k$_3$oːʑ/		*!		
(b)	/iːliz$_1$ g$_{2,3}$oːʑ/			*	*!
(c)	/iːliz$_{1,2}$ k$_3$oːʑ/	*!		*	
(d) ☞	/iːlis$_{1,2}$ k$_3$oːʑ/			*	

In the case of C-manner, alignment constraints which require that C-manner nodes are aligned with the left edge of a word dominate both DEPLINK and UNIFORMITY, ensuring that a floating node lands in a word-initial position. This is seen in (232); constraints that dominate ALIGN-L to ensure that non-floating C-manner nodes do not 'drift' towards word-initial position to satisfy alignment are not shown.

(232) Lenition of voiced stops

/grweġ$_1$ + C-man$_2$ + b$_3$jan/		ALIGN-L (C-man, Wd)	MAX (C-man)	DEPLINK(Rt, C-man)	UNIFORMITY
(a)	[grweġ$_1$ b$_3$jan]		*!		
(b) ☞	[grweġ$_1$ v$_{2,3}$jan]			*	*
(c)	[grweh$_{1,2}$ b$_3$jan]	*!		*	*

11.3.3.5 Lexical insertion and the stratal affiliation of lenition

It is important to note that the 'devoicing' of the outcome of lenition, which we observe with voiceless stops, is not found when lenition itself does not involve laryngeal change: [on ˌiːliẓ ˈvɛn] 'a white church' from [ˈdʒɥɛn] 'white', rather than the logically possible *[on ˌiːlis ˈfɛn]. I suggest this shows that the choice between the C-laryngeal and C-manner allomorphs of the lenition-triggering autosegment happens at the point of lexical insertion.

If the floating C-laryngeal node were present in the input to the phonology before segments other than voiceless stops, nothing would prevent it from causing the same devoicing of initial voiced fricatives derived by lenition.[15] I assume for the sake of the argument that the mechanism here is input subcategorisation (Paster 2006; Bye 2007; Yu 2007). This point is arguable (e.g. Wolf 2008), but the bottom line is that only one lenition-triggering autosegment is chosen at the point of lexical insertion, depending on the initial segment of the mutation target. Thus, the chain shift involved in lenition does not fall within the purview of the phonological component. In addition, this type of allomorph selection can also explain the lack of lenition of segments such as [d], [dʒ], or [n].

Importantly, the C-laryngeal autosegment involved in lenition can interact with lexical items both to its right and to its left. This indicates that it must be inserted at the postlexical level. In terms of the stratal model, this makes an important prediction: lenition may never interact with word- and stem-level phonology. In this respect, it contrasts with restricted spirantisation, which happens at the word level and may disrupt normal word-level processes such as coalescence with onset [i] (so that 'his horses' is [i ˈhjɛzəġ] and not *[i ˈhɛzəġ] as would be expected given unmutated [tʃɛzəġ] and the /tʃ/ → [h] pattern of mutation). This explains why there is no evidence for underlying initial [g] rather than [dʒ] before front high vowels, as described in section 10.1.1.1: by the time lenition happens, both underlying /g/ and underlying /dʒ/ in this position have already been mapped to [dʒ], and even if some of the instances of [dʒ] were underlyingly /g/, this fact is no longer recoverable. Thus, the stratal model correctly predicts the impossibility of the unattested paradigm [ˈdʒiːr] 'word' ~ [i hiːr] 'his word' in Bothoa Breton.

11.3.4 Lenition-and-provection

Finally, we consider the so-called 'lenition-and-provection'; this broadly corresponds to the 'mixed mutation' of the written language (e.g. Kennard and Lahiri forthcoming). As the name suggests, the effects of this mutation are essentially the composition of lenition and provection: voiceless stops remain unaffected, while for [d(ʒ)], voiced fricatives, sonorants, and vowels the effect of lenition-and-provection is simply devoicing. In the case of voiced stops, however, lenition-and-provection consists of both spirantisation and devoicing; for [gw] and [dʒɥ], the outcome is the devoicing of the result of stop deletion. A summary is given in Table 11.4.

Lenition-and-provection is attested after the word [ma] 'if', as well as two verbal particles, which apparently do not have any other segmental content in this dialect.

(233) [∅]
   'particle used between a verb and any preverbal constituent except a subject or a direct object'
   [deska]   deska   '(s)he studies'
   ba   ˈdʒɥɛngãm   ∅   ˌteska   ˈmaːd̥
   ba   Gwengamp   e   teska   mad
   'He studies well in Guingamp'

I propose that lenition-and-provection in Bothoa Breton is best analysed as lenition triggered by [h]-final items, i.e. that 'if' is a lenition trigger which is underlyingly represented as /mah/ on the segmental level; similarly, the empty particles are actually lenition-triggering /h/ morphemes. Lenition applies as normal if it can (i.e. delinking C-manner features as appropriate), while [h] behaves exactly as it does in provection. No special mechanisms are needed to derive this mutation.

11.4 Ternary contrasts and markedness relations in Bothoa Breton laryngeal phonology

In this section I summarise the evidence for a surface ternary distinction in laryngeal specifications in Bothoa Breton. In this chapter, I have

Table 11.4 The lenition-and-provection mutation in Bothoa Breton

Process	No change			Devoicing				Deletion				Spirantisation				Prefixation of [h]						
Unmutated	p	t	tʃ	k	d	dʒ	v	z	ʒ	gw	dʒɥ	b	m	gw	V	w	j	l	n	m
Mutated	p	t	tʃ	k	t	tʃ	f	s	ʃ	hw	f	f	f	hw	hV	hw	hj	hl	hn	hm

proposed that such a ternary surface distinction exists and that it is best expressed using geometric means in a privative-feature context. Both of these propositions are of theoretical import.

The ternary distinction is important because it is a surface one. In the phonological literature, and especially in the OT context, claims to ternary contrast have usually relied on analyses where a three-way contrast exists in underlying representations and manifests itself in three-way distinctions in phonological behaviour. Other claims for a surface ternary distinction rely largely on phonetic measurements rather than on phonological behaviour. The importance of Bothoa Breton in this context is that, as I argue, it shows robust evidence of a three-way phonological distinction in surface representation, meaning that this evidence for ternarity cannot be written off as either an artefact of the analysis (as with underlying ternarity cases) or as potentially irrelevant to phonological computation. The Breton data thus show conclusively that a theory of phonology must be able to accommodate ternary contrasts.

However, while proponents of ternarity have tended to emphasise its importance as a conclusive argument for binary features and against privative frameworks, I argue here that the Breton data in fact show that ternary distinctions can, and at least in this case should, be analysed in a privative theory. The reason, I argue, is that only a privative approach provides us with an adequate account of the markedness asymmetries observed in Bothoa Breton laryngeal phonology. These asymmetries also support a substance-free view of phonology, in that they are of a type that has usually been associated with a type of phonetic implementation of laryngeal contrasts that differs from that found in Breton.

11.4.1 Surface ternarity in Breton

An important feature of the analysis proposed in this chapter is the distinction between contrastive non-specification for a feature (formalised as the *presence* of a bare node) and underspecification, formalised as the lack of the relevant *node*. The difference between laryngeally unspecified segments and those with a bare C-laryngeal node has both phonological and phonetic consequences. Phonologically, the former only participate in the sharing of the C-laryngeal node ('provection') and are inert in processes implicating C-laryngeal *features*, unless they acquire a C-laryngeal node from a floating element. Phonetically, I suggested that the laryngeal underspecification of (in particular) word-final elements is responsible for pre-sonorant voicing found across word boundaries.

While the phonological evidence for this type of surface underspecification is relatively unobjectionable in a substance-free theory of phonology, the phonetic evidence needs to be interpreted carefully. This is particularly true when the phonological evidence hinges at least in part on morphologised processes such as initial mutation. Perhaps even more seriously, some recent results regarding pre-sonorant and passive voicing (Strycharczuk 2012; Strycharczuk and Simon 2013; Strycharczuk et al. 2014) seem to undermine the proposal that the voicing of laryngeally underspecified segments is a gradient function of their phonetic environment, as suggested by authors such as Keating (1988a, 1990b, 1996), Hsu (1998), and Colina (2009).

In this section I provide more evidence for the existence of a surface ternary contrast in Breton, and then argue that while the view of variable, or 'passive', voicing as being solely the product of gradient interpolation which results from the lack of a laryngeal specification is probably too simplistic, a more nuanced theory of the phonetics–phonology interface, like the one sketched in section 2.3, based on the window model of coarticulation, can accommodate the facts without sacrificing the more modular approach.

11.4.1.1 Further evidence for ternarity

The argument for ternary contrast in laryngeal specifications relies on postulating different phonological representations for obstruents in positions where laryngeal contrast is licensed (e.g. in onsets) and in positions of neutralisation (e.g. word-finally). Thus, a valid potential objection is that the realisational differences observed between these positions do not reflect differences in phonological specifications, but are instead contextually determined outside the representational system. In other words, if a word-initial [t] and a phrase-final [d̥], both phonetically ⟦t⟧ (at least in some contexts), appear in complementary contexts, why can they not be collapsed representationally? Such thinking is most pronounced in 'polysystemic' approaches (see in particular Lodge 2009), but we also find phonological specification relativised to position in other contrast-based approaches, for instance in work by Dyck (1995, 1996).

In this section I consider two phenomena that show the clearest evidence for a phonological, representational distinction between word-final and non-final obstruents in Bothoa Breton that allows us to exclude such an analysis of the facts and uphold surface ternarity.

11.4.1.1.1 'Phantom [h]'

A very small number of lexical items behave as if they began with a voiceless consonant: examples are [om] 'our' and [i] 'her'. First, there is no voicing of obstruents before these words, even though they are vowel-initial and would thus be expected to trigger voicing of a final obstruent. Second, the lack-of-release phenomena associated with word-final nasal-stop sequences are also absent, and instead we find voiceless, released stops. Humphreys (1995) calls this feature 'phantom [h]'.

(234) 'Phantom [h]'
   (a) [tut om ˈamzər]   *tout hon amzer*   'all our time'
   (b) *[tud om ˈamzər]
   (c) [gãnt i hwɛːr]   *gant he c'hoar*   'with her sister'
   (d) *[gãː i ˈhwɛːr]

I suggest this is best analysed as an instance of a floating C-lar[vcl] feature. It can dock to a preceding obstruent because the concatenation by necessity happens postlexically, and the ranking at the word level always produces delaryngealisation of the final obstruents. Thus the floating C-laryngeal node, with its associated feature, docks to the preceding obstruent, just as the bare C-laryngeal node does in lenition.

(235) Docking of floating C-lar[vcl]

tu ḍ → t {h} om

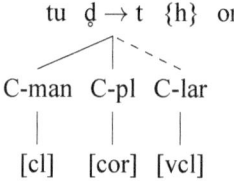

C-man C-pl C-lar
 | | |
[cl]   [cor] [vcl]

However, when there is no preceding obstruent, the floating feature simply fails to surface, with no epenthesis of a root node deployed to rescue it.

(236) Floating C-lar[vcl] only surfaces following an obstruent

			Dep(Root)	Max(C-lar[vcl])	*C-lar	DepLink (Rt) (C-lar[vcl])
/tuḍ {C-lar[vcl]}om/	(a)		[tuḍ om]		*!	*	
	(b)	☞	[tut om]			**	*
	(c)		[tuḍ hom]	*!		**	
/{C-lar[vcl]}om/	(d)	☞	[om]			*	
	(e)		[hom]	*!		*	

Importantly, this phenomenon is apparently not observed before a surface word-initial [h]. Granted, consonants in sandhi are normally voiceless before [h], but that is to be expected if sandhi is a phonetic process, since phonological [h] is normally ⟦h⟧ rather than ⟦ɦ⟧ word-initially. The fact that there is no spreading in a syntagm like ⟦ˌdɛn: ˈhiːr⟧ (phonologically [ˌdɛnḍ ˈhiːr]) 'long tooth' confirms that the C-laryngeal node may not spread across a word boundary, agreeing with the conclusion reached in section 11.2.2 on the basis of provection. Further, the

Laryngeal phonology 213

feature C-laryngeal[voiceless] also fails to spread to the preceding consonant in ⟦ˌdɛnː ˈhiːr⟧, even though spreading of [voiceless] *is* allowed across word boundaries, as shown by the 'failure of lenition'. The reason is that there is in fact no domain for such spreading in the case of an ordinary obstruent-final word since the final obstruent has been delaryngealised on the word level, and the domain can only be created by a floating C-laryngeal node – whether present lexically (as with 'phantom [h]') or inserted by mutation. This is schematised in (237).

(237) C-lar[vcl] can only spread to a node

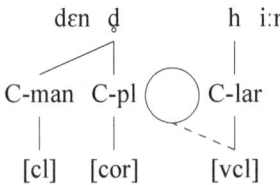

The importance of the 'phantom [h]' phenomenon lies in the fact that it establishes a firm distinction between delaryngealised word-final obstruents that do not receive a C-laryngeal node via spreading from a following word or a floating node and word-final obstruents that do receive a C-laryngeal specification, either from the floating C-laryngeal[voiceless] feature (in 'phantom [h]') or from a floating C-lar node provided by the mutation mechanism. The former are realised with the usual contextual voicing and lack of release, while the latter show no signs of neutralisation of the laryngeal contrast. This provides confirmation that delaryngealisation in word-final position is not simply a matter of contextual realisation of the same phonological representations as those found elsewhere

11.4.1.1.2 Exceptional sandhi
If we accept that a floating C-laryngeal feature can be not just introduced by mutation but also present underlyingly in the lexical representation of some morphemes, then by Richness of the Base we should also expect the possibility that a bare C-laryngeal floating node can be found with the same status. If that were so, we would expect it to show the same sort of behaviour as one created by mutation. Specifically, we would expect it to induce voicing of a following voiceless stop when there is no suitable landing site for C-lar to its left but devoicing of the entire cluster when such a site is found, via leftwards docking of the node and spreading of the C-lar[vcl] feature. In other words, we expect an alternation between a voiced stop – phrase-initially or after a sonorant or a vowel – and a voiceless stop (triggering assimilation) after an obstruent.

This prediction is entirely correct. Just such an alternation is found in most varieties of Breton, and it has for this reason attracted some comment in the generative phonological literature (see section 11.5 for explicit discussion of previous analyses).

Traditionally, the phenomenon is described as the *devoicing* of some word-initial *voiced* stops when preceded by any obstruent. Some Bothoa examples are given in (238). In some cases the word-final consonant in the examples is obscured by sandhi, but the devoicing is still present. To clarify this, I put the surface-phonological segment in parentheses, even if it may not actually be present in the phonetic surface form.

(238) Exceptional sandhi in Bothoa Breton
    (a) [ba]   *ba*   'in'
    (b) [ˈlakaḍ o vaːs pa stʃøːl]   *lakaat ur vazh ba skeul*   'put a step into a ladder'
    (c) [də]   *da*   'to'
    (d) [o ˈvwɛrp ten]   *ur voereb din*   'an aunt of mine'
    (e) [ˈhem(p) tə n oˈværn]   *eomp d'an oferenn*   'we go to Mass'
    (f) [ˈgãnḍ]   *gant*   'with, by'
    (g) [də ˌgas ˈkãntæ]   *da gas gante*   'in order to carry with them'
    (h) [ˈdɛːbə vẽj(tʃ) ˈkãntæ]   *debret a vent gante*   'they are eaten by them'
    (i) [bəˈnakəḍ]   *bennak*   'any'
    (j) [o ˈmãm(p) pəˈnakəḍ]   *ur mempr bennak*   'any member'

Other words in this category are [dəʐ] 'of', [zə] 'that', [ˈzeː] 'this one', and [beḍ] 'been'.

The pattern can be analysed by postulating that the relevant words do not begin with a voiced obstruent lexically, but instead have a floating C-lar node before a C-lar[vcl] stop. Thus, if the preposition [gãnḍ] is underlyingly /{C-lar}kãnḍ then the derivation of the relevant part of the phrase [də gas kãntæ] is as shown in (239).

(239) Exceptional devoicing sandhi

    ga ʐ → s   k ãntæ
       ⌈˙˙˙ |
   C-pl C-lar C-lar
    | ˙˙˙⌋
  [cor]   [vcl]

Conversely, when there is no preceding obstruent for C-lar to dock to, the floating C-lar node instead docks to the right, inducing voicing and creating the appearance of an underlying voiced stop.

The similarity between this 'devoicing sandhi' and lenition is not at all accidental. The devoicing sandhi is well known across Breton varieties, although many sources describe it rather unsystematically, and treat it together with phonological provection in compounds. It is notable, however, how many examples of this phenomenon involve prepositions and the lexical item *bennak* 'any'. Thus, for instance, Le Dû (1978: 145) lists the following items as triggers of devoicing sandhi in the Plougrescant dialect (I give the spelling following Le Dû 2012): *bennag* 'any', *dinan* 'under', *du-mañ* 'at my place', *du-ze* 'at your place', *da* 'to', *diwar* 'on', *douz* (variant of *ouz*) 'from', and *gand* 'with'. Crahé (2013) states that the prepositions [dø] 'to', [gøt] 'with', and [doh] 'against' (i.e. *da, gant, ouzh*) always undergo devoicing sandhi in Languidic. The list of items participating in devoicing sandhi in Île de Groix (Ternes 1970: 71) includes the prepositions [də] 'to' (*da*), [dar] 'by' (*dre*), and [dʒed] 'with' (*gant*).

The relationship between prepositions and lenition is diachronically clear: in Brythonic languages, many prepositions (and generally unstressed items) have undergone lenition diachronically (perhaps under the influence of a preceding particle that was subsequently lost): for instance, Breton *gant* (Welsh *gan*) descends from a form with initial [k]: Old Welsh *can*, Old Cornish *cant, cans*. In fact, this particular preposition also retains traces of its historical initial [k] in Welsh. As Morgan (1952: 452) notes, although modern Welsh uses only *gan*, when preceded by *a* 'and' – an item that triggers spirantisation of initial [k] to [χ] but leaves initial [g] intact – it behaves as if it were [k]-initial: *a chan* 'and with'. This behaviour is shared with other prepositions in Welsh, e.g. *ger* 'near', *a cher* 'and near'; *dan* 'under', *a than* 'and under'. Presumably these Welsh examples could be analysed similarly, as having [k] or [t] initially preceded by a floating element that normally induces voicing but is lost when mutation to a fricative ensues.

Thus, for many of the lexical items showing exceptional devoicing sandhi we can reasonably hypothesise lenition as a diachronic scenario: Bothoa Breton [bəˈnakəd̯] 'any' similarly corresponds to Middle Breton *pennac* (Lewis and Piette 1962; Schrijver 2011a). The similarity between the phonological analysis of devoicing sandhi and of lenition is not at all accidental.

The existence of devoicing sandhi provides further evidence for the analysis of lenition in section 11.3.3, and has the advantage of not involving the potentially morphological operation of consonant mutation. That analysis, in turn, crucially depends on the absence of a laryngeal specification in word-final obstruents as a matter of phonological representation.

As we saw in section 11.2.2, laryngeally specified obstruents, when adjacent, undergo 'provection', i.e. they are devoiced (via coalescence of C-lar nodes). This process is active at the word level, but clearly absent postlexically, since obstruent clusters across a word boundary are only obligatorily voiceless in the tightly circumscribed cases of lenition and devoicing sandhi.[16] By implication, outside these contexts such clusters are representationally distinct from word-internal, provected sequences, further confirming that word-final obstruents do indeed have a phonological representation distinct from obstruents in positions where laryngeal contrast is licensed.

11.4.1.2 Surface underspecification and (lack of) contrast
Having established that there is indeed a phonological distinction between obstruents in word-final position and elsewhere in terms of laryngeal specification, we turn to the question of whether this phonological hypothesis can be reconciled with phonetic data. In order to do this, a discussion of the phonetic consequences of surface underspecification is in order. This is so because surface underspecification has played a prominent role in debates around the division of labour between automatic and language-specific (hence learned) mechanisms of phonetic implementation. Therefore, establishing the limits of arbitrariness in surface underspecification provides a good testing ground for substance-free phonology, inasmuch as it represents one of the most apparent phenomena of what was called in Chapter 2 the 'phonetics–phonology interface'.

11.4.1.2.1 The standard view: underspecification and interpolation
The 'textbook' view of surface underspecification highlights the idea that the lack of phonological specification for a feature translates into the lack of a phonetic target for the realisation of that feature. Consequently, it is proposed that the relevant dimensions of phonetic implementation are governed deterministically by the phonetic context. Evidence to this effect was amassed in the area of tone (Pierrehumbert 1980; Pierrehumbert and Beckman 1988; Davison 1992; Myers 1998), vowel quality (van Bergem 1994; Choi 1995), nasality (Cohn 1993; Huffman 1993), and consonantal place of articulation (Keating 1988b).

Surface underspecification theory has been applied in the realm of laryngeal features to explain the variability in the voicing of obstruents in languages such as English, German, and Ecuadorian Spanish. Thus, Jansen (2004: §§2.2.2, 2.3.1) suggests that in languages such as English or German the voicing of postvocalic obstruents may be due to overspill of the relatively easily maintained voicing from the preceding vowel (Westbury and Keating 1986), and Jessen and Ringen (2002) interpret the variable voicing of stops that they find in German as reflecting the lack of a phonological specification for laryngeal features. It is worth emphasising here that this picture is not at all specific to laryngeal phonology: for instance, Sen (2015) argues that precisely the same architecture must have been at play in the case of Latin *l*-darkening and vowel-consonant coarticulation, where he also posits a surface ternary contrast with one underspecified member.

Crucially, these proposals tend (more or less explicitly) to treat the variability found in the realisation of surface-underspecified structures as an automatic phenomenon outwith cognitive control. This view is closely related to the idea, discussed in Chapter 2, that language-specific aspects of linguistic behaviour should be accounted for by the grammar – including the phonological grammar. If variable realisations turn out to be language-specific, they should be represented in the phonology. Since segmental phonological representations are made distinct by the use of features, language-specificity appears to rule out surface underspecification. However, this view of surface underspecification runs into empirical difficulties.

11.4.1.2.2 Interpolation and the window model of coarticulation
The idea of automatic interpolation, while attractive, has run into significant empirical difficulties, in that reliable data are now available showing that putative cases of surface underspecification may involve clearly language-specific realisations. Before we proceed, however, it is useful to distinguish between two types of surface underspecifications: those involving surface ternarity and those arising from a commitment to privative features. In this section I concentrate on the former, and return to empirical issues with the latter in section 11.4.2.

Ternarity-driven surface underspecification arises when surface-underspecified segments are assumed to be distinct from more than one type of fully specified structure. In this case, the use of surface underspecification as a theoretical device is all but unavoidable, in that the data appear to point towards a ternary distinction, which a binary-feature system with full specification is simply unable to account for. In this context, surface underspecification leads to a strong hypothesis with clear predictions: if there is a ternary contrast in surface representations, one of its members should show automatic variability. This is precisely the kind of system I hypothesise for Bothoa Breton. In fact, as will be seen, several systems of this kind proposed in the literature rely on not dissimilar data, in that surface underspecification is posited on the basis of the special behaviour of word-final obstruents in pre-sonorant position. The languages involved are Quito Spanish (Robinson 1979; Lipski 1989; Strycharczuk et al. 2014), south-western (Poznań/Kraków) Polish (e.g. Cyran 2013), Slovak (Bárkányi and Beňuš 2015), West Flemish (Strycharczuk and Simon 2013), and Central Catalan (Bermúdez-Otero 2001; Jiménez and Lloret 2008; Strycharczuk 2015).

In all these languages, some word-final obstruents (frequently only fricatives, but sometimes both stops and fricatives) appear to undergo pre-sonorant voicing. The existence of a robust contrast in intervocalic position word-medially prevents us from postulating a rule of intervocalic voicing to account for the pre-sonorant voicing word-medially. Surface underspecification in word-final position, however, provides a potential solution: if the final stop is in fact underspecified and only voiced contextually, in the phonetics, the paradox is resolved.

However, as discussed above, the strong prediction made by surface underspecification in these cases is that the voicing should be gradient and automatic. Such gradient realisations are indeed found, for instance in one subset of Quito Spanish speakers examined by Strycharczuk et al. (2014). However, in many other cases, pre-sonorant voicing is either fully categorical, as in Central Catalan (Strycharczuk 2015), or, interestingly, categorical but optional, as in another subset of Quito Spanish speakers (Strycharczuk et al. 2014), in West Flemish (Strycharczuk and Simon 2013), and in Slovak (Bárkányi and Beňuš 2015). In the latter case, speakers use either fully voiced or fully voiceless realisations in the pre-sonorant context, but not the partially voiced ones expected under an interpolation account.[17]

These facts clearly falsify the strong prediction that if a segment is underspecified for laryngeal features in the surface representations, then it will demonstrate gradient voicing effects. However, I suggest that such 'categorical variation' is fully consistent with the window model of coarticulation (Keating 1988b, 1990a). A key insight of the window model is that lack of contrast (i.e. phonological underspecification) corresponds to a wide range of *allowed* realisations; it follows that the observed range of variation may in fact be quite broad. If the window is sufficiently wide, there may be more than one path through it: 'Depending on the particular context, a path through a segment might pass through the entire range of values in the window, or span only a more limited range within the window' (Keating 1990a: 457). In other words, gradient automatic interpolation should not be the only possible phonetic realisation of surface underspecification. As discussed in Chapter 2, categorical distributions in the data can arise from the fact that certain pressures, such as discrete contextual factors, mechanical properties, or social functions, can enforce a clustering of values within the permissible window that can reach statistical significance but does not have phonological relevance. I suggest that cases such as West Flemish and Quito Spanish exemplify precisely this situation.

The phonology outputs delaryngealised obstruents in word-final position, meaning that the window is very wide and *both* fully voiced and voiceless realisations are possible. However, at least in the case of fricatives we can expect that most instances of fricatives in this position will be either fully voiced or fully voiceless, given the diachronic scenario for the rise of the pattern sketched by Strycharczuk and Simon (2013). Faced with the frequent incidence of such fully voiced segments, learners can assign it either phonological significance (as appears to have happened in Central Catalan) or some other kind of meaning, for instance social-indexical (Carr 2000).

Under this view, the phonology–phonetics interface introduces a degree of language-specificity into the realisation of surface-underspecified segments by exploiting the latitude 'within the window' left by the lack of phonological specification. The interface may leave the realisation to automatic processes, or it may narrow down the range of variation in response to non-phonological factors. It is in this component of the grammar that we may expect to identify the effects of social factors (Fruehwald 2013; MacKenzie 2013) or the use of speakers' phonetic knowledge (Kingston and Diehl 1994), perhaps for the purposes of enhancement (Stevens and Keyser 1989, 2010; Avery and Idsardi 2001; Keyser and Stevens 2006; Hall 2011).

Thus, a non-trivial phonetics–phonology interface allows us to reconcile the existence of language-specificity in phonetic realisation and the absence of surface-phonological specification. This is exactly what we expect in substance-free phonology: phonetic realisation is restricted to a certain degree by phonological specification, but is not fully determined by it. In particular, the phonetic realisation of surface-underspecified phonological structures demonstrates that some kinds of linguistic behaviour may be categorical in some aspects without corresponding to symbolic phonological specifications.

This argument can be flipped around: a symbolic specification can also have a conventionalised, language-specific realisation that is gradient at least in some aspects. In the next section I show how this consequence of the framework allows us to resolve empirical problems raised by a different kind of surface underspecification, which arises from a commitment to privativity.

11.4.2 The evidence against underspecification in binary contrasts

As noted above, much recent work on laryngeal phonology has suggested that laryngeal surface underspecification is found not just in cases such as Ecuadorian Spanish, West Flemish, or Breton, where it is relatively narrowly circumscribed in prosodic terms and probably related to the suspension of phonological contrast, but also in languages such as German or English. The obstruent (or at least stop) systems of the latter are analysed in terms of a privative contrast between [spread glottis] (or [fortis], or |H|) segments, realised as segments with long-lag VOT (in the case of stops), or as voiceless segments with short-lag VOT (in the case of fricatives). This position has been defended by, among others, Iverson and Salmons (1995, 1999, 2003a, 2007); Ringen (1999); Honeybone (2001, 2005a, 2012); Jessen and Ringen (2002); Petrova et al. (2006); Helgason and Ringen (2008); Spaargaren (2009); Beckman et al. (2011); Beckman et al. (2013); Ringen and van Dommelen (2013). Similar approaches can be found in more traditional, often structuralism-inspired work, such as that by Steblin-Kamenskij (1960) and Goblirsch (2005).

This approach has been dubbed 'laryngeal realism' by Honeybone (2005a). Both phonetic and phonological evidence is presented in favour of this approach. I will not discuss the phonological evidence in much detail here, other than to note that this kind of evidence is of course acceptable in substance-free phonology in principle. The use of phonetic evidence, on the other hand, is more problematic, at least on conceptual grounds. In this section I reconsider the claims of laryngeal realism and their relationship to surface underspecification, and argue that the substance-free framework presented in this book allows us to reconcile the phonological framework of laryngeal realism with the empirical evidence.

11.4.2.1 Laryngeal realism and essentialism

A major claim within the laryngeal realism tradition is that the phonological specification goes hand in hand with phonetic realisation. In particular, the presence of 'categorical' phonetic specification can be taken as conclusive evidence for some phonological specification, and conversely, the presence of 'variable' or 'gradient' laryngeal realisation can be taken as evidence for a lack of specification – or, in our terms, surface underspecification.

Thus, for instance, Helgason and Ringen (2008) and Beckman et al. (2011) show that certain varieties of Swedish contrast [spread glottis] stops (realised with postaspiration or optional preaspiration) with fully voiced stops, and argue that the latter must have a [voice] specification, even though it appears redundant phonologically. Similarly, Iverson and Salmons (1995) and Jessen and Ringen (2002) leverage the fact that German lenis stops are pronounced without consistent voicing in all positions to argue for a phonological representation of these segments without a laryngeal specification, while Beckman et al. (2009) propose that German fricatives bear a [voice] feature, based in part on their consistent voicing across contexts (i.e. on the lack of variable voicing characteristic of stops in that language).

Such reasoning is inconsistent with substance-free phonology. Conceptually, substance-free phonology rejects the tight coupling of phonological representation and phonetic realisation that these approaches require. These 'essentialist' (the term is due to Kingston et al. 2009) views undermine the independence of the phonological and the phonetic components of grammar, by uncritically identifying 'categorical' behavioural phenomena with symbolic phonological events.

A more serious problem is empirical. The essentialist approach is, in principle, more restrictive than the substance-free position, since it predicts that certain kinds of phonetic realisation of laryngeal contrast are incompatible with certain types of phonological specification. In particular, it is predicted that a language like Breton as analysed here should not exist: a language with prevoiced obstruents should treat [voice] as the marked value rather than [voiceless] (or [spread glottis]). Thus, either the analysis is incorrect or the predictions of laryngeal realism need to be re-examined.

11.4.2.2 Variability in laryngeal contrast realisation

To approach this re-examination, it is useful to consider an important difference in the empirical predictions of laryngeal realism and substance-free phonology. It concerns the realisation of the 'lenis' (i.e. non-[spread glottis]) segments. Under laryngeal realism, they lack any laryngeal feature, and thus are surface-underspecified. This fact leads proponents of laryngeal realism to predict that such segments will *always* be variably ('passively') voiced. As noted above, this source of surface underspecification is different from the contrast-based one discussed in the previous section: in this scenario, lack of specification follows from the standard procedure for privative feature assignment, not from lack of contrast.

This proposal appears to work well enough for languages such as German (Jessen and Ringen 2002), English (Jansen 2007b), or Turkish (Kallestinova 2004). However, there also exist languages with (post-)aspiration in (pre-stress) fortis stops where lenis stops do *not* show this kind of 'passive' voicing. One type, already referred to above with Swedish as an example, shows 'overspecified', fully voiced lenis stops, and thus is potentially amenable to a privative-feature analysis (if not a parsimonious one). A second type is more problematic. It is exemplified by Icelandic (e.g. Löfqvist and Yoshioka 1981), Danish (e.g. Hutters 1985), and Scottish Gaelic (Ladefoged et al. 1998; Nance and Stuart-Smith 2013). In these languages, lenis stops are 'voiceless unaspirated': they lack any partial ('passive') voicing, which indicates the presence of a devoicing (glottal spreading) gesture, of a smaller magnitude than that associated with (post-)aspiration, but a gesture nonetheless. This appears clearly incompatible with the strong prediction that laryngeally unspecified segments do not show any cognitively controlled variation in their phonetic realisation.

In fact, the variability in the realisation of the lenis series appears to be under cognitive control even in cases where proponents of laryngeal realism have claimed it to be automatic. Thus, Docherty (1992) describes significant variation in the amount of voicing in British varieties of English depending on, among other factors, social variation. Docherty et al. (2014) describe finely grained variation in VOT in lenis stops in a range of Northern English and Scottish varieties of English, showing it to be driven by extralinguistic factors such as geography and social identity. Perhaps most spectacularly, Scobbie (2006) shows, in a study of Shetland Scottish English, that speakers may vary the voice onset time of stops across the entire possible range (i.e. between full prevoicing and short-lag VOT 'voicelessness'), as long as a VOT contrast between the two series is maintained.

In fact, a not dissimilar amount of variability is found in the realisation of the *marked* values of laryngeal features. Thus, in languages such as Swedish, Welsh (Morris 2010; Iosad 2016), or English (Docherty and Foulkes 1999; Jones and Llamas 2003; Hejná 2015) 'fortis' stops can be realised with post- or preaspiration, depending on their position in the syllable but also, for instance, on social factors. In many varieties of English fortis stops are realised with glottal spreading (aspiration) in the onset but with glottal narrowing (glottalisation or even ejectivity; Gordeeva and Scobbie 2013) in the coda; Hejná and Scanlon (2015) report that some varieties of English show both preaspiration and glottalisation of postvocalic fortis stops. This is a major issue for essentialist approaches such as orthodox laryngeal realism that specifically identify the 'fortis' feature of English with [spread glottis], since glottal spreading is not an invariant cue to fortis status. On the other hand, this diversity in realisation is exactly what is expected under the substance-free approach.

11.4.2.3 A substance-free interpretation

How do we deal with this variability? In the grammatical architecture proposed in this book, the variability resides in a non-trivial phonetics–phonology interface. Just as the facts of fine-grained vowel allophony and incremental ('neo-Grammarian') sound change in vowels were used in Chapter 2 to justify the existence of such a phonetics–phonology interface, so the same kind of variation in laryngeal feature specifications can be accounted for given a sufficiently contentful theory of this interface. Beckman et al. (2013) concede this point when they envisage a post-phonological, language-specific component that assigns 'degrees of permitted voicing' to lenis stops to account for the existence of languages like Danish or Icelandic. Although I do not offer an explicit theory of this interface here, in this section I lay out a vision of what it should be able to do in order to account for variability in laryngeal feature specification.

As noted above, just as the existence of a categorical distribution in the phonetics does not per se prove the existence of a phonological specification, so the existence of variation does not necessarily point towards an absence of a symbolic specification. In laryngeal realism, lenis stops in languages like English are assumed to be voiced passively because the voicing is phonetically automatic (which, as we have seen, is likely to be untrue) and because the phonological evidence leads analysts to treat fortis stops as being more marked (in a privative-feature context) than lenis ones. As we have seen in the analysis of Breton, however, it is perfectly possible for two obstruent series to show a markedness asymmetry, whilst at the same time bearing *some* phonological specification. In Breton, voiceless stops are C-laryngeal[voiceless], voiced stops are C-laryngeal, and only delaryngealised, positionally restricted stops are in fact laryngeally unspecified. This specification arises from the operation of the SDA: if [voiceless] (or [fortis], or [spread glottis]) is contrastive within the subinventory containing stops, then lenis stops receive the bare C-laryngeal specification.

It is perfectly conceivable that the SDA will create very similar representations for languages like English, German, or Swedish. Thus, we would expect, contrary to the predictions of laryngeal realism, that the lenis stops in these languages are not unspecified: instead, they have a bare C-laryngeal node.

How is this bare node to be realised? Under the substance-free approach, this is a matter of the phonetics–phonology interface, which is subject to a range of influences. Ultimately, this realisation is language-specific, conventional, and potentially variable: exactly what typological study appears to show. In terms of the present model, *phonologically* there is probably no significant difference between the laryngeal systems of languages such as Icelandic, Breton, Welsh, and Swedish. They all contrast a C-lar['fortis'] specification with a bare C-lar specification that has different phonetic cues but is still not equivalent to surface underspecification.

Thus, variable but non-automatic voicing in languages like English can be accounted for in the following way. The bare C-laryngeal specification restricts the window of possible realisations somewhat: since bare C-laryngeal nodes are distinct from C-laryngeal ['fortis'] representations, they should have distinct realisations (the Interface Interpretation Principle, Chapter 2). Thus, the bare C-laryngeal node *is* associated with certain instructions to the articulatory module; however, these instructions do not necessarily imply the production of consistent closure voicing. I follow the lead of Kingston et al. (2009), who argue (following Westbury 1983; Westbury and Keating 1986) that enlargement of the supraglottal cavity in English in lenis stops is in fact controlled, even though it does not always create a transglottal pressure differential that is sufficient to sustain full closure voicing. The upshot is that the phonetic variability of stop voicing is not an automatic aerodynamic consequence of the lack of any activity cuing laryngeal features. Put more bluntly, there is probably no 'passive' voicing in English, and, by extension, possibly in other languages with similar laryngeal systems. In other languages, the bare C-laryngeal node is interpreted differently, but again entirely conventionally: in Swedish, such representations are interpreted with full voicing, whilst in Icelandic they correspond to voiceless unaspirated stops. In the two latter cases, categorical realisation follows from the presence of a phonological specification, but, unlike orthodox laryngeal realism, this does not require postulating a redundant featural specification.

A question remains: if there is so much conceptual leeway in the interpretation of such structures, why *are* their realisations so similar cross-linguistically? The answer, I suggest, is connected to the proposals of Kingston and Diehl (1994, 1995) and Kingston et al. (2008), who emphasise the lack of consistent, invariant phonetic cues for phonological features (cf. also e.g. Stevens and Blumstein 1981; Lisker 1986). Instead, Kingston, Diehl and colleagues argue that speakers (and listeners) attend to a number of covarying acoustic properties that the human auditory system automatically integrates into a set of what they call 'intermediate perceptual properties' (IPPs). Crucially, more than one acoustic cue (such as closure voicing or F_0 and F_1 movements) may contribute to a single IPP. Conversely, not all the 'raw' acoustic cues must be present to create the necessary auditory percept.

Importantly, the IPPs themselves are not linguistic: as discussed by Kingston et al. (2008), they are part of the general human auditory system. I suggest that this line of thought, which ties specifically linguistic entities (features) to a necessarily limited set of non-linguistic ones, puts us in a position to explain the typological recurrence of certain mappings between phonetics and phonology without recourse to a strong Universal Grammar with a highly deterministic interface and thus phonetically trivial representations (for a similar approach, see Samuels 2011). This goes a long way towards resolving the apparent overgeneration problem faced by the substance-free approach.

For our purposes, it is sufficient to assume that the bare C-laryngeal feature specification in systems where it contrasts with a 'fortis' type of laryngeal specification can vary across, or indeed within, languages. I suggest that speakers of different languages are attuned to the different cues which contribute to the various IPPs to a different degree, which produces the variation.

To summarise this discussion, I have argued that an adequate theory of featural structure should be able to distinguish between two sorts of 'variable' realisations. One type, corresponding to phonological surface underspecification, involves the complete absence of specific instructions to the phonetics–phonology interface, although the interface may still choose to make certain statistically detectable distinctions. Another type, corresponding to contrastive non-specification, may also lead to variable realisations, as speakers do not attend to all components of the IPP conventionally associated with the relevant featural specification in equal measure. Of course, this means that it is not possible to distinguish between the two types of variation merely in terms of a distinction between 'categorical' and 'gradient'; instead, the decision should be made on the basis of both a phonological analysis and a deep understanding of the phonetic factors involved. I suggest that the approach presented here can be helpful in finding a principled basis for the delineation between phonetics and phonology (Cohn 2006; Scobbie 2007).

11.5 Markedness relationships in Breton

Another innovative aspect of the analysis of Breton laryngeal phonology offered here is that I treated voiceless obstruents as being more marked phonologically than lenis ones. In the previous section I argued that, given an appropriate theory of the phonetics–phonology interface, this does not conflict with the phonetic implementation of the laryngeal contrast. In this section, I turn to the phonological aspect of this proposal. I argue that it represents an explicit geometric formalisation of an insight that has already been expressed in different forms in much of the existing work on the topic.

To demonstrate this, I compare the proposal in this chapter with two previously published analyses of sandhi (including irregular devoicing sandhi) in Île de Groix Breton, a Vannetais variety described in structuralist terms by Ternes (1970): those by Krämer (2000) and Hall (2009). Both of these authors recognise a ternary contrast in laryngeal state underlyingly, although not in the surface phonology, but they either make no explicit commitments as to the relative markedness of voiced and voiceless obstruents (Krämer 2000) or treat voiced obstruents as being more marked (Hall 2009). I will argue that the present approach enables us to better capture the correct generalisations.

11.5.1 Ternary contrast with binary features: Krämer (2000)

Krämer (2000) presents an analysis of laryngeal phenomena, with a focus on sandhi. He argues that a ternary contrast is required for Breton, formalising it using binary features, as a contrast between [Øvoice], [+voice], and [-voice], à la Inkelas (1994). However, Krämer (2000) suggests that this ternary contrast is reduced to a binary one by the grammar, with [Øvoice] obstruents not allowed on the surface.

11.5.1.1 The analysis

Krämer's analysis is rather complicated, so I will not reproduce it in detail here. His basic assumption is that the pre-sonorant voicing of word-final obstruents in sandhi is a phonological process which associates the feature [+voice] with these segments, rather than a phonetic implementation phenomenon as I argued above. Under this assumption, Krämer (2000) suggests that the voicing is due to a conjunction of the following constraints:

- ALIGN(stem, L, σ, L): align the left edge of a stem with the left edge of a syllable.
- ONSET VOICING: onset segments are voiced.

In general, ONSET VOICING is dominated by faithfulness, meaning that word-medial onsets are not affected: [ˈʃukət] 'sit (pl.)!'. However, Krämer (2000) assumes that consonants are resyllabified across a word boundary. Such resyllabification creates violations of ALIGN-L(stem, σ). The conjoined constraint comes into action when an onset containing a voiceless segment also forces a violation of the alignment constraint. This rules out the candidate [ʃu.k#əzaj] for 'sit here!'; instead, ONSET VOICING picks [ʃu.g#əzaj] as the winner.

As for sandhi before obstruents, where there is no resyllabification, Krämer (2000) ascribes the agreement in voicing in obstruent clusters straddling a word boundary to assimilation, coupled with the preservations of laryngeal features in the onset, as in [atʃyˈpaʒ ˈbaːk] 'boat crew'.

Finally, Krämer (2000) explains devoicing sandhi via underspecification in underlying forms. Recall that devoicing sandhi are associated with three types of contexts:

- lexically arbitrary items such as [bəˈnak] 'any', [atʃyˈpaʃ pəˈnak] 'any crew'
- words undergoing the lenition mutation
- words in tightly knit compounds.

Krämer (2000) concentrates on the first type and proposes that the initial segment in words triggering devoicing sandhi is laryngeally unspecified in underlying representation. When there is a preceding obstruent, that obstruent is devoiced by final devoicing, the assimilation constraint requires the entire cluster to be [–voice], and IDENTONSET[+voice] is inactive due to the absence of a voicing specification in the input for the word-initial consonant. In isolation, on the other hand, the word for 'any' receives an initial voiced segment because of ONSET VOICING.

11.5.1.2 Empirical issues
The most obvious issue with Krämer's (2000) analysis is that it assumes pre-sonorant voicing to be a (presumably categorical) phonological

process. As discussed in section 7.3.2, the voicing of word-final obstruents in pre-sonorant position appears to be a variable process rather than a categorical assimilation, at least in Bothoa Breton. However, given that no instrumental data are available either for the Bothoa dialect or Île de Groix, this argument cannot be considered very strong.

Nevertheless, the analysis faces some empirical problems on its own terms. First, as Hall (2009) points out, Krämer (2000) assumes that sandhi voicing before nasals is due to resyllabification of the obstruent into a complex onset: [tri'zek] 'thirteen', [trize.'g#miːs] 'thirteen months'; yet nasals appear to be impossible in (rising-sonority) complex onsets in Breton.

Second, it appears that Krämer (2000) counterfactually predicts that word-final obstruent clusters should undergo pre-sonorant voicing. Consider (240), taken from Ternes (1970: 98), who says that 'consonant groups of two paired consonants [i.e. obstruents] generally remain voiceless before a vowel'.[18]

(240) No pre-sonorant voicing of obstruent clusters
  (a) [pə'noʃt]   penaos   'how'
  (b) [pə'noʃt un am'zeir]   penaos un amzer   'what weather!'
  (c) *[pə'noʒd un am'zeir]

Under Krämer's assumptions, the correct syllabification for the form in (240b) is [pə'noʃ.t#un am'zeir], with a mismatch between syllable and stem boundaries that is expected to trigger pre-sonorant voicing. Given that both the pro-assimilation constraint and the conjoined constraint triggering onset voicing have to dominate the constraint requiring final devoicing, it appears that the expected winner in this case is, incorrectly, the candidate with pre-sonorant voicing.

(241) Analysis of sandhi voicing in clusters

/pə'noʃt un am'zeir/	ALIGN-L (stem, σ)& ONSET VOICING	AGREE [voi]	IDENT-IO [voi]	ONSET VOICING
(a) ☹ [pə'noʃ.t# un am'zeir]	*!			*
(b) ☞ [pə'noʒ.d# un am'zeir]			*	
(c) [pə'noʃ.d# un am'zeir]		*!		

A potentially even more serious empirical problem with Krämer's analysis is that he ignores the two other groups of triggering contexts for devoicing sandhi: the lenition mutation and tightly knit compounds.

With regard to lenition, for lenited words to demonstrate the same behaviour as words such as [bə'nak] 'any' as triggers of devoicing sandhi, lenition would have to be a process that deletes the input specification for [-voice] stops (and only these segments) before the operation of phonological rules, since the absence of specification in the input to phonology is crucial for both sandhi devoicing and onset voicing to be possible in Krämer's analysis. Such a 'precompilation' approach to mutation is not unprecedented in the literature (e.g. Hayes 1990; Stewart 2004; Green 2006; Hannahs 2013), so perhaps in this case Krämer's analysis could be salvaged.

However, it seems that Krämer (2000) is unable to cope with the existence of morphology-dependent devoicing. As discussed in section 11.2.2, obstruents adjacent within certain phonological domains undergo 'provection', i.e. across-the-board devoicing; however, when the same morphemes are adjacent in a larger domain, normal word-level phonology applies with no spreading across the prosodic word boundary, leading to minimal pairs such as those shown in (242) (cf. Le Dû 1986).

(242) Bothoa (Humphreys 1995)
    (a) [ə ˌhas'pjan]   *ur c'hazh-bihan*   'a kitten'
    (b) [ə 'ha:z̥ 'bjan]   *ur c'hazh bihan*   'a small cat'

(243) Berrien (Ploneis 1983)
    (a) ['gwi:nis'ty]   *gwiniz-du*   'buckwheat'
    (b) ['gwi:niz 'dy:]   *gwiniz du*   'black wheat'

Crucially, the choice between voicing and devoicing sandhi does *not* depend on the lexical identity of the second stem, as would be expected if the devoicing sandhi were triggered by the lexical underspecification of the stem-initial consonant. Instead, the sandhi depends on the domain structure: in the analysis in section 11.2.2, it is the prosodic domain structure that determines whether C-laryngeal sharing ('provection') is possible in this context. The relationship between provection and domain structure in examples like (242) and (243) is confirmed by their prosodic differences: in Bothoa [ˌkas'pjan], the stress on the first syllable is demoted to secondary status, unlike in the noun phrase ['ka:z̥ 'bjan] with no provection, and in Berrien ['gwi:nis'ty] we observe the lack of vowel lengthening in *du*, in contrast to the noun phrase ['gwi:niz 'dy:]; in the latter case the lengthening is presumably driven by word minimality, and the absence of this requirement in (243b) is again due to differences in domain structure.

To summarise, Krämer (2000) proposes that sandhi devoicing is purely a function of the featural content of the second segment in the cluster. This approach is belied by the influence of domain structure on devoicing

Laryngeal phonology 229

sandhi; this, coupled with the issues in analysing word-final clusters, means that it cannot derive the facts completely.

11.5.2 Ternary contrast with privative features: Hall (2009)

Hall (2009) proposes an analysis of (some of) the Breton facts that shares many theoretical assumptions with the present approach, in particular in its use of privative features and of the contrastive hierarchy. On the other hand, Hall (2009) follows the broad outlines of Krämer's (2000) analysis in many respects. In particular, Hall (2009) also treats final devoicing and pre-sonorant voicing as categorical phonological processes, and derives devoicing sandhi as due to input underspecification. However, probably the biggest difference vis-à-vis the present account is the treatment of voiced obstruents as more marked than voiceless ones: Hall (2009) suggests that voiceless obstruents are specified as ⟨x, Lar⟩, voiced obstruents are ⟨x, Lar, [voice]⟩, and sonorants are both ⟨x, Lar, [voice]⟩ and ⟨x, [sonorant]⟩, where [sonorant] is essentially equivalent to the [sonorant voice] of Rice and Avery (1989), Rice (1992, 1993), and Avery (1996).

Hall (2009) sees sandhi as mainly driven by a constraint he calls DISALIGN-R(ω, Lar), which prohibits right edges of words from coinciding with right edges of laryngeal domains. This constraint can be satisfied either by removing the laryngeal specification of the word-final segment or by making the domain of the Laryngeal node straddle the word boundary. In that sense, the two analyses considered here are similar, since they both assume that at least some of the sandhi phenomena are used to signal a boundary mismatch.

Hall (2009) manages to solve some problems facing Krämer (2000). In particular, his account does not rely on complex onsets with nasals, which are usually disallowed in Breton: the voicing assimilation in [triˈzeg ˈmiːs] 'thirteen months' is triggered by DISALIGN-R(ω, Lar), not by resyllabification across a word boundary.

Empirically, the account by Hall (2009) shares some of the drawbacks of Krämer's (2000), in particular with respect to the prediction of pre-sonorant voicing in word-final clusters, as in (240)[19] and to the difficulty in deriving domain related effects. In addition, as Hall (2009) acknowledges, he has to account for the difference between word-internal consonant sequences, which are always voiceless (with the exception of some obvious French borrowings) and those straddling a word boundary, where doubly linked [voice] is allowed.

In representational terms, the difference between the analysis offered here and that by Hall (2009) lies in the relative markedness of obstruents: for Hall, voiced obstruents are more marked (have more structure) than voiceless ones. At the same time he also recognises the need for a constraint DEFAULT VOICING. Although he does not discuss it in detail, it seems he follows Krämer (2000) in treating it as necessary to derive the voicing of input-underspecified obstruents. In this respect, Hall (2009) actually deviates – implicitly – from most of the existing literature on Breton laryngeal phonology.

11.5.3 Laryngeal markedness in Breton

The insight that voiceless obstruents in Breton are more marked than voiced ones is, in fact, not new, although it has been expressed in the literature so far in a variety of ways. Thus, Carlyle (1988), in an analysis of the relationship between obstruent laryngeal specification and quantity in Lanhouarneau Breton (a Léonais variety), proposes that there is in fact no laryngeal contrast between obstruents in underlying representations: instead, the distinction is expressed purely by quantity. Specifically, at one point in the derivation redundancy rules assign [+voice] values to (some) singleton obstruents and [-voice] values to all long obstruents (and to some singletons). Thus, in her analysis, voiceless obstruents are more marked, because they correspond to larger structures.

Carlyle's analysis is based on a relationship between obstruent voicing and vowel quantity that has broken down in Bothoa Breton (unlike most other varieties of the language), and is thus not directly applicable, but it does demonstrate the viability of this approach to markedness. Krämer (2000), on the other hand, does not make his commitment to the relative markedness of obstruents as explicit. However, the constraint ONSET VOICING expresses exactly the same insight: all other things being equal, voiced obstruents are preferred to ('are less marked than') voiceless ones, exactly as proposed here. This commitment is difficult to express, because otherwise Krämer (2000) uses a binary feature system, which has no 'inbuilt' way to express markedness relationships.

Hall (2009) follows Krämer (2000) in viewing voiced obstruents as *computationally unmarked* (hence the constraint DEFAULT VOICING), but assumes that they are more marked representationally, in that they bear a privative [voice] feature that voiceless obstruents lack. Thus, DEFAULT VOICING requires the epenthesis of a 'bigger' structure – the treelet ⟨Lar, [voice]⟩.

While this approach to voicing sandhi is not necessarily problematic empirically, it remains incomplete. As we saw in section 11.2, there is ample evidence for the phonological activity of the feature associated with voiceless obstruents, while in Hall's (2009) system provection processes would have had to be treated as subtractive ones. Once again, this is not problematic per se, and certainly does not represent a fatal flaw compared with the present analysis, because the latter also needs subtraction to account for some aspects of Breton laryngeal phonology (specifically the voicing of stops in connection with the lenition mutation).

However, I suggest that the present analysis sufficiently motivates the nature of voicing in lenition as subtraction-triggering addition of a floating node, since it is underpinned by the analysis of devoicing sandhi as spreading of [voiceless] in a domain created by the docking of this floating C-laryngeal node. A subtractive analysis of provection, as far as I can see, would have no independent confirmation of this sort.

On the conceptual level, the ambiguous behaviour of [±voice] in terms of markedness in Breton finds a ready explanation in the present proposal. The three possible representations ⟨x⟩, ⟨x, C-lar⟩, and ⟨x, C-lar, [voiceless]⟩ form a complexity hierarchy. Final laryngeal neutralisation, which is driven by the pure markedness constraint *C-lar, prefers structural reduction to ⟨x⟩. However, the augmentation constraint driven by the alignment constraint that disprefers bare root nodes triggers a process that appears to be an increase in markedness along the structural hierarchy, adding a C-laryngeal node only at the left edge of a syllable.

However, the augmentation constraint can only trigger a minimal increase in structural markedness, due to the logic of minimal violation. Recall that the constraint ALIGN-L(σ, C-lar) triggers a violation of DEP(C-lar) when dealing with delaryngealised obstruents in the input (which can be provided by the rich base or created in the process of mutation), but it cannot force the epenthesis of a larger structure (such as C-lar[vcl]), since candidates which epenthesise the latter incur gratuitous violations of other DEP constraints *in addition* to DEP(C-lar). Hence, we find evidence *both* of the relative unmarkedness of voiced obstruents (as evidenced by their appearance as the outcome of epenthesis) and of the greater markedness of voiceless ones (as evidenced in the phonological activity of the feature [voiceless]). Thus, I suggest that the present analysis provides the most straightforward and consistent account of markedness relationships in Breton. Although this comes at the cost of abandoning some assumptions regarding the phonetic implementation of laryngeal contrasts, this possibility is explicitly predicted by the substance-free approach to phonology proposed here.

Notes

1. See Iosad (2012c) for an analysis of Friulian 'final devoicing' with Preservation of the Marked. Similarly, in some Breton dialects (e.g. in Plougrescant) voiceless fricatives are protected from pre-sonorant voicing word-finally, which can be analysed as (selective) preservation of C-lar[vcl].
2. See also work such as that by Smith (2012), which explicitly treats them as *non-heads*.
3. In some neighbouring dialects, the pattern with a surface [h] is much more regular, and appears not only following vowels but also following sonorants,

e.g. at Saint-Gelven (around 12 km south by south-east of Bothoa) one finds [ˈdʒɥɛlhãw] 'best' (*gwellañ*), Bothoa [ˈdʒɥɛlã] (Humphreys 1995: 267).
4. 'Cet assourdissement est généralement accompagné de l'abrégement de la voyelle.'
5. The actual form given by Humphreys (1995: 268) is [neˈvɛːɒh], but this could easily be a misprint (*<néve:òh> for <névé:òh> in Humphreys' 1995 transcription).
6. '[C]ertains syntagmes à sourdure étroite, qu'on pourrait considérer comme des composés en voie d'integration.' This 'provection in common phrases' is quite common across Breton dialects; see Jackson (1967: §§487–9).
7. Two further examples are less conclusive: [ˈbrastər] 'size' (from [ˈbraːẓ] 'big') and [ˈzɛstər] or [ˈzɛhtər] 'dryness' from [ˈzɛːh] 'dry'. In the case of [ˈbrastər], the underlying voicing specification of the final consonant is unclear: apart from [ˈbrastər], other derivatives from this root are the comparative and superlative forms [ˈbrasɒh] and [ˈbrasã] and the causative/inchoative verb [ˈbrasaḍ], which have both undergone morphological provection (as also shown by the vowel shortening). In [ˈzɛhtər]/[ˈzɛstər], the highly irregular alternation between [h] and [s]/[z] complicates matters.
8. Admittedly [zl] is very infrequent, being found only across a morpheme boundary. However, [sl] appears to be in the same position: in fact Humphreys (1995) records this sequence only in [ˌdisˈliːvo] 'discolour' and its derivatives, so it does not appear that there is a particular reason to suppose that the choice of [dis] over [diz] before [l] is phonologically driven. Similarly, [sm] is only found in words involving the [dis] suffix, whereas [zm] is also possible, if rare and only across morpheme boundaries.
9. I assume MAXFLOAT (Wolf 2005, 2007b) is not part of CON; see section 4.2.6.
10. The only other 'voiceless sonorant' that can appear initially is [hj], but it appears to be unaffected. Initial [h] is also immune: [mə ˈhãw̃n] 'my name' (*va hañv*), [mə ˈhjɒːl] (*va heol*) 'my sun' from [ˈhãw̃n], [hjɒːl].
11. Of course, this claim cannot be taken for granted; in general, the study of whether initial mutations in the Celtic languages produce complete neutralisations is still largely in its infancy, although Welby, Ní Chiosáin & Ó Raghallaigh (2011) report some cases of incomplete neutralisations for Irish.
12. Humphreys (1995) also proposes that [dæhˈmaːḍ] might also be analysed as two words, which would means that [h.C] sequences with sonorants are in fact never tolerated. Historically, [dæhˈmaːḍ] is derived from [ˈdæh] 'thing' (*dalcʰh*) and [ˈmaːḍ] 'good', used as an intensifier, but it is not obvious that the derivation can be sustained synchronically.
13. Note, however, that, as discussed in section 11.3.2.4, prohibiting mutation from looking further than one segment from the edge is problematic for analysing the lenition of [ɽ]/[hr].
14. This constitutes another argument against a unitary segment [r], since if the rhotic had been able to have a C-lar specification, we would expect it

to pattern with obstruents in blocking lenition. It does not, as the example shows.
15. As indeed it does in other Breton dialects (Falc'hun 1938, 1951; Jackson 1967).
16. This is not necessarily true of all Breton varieties, at least for some contexts. Thus, in Plougrescant (Le Dû 1978) clusters involving fricatives are always voiceless, even across a word boundary.
17. In fact, it may be the case that something like this categorical but optional pattern is found in Breton. Humphreys (1995) claims that (at least underlyingly voiceless) fricatives can be fully voiceless word-finally before a vowel, even though normally obstruents are at least partially voiced in this position. No such phenomenon is noted for stops.
18. '[L]es [...] groupes consonantiques à *deux* consonnes appariées restent en général sourds devant voyelle.'
19. However, Hall (2009) does not consider the phonology of obstruent clusters in his brief paper, so it is not entirely clear what exactly the predictions would be.

12

Conclusion

In this book I have offered both a programmatic account of a substance-free approach to the analysis of phonological patterning and an extended discussion of the sound patterns of a Breton variety. It has thus been my intention not only to provide a framework of assumptions that is capable of providing new theoretical insights but also to show the viability of my chosen approach in facing phonological data. By way of conclusion, in this brief chapter I point out three main themes that a theoretical phonologist (or a phonetician or morphologist interested in how 'their' module interacts with phonology) might find useful.

First, I have insisted on a substance-free approach to phonological representation. Under this view, the mapping between phonological symbols and phonetic realisation is not at all fixed, certainly not by any innate mechanism, and is instead language-specific (hence learned), subject to a range of influences both from phonology and other cognitive components, and – in principle – arbitrary. This last point is perhaps the most contentious one. However, the mainstream generative position – that representations are trivially recoverable from pronunciation – appears to be untenable. It is incompatible with a number of empirical facts, such as:

- cross-linguistic differences in the realisation of 'the same' phonological representation
- fine-grained within-speaker variation
- gradual Neogrammarian sound change without changes to phonological patterning ('sound change without phonological change').

All this, coupled with significant evidence of non-categorical behaviour in many processes formerly assumed to be featural, leads us towards an abandonment of a maximalist approach based on universal features. Once we abandon this tight coupling between representation and substance, we are left with the question of how this mapping can be constrained. Crucially, in a modular framework it appears the correct answer is that, *in principle*, it cannot. This is because any such restrictions – which are normally connected to factors such as perceptibility (or perceptual reliability), learnability, biases, or even sheer frequency – cannot be *phonological*. Their role cannot be denied, of course, but there is, I suggest, no good reason to account for these effects in the phonological grammar itself, which concentrates on 'core' phonological phenomena such as contrast and morphophonological alternations.

The most obviously relevant feature of Breton phonology in this respect is the behaviour of laryngeal features. Across different contexts, there is, as I have shown, ample evidence for the phonological activity of voiceless obstruents, and very little – if any – for any similar status for voiced obstruents. This type of *phonological* behaviour is not at all unprecedented. However, in most if not all previously described cases of such systems the *phonetic* realisation of the marked series has belonged to a particular type, namely showing laryngeal activity other than voicing. In Breton, despite clear phonological similarities to languages such as English or Icelandic, the phonetic realisation is more similar to 'voicing' languages such as French or Russian. Thus, the hypothesis that phonological specification can be inferred purely from phonetic realisation appears to be falsified: the substance-free approach is more powerful than a more restricted 'laryngeal realism', but more empirically adequate.

This case also probably underscores the non-phonological nature of the phonology–phonetics mapping. The patterning of the 'voiceless' stops in Breton is very similar to that in Welsh, where the system is much more compatible with the predictions of 'laryngeal realism' (e.g. Ball and Williams 2001); the difference between the two languages lies in the mapping from phonology to phonetics, not in the phonology as such. This change in the mapping is commonly assumed to have been triggered by contact with Romance varieties – an extraphonological event that has not had an impact on the phonology of the language, and hence outside the purview of the grammar.[1] It is also worth noting that there are, not unexpectedly, also some differences between the phonological grammars of Breton and Welsh (for discussion, see Parry-Williams 1913). This includes, notably, final devoicing, a pattern that is at face value more characteristic of 'voicing' languages, and hence might be seen as an instance of phonologically relevant contact influence. However, Breton shares final devoicing also with Cornish (although it is more restricted in the latter), a language that did not undergo significant Romance influence (discounting lexical loans), which allows us to conclude that the contact with Romance does not, after all, *necessarily* have to be relevant in this respect.

Further work on featural representations in a substance-free framework is possible, but it is important to emphasise, following Hall (2010, 2014), that the arbitrariness of the phonology–phonetics mapping should not be seen as a carte blanche for highly abstract analyses that postulate features covering a priori implausible classes of segments simply because they participate in an apparent pattern. This work should proceed by closely examining the evidence for and against each such pattern being part of the phonology, and also for and against the existence of a unitary process. This can only be done via detailed analysis informed by the entire phonology of the language, and I hope that this book's extended example shows the viability of such an enterprise.

A second major topic of this book is the relationship between phonological structure and phonological activity. I have argued, following authors such as Causley (1999) and de Lacy (2006), that the kinds of phonological behaviour commonly ascribed to 'markedness' (Rice 2003) can be accounted for by the interaction of structure in representations (implemented here through a privative featural system) and the computation (i.e. stringent violation sets). Of course, given the substance-free assumptions of the representational system, 'markedness' as understood here cannot have, as its proximate cause, any kind of functional explanation. Although this result is at odds with much existing work on the typology of markedness, it is, I suggest, a highly welcome one.

As Rice (2009) has shown, phonetic substance becomes increasingly important as a guide to the shape of markedness-based phonological patterns when the number of contrasts a language makes in the relevant dimensions also increases. In other words, languages with relatively crowded (sub)inventories will tend to follow the predictions of substance-based theories of markedness, whereas languages that make relatively few contrasts show more freedom in what is treated as 'marked' or 'unmarked' in phonological patterning. The featural proposal adopted in this book provides a direct connection between the sparseness of the contrastive space and unmarkedness. 'Unmarked' behaviour follows from the absence of phonological structure: a representation where some feature is absent will be a preferred outcome of neutralisation in weak positions, since such neutralisation is expressed as deletion of structure, and a preferred target of assimilation, since feature co-occurrence constraints will be unable to block assimilation; this is the behaviour Rice (2003) designates as 'submergence of the unmarked'. Similarly, a structure lacking a feature will be unable to be targeted by faithfulness constraints, which are required to account for 'triumph of the marked' behaviour.

Causley (1999) provides an extended exposition of this argument. In this book, I take these ideas further by proposing an explicit relationship between the structure of inventories and featural representations. This comes from adopting Ghini's (2001b) proposal to assign privative specifications on the basis of a contrastive hierarchy. In this view, a feature is normally present in the representations precisely *because* it is needed to establish some contrast. When a contrast is absent, there is no need to use features, and hence a smaller, underspecified structure results. Such underspecified structures in smaller (sub)inventories can show variation in their realisation (Lorentz 2007; Morén 2007). Phonologically, such underspecified representations will show unmarked behaviour, and in the absence of significant pressure to be distinct from other contrastive units we also expect more leeway in the segment's phonetic realisation. This is exactly the observation made by Rice (2009): absence of contrast leads to greater freedom in the choice of phonetic implementation.

None of these conclusions is meant to undermine the study of the relationship between markedness and phonetic salience (e.g. Steriade 2001) or markedness and information load (e.g. Hume 2004; Hall 2013). It is highly plausible that especially in relatively crowded contrastive spaces such factors will play an important role in guiding how particular representations are phonetically implemented. However, I suggest here that such factors do not enter into the phonological grammar per se: instead, within the grammar markedness relationships are categorical and flow from the structure of phonological representations and from the ranking of relevant constraints. Gradient aspects of markedness are real, but do not concern the phonological computation directly.

This kind of division of labour where (some) categorical aspects of some phenomena are within the purview of phonology, but gradience is due to extraphonological factors, is a characteristic example of the substance-free phonological architecture. I suggest that such an approach can be fruitful in addressing other areas that show similar 'intertwining' or categorical and gradient influences.

Finally, I have tried in this book to emphasise the importance of both representational and computational solutions to phonological problems. Although the focus has been mostly on the representational side, I have made several arguments more directly relevant to the study of phonological computation. I have concentrated in particular on the stratal approach to morphology–phonology interactions. For the purposes of this book, it has been attractive both empirically – it makes better predictions regarding the source of cyclic transfer in Bothoa Breton – and conceptually – it allows to restrict the flow of information between the phonological module and the morphosyntax in a way that is consistent with modularist assumptions. Perhaps the most positive aspect of adopting a stratal framework, however, is that it is consistent with the overall substance-free ethos of not trying to make the phonological module alone responsible for all the *explananda* we can identify. In the stratal framework, morphology–phonology interactions follow from the architecture of grammar, so that the phonological domains and type of grammar are determined on independent, morphosyntactic grounds, and the phonology does not need devices whose sole purpose is to explain (for instance) cyclic misapplication. Once again, a proper division of labour opens the way to an overall more insightful account of phonological patterning.

Of course, an analysis of a single language based on imperfect data – such as the one provided here – cannot be said to settle matters of phonological architecture conclusively. I do hope, however, that I have been successful in demonstrating the coherence and viability of an approach that takes formal phonology seriously and delineates a well-defined set of questions that it may be able to answer. Much further work remains to test and challenge the assumptions made throughout this book, but if it allows the reader to revisit new (and old) questions in light of these assumptions, it will have served its purpose.

Note

1. Cf. the notion of 'legacy specification' in Dutch, which has undergone a similar shift, proposed by Iverson & Salmons (2003b), and see Simon (2011) on the mechanism of this contact.

References

Aaronson, Scott (2013), 'Why philosophers should care about computational complexity', in Brian Jack Copeland, Carl Posy and Oron Shagrir (eds), *Computability: Gödel, Turing, Church, and beyond*, Cambridge, MA: MIT Press, pp. 261–328.
Adkins, Madeleine (2013), 'Will the real Breton please stand up? Language revitalisation and the problem of authentic language', *International Journal of the Sociology of Language* 223: 55–70.
Alderete, John (1999), 'Head dependence in stress-epenthesis interaction', in Marc van Oostendorp and Ben Hermans (eds), *The derivational residue in phonological Optimality Theory* (Linguistik Aktuell 28), Amsterdam: John Benjamins, pp. 29–50.
Alderete, John (2008), 'Using learnability as a filter on factorial typology: A new approach to Anderson and Browne's generalisation', *Lingua* 118(8): 1177–220.
Altshuler, Daniel (2009), 'Quantity-insensitive iambs in Osage', *International Journal of American Linguistics* 75(3): 365–98.
Anderson, John and Colin Ewen (1987), *Principles of Dependency Phonology*, Cambridge: Cambridge University Press.
Anderson, Stephen R. (1981), 'Why phonology isn't "natural"', *Linguistic Inquiry* 12(4): 493–539.
Anderson, Stephen R. (1985), *Phonology in the twentieth century*, Chicago: University of Chicago Press.
Archangeli, Diana (1988), 'Aspects of underspecification theory', *Phonology* 5: 183–207.
Archangeli, Diana and Douglas Pulleyblank (1994), *Grounded phonology*, Cambridge, MA: MIT Press.
Areces, Carlos and Patrick Blackburn (2001), 'Bringing them all together', *Journal of Logic and Computation* 11(5): 657–69.
Atkinson, Quentin D. (2011), 'Phonemic diversity supports a serial founder effect model of language expansion from Africa', *Science* 332(6027): 346–9.
Avery, Peter (1996), *The representation of voicing contrasts*, Toronto: University of Toronto PhD thesis.

Avery, Peter and William J. Idsardi (2001), 'Laryngeal dimensions, completion, and enhancement', in T. Alan Hall (ed.), *Distinctive feature theory* (Phonetics and Phonology 2), Berlin: Mouton de Gruyter, pp. 41–71.

Avery, Peter and Keren Rice (1989), 'Segmental structure and coronal underspecification', *Phonology* 6(2): 179–200.

Awbery, Gwenllian M. (1984), 'Phonotactic constraints in Welsh', in Martin J. Ball and Glyn E. Jones (eds), *Welsh phonology: Selected readings*, Cardiff: University of Wales Press, pp. 65–104.

Awbery, Gwenllian M. (1986), *Pembrokeshire Welsh: A phonological study*, Llandysul: Welsh Folk Museum.

Bach, Emmon and Robert T. Harms (1972), 'How do languages get crazy rules?', in Robert P. Stockwell and Ronald K. S. Macaulay (eds), *Linguistic change and generative theory*, Bloomington: Indiana University Press, pp. 1–21.

Backley, Phillip (2011), *An introduction to Element Theory*, Edinburgh: Edinburgh University Press.

Baković, Eric (2004), 'Unbounded stress and factorial typology', in John J. McCarthy (ed.), *Optimality Theory in phonology: A reader*, Oxford: Blackwell, pp. 202–14.

Ball, Martin J. and Briony Williams (2001), *Welsh phonetics* (Welsh Studies 17), Lewiston, Queenston, Lampeter: Edwin Mellen Press.

Bárkányi, Zsuzsanna and Štefan Beňuš (2015), 'Prosodic conditioning of pre-sonorant voicing', in The Scottish Consortium for ICPhS 2015 (ed.), *Proceedings of the 18th International Congress of Phonetic Sciences*, Glasgow: University of Glasgow.

Barnes, Jonathan (2006), *Strength and weakness at the interface: Positional neutralisation in phonetics and phonology*, Berlin: Walter de Gruyter.

Barnes, Jonathan (2007), 'Phonetics and phonology in Russian unstressed vowel reduction: A study in hyperarticulation', MS, Boston University.

Baroni, Marco and Laura Vanelli (2000), 'The relationship between vowel length and consonantal voicing in Friulian', in Lori Repetti (ed.), *Phonological theory and the dialects of Italy* (Current Issues in Linguistic Theory 212), Amsterdam: John Benjamins, pp. 13–44.

Becker, Michael, Nihan Ketrez and Andrew Nevins (2011), 'The Surfeit of the Stimulus: Analytic biases filter lexical statistics in Turkish laryngeal alternations', *Language* 87(1): 84–125.

Becker, Michael, Andrew Nevins and Jonathan Levine (2012), 'Asymmetries in generalizing alternations to and from initial syllables', *Language* 88(2): 231–68.

Beckman, Jill (1998), *Positional faithfulness*, Amherst: University of Massachusetts, Amherst PhD thesis.

Beckman, Jill, Pétur Helgason, Bob McMurray and Catherine Ringen (2011), 'Rate effects on Swedish VOT: Evidence for phonological overspecification', *Journal of Phonetics* 39(1): 39–49.

Beckman, Jill, Michael Jessen and Catherine Ringen (2009), 'German fricatives: Coda devoicing or positional faithfulness?', *Phonology* 26(2): 231–68.

Beckman, Jill, Michael Jessen and Catherine Ringen (2013), 'Empirical evidence for laryngeal features: Aspirating vs. true voice languages', *Journal of Linguistics* 49(2): 259–84.
Benua, Laura (1997), *Transderivational identity*, Amherst: University of Massachusetts, Amherst PhD thesis.
Bermúdez-Otero, Ricardo (1999), *Constraint interaction in language change: Quantity in English and Germanic*, Manchester, Santiago de Compostela: University of Manchester, Universidad de Santiago de Compostela PhD thesis.
Bermúdez-Otero, Ricardo (2001), 'Voicing and continuancy in Catalan: A non-vacuous Duke-of-York gambit and a Richness-of-the-Base paradox', MS, University of Manchester.
Bermúdez-Otero, Ricardo (2003), 'The acquisition of phonological opacity', in Jennifer Spenader, Anders Eriksson and Östen Dahl (eds), *Variation within Optimality Theory: Proceedings of the Stockholm workshop on 'Variation within Optimality Theory'*, Stockholm: Stockholm University, pp. 25–36.
Bermúdez-Otero, Ricardo (2006), 'Morphological structure and phonological domains in Spanish denominal derivation', in Fernando Martínez-Gil and Sonia Colina (eds), *Optimality-theoretic studies in Spanish phonology* (Linguistik Aktuell/Linguistics Today 99), Amsterdam: John Benjamins, pp. 278–311.
Bermúdez-Otero, Ricardo (2007a), 'Diachronic phonology', in Paul de Lacy (ed.), *The Cambridge handbook of phonology*, Cambridge: Cambridge University Press, pp. 497–518.
Bermúdez-Otero, Ricardo (2007b), 'Marked phonemes vs marked allophones: Segment evaluation in Stratal OT', MS, University of Manchester.
Bermúdez-Otero, Ricardo (2011), 'Cyclicity', in Marc van Oostendorp, Colin J. Ewen, Elizabeth Hume and Keren Rice (eds), *The Blackwell companion to phonology*, Oxford: Blackwell, pp. 2019–48.
Bermúdez-Otero, Ricardo (2012), 'The architecture of grammar and the division of labour in exponence', in Jochen Trommer (ed.), *The phonology and morphology of exponence: The state of the art* (Oxford Studies in Theoretical Linguistics 41), Oxford: Oxford University Press, pp. 8–83.
Bermúdez-Otero, Ricardo (2013), 'The Spanish lexicon stores stems with stem vowels, not roots with inflectional class features', *Probus* 25(1): 3–103.
Bermúdez-Otero, Ricardo (2015), 'Amphichronic explanation and the life cycle of phonological processes', in Patrick Honeybone and Joseph C. Salmons (eds), *The Oxford handbook of historical phonology*, Oxford: Oxford University Press, pp. 374–99.
Bermúdez-Otero, Ricardo and Ana R. Luís (2009), 'Cyclic domains and prosodic spans in the phonology of European Portuguese functional morphs', presentation at the 6th Old World Conference in Phonology, Edinburgh.
Bethin, Christina Y. (1992), *Polish syllables: The role of prosody in phonology and morphology*, Columbus: Slavica Publishers.

Bever, Thomas G. (1992), 'The logical and extrinsic sources of modularity', in Megan R. Gunnar and Michael Maratsos (eds), *Modularity and constraints in language and cognition*, Hillsdale, NJ: Erlbaum, pp. 179–212.
Bickmore, Lee S. (2000),'Downstep and fusion in Namwanga', *Phonology* 17(3): 297–331.
Bird, Steven (1995), *Computational phonology: A constraint-based approach*, Cambridge: Cambridge University Press.
Bird, Steven and Ewan Klein (1994), 'Phonological analysis in typed feature systems', *Computational Linguistics* 20(3): 455–91.
Blackburn, Patrick (2000), 'Representation, reasoning, and relational structures: A hybrid logic manifesto', *Logic Journal of IGPL* 8(3): 339–65.
Blaho, Sylvia (2008), *The syntax of phonology: A radically substance-free approach*, Tromsø: University of Tromsø PhD thesis.
Blevins, Juliette (2004), *Evolutionary phonology: The emergence of sound patterns*, Cambridge: Cambridge University Press.
Blevins, Juliette (2006), 'A theoretical synopsis of Evolutionary Phonology', *Theoretical Linguistics* 32(2): 117–66.
Bobaljik, Jonathan David (2008), 'Paradigms, optimal and otherwise: A case for scepticism', in Asaf Bachrach and Andrew Nevins (eds), *Inflectional identity*, Oxford: Oxford University Press, pp. 29–54.
Boersma, Paul (1998), *Functional phonology: Formalizing the interactions between articulatory and perceptual drives*, Amsterdam: University of Amsterdam PhD thesis.
Boersma, Paul and Silke Hamann (2008),'The evolution of auditory dispersion in bidirectional constraint grammars', *Phonology* 25(2): 217–70.
Boersma, Paul, Paola Escudero and Rachel Hayes (2003), 'Learning abstract phonological from auditory phonetic categories: An integrated model for the acquisition of language-specific sound categories', in Maria-Josep Solé, Daniel Recasens and Joaquin Romero (eds), *Proceedings of the 15th International Congress of Phonetic Sciences*, Barcelona: Universitat Autònoma de Barcelona, pp. 1013–16.
Bothorel, André (1982), *Étude phonetique et phonologique du breton parlé à Argol (Finistère-Sud)*, Spezed: Diffusion Breizh.
Braver, Aaron (2011), 'Incomplete neutralisation in American English flapping: A production study', in *Proceedings of the 34th Annual Penn Linguistics Colloquium* 17: 31–40.
Broudic, Fañch (1995), *La pratique du breton de l'Ancien Régime à nos jours*, Rennes: Presses universitaires de Rennes.
Browman, Catherine and Louis Goldstein (1990), 'Articulatory gestures as phonological units', *Phonology* 6(2): 201–51.
Buckley, Eugene (1992), *Theoretical aspects of Kashaya phonology and morphology*, Berkeley: University of California, Berkeley PhD thesis.
Burton-Roberts, Noel (2000), 'Where and what is phonology?', in Noel Burton-Roberts, Philip Carr and Gerard Docherty (eds), *Phonological*

knowledge: Concepts and empirical issues, Oxford: Oxford University Press, pp. 39–66.

Bye, Patrik (2007), 'Allomorphy – selection, not optimisation', in Sylvia Blaho, Patrik Bye and Martin Krämer (eds), *Freedom of analysis?* (Studies in Generative Grammar 95), Berlin: Mouton de Gruyter, pp. 63–92.

Bye, Patrik and Peter Svenonius (2012), 'Non-concatenative morphology as epiphenomenon', in Jochen Trommer (ed.), *The phonology and morphology of exponence: The state of the art* (Oxford Studies in Theoretical Linguistics 41), Oxford: Oxford University Press, pp. 427–95.

Cable, Seth (2004), 'Phonological noun–verb dissimilarities in Optimal Paradigms', MS, University of Massachusetts, Amherst.

Calabrese, Andrea (2005), *Markedness and economy in a derivational model of phonology* (Studies in Generative Grammar 80), Berlin: Mouton de Gruyter.

Calamaro, Shira and Gaja Jarosz (2014), 'Learning general phonological rules from distributional information: A computational model', *Cognitive Science* 39(3): 647–66.

Carlyle, Karen Ann (1988), *A syllabic phonology of Breton*, Toronto: University of Toronto PhD thesis.

Carr, Philip (2000), 'Scientific realism, sociophonetic variation, and innate endowments in phonology', in Noel Burton-Roberts, Philip Carr and Gerard Docherty (eds), *Phonological knowledge: Concepts and empirical issues*, Oxford: Oxford University Press, pp. 67–104.

Casali, Roderic (1998), *Resolving hiatus*, New York: Garland.

Causley, Trisha (1999), *Complexity and markedness in Optimality Theory*, Toronto: University of Toronto PhD thesis.

Charles-Luce, Jan and Daniel A. Dinnsen (1987), 'A reanalysis of Catalan devoicing', *Journal of Phonetics* 15(1): 187–90.

Cheveau, Loïc (2006), 'Les mutations consonantiques en breton vannetais littéraire et en breton lorientais', *Journal of Celtic Linguistics* 10: 1–15.

Cheveau, Loïc (2007), *Approche phonologique, morphologique et syntaxique du breton du Grand Lorient (bas-vannetais)*, Rennes: Université Rennes 2 Haute-Bretagne PhD thesis.

Choi, John D. (1995), 'An acoustic-phonetic underspecification account of Marshallese vowel allophony', *Journal of Phonetics* 23(3): 323–47.

Chomsky, Noam and Morris Halle (1967), *The sound pattern of English*, New York: Harper and Row.

Clements, G. Nick (1991a), 'Place of articulation in consonants and vowels: A unified theory', in *Working papers of the Cornell Phonetics Laboratory* 5: 77–123.

Clements, G. Nick (1991b), 'Vowel height assimilation in Bantu', in *Working papers of the Cornell Phonetics Laboratory* 5: 37–76.

Clements, G. Nick (2003), 'Feature economy in sound systems', *Phonology* 20(3): 287–333.

Clements, G. Nick and Elizabeth V. Hume (1995), 'The internal organisation of speech sounds', in John Goldsmith (ed.), *The handbook of phonological theory*, Oxford: Blackwell, pp. 245–306.

Coetzee, Andries and Joe Pater (2011), 'The place of variation in phonological theory', in John Goldsmith, Jason Riggle and Alan Yu (eds), *The handbook of phonological theory*, 2nd edn, Oxford: Wiley-Blackwell, pp. 401–34.

Cohn, Abigail C. (1990), *Phonetic and phonological rules of nasalisation*, Los Angeles: University of California, Los Angeles PhD thesis.

Cohn, Abigail C. (1993), 'Nasalisation in English: Phonology or phonetics', *Phonology* 10(1): 43–81.

Cohn, Abigail C. (1998), 'The phonetics–phonology interface revisited: Where's phonetics?', in *Proceedings of the 1998 Texas Linguistics Society conference*, Austin: University of Texas, Austin, pp. 25–40.

Cohn, Abigail C. (2006), 'Is there gradient phonology?', in Gisbert Fanselow, Caroline Féry, Ralf Vogel and Matthias Schlesewsky (eds), *Gradience in grammar: Generative perspectives*, Oxford: Oxford University Press, pp. 25–44.

Cohn, Abigail C. (2010), 'Laboratory Phonology: Past successes and current questions, challenges, and goals', in Cecile Fougéron, Barbara Kühnert, Mariapaola D'Imperio and Nathalie Vallée (eds), *Laboratory Phonology 10*, Berlin: Mouton de Gruyter, pp. 3–30.

Cohn, Abigail C. (2011), 'Features, segments, and the sources of phonological primitives', in G. Nick Clements and Rachid Ridouane (eds), *Where do phonological features come from?* (Language Faculty and Beyond 6), Amsterdam: John Benjamins, pp. 13–42.

Coleman, John (1998), *Phonological representations: Their names, forms and powers* (Cambridge Studies in Linguistics 85), Cambridge: Cambridge University Press.

Colina, Sonia (2009), 'Sibilant voicing in Ecuadorian Spanish', *Studies in Hispanic and Lusophone Linguistics* 2(1): 1–18.

Collie, Sarah (2007), *English stress preservation and Stratal Optimality Theory*, Edinburgh: University of Edinburgh PhD thesis.

Coltheart, Max (1999), 'Modularity and cognition', *Trends in Cognitive Science* 3(3): 115–20.

Cooper, Sarah (2015), *Intonation in Anglesey Welsh*, Bangor: Bangor University PhD thesis.

Cornillet, Gérard (2006), *Wörterbuch Bretonisch-Deutsch, Deutsch-Bretonisch*, Hamburg: Helmut Buske Verlag.

Cowper, Elizabeth and Daniel Currie Hall (2014), '*Reductiō ad discrīmen*: Where features come from', in Martin Krämer, Sandra Ronai and Peter Svenonius (eds), *Nordlyd* 41(2), *Special issue on features*: 145–64.

Crahé, Maxime-Morvan (2013), *Le breton du Languidic: Étude phonétique, morphologique et syntaxique d'un sous-dialecte du breton vannetais*, Rennes: Université Rennes 2 Basse-Bretagne PhD thesis.

Crowhurst, Megan J. and Mark Hewitt (1997), *Boolean operations and constraint interactions in Optimality Theory*, MS.
Cyran, Eugeniusz (2010), *Complexity scales and licensing in phonology* (Studies in Generative Grammar 105), Berlin: Mouton de Gruyter.
Cyran, Eugeniusz (2013), *Polish voicing: Between phonology and phonetics*, Lublin: Wydawnictwo KUL.
Davison, Deborah (1992), 'Parametric variation in pitch realisation of "neutral tone" in Mandarin', *BLS* 18(2): 67–79.
de Boer, Bart (2000), 'Self-organisation in vowel systems', *Journal of Phonetics* 28(4): 441–65.
de Boer, Bart (2001), *The origins of vowel systems* (Oxford Studies in the Evolution of Language 1), Oxford: Oxford University Press.
de Lacy, Paul (2002), 'The interaction of tone and stress in Optimality Theory', *Phonology* 19(1): 1–32.
de Lacy, Paul (2004), 'Markedness conflation in Optimality Theory', *Phonology* 21(2): 145–99.
de Lacy, Paul (2006), *Markedness: Reduction and preservation in phonology*, Cambridge: Cambridge University Press.
Denez, Per (1977), *Description structurale d'un parler breton (Douarnenez)*, Rennes: Université Rennes 2 Haute-Bretagne PhD thesis.
Di Paolo, Marianna and Alice Faber (1990), 'Phonation differences and the phonetic content of the tense–lax contrast in Utah', *Language Variation and Change* 2(2): 155–204.
Dillon, Brian, Ewan Dunbar and William Idsardi (2012), 'A single-stage approach to learning phonological categories: Insights from Inuktitut', *Cognitive Science* 37(2): 344–77.
D'Imperio, Mariapaola and Sam Rosenthall (1999), 'Phonetics and phonology of main stress in Italian', *Phonology* 16(1): 1–28.
Dinnsen, Daniel A. and Jan Charles-Luce (1984), 'Phonological neutralisation, phonetic implementation and individual differences', *Journal of Phonetics* 12(1): 49–60.
Dmitrieva, Olga, Allard Jongman and Joan Sereno (2010), 'Phonological neutralisation by native and non-native speakers: The case of Russian final devoicing', *Journal of Phonetics* 38(3): 483–92.
Docherty, Gerard J. (1992), *The timing of voicing in British English obstruents* (Netherlands Phonetics Archives 9), Berlin, New York: Foris Publications.
Docherty, Gerard J. and Paul Foulkes (1999), 'Derby and Newcastle: Instrumental phonetics and variationist studies', in Paul Foulkes and Gerard J. Docherty (eds), *Urban voices*, London: Arnold, pp. 47–71.
Docherty, Gerry, Damien Hall, Carmen Llamas, Jennifer Nycz and Dominic Watt (2014), 'Language and identity on the Scottish/English border', in Dominic Watt and Carmen Llamas (eds), *Language, borders and identity*, Edinburgh: Edinburgh University Press.

Donohue, Mark and Johanna Nichols (2011), 'Does phoneme inventory size correlate with population size?', *Linguistic Typology* 15(2): 161–70.
Dresher, B. Elan (2003), 'The contrastive hierarchy in phonology', *Toronto Working Papers in Linguistics* 20: 47–62.
Dresher, B. Elan (2009), *The contrastive hierarchy in phonology*, Cambridge: Cambridge University Press.
Dresher, B. Elan (2014), 'The arch not the stones: Universal feature theory without universal features', in Martin Krämer, Sandra Ronai and Peter Svenonius (eds), *Nordlyd* 41(2), *Special issue on features*: 165–81.
Dresher, B. Elan and Harry van der Hulst (1998), 'Head-dependent asymmetries in phonology: Visibility and complexity', *Phonology* 15(3): 317–52.
Dresher, B. Elan, Glyne Piggott and Keren Rice (1994), 'Contrast in phonology: Overview', *Toronto Working Papers in Linguistics* 14: iii–xvii.
Dressler, Wolfgang U. (1973), *Allegroregeln rechtfertigen Lentoregeln: Sekundäre Phoneme des Bretonischen* (Innsbrucker Beiträge zur Sprachwissenschaft 9), Innsbruck: Institut für vergleichende Sprachwissenschaft der Universität Innsbruck.
Dressler, Wolfgang U. and Josef Hufgard (1980), *Études phonologiques sur le breton sud-bigouden*, Vienna: Verlag der österreichischen Akademie der Wissenschaften.
Dyck, Carrie (1995), *Constraining the phonology–phonetics interface, with exemplification from Spanish and Italian dialects*, Toronto: University of Toronto PhD thesis.
Dyck, Carrie (1996), 'The interface between underspecified phonological representations and specified phonetic representations', in Ursula Kleinhenz (ed.), *Interfaces in phonology* (Studia Grammatica 41), Berlin: Akademie Verlag, pp. 279–93.
Ellis, Jeffrey (1965), 'The grammatical status of initial mutation', *Lochlann* 3: 315–29.
Ernestus, Mirjam and R. Harald Baayen (2006), 'The functionality of incomplete neutralisation in Dutch: The case of past-tense formation', in Louis M. Goldstein, D. H. Whalen and Catherine T. Best (eds), *Phonetics and phonology: Laboratory Phonology 8*, Berlin: Mouton de Gruyter, pp. 27–49.
Ernestus, Mirjam and R. Harald Baayen (2007), 'Intraparadigmatic effects on the perception of voice', in Jeroen van de Weijer and Jan Erik van der Torre (eds), *Voicing in Dutch* (Current Issues in Linguistic Theory 286), Amsterdam: John Benjamins, pp. 153–73.
Escudero, Paola and Paul Boersma (2003), 'Modelling the perceptual development of phonological contrasts with Optimality Theory and the Gradual Learning Algorithm', in Sudha Arunachalam, Elsi Kaiser and Alexander Williams (eds), *Proceedings of the 25th Annual Penn Linguistics Colloquium*, pp. 71–85.
Evans, Nicholas and Stephen C. Levinson (2009), 'The myth of language universals: Language diversity and its importance for cognitive science', *Behavioral and Brain Sciences* 32(5): 429–48.

Evenou, Erwan (1987), *Studi fonologel brezhoneg Lanijen (kanton ar Faouet, Kernev)*, Rennes: Université Rennes 2 Haute-Bretagne PhD thesis.

Evenou, Yvon (1989), 'Description phonologique du breton de Lanvénégen', *Klask* 1: 17–55.

Ewen, Colin J. (1995), 'Dependency relations in phonology', in John Goldsmith (ed.), *The handbook of phonological theory*, Oxford: Blackwell, pp. 570–85.

Falc'hun, François (1938), 'Recherches sur la sonorité des groupes consonantiques en breton', *Études celtiques* 3: 335–61.

Falc'hun, François (1951), *Le système consonantique du breton*, Rennes: Pilhon.

Falc'hun, François (1981), *Perspectives nouvelles sur l'histoire de la langue bretonne*, Paris: Union générale d'éditions.

Favereau, Francis (1984), *Langue quotidienne, langue technique et langue littéraire dans le parler et la tradition orale de Poullaouen*, Rennes: Université Rennes 2 Haute-Bretagne PhD thesis.

Favereau, Francis (1997), *Geriadur ar brezhoneg a-vremañ/Dictionnaire du breton contemporain*, Brest: Skol Vreizh.

Favereau, Francis (2001), *Grammaire du breton contemporain*, Morlaix: Skol Vreizh.

Fisher, William M. and Ira J. Hirsch (1976), 'Intervocalic flapping in English', *CLS* 12(1): 183–98.

Flemming, Edward (2002), *Auditory representations in phonology*, London, New York: Routledge.

Flemming, Edward (2005), 'Deriving natural classes in phonology', *Lingua* 115(3): 287–309.

Flemming, Edward and Stephanie Johnson (2007), 'Rosa's roses: Reduced vowels in American English', *Journal of the International Phonetic Association* 37(1): 83–96.

Fleuriot, Léon (1964), *Le vieux breton: Éléments d'une grammaire*, Paris: Klincksieck.

Fodor, Jerry (1983), *Modularity of the mind: An essay on faculty psychology*, Cambridge, MA: MIT Press.

Foley, James (1977), *Foundations of theoretical phonology* (Cambridge Studies in Linguistics 20), Cambridge: Cambridge University Press.

Fourakis, Marios and Gregory K. Iverson (1984), 'On the "incomplete neutralisation" of German final obstruents', *Phonetica* 31: 140–9.

Fox, Robert A. and Dale Terbeek (1977), 'Dental flaps, vowel duration, and rule ordering in American English', *Journal of Phonetics* 5(1): 27–34.

Fruehwald, Josef (2013), *Phonological involvement in phonetic change*, Philadelphia, PA: University of Pennsylvania PhD thesis.

Fruehwald, Josef (2016), 'The early influence of phonology on phonetic change', *Language* 92(2): 376–410.

George, Ken (1999), 'Mid-length vowels in Cornish', *Journal of Celtic Linguistics* 6: 103–24.

Ghini, Mirco (2001a), *Asymmetries in the phonology of Miogliola* (Studies in Generative Grammar 60), Berlin: Mouton de Gruyter.

Ghini, Mirco (2001b), 'Place of articulation first', in T. Alan Hall (ed.), *Distinctive feature theory* (Phonetics and Phonology 2), Berlin: Mouton de Gruyter, pp. 147–76.

Goblirsch, Kurt Gustav (2005), *Lautverschiebungen in den germanischen Sprachen*, Heidelberg: Universitätsverlag Winter.

Gordeeva, Olga B. and James M. Scobbie (2013), 'A phonetically versatile contrast: Pulmonic and glottalic voicelessness in Scottish English obstruents and voice quality', *Journal of the International Phonetic Association* 43(3): 249–71.

Gordon, Matthew (2000), 'Re-examining default-to-opposite stress', *BLS* 26: 101–12.

Gordon, Matthew J. (2002), 'Investigating chain shifts and mergers', in J. K. Chambers, Peter Trudgill and Natalie Schilling-Estes (eds), *Handbook of language variation and change*, Oxford: Blackwell, pp. 244–66.

Gorman, Kyle (2013), *Generative phonotactics*, Philadelphia, PA: University of Pennsylvania PhD thesis.

Green, Anthony Dubach (2006), 'The independence of phonology and morphology: The Celtic mutations', *Lingua* 116(11): 1946–85.

Green, Anthony Dubach (2007), *Phonology limited*, Potsdam: Universitätsverlag.

Greene, David (1967), 'Varia: Provection and *calediad*', *Studia Celtica* 2: 101–4.

Guillevic, Augustin and Pierre Le Goff (1902), *Grammaire bretonne du dialecte de Vannes*, Vannes: Lafolye Frères.

Gussmann, Edmund (2007), *The phonology of Polish*, Oxford: Oxford University Press.

Hale, Mark and Charles Reiss (2000a), '"Substance abuse" and "dysfunctionalism": Current trends in phonology', *Linguistic Inquiry* 31(1): 157–69.

Hale, Mark and Charles Reiss (2000b), 'Phonology as cognition', in Noel Burton-Roberts, Philip Carr and Gerard Docherty (eds), *Phonological knowledge: Concepts and empirical issues*, Oxford: Oxford University Press, pp. 161–84.

Hale, Mark and Charles Reiss (2008), *The phonological enterprise*, Oxford: Oxford University Press.

Hale, Mark, Madelyn Kissock and Charles Reiss (2007), 'Microvariation, variation, and the features of universal grammar', *Lingua* 117(4): 645–65.

Hall, Daniel Currie (2007), *The role and representation of contrast in phonological theory*, Toronto: University of Toronto PhD thesis.

Hall, Daniel Currie (2009), 'Laryngeal neutralization in Breton: Loss of voice and loss of contrast', in Frédéric Mailhot (ed.), *Proceedings of the 2009 annual conference of the Canadian Linguistic Association*, Toronto: Canadian Linguistic Association, <http://homes.chass.utoronto.ca/~cla-acl/actes2009/CLA2009_Hall.pdf> (last accessed 24 August 2016).

Hall, Daniel Currie (2010), 'Probing the unnatural', *Linguistics in the Netherlands* 27: 73–85.

Hall, Daniel Currie (2011), 'Phonological contrast and its phonetic enhancement: Dispersedness without dispersion', *Phonology* 28(1): 1–54.
Hall, Daniel Currie (2014), 'On substance in phonology', in Laura Teddiman (ed.), *Proceedings of the 2014 annual conference of the Canadian Linguistic Association*, Toronto: Canadian Linguistic Association, <http://cla-acl.ca/wp-content/uploads/Hall-2014.pdf> (last accessed 24 August 2016).
Hall, Kathleen Currie (2013), 'A typology of intermediate phonological relationships', *The Linguistic Review* 30(2): 215–75.
Halle, Morris (1995), 'Feature geometry and feature spreading', *Linguistic Inquiry* 26(1): 1–46.
Hammarberg, Robert (1976), 'The metaphysics of coarticulation', *Journal of Phonetics* 4(4): 353–63.
Hammer, Françoise (1969), *Der bretonische Dialekt von Plouharnel*, Kiel: Christian-Albrechts-Universität zu Kiel PhD thesis.
Hannahs, S. J. (2013), 'Celtic initial mutation: Pattern extraction and subcategorisation', *Word Structure* 6(1): 1–20.
Harris, Alice C. (2008), 'On the explanation of typologically unusual structures', in Jeff Good (ed.), *Linguistic universals and language change*, Oxford: Oxford University Press, pp. 54–76.
Harris, Alice C. (2010), 'Explaining typologically unusual structures: The role of probability', in Michael Cysouw and Jan Wohlgemuth (eds), *Rethinking universals: How rarities affect linguistic theory* (Empirical Approaches to Language Typology 45), Berlin: Mouton de Gruyter, pp. 91–103.
Harris, John (1994), *English sound structure*, Oxford: Blackwell.
Harris, John (1997), 'Licensing Inheritance: An integrated theory of neutralisation', *Phonology* 14(3): 315–70.
Harris, John (2005), 'Vowel reduction as information loss', in Philip Carr, Jacques Durand and Colin J. Ewen (eds), *Headhood, elements, specification, and contrastivity: Papers in honour of John Anderson* (Current Issues in Linguistic Theory 259), Amsterdam: John Benjamins, pp. 119–32.
Harris, John (2009), 'Why final obstruent devoicing is weakening', in Kuniya Nasukawa and Phillip Backley (eds), *Strength relations in phonology* (Studies in Generative Grammar 103), Berlin: Mouton de Gruyter, pp. 9–46.
Harris, John and Geoff Lindsey (1995), 'The elements of phonological representation', in Jacques Durand and Francis Katamba (eds), *Frontiers of phonology: Atoms, structures, derivations*, Harlow: Longman, pp. 34–79.
Haspelmath, Martin (2006), 'Against markedness (and what to replace it with)', *Journal of Linguistics* 42(1): 25–70.
Hay, Jennifer and Laurie Bauer (2007), 'Phoneme inventory size and population size', *Language* 83(2): 388–400.
Hayes, Bruce (1986), 'Inalterability in CV phonology', *Language* 62(2): 321–51.
Hayes, Bruce (1990), 'Precompiled phrasal phonology', in Sharon Inkelas and Draga Zec (eds), *The phonology–syntax connection*, Chicago: University of Chicago Press, pp. 85–108.

Heinz, Jeffrey (2009), 'On the role of locality in learning stress patterns', *Phonology* 26(2): 303–51.
Hejná, Michaela (2015), *Pre-aspiration in Welsh English: A case study of Aberystwyth*, Manchester: University of Manchester PhD thesis.
Hejná, Michaela and Jane Scanlon (2015), 'New laryngeal allophony in Manchester English', in The Scottish Consortium for ICPhS 2015 (ed.), *Proceedings of the 18th International Congress of Phonetic Sciences*, Glasgow: University of Glasgow.
Helgason, Pétur and Catherine Ringen (2008), 'Voicing and aspiration in Swedish stops', *Journal of Phonetics* 36(4): 607–28.
Hemon, Roparz (1940), *Grammaire bretonne*, Brest: Gwalarn.
Hemon, Roparz (1975), *A historical phonology and syntax of Breton*, Dublin: Dublin Institute for Advanced Studies.
Hemon, Roparz and Ronan Huon (2005), *Dictionnaire breton/français et français/breton*, 11th edn, Lannuon: Al Liamm.
Hennessey, Jr., John S. (1990), 'Spirantisation to lenition in Breton: Interpretation of morphological variability', in Martin J. Ball, James Fife, Erich Poppe and Jenny Rowland (eds), *Celtic linguistics/Ieithyddiaeth Geltaidd: Readings in the Brythonic languages. Festschrift for Arwyn T. Watkins* (Current Issues in Linguistic Theory 68), Amsterdam: John Benjamins, pp. 209–24.
Hewitt, Stephen (1973), *The degree of acceptability of Modern Literary Breton to native Breton speakers*, Unpublished Diploma in Linguistics, University of Cambridge.
Hjelmslev, Louis (1943), *Omkring sprogteoriens grundlæggelse*, Copenhagen: Ejnar Munksgaard.
Hjelmslev, Louis (1975), *Résumé of a theory of language*, Copenhagen: Nordisk Sprog- og Kulturforlag.
Hock, Hans Heinrich (1999), 'Finality, prosody, and change', in Osamu Fujimura, Brian D. Joseph and Bohumil Palek (eds), *Proceedings of LP'98: Item order in language and speech*, vol. 1, Prague: Karolinum, pp. 15–30.
Honeybone, Patrick (2001), 'Lenition inhibition in Liverpool English', *English Language and Linguistics* 5(2): 213–49.
Honeybone, Patrick (2002), *Germanic obstruent lenition: Some mutual implications of theoretical and historical phonology*, Newcastle upon Tyne: University of Newcastle upon Tyne PhD thesis.
Honeybone, Patrick (2005a), 'Diachronic evidence in segmental phonology: The case of obstruent laryngeal specification', in Marc van Oostendorp and Jeroen van de Weijer (eds), *The internal organisation of phonological segments* (Studies in Generative Grammar 77), Berlin: Mouton de Gruyter, pp. 319–54.
Honeybone, Patrick (2005b), 'Sharing makes us stronger: Process inhibition and segmental structure', in Philip Carr, Jacques Durand and Colin J. Ewen (eds), *Headhood, elements, specification, and contrastivity: Papers in honour of John Anderson* (Current Issues in Linguistic Theory 259), Amsterdam: John Benjamins, pp. 167–92.

Honeybone, Patrick (2012), 'Lenition in English', in Terttu Nevalainen and Elizabeth Closs Traugott (eds), *Handbook on the history of English: Rethinking approaches to the history of English*, Oxford: Oxford University Press, pp. 773–87.
Hsu, Chai-Shune K. (1998), 'Voicing underspecification in Taiwanese word-final consonants', *UCLA Working Papers in Phonetics* 90: 90–105.
Huffman, Marie (1993), 'Phonetic patterns of nasalisation and implications for feature specification', in Marie Huffman and Rena Krakow (eds), *Nasals, nasalisation, and the velum*, San Diego: Academic Press, pp. 303–27.
Hume, Elizabeth (2004), 'Deconstructing markedness: A predictability-based approach', *BLS* 30(1): 182–98.
Hume, Elizabeth (2011), 'Markedness', in Marc van Oostendorp, Colin J. Ewen, Elizabeth Hume and Keren Rice (eds), *The Blackwell companion to phonology*, Oxford: Blackwell.
Humphreys, Humphrey Lloyd (1972), 'Les sonants fortes dans le parler haut cornouaillais de Bothoa (Saint-Nicholas-du-Pelem, Côtes-du-Nord)', *Études celtiques* 13(1): 259–79.
Humphreys, Humphrey Lloyd (1990), 'Traditional morphological processes and their vitality in Modern Breton and Welsh', in Martin J. Ball, James Fife, Erich Poppe and Jenny Rowland (eds), *Celtic linguistics/Ieithyddiaeth Geltaidd: Readings in the Brythonic languages. Festschrift for Arwyn T. Watkins* (Current Issues in Linguistic Theory 68), Amsterdam: John Benjamins, pp. 129–59.
Humphreys, Humphrey Lloyd (1995), *Phonologie et morphosyntaxe du parler breton de Bothoa en Saint-Nicolas-du-Pélem*, Brest: Emgleo Breiz.
Hutters, Birgit (1985), 'Vocal fold adjustments in aspirated and unaspirated stops in Danish', *Phonetica* 42(1): 1–24.
Hyde, Brett (2006), 'Towards a uniform account of prominence-sensitive stress', in Eric Baković, Junko Itô and John McCarthy (eds), *Wondering at the natural fecundity of things: Essays in honour of Alan Prince*, Santa Cruz: Linguistics Research Center, pp. 139–83.
Hyman, Larry M. (2008), 'Universals in phonology', *The Linguistic Review* 25(1–2): 83–137.
Inkelas, Sharon (1994), 'The consequences of optimisation for underspecification', *NELS* 27: 287–302.
Iosad, Pavel (2012a), 'Vowel reduction in Russian: No phonetics in phonology', *Journal of Linguistics* 48(3): 521–71.
Iosad, Pavel (2012b), *Representation and variation in substance-free phonology: A case study in Celtic*, Tromsø: University of Tromsø PhD thesis.
Iosad, Pavel (2012c), 'Final devoicing and vowel lengthening in Friulian: A representational approach', *Lingua* 122(8): 922–51.
Iosad, Pavel (2014), 'The phonology and morphosyntax of mutation in Breton', *Lingue e linguaggio* 13(1): 23–42.
Iosad, Pavel (2015a), 'The phonologisation of redundancy: Length and quality in Welsh vowels', MS, University of Edinburgh.

Iosad, Pavel (2015b), '"Pitch accent" and prosodic structure in Scottish Gaelic: Reassessing the role of contact', in Martin Hilpert, Janet Duke, Christine Mertzlufft, Jan-Ola Östman and Michael Rießler (eds), *New trends in Nordic and general linguistics*, Berlin: Mouton de Gruyter, pp. 28–54.

Iosad, Pavel (2016), 'The ATR/Laryngeal connection and emergent features', in Bert Botma and Marc van Oostendorp (eds), *Primitives of phonological structure*, Oxford: Oxford University Press.

Iosad, Pavel (forthcoming a), 'Optimality Theory: Motivations and perspectives', in Anna R. K. Bosch and S. J. Hannahs (eds), *The Routledge handbook of phonology*. London, New York: Routledge.

Iosad, Pavel (forthcoming b), 'Welsh svarabhakti as stem allomorphy', *Transactions of the Philological Society*.

Itô, Junko and Armin Mester (1999), 'Realignment', in René Kager, Harry van der Hulst and Wim Zonneveld (eds), *The prosody–morphology interface*, Cambridge: Cambridge University Press, pp. 188–217.

Itô, Junko, Armin Mester and Jaye Padgett (1995), 'Licensing and underspecification in Optimality Theory', *Linguistic Inquiry* 26(4): 571–613.

Iverson, Gregory K. and Joseph C. Salmons (1995), 'Aspiration and laryngeal representation in Germanic', *Phonology* 12(3): 369–96.

Iverson, Gregory K. and Joseph C. Salmons (1999), 'Laryngeal bias in Germanic', *Linguistische Berichte* 178: 135–51.

Iverson, Gregory K. and Joseph C. Salmons (2003a), 'Laryngeal enhancement in early Germanic', *Phonology* 20(1): 43–74.

Iverson, Gregory K. and Joseph C. Salmons (2003b), 'Legacy specification in the laryngeal phonology of Dutch', *Journal of Germanic Linguistics* 15(1): 1–26.

Iverson, Gregory K. and Joseph C. Salmons (2007), 'Domains and directionality in the evolution of German final fortition', *Phonology* 24(1): 121–45.

Iverson, Gregory K. and Joseph C. Salmons (2011), 'Final laryngeal neutralisation and final devoicing', in Marc van Oostendorp, Colin J. Ewen, Elizabeth Hume and Keren Rice (eds), *The Blackwell companion to phonology*, Oxford: Blackwell.

Jackendoff, Ray (1987), *Consciousness and the computational mind*, Cambridge, MA: MIT Press.

Jackendoff, Ray (1992), *Languages of the mind*, Cambridge, MA: MIT Press.

Jackendoff, Ray (1997), *The architecture of the language faculty*, Cambridge, MA: MIT Press.

Jackendoff, Ray (2000), 'Fodorian modularity and representational modularity', in Yosef Grodzinsky, Lew Shapiro and David Swinney (eds), *Language and the brain: Representation and processing*, San Diego: Academic Press, pp. 4–30.

Jackendoff, Ray (2002), *Foundations of language: Brain, memory, grammar, evolution*, Oxford: Oxford University Press.

Jackson, Kenneth Hurlstone (1960), 'The phonology of the Breton dialect of Plougrescant', *Études celtiques* 9: 327–404.

Jackson, Kenneth Hurlstone (1967), *A historical phonology of Breton*, Dublin: Dublin Institute for Advanced Studies.
Jackson, Kenneth Hurlstone (1972), 'The regular and irregular verbs at Plougrescant', in Herbert Pilch and Joachim Thurow (eds), *Indo-Celtica: Gedächtnisschrift für Alf Sommerfelt* (Commentationes Societatis Linguisticae Europeae 2), Oxford: Max Hueber Verlag, pp. 73–88.
Jaker, Alessandro (2011), *Prosodic reversal in Dogrib (Weledeh dialect)*, Stanford, CA: Stanford University PhD thesis.
Jakobson, Roman and Morris Halle (1956), *Fundamentals of language*, The Hague: Mouton.
Jakobson, Roman, Gunnar Fant and Morris Halle (1951), *Preliminaries to speech analysis*, Cambridge, MA: MIT Press.
Jansen, Wouter (2004), *Laryngeal contrast and phonetic voicing: A Laboratory Phonology approach to English, Hungarian and Dutch*, Groningen: University of Groningen PhD thesis.
Jansen, Wouter (2007a), 'Dutch regressive voicing assimilation as a "low level phonetic process": Acoustic evidence', in Jeroen van de Weijer and Jan Erik van der Torre (eds), *Voicing in Dutch* (Current Issues in Linguistic Theory 286), Amsterdam: John Benjamins, pp. 123–51.
Jansen, Wouter (2007b), 'Phonological "voicing", phonetic voicing, and assimilation in English', *Language Sciences* 29(2–3): 270–93.
Jessen, Michael and Catherine Ringen (2002), 'Laryngeal features in German', *Phonology* 19(2): 189–218.
Jiménez, Jesús and Maria-Rosa Lloret (2008), 'Asimetrías perceptivas y similitud articulatoria en la asimilación sonoridad del catalán', *Cuadernos de Lingüística del I. U. I. Ortega y Gasset* 15: 71–90.
Jones, Mari C. (1995), 'At what price language maintenance? Standardisation in Modern Breton', *French Studies* 49(4): 424–38.
Jones, Mark J. and Carmen Llamas (2003), 'Fricated pre-aspirated /t/ in Middlesbrough English: An acoustic study', in Maria-Josep Solé, Daniel Recasens and Joaquin Romero (eds), *Proceedings of the 15th International Congress of Phonetic Sciences*, Barcelona: Universitat Autònoma de Barcelona, pp. 655–8.
Jurgec, Peter (2010), *Feature spreading 2.0: A unified theory of assimilation*, Tromsø: University of Tromsø PhD thesis.
Kager, René (1999), 'Surface opacity of metrical structure in Optimality Theory', in Marc van Oostendorp and Ben Hermans (eds), *The derivational residue in phonological Optimality Theory* (Linguistik Aktuell 28), Amsterdam: John Benjamins, pp. 207–46.
Kaisse, Ellen M. and April McMahon (2011), 'Lexical Phonology and the lexical syndrome', in Marc van Oostendorp, Colin J. Ewen, Elizabeth Hume and Keren Rice (eds), *The Blackwell companion to phonology*, Oxford: Blackwell.
Kallestinova, Elena (2004), 'Voice and aspiration of stops in Turkish', *Folia Linguistica* 38(1–2): 117–43.

Kaye, Jonathan (1990), '"Coda" licensing', *Phonology* 7(2): 301–30.
Keating, Patricia (1988a), 'Underspecification in phonetics', *Phonology* 5(2): 275–92.
Keating, Patricia (1988b), 'The window model of coarticulation: Articulatory evidence', *UCLA Working Papers in Phonetics* 69: 3–29.
Keating, Patricia (1990a), 'The window model of coarticulation: Acoustic evidence', in John Kingston and Mary Beckman (eds), *Papers in Laboratory Phonology 1*, Cambridge: Cambridge University Press, pp. 451–70.
Keating, Patricia (1990b), 'Phonetic representations in a generative grammar', *Journal of Phonetics* 18(3): 321–34.
Keating, Patricia (1996), 'The phonology–phonetics interface', in Ursula Kleinhenz (ed.), *Interfaces in phonology* (Studia Grammatica 41), Berlin: Akademie Verlag, pp. 262–78.
Keating, Patricia and Aditi Lahiri (1993), 'Fronted velars, palatalised velars, and palatals', *Phonetica* 50(2): 73–101.
Kennard, Holly J. (2014), 'The persistence of verb second in negative utterances in Breton', *Journal of Historical Linguistics* 4(1): 1–39.
Kennard, Holly J. and Aditi Lahiri (forthcoming), 'Mutation in Breton verbs: Pertinacity across generations', *Journal of Linguistics*.
Kenstowicz, Michael (1996), 'Base-identity and uniform exponence: Alternatives to cyclicity', in Jacques Durand and Bernard Laks (eds), *Current trends in phonology: Models and methods*, Salford: European Studies Research Institute, University of Salford, pp. 363–93.
Kenstowicz, Michael (1997), 'Quality-sensitive stress', *Rivista di linguistica* 9: 157–87.
Kervella, Frañsez (1946), *Yezhadur bras ar brezhoneg*, La Baule: Skridou Breizh.
Keyser, Samuel Jay and Kenneth N. Stevens (2006), 'Enhancement and overlap in the speech chain', *Language* 82(1): 33–63.
Kingston, John (2007), 'The phonetics–phonology interface', in Paul de Lacy (ed.), *The Cambridge handbook of phonology*, Cambridge: Cambridge University Press, pp. 401–34.
Kingston, John and Randy L. Diehl (1994), 'Phonetic knowledge', *Language* 70(3): 419–54.
Kingston, John and Randy L. Diehl (1995), 'Intermediate properties in the perception of distinctive feature values', in Amalia Arvaniti and Bruce Connell (eds), *Phonology and phonetic evidence: Papers in Laboratory Phonology IV*, Cambridge: Cambridge University Press, pp. 7–27.
Kingston, John, Randy L. Diehl, Cecilia J. Kirk and Wendy A. Castleman (2008), 'On the internal perceptual structure of distinctive features: The [voice] contrast', *Journal of Phonetics* 36(1): 28–54.
Kingston, John, Aditi Lahiri and Randy L. Diehl (2009), 'Voice', MS, University of Massachusetts, Amherst, University of Oxford, University of Texas, Austin.

Kiparsky, Paul (1982), 'Lexical Phonology and Morphology', in In-Seok Yang (ed.), *Linguistics in the morning calm: Selected papers from SICOL-1981*, vol. 1, Seoul: Hanshin Publishing, pp. 3–91.
Kiparsky, Paul (1985), 'Some consequences of Lexical Phonology', *Phonology Yearbook* 2: 85–138.
Kiparsky, Paul (2000), 'Opacity and cyclicity', *The Linguistic Review* 17(2–4): 351–67.
Kiparsky, Paul (2006), 'The Amphichronic Program vs. Evolutionary Phonology', *Theoretical Linguistics* 32(2): 217–36.
Kiparsky, Paul (2008a), 'Universals constrain change; change results in typological generalisations', in Jeff Good (ed.), *Linguistic universals and language change*, Oxford: Oxford University Press, pp. 23–53.
Kiparsky, Paul (2008b), 'Fenno-Swedish quantity: Contrast in Stratal OT', in Bert Vaux and Andrew Nevins (eds), *Rules, constraints and phonological phenomena*, Oxford: Oxford University Press, pp. 185–220.
Kiparsky, Paul (2011), 'Chains or strata? The case of Maltese', MS, Stanford University.
Kirby, Simon, Tom Griffiths and Kenny Smith (2014), 'Iterated learning and the evolution of language', *Current Opinion in Neurobiology* 28: 108–14.
Kirchner, Robert (1997), 'Contrastiveness and faithfulness', *Phonology* 14(1): 83–111.
Kirchner, Robert (2000), 'Geminate inalterability and lenition', *Language* 76(3): 509–46.
Köhnlein, Björn (2016), 'Contrastive foot structure in Franconian tone accent systems', *Phonology* 31(3): 87–123.
Kraehenmann, Astrid (2001), 'Swiss German stops: Geminates all over the word', *Phonology* 18(1): 109–45.
Kraehenmann, Astrid (2003), *Quantity and prosodic asymmetries in Alemannic: Synchronic and diachronic perspectives*, Berlin: Mouton de Gruyter.
Kraehenmann, Astrid and Aditi Lahiri (2008), 'Duration differences in the articulation and acoustics of Swiss German word-initial geminate and singleton stops', *Journal of the Acoustical Society of America* 123(6): 4446–55.
Krämer, Martin (2000), 'Voicing alternations and underlying representations: The case of Breton', *Lingua* 110(9): 639–63.
Krämer, Martin (2009), *The phonology of Italian*, Oxford: Oxford University Press.
Krämer, Martin (2012), *Underlying representations* (Key Topics in Phonology 2), Cambridge: Cambridge University Press.
Kurisu, Kazutaka (2001), *The phonology of morpheme realisation*, Santa Cruz: University of California, Santa Cruz PhD thesis.
Labov, William (1994), *Principles of linguistic change. Vol. 1: Internal factors*, Oxford: Blackwell.
Labov, William (2010), *Principles of linguistic change. Vol. 3: Cognitive and cultural factors*, Malden, MA: Wiley-Blackwell.

Labov, William, Ingrid Rosenfelder and Josef Fruehwald (2013), 'One hundred years of sound change in Philadelphia: Linear incrementation, reversal, and reanalysis', *Language* 89(1): 30–65.

Ladd, D. Robert (2011), 'Phonetics in phonology', in John Goldsmith, Jason Riggle and Alan Yu (eds), *The handbook of phonological theory*, 2nd edn, Oxford: Wiley-Blackwell, pp. 348–73.

Ladd, D. Robert (2014), *Simultaneous structure in phonology*, Oxford: Oxford University Press.

Ladefoged, Peter (1984), '"Out of chaos, comes order": Physical, biological, and structural patterns in phonetics', in M. P. R. van den Broecke and A. Cohen (eds), *Proceedings of ICPhS X*, Dordrecht: Foris, pp. 83–95.

Ladefoged, Peter, Jenny Ladefoged, Alice Turk, Kevin Hind and St. John Skilton (1998), 'Phonetic structures of Scottish Gaelic', *Journal of the International Phonetic Association* 28(1): 1–41.

Le Clerc, Louis (1908), *Grammaire bretonne du dialecte de Tréguier*, Saint-Brieuc: Prud'homme.

Le Dû, Jean (1978), *Le parler breton de la presqu'île de Plougrescant*, Brest: Université de Bretagne Occidentale PhD thesis.

Le Dû, Jean (1986), 'A sandhi survey of the Breton language', in Henning Andersen (ed.), *Sandhi phenomena in the languages of Europe* (Trends in Linguistics 33), Berlin, New York, Amsterdam: Mouton de Gruyter, pp. 435–50.

Le Dû, Jean (1997), 'Le breton au XXe siècle: Renaissance ou création?', *Zeitschrift für celtische Philologie* 49–50: 414–31.

Le Dû, Jean (2001), *Nouvel atlas linguistique de la Basse-Bretagne*, Brest: CRBC.

Le Dû, Jean (2012), *Le trégorrois à Plougrescant: Dictionnaire breton-français*, Brest: Emgleo Breiz.

Le Gall, J. (1903), 'Quelques recherches sur l'accent, le timbre et la quantité des voyelles dans le dialecte breton de Botsorhel', *Annales de Bretagne* 19(2): 249–66.

Le Pipec, Erwan (2000), *Le breton de Malguénac: Quelques aspects*, Lannion: Hor Yezh.

Le Pipec, Erwan (2008), *Etude pluridimensionnelle d'un parler: Description, émergence et aspects sociolinguistiques du breton de Malguénac*, Rennes: Université Rennes 2 Haute-Bretagne PhD thesis.

Le Pipec, Erwan (2013), 'Les trois ruptures sociolinguistiques du breton', *International Journal of the Sociology of Language* 223: 103–16.

Le Roux, Pierre (1924–63), *Atlas linguistique de la Basse-Bretagne*, Rennes, Paris: Plihon, Champion.

Lewis, Henry and J. R. F. Piette (1962), *Llawlyfr Llydaweg Canol*, Caerdydd: Gwasg Prifysgol Cymru.

Liljencrants, Johan and Björn Lindblom (1972), 'Numerical simulation of vowel quality systems: The role of perceptual contrast', *Language* 48(4): 839–62.

Lipski, John (1989), '/s/-voicing in Ecuadoran Spanish: Patterns and principles of consonantal modification', *Lingua* 79(1): 49–71.

Lisker, Leigh (1986), '"Voicing" in English: A catalogue of acoustic features signaling /b/ versus /p/ in trochees', *Language and Speech* 29(1): 3–11.
Lodge, Ken (2009), *Fundamental concepts in phonology*, Edinburgh: Edinburgh University Press.
Löfqvist, Anders and Hirohide Yoshioka (1981), 'Laryngeal activity in Icelandic obstruent production', *Nordic Journal of Linguistics* 4(1): 1–18.
Lombardi, Linda (1990), 'The nonlinear organisation of the affricate', *Natural Language and Linguistic Theory* 8(3): 375–425.
Lombardi, Linda (1995a), *Laryngeal features and laryngeal neutralisation*, New York, London: Garland Publishing.
Lombardi, Linda (1995b), 'Laryngeal features and privativity', *The Linguistic Review* 12(1): 35–60.
Lombardi, Linda (1999), 'Positional faithfulness and voicing assimilation in Optimality Theory', *Natural Language & Linguistic Theory* 17: 267–302.
Lombardi, Linda (2001), 'Why Place and Voice are different: Constraint-specific alternations in Optimality Theory', in Linda Lombardi (ed.), *Segmental phonology in Optimality Theory: Constraints and representation*, Cambridge: Cambridge University Press, pp. 13–45.
Lorentz, Ove (2007), 'Privativity and allophony in small inventories', MS, University of Tromsø.
Lowenstamm, Jean (1996), 'CV as the only syllable type', in Jacques Durand and Bernard Laks (eds), *Current trends in phonology: Models and methods*, Salford: European Studies Research Institute, University of Salford, pp. 419–41.
McCarthy, John J. (1988), 'Feature geometry and dependency: A review', *Phonetica* 45: 84–108.
McCarthy, John J. (2004), 'Optimal Paradigms', in Laura J. Downing, Alan Tracy Hall and Renate Raffelsiefen (eds), *Paradigms in phonological theory*, Oxford: Oxford University Press, pp. 170–210.
McCarthy, John J. (2005), 'The length of stem-final vowels in Colloquial Arabic', in Mohammad T. Alhaway and Elabbas Benmamoun (eds), *Perspectives on Arabic linguistics XVII–XVIII*, Amsterdam: John Benjamins, pp. 1–26.
McCarthy, John J. (2007), *Hidden generalisations: Phonological opacity in Optimality Theory* (Advances in Optimality Theory 1), London: Equinox.
McCarthy, John J. and Joe Pater (eds) (2016), *Harmonic Grammar and Harmonic Serialism*, London: Equinox.
McKenna, Malachy (1988), *A handbook of modern spoken Breton*, Tübingen: Günter Narr Verlag.
MacKenzie, Laurel (2013), 'Variation in English auxiliary realisation: A new take on contraction', *Language Variation and Change* 25(1): 17–41.
MacKenzie, Laurel and Meredith Tamminga (2013), 'Two case studies on the non-local conditioning of variation', Presentation at the 2013 Annual Meeting of the Linguistic Society of America.
Mackenzie, Sara (2013), 'Laryngeal co-occurrence restrictions in Aymara: Contrastive representations and constraint interaction', *Phonology* 30(2): 297–345.

McMahon, April (2000), *Lexical Phonology and the history of English* (Cambridge Studies in Linguistics 91), Cambridge: Cambridge University Press.

Maddieson, Ian and Richard Wright (1995), 'The vowels and consonants of Amis: A preliminary phonetic report', *UCLA Working Papers in Phonetics* 91: 45–66.

Madeg, Mikael (2010), *Traité de prononciation du breton de Nord-Ouest*, Brest: Emgleo Breiz.

Maguire, Warren (2008), *What is a merger, and can it be reversed? The origin, status and reversal of the 'NURSE–NORTH merger' in Tyneside English*, Newcastle upon Tyne: University of Newcastle upon Tyne PhD thesis.

Maguire, Warren, Lynn Clark and Kevin Watson (2013), 'Introduction: What are mergers and can they be reversed?', *English Language and Linguistics* 17(2): 229–39.

Manaster Ramer, Alexis (1996), 'A letter from an incompletely neutral phonologist', *Journal of Phonetics* 24(4): 477–89.

Martinet, André (1955), *Économie des changements phonétiques*, Bern: Francke.

Mielke, Jeff (2003), 'The interplay of speech perception and phonology: Experimental evidence from Turkish', *Phonetica* 60(3): 208–29.

Mielke, Jeff (2005), 'Ambivalence and ambiguity in laterals and nasals', *Phonology* 22(2): 169–203.

Mielke, Jeff (2007), *The emergence of distinctive features*, Oxford: Oxford University Press.

Mielke, Jeff (2013), 'Phonologisation and the typology of feature behavior', in Alan C. L. Yu (ed.), *Origins of sound change: Approaches to phonologisation*, Oxford: Oxford University Press, pp. 165–80.

Mielke, Jeff, Lyra Magloughlin and Elizabeth Hume (2010), 'Evaluating the effectiveness of Unified Feature Theory and three other feature systems', in John A. Goldsmith, Elizabeth Hume and W. Leo Wetzels (eds), *Tones and features: Phonetic and phonological perspectives* (Studies in Generative Grammar 107), Berlin: De Gruyter, pp. 223–63.

Mihm, Arend (2007), 'Theorien der Auslautverhärtung im Spannungsverhältnis zwischen Normsetzung und Sprachwirklichkeit', *Deutsche Sprache* 35(2): 95–118.

Milroy, James and John Harris (1980), 'When is a merger not a merger? The MEAT/MATE problem in a presentday English vernacular', *English World-Wide* 1: 199–210.

Mohanan, K. P. (1986), *The theory of lexical phonology*, Dordrecht: Foris.

Moran, Steven, Daniel McCloy and Richard Wright (2012), 'Revisiting population size vs. phoneme inventory size', *Language* 88(4): 877–93.

Morén, Bruce (2001), *Distinctiveness, coercion, and sonority: A unified theory of weight*, London, New York: Routledge.

Morén, Bruce (2003), 'The Parallel Structures Model of feature geometry', *Working Papers of the Cornell Phonetics Laboratory* 15: 194–270.

Morén, Bruce (2006), 'Consonant–vowel interactions in Serbian: Features, representations and constraint interactions', *Lingua* 116(8): 1198–244.

Morén, Bruce (2007), 'The division of labour between segment-internal structure and violable constraints', in Sylvia Blaho, Patrik Bye and Martin Krämer (eds), *Freedom of analysis?* (Studies in Generative Grammar 95), Berlin: Mouton de Gruyter, pp. 313–44.

Morén-Duolljá, Bruce (2013), 'The prosody of Swedish underived nouns: No lexical tones required', in Sylvia Blaho, Martin Krämer and Bruce Morén-Duolljá (eds), *Nordlyd* 40(1), 196–248.

Moreton, Elliott (2004), 'Non-computable functions in Optimality Theory', in John J. McCarthy (ed.), *Optimality Theory in phonology*, Oxford: Blackwell, pp. 141–64.

Moreton, Elliott (2006), 'Analytic bias and phonological typology', *Phonology* 25(1): 83–127.

Morgan, Thomas John (1952), *Y treigladau a'u cystrawen*, Caerdydd: Gwasg Prifysgol Cymru.

Morley, Rebecca L. (2015), 'Can phonological universals be emergent? Modeling the space of sound change, lexical distribution, and hypothesis selection', *Language* 91(2): e40–e70.

Morris, Jonathan (2010), 'Phonetic variation in North Wales: Preaspiration', in *Proceedings of the Second Summer School on Sociolinguistics, University of Edinburgh*.

Myers, Scott (1998), 'Surface underspecification of tone in Chichewa', *Phonology* 15(3): 367–91.

Myers, Scott (2000), 'Boundary disputes: The distinction between phonetic and phonological sound patterns', in Noel Burton-Roberts, Philip Carr and Gerard Docherty (eds), *Phonological knowledge: Concepts and empirical issues*, Oxford: Oxford University Press, pp. 245–72.

Nance, Claire and Jane Stuart-Smith (2013), 'Pre-aspiration and post-aspiration in Scottish Gaelic stop consonants', *Journal of the International Phonetic Association* 43(2): 129–52.

Nesset, Tore (2002), 'Dissimilation, assimilation and vowel reduction: Constraint interaction in East Slavic dialects with so-called assimilative *akan'je* and *jakanje*', *Poljarnyj vestnik* 5: 77–101.

Nettle, Daniel (1999a), 'Is the rate of linguistic change constant?', *Lingua* 108(2–3): 119–36.

Nettle, Daniel (1999b), 'Using Social Impact Theory to simulate language change', *Lingua* 108(2–3): 95–117.

Nevins, Andrew (2009), 'On formal universals in phonology', *Behavioral and Brain Sciences* 32(5): 461–2.

Nevins, Andrew (2010), *Locality in vowel harmony* (Linguistic Inquiry Monograph 55), Cambridge, MA: MIT Press.

Newmeyer, Frederick (2005), *Possible and probable languages: A generative perspective on linguistic typology*, Oxford: Oxford University Press.

Noske, Manuela (1997), 'Feature spreading as dealignment: The distribution of [ç] and [x] in German', *Phonology* 14(2): 221–34.

Odden, David (1988), 'Anti-antigemination and the OCP', *Linguistic Inquiry* 19(3): 451–75.
Odden, David (1994), 'Adjacency parameters in phonology', *Language* 70(2): 289–330.
Odden, David (2010), 'Features impinging on tone', in John A. Goldsmith, Elizabeth Hume and W. Leo Wetzels (eds), *Tones and features: Phonetic and phonological perspectives* (Studies in Generative Grammar 107), Berlin: De Gruyter, pp. 81–107.
Odden, David (2013), 'Formal Phonology', in Sylvia Blaho, Martin Krämer and Bruce Morén-Duolljá (eds), *Nordlyd* 40(1): 24–43.
Ohala, John J. and Maria-Josep Solé (2010), 'Turbulence and phonology', in Susanne Fuchs, Martine Toda and Marzena Żygis (eds), *Turbulent sounds: Interdisciplinary guide* (Interface Explorations 21), Berlin: Mouton de Gruyter, pp. 37–101.
Oudeyer, Pierre-Yves (2005), 'The self-organisation of speech sounds', *Journal of Theoretical Biology* 233(3): 435–49.
Parry-Williams, Thomas Herbert (1913), *Some points of similarity in the phonology of Welsh and Breton*, Paris: Champion.
Paster, Mary (2006), *Phonological conditions on affixation*, Berkeley: University of California, Berkeley PhD thesis.
Pater, Joe (2000), 'Non-uniformity in English secondary stress: The role of ranked and lexically specific constraints', *Phonology* 17(2): 237–74.
Pater, Joe (2009), 'Morpheme-specific phonology: Constraint indexation and inconsistency resolution', in Steve Parker (ed.), *Phonological argumentation: Essays on evidence and motivation* (Advances in Optimality Theory 5), London: Equinox, pp. 123–54.
Peperkamp, Sharon, Rozenn Le Calvez, Jean-Pierre Nadal and Emmanuel Dupoux (2006), 'The acquisition of allophonic rules: Statistical learning with linguistic constraints', *Cognition* 101(3): B31–B41.
Petrova, Olga, Rosemary Plapp, Catherine Ringen and Szilard Szentgyörgyi (2006), 'Voice and aspiration: Evidence from Russian, Hungarian, German, Swedish and Turkish', *The Linguistic Review* 23(1): 1–35.
Picanço, Gessiane (2005), *Mundurukú: Phonetics, phonology, synchrony, diachrony*, Vancouver: University of British Columbia PhD thesis.
Pierrehumbert, Janet (1980), *The phonetics and phonology of English intonation*, Cambridge, MA: Massachusetts Institute of Technology PhD thesis.
Pierrehumbert, Janet (1990), 'Phonological and phonetic representation', *Journal of Phonetics* 18(3): 375–94.
Pierrehumbert, Janet (2001), 'Exemplar dynamics: Word frequency, lenition, and contrast', in Joan Bybee and Paul J. Hopper (eds), *Frequency effects and emergent grammar*, Amsterdam: John Benjamins, pp. 137–58.
Pierrehumbert, Janet (2002), 'Word-specific phonetics', in Carlos Gussenhoven and Natasha Warner (eds), *Laboratory Phonology 7*, Berlin, New York: Mouton de Gruyter, pp. 101–40.

Pierrehumbert, Janet (2006), 'The next toolkit', *Journal of Phonetics* 34(4): 516–30.
Pierrehumbert, Janet and Mary Beckman (1988), *Japanese tone structure* (Linguistic Inquiry Monograph 15), Cambridge, MA: MIT Press.
Pierrehumbert, Janet, Mary Beckman and D. Robert Ladd (2000), 'Conceptual foundations of phonology as a laboratory science', in Noel Burton-Roberts, Philip Carr and Gerard Docherty (eds), *Phonological knowledge: Concepts and empirical issues*, Oxford: Oxford University Press, pp. 273–304.
Piggott, Glyne L. (1992), 'Variability in feature dependency: The case of nasality', *Natural Language & Linguistic Theory* 10(1): 33–77.
Ploneis, Jean-Marie (1983), *Au carrefour des dialectes bretons: Le parler de Berrien. Essai de description phonématique et morphologique*, Paris: SELAF.
Plourin, Jean-Yves (1985), 'L'accentuation en Haute-Cornouaille et en bas-vannetais', *La Bretagne Linguistique* 1: 103–15.
Port, Robert F. and Adam P. Leary (2005), 'Against formal phonology', *Language* 81(4): 927–64.
Port, Robert F. and Michael O'Dell (1985), 'Neutralisation of syllable-final voicing in German', *Journal of Phonetics* 13(4): 455–71.
Potts, Christopher and Geoffrey K. Pullum (2002), 'Model theory and the content of OT constraints', *Phonology* 19(3): 361–93.
Press, Ian (1986), *A grammar of Modern Breton*, Berlin: Mouton de Gruyter.
Press, Ian (2004), *Standard Breton*, Munich: LINCOM Europa.
Prince, Alan S. (1992), 'Quantitative consequences of rhythmic organisation', *CLS* 25(2): 355–98.
Prince, Alan S. and Paul Smolensky (1993), *Optimality Theory: Constraint interaction in generative grammar*, Technical report, New Brunswick, NJ, Boulder, CO: Rutgers University Center for Cognitive Science, University of Colorado, Boulder.
Prinz, Jesse J. (2006), 'Is the mind really modular?', in Robert J. Stainton (ed.), *Contemporary debates in cognitive science* (Contemporary Debates in Philosophy 7), Oxford: Blackwell, pp. 22–36.
Przezdziecki, Marek (2005), *Vowel harmony and coarticulation in three dialects of Yorùbá: Phonetics determining phonology*, Ithaca, NY: Cornell University PhD thesis.
Pulleyblank, Douglas (2006), 'Minimizing UG: Constraints upon constraints', *WCCFL* 25: 15–39.
Pyatt, Elizabeth J. (1997), *An integrated model of the syntax and phonology of Celtic mutation*, Cambridge, MA: Harvard University PhD thesis.
Pyatt, Elizabeth J. (2003), 'Relativised mutation domains in the Celtic languages', in Elsi Kaiser and Sudha Arunachalam (eds), *Proceedings from the Penn Linguistics Colloquium 26*, Philadelphia: University of Pennsylvania.
Pycha, Anne (2009), 'Lengthened affricates as a test case for the phonetics–phonology interface', *Journal of the International Phonetic Association* 39(1): 1–31.

Pycha, Anne (2010), 'A test case for the phonetics–phonology interface: Gemination restrictions in Hungarian', *Phonology* 27(1): 119–52.
Pylyshyn, Zenon (1984), *Computation and cognition: Towards a foundation for cognitive science*, Cambridge, MA: MIT Press.
Ramsammy, Michael (2015), 'The life cycle of phonological processes: Accounting for dialectal microtypologies', *Language and Linguistics Compass* 9(1): 33–54.
Reiss, Charles (2003), 'Quantification in structural descriptions: Attested and unattested patterns', *The Linguistic Review* 20(2–4): 305–38.
Reiss, Charles (2007), 'Modularity in the sound domain: Implications for the purview of Universal Grammar', in Charles Reiss and Gillian Ramchand (eds), *The Oxford handbook of linguistic interfaces*, Oxford: Oxford University Press, pp. 53–80.
Rice, Curt (1992), *Binarity and ternarity in metrical systems: Parametric extensions*, Austin: University of Texas, Austin PhD thesis.
Rice, Keren (1992), 'On deriving sonority: A structural account of sonority relationships', *Phonology* 9(1): 61–99.
Rice, Keren (1993), 'A reexamination of the feature [sonorant]: The status of "sonorant obstruents"', *Language* 69(2): 308–44.
Rice, Keren (1994), 'Laryngeal features in Athapaskan languages', *Phonology* 11(1): 107–47.
Rice, Keren (1996), 'Default variability: The coronal–velar relationship', *Natural Language & Linguistic Theory* 14(3): 493–543.
Rice, Keren (2003), 'Featural markedness in phonology: Variation', in Lisa Cheng and Rint Sybesma (eds), *The second Glot International state-of-the-article book: The latest in linguistics* (Studies in Generative Grammar 61), Berlin: Mouton de Gruyter, pp. 389–430.
Rice, Keren (2007), 'Markedness in phonology', in Paul de Lacy (ed.), *The Cambridge handbook of phonology*, Cambridge: Cambridge University Press, pp. 79–97.
Rice, Keren (2009), 'Nuancing markedness: A place for contrast', in Eric Raimy and Charles Cairns (eds), *Contemporary views on architecture and representations in phonology* (Current Studies in Linguistics 48), Cambridge, MA: MIT Press, pp. 311–21.
Rice, Keren (2011), 'What is universal? Some remarks on featural markedness in phonology', presentation at NELS 42, University of Toronto.
Rice, Keren and Peter Avery (1989), 'On the relation between sonorancy and voicing', in Barbara Brunson, Strang Burton and Tom Wilson (eds), *Toronto Working Papers in Linguistics* 10: 65–82.
Ringen, Catherine (1999), 'Aspiration, preaspiration, deaspiration, sonorant devoicing and spirantisation in Icelandic', *Nordic Journal of Linguistics* 22(2): 137–56.
Ringen, Catherine and Wim A. van Dommelen (2013), 'Quantity and laryngeal contrasts in Norwegian', *Journal of Phonetics* 41(6): 479–90.

Robbins, Philip (2010), 'Modularity of mind', in Edward N. Zalta (ed.), *The Stanford Encyclopedia of Philosophy*, Stanford, CA: CSLI.
Robinson, Kimball (1979), 'On the voicing of intervocalic /s/ in the Ecuadorian highlands', *Romance Philology* 33: 137–43.
Rubach, Jerzy (2000), 'Backness switch in Russian', *Phonology* 17(1): 39–64.
Rubach, Jerzy (2005), 'Mid vowel fronting in Ukrainian', *Phonology* 22(1): 1–36.
Rubach, Jerzy (2008), 'Prevocalic faithfulness', *Phonology* 25(3): 433–68.
Saba Kirchner, Jesse (2010), *Minimal reduplication*, Santa Cruz: University of California, Santa Cruz PhD thesis.
Sagey, Elizabeth (1986), *The representation of features and relations in nonlinear phonology*, Cambridge, MA: Massachusetts Institute of Technology PhD thesis.
Samuels, Bridget (2011), *Phonological architecture: A biolinguistic perspective* (Oxford Studies in Biolinguistics 2), Oxford: Oxford University Press.
Sandler, Wendy (1993), 'Sign language and modularity', *Lingua* 89(4): 315–51.
Schane, Sanford S. (1984), 'The fundamentals of Particle Phonology', *Phonology Yearbook* 1: 129–55.
Scheer, Tobias (2004), *A lateral theory of phonology. What is CVCV and why should it be?* (Studies in Generative Grammar 68), Berlin: Mouton de Gruyter.
Scheer, Tobias (2010), *A guide to morphosyntax–phonology interface theories: How extra-phonological information is treated in phonology since Trubetzkoy's Grenzsignale*, Berlin: Mouton de Gruyter.
Scheer, Tobias (2014), 'Spell-Out, post-phonological', in Eugeniusz Cyran and Jolanta Szpyra-Kozłowska (eds), *Crossing phonetics–phonology lines*, Newcastle upon Tyne: Cambridge Scholars Publishing, pp. 255–75.
Schrijver, Peter (2011a), 'Middle and Early Modern Breton', in Elmar Ternes (ed.), *Brythonic Celtic/Britannisches Keltisch* (Münchner Forschungen zur Historischen Sprachwissenschaft 11), Bremen: Hempen Verlag, pp. 359–430.
Schrijver, Peter (2011b), 'Old British', in Elmar Ternes (ed.), *Brythonic Celtic/Britannisches Keltisch* (Münchner Forschungen zur Historischen Sprachwissenschaft 11), Bremen: Hempen Verlag, pp. 1–84.
Scobbie, James M. (1995), 'What do we do when phonology is powerful enough to imitate phonetics? Comments on Zsiga', in Amalia Arvaniti and Bruce Connell (eds), *Phonology and phonetic evidence: Papers in Laboratory Phonology IV*, Cambridge: Cambridge University Press, pp. 303–14.
Scobbie, James M. (1997), *Autosegmental representation in a declarative constraint-based framework*, New York: Garland.
Scobbie, James M. (2006), 'Flexibility in the face of incompatible English VOT systems', in Louis M. Goldstein, D. H. Whalen and Catherine T. Best (eds), *Phonetics and phonology: Laboratory Phonology 8*, Berlin: Mouton de Gruyter, pp. 367–92.
Scobbie, James M. (2007), 'Interface and overlap in phonetics and phonology', in Charles Reiss and Gillian Ramchand (eds), *The Oxford handbook of linguistic interfaces*, Oxford: Oxford University Press, pp. 17–52.

Scobbie, James M., John S. Coleman and Steven Bird (1996), 'Key aspects of declarative phonology', in Jacques Durand and Bernard Laks (eds), *Current trends in phonology: Models and methods*, Salford: European Studies Research Institute, University of Salford, pp. 685–710.
Sebregts, Koen (2014), *The sociophonetics and phonology of Dutch /r/*, Utrecht: Utrecht University PhD thesis.
Sen, Ranjan (2015), *Syllable and segment in Latin*, Oxford: Oxford University Press.
Silverman, Daniel (1997), *Phasing and recoverability*, New York: Garland.
Silverman, Daniel (2003), 'On the rarity of pre-aspirated stops', *Journal of Linguistics* 39(3): 575–98.
Simon, Ellen (2011), 'Laryngeal stop systems in contact: Connecting present-day acquisition findings and historical contact hypotheses', *Diachronica* 28(2): 225–54.
Sinou, André (1999), *Le breton de Léchiagat: Phonologie*, Lannion: Hor Yezh.
Sinou, André (2000), *Brezhoneg Lechiagad: Geriaoueg*, Lannion: Hor Yezh.
Slowiaczek, Louisa and Daniel A. Dinnsen (1985), 'On the neutralizing status of Polish word-final devoicing', *Journal of Phonetics* 13: 325–41.
Slowiaczek, Louisa M. and Helena J. Szymanska (1989), 'Perception of word-final devoicing in Polish', *Journal of Phonetics* 17(3): 205–12.
Smith, Jennifer L. (2002), *Phonological augmentation in prominent positions*, Amherst: University of Massachusetts, Amherst PhD thesis.
Smith, Jennifer L. (2004), 'Making constraints positional: Toward a compositional model of CON', *Lingua* 114(12): 1433–64.
Smith, Jennifer L. (2012), 'The formal definition of the ONSET constraint and implications for Korean syllable structure', in Toni Borowsky, Shigeto Kawahara, Takahito Shinya and Mariko Sugahara (eds), *Prosody matters: Essays in honor of Elisabeth Selkirk*, London: Equinox, pp. 73–108.
Solé, Maria Josep (2002), 'Aerodynamic characteristics of trills and phonological patterning', *Journal of Phonetics* 30(4): 655–88.
Sommerfelt, Alf (1962), 'Notes sur le parler de Dourduff en Plouézoch, Finistère', *Lochlann* 2: 58–92.
Sommerfelt, Alf (1978), *Le breton parlé à Saint-Pol-de-Léon*, Oslo, Bergen, Tromsø: Universitetsforlaget.
Spaargaren, Magdalena Jeannette (2009), *Change in obstruent laryngeal specification in English: Historical and theoretical phonology*, Edinburgh: University of Edinburgh PhD thesis.
Steblin-Kamenskij, M. I. (1960), 'Den islandske klusilforskyvning i fonologisk fremstilling', *Arkiv för nordisk filologi* 75: 74–83.
Stephens, Janig (1993), 'Breton', in Martin J. Ball and James Fife (eds), *The Celtic languages*, London, New York: Routledge, pp. 349–409.
Steriade, Donca (1987), 'Redundant values', in Anna Bosch, Barbara Need and Eric Schiller (eds), *Papers from the parasession on metrical and autosegmental phonology*, Chicago: Chicago Linguistics Society, pp. 339–62.

Steriade, Donca (1993), 'Orality and markedness', *BLS* 25: 334–7.
Steriade, Donca (1994), 'Positional neutralisation', MS, Massachusetts Institute of Technology.
Steriade, Donca (1995), 'Underspecification and markedness', in John Goldsmith (ed.), *The handbook of phonological theory*, Oxford: Blackwell, pp. 114–74.
Steriade, Donca (1997), 'Phonetics in phonology: The case of laryngeal neutralisation', MS, Massachusetts Institute of Technology.
Steriade, Donca (2001), 'The phonology of perceptibility effects: The p-map and its consequences for prosodic organisation', MS, Massachusetts Institute of Technology.
Stevens, Kenneth N. and Sheila E. Blumstein (1981), 'The search for invariant acoustic correlates of phonetic features', in Peter D. Eimas and Joanne L. Miller (eds), *Perspectives on the study of speech*, Hillsdale, NJ: Lawrence Erlbaum Associates, pp. 1–38.
Stevens, Kenneth N. and Samuel Jay Keyser (1989), 'Primary features and their enhancement in consonants', *Language* 65(1): 81–106.
Stevens, Kenneth N. and Samuel Jay Keyser (2010), 'Quantal theory, enhancement and overlap', *Journal of Phonetics* 38(1): 10–19.
Stewart, Jr., Thomas W. (2004), *Mutation as morphology: Bases, stems and shapes in Scottish Gaelic*, Columbus, OH: Ohio State University PhD thesis.
Struijke, Caro (2000), *Existential faithfulness: A study of reduplicative TETU, feature movement, and dissimilation*, College Park, MD: University of Maryland, College Park PhD thesis.
Strycharczuk, Patrycja (2012), *Phonetics–phonology interaction in pre-sonorant voicing*, Manchester: University of Manchester PhD thesis.
Strycharczuk, Patrycja (2015), 'Manner asymmetries in Central Catalan prevocalic voicing', *Language Sciences* 47: 84–106.
Strycharczuk, Patrycja and Ellen Simon (2013), 'Obstruent voicing before sonorants: The case of West-Flemish', *Natural Language and Linguistic Theory* 31(2): 563–88.
Strycharczuk, Patrycja, Marijn van 't Veer, Martine Bruil and Kathrin Linke (2014), 'Phonetic evidence on phonology–morphosyntax interactions: Sibilant voicing in Quito Spanish', *Journal of Linguistics* 50(2): 403–53.
Stump, Gregory T. (1987), 'On incomplete mutations in Breton', in Brian Joseph and Arnold Zwicky (eds), *A Festschrift for Ilse Lehiste* (Ohio State University Working Papers in Linguistics 35), pp. 1–10.
Stump, Gregory T. (1988), 'Nonlocal spirantisation in Breton', *Journal of Linguistics* 24(2): 457–81.
Tamminga, Meredith, Laurel MacKenzie and David Embick (2016), 'The dynamics of variation in individuals', *Linguistic Variation* 16(2).
Teeple, David (2009), *Biconditional prominence correlation*, Santa Cruz: University of California, Santa Cruz PhD thesis.
Ternes, Elmar (1970), *Grammaire structurale du breton de l'Île de Groix (dialecte occidental)*, Heidelberg: Carl Winter Universitätsverlag.

Ternes, Elmar (1993), 'The Breton language', in Donald Macaulay (ed.), *The Celtic languages*, Cambridge: Cambridge University Press, pp. 371–452.
Ternes, Elmar (2011), 'Neubretonisch', in Elmar Ternes (ed.), *Brythonic Celtic/ Britannisches Keltisch* (Münchner Forschungen zur Historischen Sprachwissenschaft 11), Bremen: Hempen Verlag, pp. 431–530.
Thibault, E. (1914), 'Notes sur le parler breton de Cléguérec (Morbihan)', *Révue celtique* 35: 1–28, 169–92, 431–40.
Thomas, Ceinwen H. (1967), 'Welsh intonation: A preliminary study', *Studia Celtica* 2: 8–28.
Timm, Lenora A. (1984), 'The segmental phonology of Carhaisien Breton', *Zeitschrift für celtische Philologie* 40(1): 118–92.
Timm, Lenora A. (1985), 'Breton mutations: Literary vs. vernacular usages', *Word* 36(2): 95–107.
Topintzi, Nina (2010), *Onsets*, Cambridge: Cambridge University Press.
Trépos, Pierre (1966), *Grammaire bretonne*, Rennes: Imprimerie Simon.
Trommer, Jochen (2011), *Phonological aspects of Western Nilotic mutation morphology*, Habilitationsschrift, Universität Leipzig.
Trommer, Jochen (2013), 'Stress uniformity in Albanian: Morphological arguments for cyclicity', *Linguistic Inquiry* 44(1): 109–43.
Trommer, Jochen (2014), 'Moraic prefixes and suffixes in Anywa', *Lingua* 140: 1–34.
Trommer, Jochen and Eva Zimmermann (2014), 'Generalised mora affixation and quantity-manipulating morphology', *Phonology* 31(3): 463–510.
Trubetzkoy, Nikolai S. (1939), *Grundzüge der Phonologie*, Prague: Le cercle linguistique de Prague.
Trudgill, Peter (2011), *Sociolinguistic typology: Social determinants of linguistic complexity*, Oxford: Oxford University Press.
Turton, Danielle (2014), *Variation in English /l/: Synchronic reflections on the life cycle of phonological processes*, Manchester: University of Manchester PhD thesis.
Uffmann, Christian (2005), 'Optimal geometries', in Marc van Oostendorp and Jeroen van de Weijer (eds), *The internal organisation of phonological segments* (Studies in Generative Grammar 77), Berlin: Mouton de Gruyter, pp. 27–92.
Uffmann, Christian (2007), 'Restraining GEN', in Sylvia Blaho, Patrik Bye and Martin Krämer (eds), *Freedom of analysis?* (Studies in Generative Grammar 95), Berlin: Mouton de Gruyter, pp. 281–312.
Uffmann, Christian (2013), 'Set the controls for the heart of the alternation: Dahl's Law in Kitharaka', in Sylvia Blaho, Martin Krämer and Bruce Morén-Duolljá (eds), *Nordlyd* 40(1): 323–37.
van Alphen, Petra M. (2007), 'Prevoicing in Dutch initial plosives: Production, perception, and word recognition', in Jeroen van de Weijer and Jan Erik van der Torre (eds), *Voicing in Dutch* (Current Issues in Linguistic Theory 286), Amsterdam: John Benjamins, pp. 99–124.

van Bergem, Dick R. (1994), 'A model of coarticulatory effects on the schwa', *Speech Communication* 14(2): 143–62.

van de Vijver, Ruben and Dinah Baer-Henney (2014), 'Developing biases', *Frontiers in Psychology* 5, <http://journal.frontiersin.org/article/10.3389/fpsyg.2014.00634/full> (last accessed 24 August 2016).

van der Hulst, Harry (1993), 'Units in the analysis of signs', *Phonology* 10(2): 209–41.

van Oostendorp, Marc (2000), *Phonological projection: A theory of feature content and prosodic structure* (Studies in Generative Grammar 47), Berlin: Mouton de Gruyter.

van Oostendorp, Marc (2003), 'Ambisyllabicity and fricative voicing in West Germanic dialects', in Caroline Féry and Ruben van de Vijver (eds), *The syllable in Optimality Theory*, Cambridge: Cambridge University Press, pp. 304–37.

van Oostendorp, Marc (2007), 'Derived environment effects and Consistency of Exponence', in Sylvia Blaho, Patrik Bye and Martin Krämer (eds), *Freedom of analysis?* (Studies in Generative Grammar 95), Berlin: Mouton de Gruyter, pp. 123–49.

van Oostendorp, Marc (2008), 'Incomplete devoicing in formal phonology', *Lingua* 118(9): 1362–74.

van Rooy, Bertus, Daan Wissing and Dwayne D. Paschall (2003), 'Demystifying incomplete neutralisation during final devoicing', *Southern African Linguistics and Applied Language Studies* 21(1–2): 49–66.

van 't Veer, Marijn (2015), *Building a phonological inventory: Feature co-occurrence constraints in acquisition*, Leiden: Leiden University PhD thesis.

Vaux, Bert (2008), 'Why the phonological component must be serial and rule-based', in Bert Vaux and Andrew Nevins (eds), *Rules, constraints and phonological phenomena*, Oxford: Oxford University Press, pp. 20–61.

Walker, Rachel (2000), 'Mongolian stress, licensing and factorial typology', MS.

Walker, Rachel (2005), 'Weak triggers in vowel harmony', *Natural Language & Linguistic Theory* 23(4): 917–89.

Walker, Rachel (2011), *Vowel patterns in language* (Cambridge Studies in Linguistics 125), Cambridge: Cambridge University Press.

Warner, Natasha, Allard Jongman, Joan Sereno and R. Rachèl Kemps (2004), 'Incomplete neutralisation and other sub-phonemic durational differences in production and perception: Evidence from Dutch', *Journal of Phonetics* 32(2): 251–76.

Wedel, Andrew B. (2007), 'Feedback and regularity in the lexicon', *Phonology* 24(1): 147–85.

Welby, Pauline, Máire Ní Chiosáin and Brian Ó Raghallaigh (2011), 'A phonetic investigation of Irish eclipsis: Preliminary results and challenges', in *Proceedings of ICPhS XVII, Hong Kong*, pp. 2122–5.

Wells, John C. (1979), 'Final voicing and vowel length in Welsh', *Phonetica* 36(4–5): 344–60.

Westbury, John R. (1983), 'Enlargement of the supraglottal cavity and its relation to stop consonant voicing', *Journal of the Acoustical Society of America* 73(4): 1322–36.
Westbury, John R. and Patricia Keating (1986), 'On the naturalness of stop consonant voicing', *Journal of Linguistics* 22(1): 145–66.
Wetzels, W. Leo and Joan Mascaró (2001), 'The typology of voicing and devoicing', *Language* 77(2): 207–44.
Wichmann, Søren, Taraka Rama and Eric W. Holman (2011), 'Phonological diversity, word length, and population sizes across languages: The ASJP evidence', *Linguistic Typology* 15(2): 177–97.
Williams, Briony (1999), 'The phonetic manifestation of stress in Welsh', in Harry van der Hulst (ed.), *Word prosodic systems in the languages of Europe* (Empirical Approaches to Language Typology 20), Berlin: Mouton de Gruyter, pp. 311–54.
Willis, Penny (1986), *The initial consonant mutations in Welsh and Breton*, Bloomington: Indiana University Linguistics Club.
Wmffre, Iwan (1999), *Central Breton* (Languages of the World/Materials 152), Munich: LINCOM Europa.
Wmffre, Iwan (2007a), *Breton orthographies and dialects: The twentieth-century orthography war in Brittany. Vol. 1* (Contemporary Studies in Descriptive Linguistics 18), Frankfurt am Main: Peter Lang.
Wmffre, Iwan (2007b), *Breton orthographies and dialects: The twentieth-century orthography war in Brittany. Vol. 2* (Contemporary Studies in Descriptive Linguistics 19), Frankfurt am Main: Peter Lang.
Wohlgemuth, Jan (2010), 'Language endangerment, community size, and typological rarity', in Michael Cysouw and Jan Wohlgemuth (eds), *Rethinking universals: How rarities affect linguistic theory* (Empirical Approaches to Language Typology 45), Berlin: Mouton de Gruyter, pp. 255–77.
Wolf, Matthew (2005), 'An autosegmental theory of quirky mutations', *WCCFL* 24: 370–8.
Wolf, Matthew (2007a), 'What constraint connectives should be permitted in OT?', in Michael Becker (ed.), *University of Massachusetts Occasional Papers in Linguistics 36: Papers in theoretical and computational phonology*, Amherst: GLSA, pp. 151–79.
Wolf, Matthew (2007b), 'For an autosegmental theory of mutation', in Michael O'Keefe, Ehren Reilly and Adam Werle (eds), *University of Massachusetts Occasional Papers in Linguistics 32: Papers in Optimality Theory III*, Amherst: GLSA, pp. 315–404.
Wolf, Matthew (2008), *Optimal interleaving: Serial phonology–morphology interaction in a constraint-based model*, Amherst: University of Massachusetts, Amherst PhD thesis.
Yang, Charles D. (2002), *Knowledge and learning in natural language*, Oxford: Oxford University Press.
Yang, Charles D. (2004), 'Universal Grammar, statistics, or both?', *Trends in Cognitive Science* 8(10): 451–6.

Yip, Moira (2005), 'Variability in feature affiliations through violable constraints: The case of [lateral]', in Marc van Oostendorp and Jeroen van de Weijer (eds), *The internal organisation of phonological segments* (Studies in Generative Grammar 77), Berlin: Mouton de Gruyter, pp. 63–92.

Youssef, Islam (2010), 'Laryngeal assimilation in Buchan Scots', *English Language and Linguistics* 14(3): 321–45.

Youssef, Islam (2013), *Place assimilation in Arabic: Contrasts, features, and constraints*, Tromsø: University of Tromsø PhD thesis.

Youssef, Islam (2015), 'Vocalic labialisation in Baghdadi Arabic: Representation and computation', *Lingua* 160: 74–90.

Yu, Alan C. L. (2004), 'Explaining final obstruent voicing in Lezgian: Phonetics and history', *Language* 80(1): 73–97.

Yu, Alan C. L. (2007), *A natural history of infixation*, Oxford: Oxford University Press.

Zimmermann, Eva (2013a), 'Vowel deletion as mora usurpation: The case of Yine', *Phonology* 30(1): 125–63.

Zimmermann, Eva (2013b), 'Non-concatenative allomorphy is generalized prosodic affixation: The case of Upriver Halkomelem', *Lingua* 134: 1–26.

Zoll, Cheryl (1997), 'Conflicting directionality', *Phonology* 14(2): 263–86.

Zoll, Cheryl (2004), 'Positional faithfulness and licensing', in John J. McCarthy (ed.), *Optimality Theory in phonology*, Oxford: Blackwell, pp. 356–78.

Zsiga, Elizabeth (1995), 'An acoustic and electropalatographic study of lexical and postlexical palatalisation in American English', in Amalia Arvaniti and Bruce Connell (eds), *Phonology and phonetic evidence: Papers in Laboratory Phonology IV*, Cambridge: Cambridge University Press, pp. 282–302.

Zsiga, Elizabeth (2000), 'Phonetic alignment constraints: Consonant overlap and palatalisation in English and Russian', *Journal of Phonetics* 28(1): 69–102.

Zue, Victor W. and Martha Laferriere (1979), 'Acoustic study of medial /t, d/ in American English', *Journal of the Acoustical Society of America* 66: 1039–50.

Zuidema, Willem and Bart de Boer (2009), 'The evolution of combinatorial phonology', *Journal of Phonetics* 37(2): 125–44.

Index

acquisition and learning, 12, 16–19, 22, 28, 32–3, 34n, 40–4, 48, 59n, 63, 219, 234–5
affixation
  Generalised Nonlinear Affixation, 55, 176
  prefixation, 55–6, 83, 101, 105, 180–9, 197, 205
  suffixation, 76, 99–106, 110, 114, 119, 122n, 125–6, 129, 130–1, 133–4, 139–41, 147–51, 153, 157–60, 161n, 170–5, 179
agreement, morphosyntactic, 148, 191–3
allomorphy, 148–9, 161n, 197, 200, 204, 207
assimilation, 12, 62–3, 87–9, 164–6, 226–8; *see also* laryngeal phonology: laryngeal similation

Breton (other than Bothoa Breton)
  Argol dialect, 80
  Berrien dialect, 116, 228
  dialects, 67–71, 116, 193, 197, 232n, 233n
  Grand-Lorient dialect, 80, 197, 215
  Île de Groix dialect, 215, 225–30
  Languidic dialect, 76, 215
  Lanhouarneau dialect, 116, 230
  Malguénac dialect, 80
  Middle Breton, 161n, 215

Plougrescant dialect, 80, 116, 158–9, 161n, 178, 215, 231n
Vannetais dialects, 68, 76, 80, 95–6, 161n

Catalan, 22, 217–19,
coalescence, 55–6, 93, 126, 138–56, 158, 161n, 175–8, 191, 193, 195–6, 198, 205–7
coarticulation, 16, 164, 211, 217–19
constraints
  augmentation constraints, 52–4, 59n, 65–6, 168, 185, 231
  constraint conjunction, 13, 51, 52, 149, 226–7
  constraint schemata, 47–8, 49–52, 52–54, 59n, 137, 187
  faithfulness constraints, 50–2, 54–6, 63, 104–7, 109, 119, 128–9, 144, 149–54, 157–60, 168, 171, 183–4, 226
  markedness constraints, 42, 48–54, 61–6, 137, 141–6, 168–70, 176–7, 180, 185–6, 191, 236
contrast, phonological, 5–6, 10–11, 14–15, 21–7, 31, 33n, 37, 39–44, 61, 62–4, 76–9, 87, 124, 150, 161n, 162n, 164–5, 179, 216–19, 235; *see also* ternarity
Cornish, 95, 116, 215, 235
cyclicity, 56–9, 105–9, 126, 135–6, 150, 157–9, 185–7, 205, 207–8, 237

271

Danish, 221–2
delaryngealisation, 42, 165–70, 179, 182–5, 205–6, 212–13, 218, 223, 231
Dutch, 22, 186, 217–18, 238n

English, 16, 22, 23, 24, 26, 34n, 69, 78, 83, 85, 216, 219–25
Evenki, 12
extrametricality, 28, 104, 119–22, 178, 183

features, phonological
  arbitrariness of phonetic realisation, 12, 27, 38–9, 63, 216, 234
  emergent features, 12–14, 17, 47
  see also laryngeal phonology; Parallel Structures Model; floating autosegments; Successive Division Algorithm
floating autosegments, 55–6, 161–2n, 176–8, 182, 185, 191–2, 196, 200, 203, 205–7, 210, 212–13, 214–15, 231
French, 68–9, 72n, 78, 80, 95, 110, 118, 162n, 178, 229, 235
frequency, 16, 20–1, 28–9, 58, 235
Friulian, 22, 231n

Gaelic see Scottish Gaelic
German, 22, 24, 25, 34n, 48, 85, 105, 216, 219–21, 223
gestures, phonetic, 6, 19, 83, 93, 113, 164–5, 167, 221

hiatus, 82–3, 118, 123n, 129–30, 150, 154, 160
Hungarian, 16, 21, 33n

Icelandic, 186, 221–4, 235
interfaces
  Interface Interpretation Principle, 21, 23, 24, 26, 31, 166, 223
  phonetics–phonology interface, 22–6, 34n, 90, 114, 166, 211, 219–25
  phonology–morphology interface, 20, 56–60, 99–100, 105–7, 119, 125–6, 130–1, 148, 160, 171–7, 198, 203, 211, 228; see also cyclicity

laryngeal phonology
  laryngeal realism, 90, 219–25
  laryngeal similation, 176–89, 228
  phonetic realisation of laryngeal contrast, 79–81, 87–9, 114, 164–5, 196, 211–13
lengthening, 77, 86, 119–21, 174–7, 228
licensing, 52–4, 107, 167, 180, 186, 188, 196, 202, 211, 216; see also constraints: augmentation constraints

markedness, 15–16, 42, 61–6, 90, 208–11, 225–31
  markedness conflation, 47, 62
  markedness reduction, 62–3, 65, 127–9, 168–9, 231; see also neutralisation
  preservation of the marked, 52, 62–3, 196, 231n, 236
  see also constraints: markedness constraints
mixed mutation see mutation: lenition-and-provection
modularity, 5–21, 26, 30, 45, 47, 154, 187, 204, 206, 211, 234, 237
moraic structure, 53, 59n, 97, 102–8, 111–13, 119, 120–2, 137, 147–52, 157–60, 162n, 175–7, 183
mutation
  lenition, 133–5, 146, 154, 170, 181–2, 198–208, 212–16, 228, 231, 232n
  lenition-and-provection, 208

provection, 193–8, 208
spirantisation, 134, 140, 148, 154, 189–193, 196, 198, 207, 215

Navajo, 13, 33n
neutralisation, 21–4, 25, 27, 34n, 42, 46–7, 54, 63–6, 76, 87, 120, 163–71, 185, 198, 211, 231, 232n
nodes, feature-geometric
  bare nodes, 40–2, 163, 205, 210–13, 223–4
  C- and V-nodes, 38–9, 44, 155–6
  laryngeal nodes, 166–9, 180–9, 200–5, 210, 212–16, 222–5, 229–30
  manner nodes, 130, 143, 161n, 166, 190–1, 196, 200–2, 205–7
  place nodes, 127–8, 136, 156–7

opacity, 21–2, 34n, 46, 136, 157–61

palatalisation
  coronal palatalisation, 82–3, 138–46, 148, 152–3, 162n
  phonetic palatalisation, 82–3
  velar palatalisation, 81, 132–8, 146–7, 161n
Parallel Structures Model, 36–9, 41, 44, 48–9, 61–2, 64, 79, 132
phoneme, 14, 26, 35n, 75, 76–7, 82, 196
Polish, 22, 217
pre-sonorant voicing *see* sandhi
provection *see* mutation: provection; laryngeal phonology: laryngeal similation; moraic structure

recursion, 36–8, 41, 44, 183
Richness of the Base, 43, 45, 51, 57–8, 77, 127, 134, 160, 169–70, 185, 213, 231
Russian, 16, 22, 24, 33n, 80, 163, 235

sandhi, 84, 85–9, 114, 165, 171, 178, 180, 212, 213–16, 225–31; *see also* mutation
Scottish Gaelic, 105, 221
shortening, 77, 102, 107, 110–11, 113, 118–19, 122n, 153, 173–7, 183, 232n
Spanish, 162n, 216–19
stress, 67, 76–7, 86, 94–107, 152–3, 158–9, 162n, 173–5, 181, 183–5
  degenerate footing, 104–7
  in other dialects, 72, 76, 158, 228–9
subcategorisation, 135, 191–2, 200, 207
subtraction, 55–6, 59n, 190–1, 200, 205, 230–1
Successive Division Algorithm, 36, 40–4, 90, 223
Swedish, 220–4
syllabic structure, 31, 53, 95–6, 108–15, 119–22, 126, 146, 149–50, 154, 156–8, 167, 169–71, 173, 178, 180, 195, 196–7, 226–9, 231

ternarity, 40–1, 164–71, 208–10, 217–18, 225–31
tone accents, 96–7, 101–5
Turkish, 171, 221, 225

underspecification
  contrastive underspecification, 14–15; *see also* Successive Division Algorithm
  input underspecification, 40, 225–31, 229
  surface underspecification, 48, 164, 210–11, 216–25

variation, cross-linguistic, 7, 9–10, 12–13, 26–7, 30–1, 42, 44n, 45–7, 63–4, 221–2
  factorial typology, 13, 29–30, 48

variation, phonological, 23, 26, 28–9, 75–7, 82–3, 83–5, 87–8, 97, 98, 113–15, 129, 153, 162n, 164–6, 172–3, 177, 197, 216–25, 234, 236

vowel reduction, 76, 113–15, 124–9, 153

Welsh, 71, 85, 94n, 95, 96, 104, 116, 119, 122n, 135, 197, 215, 222–3, 235

EU representative:
Easy Access System Europe
Mustamäe tee 50, 10621 Tallinn, Estonia
Gpsr.requests@easproject.com

www.ingramcontent.com/pod-product-compliance
Lightning Source LLC
Chambersburg PA
CBHW071810300426
44116CB00009B/1261